PUBLISHING PLACE

Publishing Place

Transatlantic Modernity and Periodical Culture on Canada's East Coast

BILLY JOHNSON

McGill-Queen's University Press
Montreal & Kingston · London · Chicago

ISBN 978-0-2280-2589-4 (paper)
ISBN 978-0-2280-2590-0 (ePDF)
ISBN 978-0-2280-2591-7 (ePUB)

Legal deposit fourth quarter 2025
Bibliothèque et Archives nationales du Québec

Printed in Canada on acid-free paper that is 100% ancient-forest-free, containing 100% sustainable, recycled fibre, and processed chlorine-free.

This book has been published with the help of a grant from the Federation for the Humanities and Social Sciences, through the Awards to Scholarly Publications Program, using funds provided by the Social Sciences and Humanities Research Council of Canada.

Funded by the Government of Canada | Financé par le gouvernement du Canada | Canada | Canada Council for the Arts | Conseil des arts du Canada

We acknowledge the support of the Canada Council for the Arts.

Nous remercions le Conseil des arts du Canada de son soutien.

McGill-Queen's University Press in Montreal is on land which long served as a site of meeting and exchange amongst Indigenous Peoples, including the Haudenosaunee and Anishinabeg nations. In Kingston it is situated on the territory of the Haudenosaunee and Anishinaabek. We acknowledge and thank the diverse Indigenous Peoples whose footsteps have marked these territories on which peoples of the world now gather.

Library and Archives Canada Cataloguing in Publication

Title: Publishing place: transatlantic modernity and periodical culture on Canada's East Coast / Billy Johnson.

Names: Johnson, Billy (Lecturer in English literature and Canadian studies), author.

Description: Includes bibliographical references and index.

Identifiers: Canadiana (print) 20250214881 | Canadiana (ebook) 20250215063 | ISBN 9780228025894 (paper) | ISBN 9780228025917 (ePUB) | ISBN 9780228025900 (ePDF)

Subjects: LCSH: Canadian literature—Atlantic Provinces—History and criticism. | LCSH: Literature publishing—Atlantic Provinces—History. | LCSH: Periodicals—Publishing—Atlantic Provinces—History. | LCSH: Canadian periodicals—Atlantic Provinces—History. | LCSH: Culture in literature. | LCSH: Group identity in literature. | LCSH: Atlantic Provinces—In literature. | LCSH: Atlantic Provinces—Intellectual life. | CSH: Canadian literature (English)—Atlantic Provinces—History and criticism. | CSH: Canadian periodicals (English)—Atlantic Provinces—History.

Classification: LCC PS8131.A85 264 2025 | DDC C810.9/9715—dc23

This book was designed and typeset by Marquis Interscript in 11/14 Bembo.
Copyediting by Grace Seybold.

McGill-Queen's University Press
Suite 1720, 1010 Sherbrooke St West, Montreal, QC, H3A 2R7

Authorized safety representative in the EU: Mare Nostrum Group BV, Mauritskade 21D, 1091 GC Amsterdam, the Netherlands, gpsr@mare-nostrum.co.uk

Contents

Figures

Acknowledgments

As any book historian knows, the book is a social as well as material and textual object; writing, as solitary as it may feel, is a social act, and no book is the work of an individual. This book would not have been possible without the innumerable friends, family, teachers, and colleagues who have shaped my outlook on literature and life. Their varied influences far exceed what I can convey here, but please know, every one of you, that I am grateful.

There are several people whose contributions to the composition of this book have been more direct. I have been incredibly fortunate to have had several mentors since the idea of this project first took shape, but I am especially indebted to the formative influence of Tony Tremblay and to years of guidance from Colin Hill. I'm grateful for the invaluable advice and support that I received from Jason Haslam and Jennifer Andrews as I worked to complete this book while also navigating the precarity of the job market. The book also owes a debt to many more scholars who shaped my thinking both directly or indirectly, in particular George Elliott Clarke, David Creelman, Gwendolyn Davies, Nick Mount, Heather Murray, Cynthia Sugars, and Herb Wyile. Much of the support I've received has come from those who are close friends as well as colleagues, and for that I would like to thank Jorge Thielen-Armand, Blaise Convey, Rohan Ghatage, Kyle Kinaschuk, and Tavleen Purewal.

From 2022 to 2024, I was supported by SSHRC and Killam postdoctoral fellowships, and much of this book was written and revised during my time at Dalhousie University. I am grateful for the community I found in the English department, and thanks are due to Lynn Bennett, Bart

Vautour, and Erin Wunker for their support. Sheheryar Sheik was also a fellow at Dal during my second year there, and I am grateful for both his friendship and the delight of hearing his prose aloud. During the same period, I spent Monday afternoons at the Oxford Taproom writing in the company of writers I admire. Thank you to my fellow OWLs and to Heather Jessup for welcoming me there and for modelling what it is to foster a writerly community.

I presented parts of this book at many symposiums and conferences, but particularly those of the Association of Canadian College and University Teachers of English (ACCUTE) and the Bibliographical Society of Canada / La Société bibliographique du Canada (BSC/SBC). The feedback I received from fellow members of the BSC was helpful to my composition of this book from the first chapter to the last. Part of chapter 2 was previously published in slightly different form as "A.B. Walker's *Neith* and the Aesthetic Grammars of Black Modernism in Canada" in *Studies in Canadian Literature* 47, no. 2 (2022). My discussion of socialist feminist poetics in chapter 5 appeared in substantially different form as "*The Maritime Labor Herald* (1921–26) and the Genealogy of Socialist Feminism in Canada" in *Canadian Literature* 256 (2024). Thanks to the editors of those journals for allowing me to reprint those materials here.

It was a privilege to work with McGill-Queen's on this book. I am tremendously grateful for the advice and guidance I received from Jonathan Crago and for the care and rigour of Grace Seybold. Thanks also to Jennifer Roberts, Filomena Falocco, and Kathleen Fraser, who were essential to getting this book into print, and to the anonymous reviewers for their careful criticisms and encouragement.

Much of the research undertaken for this book was archival, and I have benefited tremendously from the work and expertise of special collections librarians, archivists, and staff at institutions throughout Canada. Special thanks are due to Fran Holyoke, Patti Auld, and Christine Lovelace at the Harriet Irving Library (University of New Brunswick), Karen Smith at the Killam Memorial Library (Dalhousie University), and Natalya Rattan and the archivists at the Thomas Fisher Rare Book Library (University of Toronto).

Finally, there are those for whom thanks will never be enough. To Anna, you've been a friend and my closest scholarly companion. To Emma, Jack, Izzy, and Ruby, you've shown me what it means to love and grow through the greatest adversity. To my parents, my first teachers, memory fades, but you've shown me – and continue to show me – that love is like poetry and art, bestowing what memory alone cannot, "life and the memory of it so compressed / they've turned into each other." And to my partner, Julia, my most constant support, I love you. This book is for you.

PUBLISHING PLACE

INTRODUCTION

Print Modernity in the East

In mid-August 1923, Arthur Huff Fauset made his way through torrential rain to the Travellers Inn in Digby, Nova Scotia. A student of anthropology and self-described "itinerant story gatherer," Fauset had spent the past six weeks collecting folklore in Black communities throughout the province.[1] Exhausted, he was ready to conclude his fieldwork, return to Philadelphia, and edit the collection that would become *Folklore from Nova Scotia* (1931). Now, anticipating the work ahead, he became doubtful.[2] He had had no trouble obtaining folktales in the communities he visited; he had collected six hundred in July alone. Yet, the "folk" he had encountered defied his expectations, and the places he had visited upset his assumptions about Nova Scotian folklife. Instead of pastoral scenes of rural isolation, Fauset had seen bustling port towns on the province's south shore, backwoods squalor in the Annapolis Valley, and a "hard proletarian people in the coke ovens" of Cape Breton.[3] To make matters worse, he was not certain that the tales he had obtained could "properly be called native folklore."[4] Too often, when asked about a story, an informant would "light up," only to reply, "Oh yes. I read one like that a long time ago in the Halifax Herald."[5] Not simply tellers of tales, here were readers of print culture. Were these folk and their tales *authentic*? Were these folk truly *folk*?

What Fauset had discovered on his voyage through Nova Scotia was the incongruence between popular images of "the folk" and the social realities of rural and urban life on Canada's east coast. The difficulty, Fauset would later explain in the introduction to *Folklore from Nova Scotia*, had much to do with the transatlantic currents that continuously shaped and reshaped the cultural life of Nova Scotia. "The folklore of the province," Fauset observed, "is a medley of tales and folk notions representing cultures from all parts of the western world, a natural situation in a maritime locality." As a result, Fauset continued, "the lore is heterogenous."[6] "Heterogenous," but not inauthentic – Fauset's "medley" thesis is, in short, a theory of transculturation. It is an account of how cultural exchange and convergence in Nova Scotia produced hybridity and precipitated change. With it, Fauset challenged the prevailing image of a primordial folk confined to the rural margins of modernity. In its place, he inscribed a plural folk shaped not by essentialism and boundedness, but by thoroughly modern processes of exchange, consumption, and conflict.

This book is about how those modern processes played out in periodicals – magazines, journals, and newspapers – published in and about Canada's east coast in the first half of the twentieth century. More particularly, it is a study of how writers and editors responded to, and in turn influenced, those processes, not by retreating into romantic nostalgia, but by imparting new meanings to the relationship between place and collective identity. The implications of Fauset's *Folklore from Nova Scotia* for the history of Canada's east coast thus extend beyond the challenge it poses to prevailing definitions of "the folk." In the context of interwar Nova Scotia, the collection defied a powerful cultural narrative that would, by the early 1930s, dominate popular perceptions of the province. This was a narrative, writes Ian McKay, that located the "true essence" of Nova Scotia in "the primitive, the rustic, the unspoiled, the picturesque, the quaint, the unchanging."[7] Fauset, however, was acutely aware that he was visiting communities shaped by successive and ongoing waves of transatlantic migration. Under such conditions, the notion of an "unchanging" cultural essence was untenable. Also untenable were antimodernist conceptions of place that imagined Canada's east coast as a premodern preserve, a haven untouched by the consequences of twentieth-century modernity. This was a province where people were more likely to recite stories read in local papers than to deliver tales unearthed from an essential, unchanging tradition. These were subjects implicated in broader North American print networks, themselves consumers of an extensive print culture. Whatever else Fauset had witnessed on his journey north, the fact of widespread mass literacy was the surest sign that old definitions of "the folk" would not suffice. This was a province awash in "that scourge of the oral culture of the Folk, the printed word."[8]

The existence of books and periodicals in twentieth-century Nova Scotia is no revelation. Since at least the end of the eighteenth century, Canada's east coast had sustained a rich serial press, and literary life in the nineteenth century was cultivated in more than a dozen magazines and a burgeoning book-publishing industry. Rather, what is significant is the discrepancy between the conditions Fauset experienced and what remains a commonplace in both cultural depictions of Canada's east coast and contemporary cultural criticism: namely, that the east coast was not a significant site of modernization, modernism, or modernity in the first half of the twentieth century. In this respect, the print ecology of the east coast offers a very different picture of social and cultural life from that projected by the antimodernist mythomoteur of twentieth-century Nova Scotia.

More than any other medium, periodicals provided the forums in which writers and editors discussed, debated, and gave imaginative expression to emergent conceptions of space, place, and identity. At the same time, editors of periodicals on the east coast situated the literary at the core of their political-cultural programs. Periodicals thus helped sustain local literary cultures while consistently emphasizing the continuing relevance of literary expression to territorial politics and identity formation. And on the east coast, as elsewhere, it was in the pages of periodicals that modernism, understood broadly as a response to the social and cultural conditions of modernity, began to take shape. As Robert Scholes and Clifford Wulfman contend of modernism globally, it "began in the magazines, and the magazines in which it began were – all of them – shaped by modernity."[9] To be sure, prior to mid-century, engagements with modernity in east-coast periodicals only rarely precipitated a break with traditional literary form. But periodicals, their editors, and their contributors consistently negotiated the "cultural dislocation and fragmentation" and "prolonged economic crisis" that distinguished late modernity in the Maritime Provinces.[10] And they did so in ways that resisted the antimodernism that has become synonymous with the "region" in the period. In the pages of east-coast periodicals from the late nineteenth century on, editors and writers engaged with the conditions of late modernity that produced new spatial understandings, debating and challenging conventional political, social, and cultural values. Any sustained analysis of these periodicals, then, is also a history of the complicated processes of political contest, cultural selection, and exclusion that have been obscured in a narrative of modern Canada that juxtaposes regional cultural decline with national cultural growth.

In this narrative of Canadian modernity, periodicals of the Maritime Provinces are deemed to have contributed little if anything to either national or transatlantic literary and print culture. This assumption has been exacerbated by the fact that twentieth-century print culture in the Maritime Provinces remains virtually unexplored. According to Gwendolyn Davies and Eric Swanick, the twentieth century "is the least studied of all periods for the Maritimes."[11] This remains true despite the resurgence of Atlantic Canadian criticism coinciding with the so-called "renaissance" of Atlantic Canadian literature from the mid-1990s to the early 2010s.[12] The result has been a much more complex picture of contemporary literary and print culture set against a comparatively reductive history of the period before mid-century. At its most extreme, the region, as Tony Tremblay observes, figures as "an anti-space of underdevelopment where myths of pastoral and monoculture, innocence and authenticity, serve as functional antitheses against which more progressive movements defined themselves."[13]

Challenging this general picture of cultural decline, the present study contends that periodicals on Canada's east coast were not only thoroughly implicated in the global flows of a reconfigured, twentieth-century modernity, but also paradigmatic of the ways in which emergent ideas of place and identity circulated in print beyond Canada's urban metropoles – the centres that generally substitute for "national culture" in histories of modern Canada. As such, this study argues that reading periodicals in and about the east coast of Canada can help us rethink the relationship between periodical form, editorial practice, and space in the twentieth century. As an inherently mobile form, the periodical – and the magazine, in particular – is especially suited to charting the translocal networks of people, ideas, literature, and culture that constituted and contested territorial allegiances at multiple scales.

MODERN PERIODICALS ON THE EAST COAST, 1895–1933

This book is a critical study of several neglected English-language periodicals – six magazines and one weekly paper – published in or about the Maritime Provinces of Canada between 1895 and 1933. It is, first and foremost, an examination of the diverse forms and genres that mediated the way many people along the east coast of Canada conceived of place, identity, and culture in a period of upheaval and transformation. This was a period characterized by rapid but uneven industrialization before the First World War, followed by sudden, severe socio-economic crisis. It was also a period of incredible transit that saw hundreds of thousands of people enter through the ports at Halifax and Saint John, and hundreds of thousands more, nearly half of the entire population still present in 1931, leave the Maritime Provinces, most for the United States.[14] And it was a period during which the epochal shifts of the modern world were acutely felt by those living on the east coast, made proximate by the Halifax Explosion, the complete collapse of local manufacturing industries, and an unprecedented postwar labour revolt. During this period, a once-promising book-publishing industry, led by such firms as J. & A. McMillan in Saint John, all but disappeared. In its wake there appeared dozens of magazines. Most were short-lived and many never gained wide circulation; but several key periodicals helped shape social and political life across the heterogeneous localities of the east coast, advancing literary, political, and spatial discourses that responded to this radically altered modern moment. The story of these periodicals, then, is also the story of the editors, writers, and readers who struggled to respond to the expanding transatlantic world into which they were thrust.

And this is also a print-cultural history of the origins of "the Maritimes" and its contested ascendence as both a coherent geographic space and a locus for identification. Magazines were central to this production of regional space. But periodicals were also significant vehicles for a countervailing discourse that questioned the primacy of place in the formation of cultural, social, and political identities. The production of local and regional space on the east coast was never neutral, but worked continuously to produce geographies of exclusion along the fault lines of race, class, and gender. The regionalism that emerged at the turn of the twentieth century actively worked to conceal internal difference with powerful narratives of cultural homogeneity, racial uniformity, and political unity. But these narratives were always subject to critique, always already contested by writers, editors, and readers who envisioned and advanced alternative forms of identity and community. Inasmuch as periodicals trace the discursive construction of the region, then, they also reveal forms of communal, class, and racial identification that challenged, directly and indirectly, the dominant discourses of emergent regionalism, the logic of liberal capitalism, and the geographies of exclusion they produced.

Attention to early-twentieth-century magazines in the Maritime Provinces thus occasions a much-needed reassessment of spatial and cultural production beyond Canada's urban metropolises, urban spaces from and against which the "regional" has been consistently defined. For those accustomed to a settler-colonial geography that continues to cast regions as the primitive, organic containers of culture, it may come as some surprise that "the Maritimes" did not exist prior to its discursive construction at the turn of the twentieth century. Cast as a natural fact of culture and geography, the region was and is generally taken to be the obverse of the modern nation-state. But the nation is not the only scale at which space is produced and communities are imagined. The region was neither the inevitable result of colonial conquest and settlement of Wabanaki lands nor the natural successor to colonial Acadia. It is neither a geographic given with prehistoric depth, nor a necessary consequence of social and cultural uniformity. Rather, it is an historically contingent space that was produced, negotiated, and contested across disparate translocalities within a rapidly expanding transatlantic world. This history of the region's discursive production, however, has been all but eclipsed by a cultural-historical narrative of regional premodernity and cultural latency that continues to identify the east coast as an elsewhere of modernity, a region against which the modern nation-state can be read and demarcated. Moving beyond the regional framework to attend to the local and translocal conditions of periodical production and circulation thus meets an urgent need to historicize the "heterogenous, unstable, even internally divided" character of regions,[15] characteristics that are too often aligned in recent criticism with the ostensibly more sophisticated sensibilities of contemporary writers and critics.

Accordingly, I do not aim to develop a broad criterion for regional literature and print culture in the modern period. Such a critical manoeuvre, I contend, is antithetical to a fuller appreciation of the manifold trajectories and temporalities of print modernity on the east coast. While the book as a whole stages an intervention into contemporary critical conversations around the locations and trajectories of modernism and modernity in the transatlantic, the critical stakes of each chapter are distinct. Conceptually as well as methodologically, however, the chapters are anchored in three interrelated themes: (1) place and identity, (2) transatlantic modernity, and (3) periodical form. In addition to charting themes through the remainder of the introduction, I turn to register both the advantages and limits presented by a focus on English-language periodicals in the period. I make no claim that the present study is all-inclusive of the variegated identities that found expression (and those that did not) in periodicals in and about the east coast. Nevertheless, the exclusion of Indigenous modernities from print culture deserves special attention, bringing much to bear on the themes that animate this study, not least of which is the intersection of place and identity.

PLACE AND IDENTITY

The idea of "place" takes on particular resonance in the context of literature and culture along Canada's east coast, where attachment to place has generally figured more prominently in critical discussions of identity and community. Commenting on the disparity produced by "asymmetrical mobility," Herb Wyile contends that "[t]his imbalance has particularly troubling implications for a region such as Atlantic Canada with a long history of occupation, a resource-based economy, and a concomitantly stronger attachment to place."[16] It was such a perceived attachment that led Gwendolyn Davies to influentially identify the "home place" as a trope that provided regional literature with "a sense of cultural continuity and psychological identification" from the 1920s on.[17] Similarly, historians Margaret Conrad and James Hiller observe that it is, in part, a "deep sense of place that sets Atlantic Canadians apart from many other North Americans."[18] By historicizing and complicating the regional framework itself, I question the extent to which attachment to place has ever been uniformly prioritized over other allegiances, affiliations, or attachments in the periodical literatures and, by extension, the political-cultural imaginaries of the east coast. Nevertheless, place and its relationship to cultural identity were at the centre of much discursive and political contest in periodicals of the modern period. As such, this relationship between place and identity forms a significant theme throughout this book.

The salience of this relationship between place and cultural identity in modern periodicals, however, is not as inconsistent with the contemporary spatial registers of Canadian cultural criticism as some recent criticism would suggest. In her 2000 essay "Notes from the Cultural Field: Canadian Literature from Identity to Hybridity," Barbara Godard addresses the shifting conditions of cultural production in Canada between the 1950s and 1990s, writing that "everything has changed under the material conditions produced by the rise of a distinctively transnational capitalism."[19] Central to her analysis of this "transformation" is the claim that "[c]riticism continues to turn around the problem of identity" but that "[l]iterature no longer 'expresses' and so binds territory."[20] Though primarily concerned with the nation's becoming "a site of profound anxiety," Godard's comments point to the extent to which, already, more than two decades ago, the disconnection of cultural identity from place had become commonplace in cultural theory in Canada as elsewhere.[21] As Doreen Massey had put it nearly a decade earlier, "place itself, the seeking after a sense of place, has come to be seen by some as necessarily reactionary."[22] Since Godard was writing, place has frequently been deemed ever more redundant and its constitutive relation to cultural identity increasingly problematic.

More recent theoretical currents, however, question the desirability of deterritorialization as a normative ideal, something to be sought after and achieved. Mobility has not undermined the relevance of place in the production of cultural identity; the particularities of place continue to influence identities as they are constituted across space and cultural boundaries. Even as increased attention to globalization and mobility spurred declarations of the "end of geography," many critics questioned the tenability of "placelessness" as a generative response to the modern world of global flows and time-space compression.[23] As Lucy Lippard argues, "even as the power of place is diminished and often lost, it continues – as an absence – to define culture and identity."[24] Important here is the recognition that place-identity, as attachment to and identification with place, does not mutually exclude cosmopolitan and diasporic identities. As Tim Cresswell points out, "cosmopolitan identity may be formed through mobility and a decrease in the importance of one's own place, but it simultaneously depends on continued variation in the world."[25] Cosmopolitanism, in other words, depends as much upon the local for intelligibility as it does upon the global for meaning.

Cresswell further points to Anna Tsing's concept of "friction" as especially useful for thinking through contemporary configurations of place and identity. For Tsing, "aspirations for global connection" take shape as they encounter the "particularities of place," or what Tsing calls the "sticky materiality of practical encounters."[26] Importantly, argues Tsing, global change is not merely experienced in "peripheral places"; rather, "global forces are themselves congeries of local/global interaction."[27] Tsing's contention that cultures are "continuously co-produced" through encounters and interaction across difference, or "friction," aligns with what Stuart Hall sees as the "constant transformation" to which identities are subject; yet it also invites critical attention to Hall's insistence that such identities "come from somewhere, have histories."[28] For Hall, cultural identities are not essences, but "the unstable points of identification or suture, which are made, within the discourses of history and culture."[29] It is with such discourses of history and culture on the east coast – the multiple and unstable points of cultural and political identification that were imagined, consolidated, negotiated, and contested in the pages of periodicals – that the present study is concerned.

Expressions of place and identity in the region's periodicals were often conflictual and never uniform. Writers and editors frequently professed strong attachments to place, yet rarely does one find deeply ingrained, shared concepts such as the "home place," an idea that many critics following Davies have identified as a central trope in the region's literature. As Davies explains, the "home place" emerged as a motif in Maritime Provinces literature in the 1920s, "in the face of social fragmentation, outmigration, and a continuing hardscrabble economy."[30] Before the end of that decade, however, responses to those same conditions seldom imagined a home place, as later writers would, "as the nurturer … of local tradition" and "a wider social universe."[31] Indeed, prior to the emergence of Maritime regionalism in the first decades of the twentieth century, the idea of a monolithic "Maritime identity" would have seemed dubious. But even as the image gained popularity in the interwar period, many writers declined to "physically and imaginatively see in the 'home place' the essence of their Maritime identity."[32] Still others imagined the region as a site of exclusion, economic exploitation, or conflict – less a home place of essential belonging than a place to be transformed or otherwise abandoned.

What such conflicting conceptions of place generally do share, however, are a foundational commitment to various forms of "Settler place-identity."[33] Interrogating the "home place" from the vantage point of contemporary Indigenous studies, Rachel Bryant examines the ways "non-Indigenous Maritime writers and readers have articulated, revised, and ultimately controlled their relationships to the places they inhabit, effectively and continuously claiming and re-imagining this region, to which they are relative newcomers, as their own intellectual property."[34] Though few of the writers examined in *Publishing Place* forged collective identities by way of the home place motif, all defined new relations to place as they grappled with feelings of "uncertainty and unbelonging"[35] – feelings to which the trope would respond. Privileging the print periodical as their chosen medium of discourse, and forgoing any thorough engagement with Indigenous place-based thought and practice, those writers and editors did not undergo an "epistemological transformation" of the sort Bryant urges. But neither were they merely "consolidating a new, perhaps slightly more *edgy* or *progressive* collective identity against their rivals."[36] Such notions of a monolithic regional identity – progressive and anti-progressive, conservative and liberal – certainly found expression in regionalist periodicals such as *Acadiensis* and *The Busy East*, but they remained always partial, incomplete, and contested. Others forged collective attachments that refuse to be subsumed under a revised concept of regional identity. Rather than recuperate modern periodicals for an expanded regional canon, then, the present study aims to unsettle the assumption that identities on the east coast were ever reducible to one dominant relation to place, much less a single coherent and bounded territory.

Ultimately, I am concerned less with deterritorialization than I am with the profound *dehistoricization* that often attends contemporary discussions of globalization, place, and literature, a lack of historical sense suggested by the "no longer" in Godard's quote above. In this, I am indebted to Michel-Rolph Trouillot's suggestion that, "since the early centuries of the Atlantic moment, identities have never been as simple as we are sometimes prone to believe."[37] At issue here is whether identification with and expression of "bounded territories" *ever* existed without substantive opposition from alternative conceptions of place and identity. Indeed, the paradox at the core of pronouncements of "newness" (of globality, interconnectedness, placelessness, etc.) and concomitant dismissals of place attachment as backward nostalgia is an implicit longing for "spatial coherences" that *never* existed.[38] As Tremblay points out in the Canadian context, what critical dismissals of place-based identity projects frequently elide is "the fact that *no* place is or ever was fixed, static, and comprehensible": "Narratives of every type and era," argues Tremblay, "have always altered the notion and representations of place, shaping its bias to the dictates of the dominant."[39] Periodicals of the modern period reveal histories of such instability and dominance, but they also reveal the extent to which writers, editors, and readers were often *conscious* of that instability in their conflictual articulations of place and identity. The vocabulary they used to discuss and debate these terms looked very different from the spatial registers of today. But periodicals of the period consistently betray discursively complex debates about the appropriate relationship between place and identity, debates that were as much an animating feature of modern periodical literature as they are the jurisdiction of contemporary criticism. Writers, editors, and readers of periodicals in and about the east coast were conscious of being subjects in and of the reconfigured spatial field of the modern world – conscious of being and becoming modern.

TRANSATLANTIC MODERNITY AND TRANSLOCALISM

Attention to print periodicals thus challenges the notion that sites of cultural production on the east coast were remote, isolated, or unresponsive to transformed social relations in an increasingly connected transatlantic world. Part of this challenge includes contesting the sublation of heterogenous localities and voices into a coherent regional culture. One aim, then, is to repudiate the view that "the Maritimes" ever was a stable and comprehensible regional space per se, and, by extension, to question the received notion that regional spaces exist in opposition to the urban as anti-spaces of modernism and modernity. This pertains particularly to the critical perception of the Maritime Provinces as a space marked by conservative nostalgia and the absence of modernization and modern culture in the early twentieth century. This is one crucial perception that periodicals there help to dispel. But part of my critical purpose is also to complicate the very claims to modernity advanced in settler-colonial discourses of regionality, then and now. This requires moving beyond the notion that the east coast was simply an "elsewhere" of modernity in order to recuperate what Trouillot calls "the hidden faces" of modernity, to investigate the ways in which "modernity disguises and misconstrues the many Others that it creates."[40] Important here is not only how the east has been "othered" in narratives of Canadian and transatlantic modernity, but also how narratives of modernity generated from within conceal their own histories of colonial violence, appropriation, class conflict, and structural exclusion.

If, as I argue, the region itself is a contingent product of modernity, its deconstruction involves interrogating the appropriations and exclusions that facilitated its emergence. It necessarily attends to the superimposition of settler-colonial geography onto Wabanaki territory, a superimposition achieved, in part, through narratives of cultural inheritance and self-indigenization in *fin-de-siècle* cultural magazines. It also needs to consider how the wedding of whiteness to "regional identity" produced concrete geographies of exclusion that situated both long-resident and diasporic Black populations outside the newly conceived region. And, finally, it must also account for the ways in which liberal and nominal recognition of racial and ethnic difference served rather to police the boundaries of regional identity than to shape new spatial understandings to the material realities of internal difference. However, it also involves recuperating those voices – Black-separatist, communist, socialist-feminist – excluded from extant literary-cultural histories of the east coast, voices that found expression in dissenting magazines and papers such as *Neith* and *The Maritime Labor Herald*. The purpose of this recovery work is not to assimilate those voices to a reformed vision of inclusive regionality, but rather to identify the multiple sites and trajectories of modernity in the east that cannot be contained within narratives of literary or cultural regionalism. These were trajectories that not only exceeded the nation-space, but also rejected the region and nation as workable, territorializing responses to modernity, and as the only scales at which political action and substantive change could be realized.

In attempting to recover both the discursive operation of colonial, racialized, and gendered exclusivities in regional magazines, *and* the significant sites of resistance that found expression in periodicals, I depend upon Trouillot's conceptualization of modernity as a "North Atlantic Universal": "particulars that have gained a degree of universality, chunks of human history that have become historical standards."[41] As such, I share Trouillot's ambivalence about "the extent to which modernity can be fully conceptualized," but similarly recognize that "the word modernity evokes sensibilities, perceptions, choices, and states of affairs that are not easily captured by other words."[42] Modernity remains a useful concept, then, not for the uncritical celebration of the modern, but as an historically and geographically rooted universal that produces geographies and subjects, centres and elsewheres, moderns and "Others." For Trouillot, the processes and assumptions of modernity, projections of "the North Atlantic experience on a universal scale," necessarily "deny their localization, the sensibilities, and the history from which they spring."[43] Yet we can recover (as Trouillot does for the Caribbean) the particularities of place as they encounter and thus shape the trajectories of modernity.

Understanding modernity as historically rooted in the North Atlantic, but necessarily reconfigured as it is routed through the east coast, thus requires a framework that stresses *translocal* connections within a *transatlantic* context. Translocalism, a concept that has gained much currency in critical geography and anthropology over the past two decades, has received far less attention in literary and cultural criticism than has the related but distinct concept of transnationalism. In one of the only articles to put "translocalism" into conversation with literatures in Canada, Julie Rak contends that "[the] translocal … can be a description of movement as well as a critique of mobility within a nation-state."[44] Significantly, Rak sees translocality as emphasizing "the importance of local places in Canada, at the same time resisting the impulse to subordinate the regional to the national in the Canadian imaginary."[45] Rak's comments here highlight the usefulness of the translocal in capturing connections and movements between localities without appealing to a national paradigm. According to this framework, it is not primarily the movements of editors, writers, and periodicals across national borders that are important, but rather the connections and flows among local sites of production, influence, and reception within a broader transatlantic context. Thus, the regionalist discourse advanced in the magazine *Acadiensis* is constituted by movements and exchanges between Saint John, Boston, and New York; the multiple lines of influence that shape Abraham Beverley Walker's rhetorical modernity in *Neith*, though rooted in Saint John, are equally routed through Atlanta, Baltimore, and Port of Spain. Every chapter in this book thus registers the varying degrees of translocal mobility and exchange that not only helped shape periodical discourse, but also constituted the sites of periodical production and reception as translocalities.

By studying modern magazines in and about the Maritime Provinces within a translocal framework, we can begin to appreciate the degree to which periodicals beyond Canada's metropolitan centres advanced spatializing and identity-forming responses to their moment. And these responses frequently contested the national and nationalist preoccupations of editors elsewhere. Scholars have long examined the contribution of literature – and periodical literature, in particular – to national belonging. Comparatively few studies, however, have examined the significance of periodicals to the discursive construction of space and place at scales other than the national. In the midst of the sweeping "nationalization of culture" between the wars, during what Benedict Anderson calls Canada's "era of high capitalist nationalism," the agonistic resistance to nationalism evident in many east-coast periodicals is, in and of itself, a significant development.[46] What is "truly remarkable" about *these* periodicals is not, as Allan Weiss remarks of modern "Canadian magazines" generally, "the extent to which editors had a nationalist purpose or consciousness," but rather the extent to which editors situated themselves in broader transatlantic dialogues to articulate loyalties and identifications independent of and sometimes beyond the nation-space.[47]

Finally, attention to these forgotten periodicals reveals significant cultural forms that have been ignored in recent criticism despite efforts to broaden the temporal and geographic scope of Canadian modernism. Such overlooked forms include the discursive constellation of Afromodernism at the turn of the century and socialist-feminist poetics before the 1930s, both of which found expression in periodicals of the east coast, in *Neith* and *The Maritime Labor Herald*, respectively. These formations remain entirely absent from modernist studies in Canada, including those purporting to "[trouble] the temporality and locatedness of cultural modernity" and draw "critical attention to alternative modernisms and other sites of cultural formation" in the early twentieth century.[48] This absence evinces what James Connolly deems the "metropolitan bias" of modernist print studies, "one strong enough to suggest, sometimes explicitly and sometimes implicitly, that modernity itself was an urban phenomenon."[49] The result is not only a spatial lacuna, according to which places and regions are simply dropped from the geography of Canadian modernism, but also a temporal narrowing, whereby the historical scope of modernism is expanded backward but its linear coherence and progression are preserved intact. Ultimately, what the critical neglect of divergent periodicals like *Neith* and *The Maritime Labor Herald* suggests is less an opportunity to expand further the spatial-temporal scope of Canadian modernism, than a need to recognize the different and sometimes incommensurate temporalities of modernity and its routes through non-metropolitan localities in the transatlantic. Periodicals, perhaps more than any other form, are uniquely suited to charting those routes.

PERIODICAL FORM

It bears repeating that, before telecommunications media such as radio and television challenged the authority of print periodicals in the mid-twentieth century, the periodical was the primary medium through which many people sought to address plural publics on issues of culture and politics, place and literature. In turn, editors and contributors helped shape the cultural politics and spatial understandings of their readerships. For this reason, periodicals constitute key records of people's discursive and imaginative engagements with ideas of place and identity under the conditions of twentieth-century modernity. Periodicals, however, are not mere repositories for isolated texts, and the emergence of periodical studies has encouraged a reconsideration of the serial as a unique form meriting special critical attention. In fact, as early as 1989, Margaret Beetham argued for the examination of the Victorian periodical as a distinct genre "associated with a set of characteristics which make it a potentially disruptive kind of text."[50] Working against the "openness" and "fluidity" of the periodical, however, are the regularity of its appearance, as well as "continuities of format, shape, and pattern of contents."[51] In one respect, this tension between the constraint and openness of the periodical form both facilitates and conditions the discursive construction of specific readerships and, in turn, the projection of political and cultural identities, in place. Yet it is also a fundamentally mobile form, circulating across distances, sometimes great, and connecting disparate contributors to diffuse readerships. It is thus useful to consider how the form of the periodical inflected the production, circulation, and reception of place, identity, and literature in the modern period, and this consideration underpins the methodology I adopt in the study of periodicals in and about the east coast.

While the treatment of periodicals as a distinct genre has been a cornerstone of nineteenth-century and Victorian studies, its application in studies of the modern period is comparatively recent. In Canada, such key studies as Ken Norris's *The Little Magazine in Canada 1925–1980* and Louis Dudek and Michael Gnarowski's *The Making of Modern Poetry in Canada* asserted the importance of particular magazines to Canadian literary modernism, but rarely do they treat periodicals as more than receptacles for individual texts. In the past two decades, however, scholars have begun to address this critical oversight. In their influential 2006 article "The Rise of Periodical Studies," Sean Latham and Robert Scholes argue that scholars in the humanities "have been too quick to see magazines merely as discrete bits of information rather than autonomous objects of study."[52] Ann Ardis and Patrick Collier note that this tendency is especially detrimental for the period 1880–1940, a period that saw a "mediamorphosis" of print and a "sea change" in the world of "book, newspaper, and periodical publishing."[53] "Studying the culture of this period," they argue, "requires renewed attention to this radically transforming print ecology."[54] The scope of this transformative period has obvious implications for the study of east-coast periodicals between 1890 and 1933, a period roughly coextensive with the "mediamorphosis" to which Ardis and Collier refer. The consideration of periodicals as "autonomous objects of study" has helped redefine modern periodical studies. Exemplary of this book-historical and bibliographic scholarship is the work of Faye Hammill and Michelle Smith, whose *Magazines, Travel, and Middlebrow Culture: Canadian Periodicals in English and French, 1925–1960* makes an invaluable contribution to the study of modern magazines in Canada. Nevertheless, though such revisionary work continues to expand the scope of modern periodical studies, it has done little to encourage attention to periodicals outside Canada's urban metropoles.

This is surprising given both the importance of periodicals to literature and cultural discourse on the east coast and the mobile nature of the periodical form itself. If, as Franco Moretti observes, "the novel is *the most centralized of all literary genres*,"[55] one might expect the repeating, serial nature of the periodical, long contrasted with the relative permanence and spatial fixity of the book, to lend itself to decentralizing tendencies and anticentric formations. Such is not the case, however, according to extant studies of modern periodicals in Canada, most of which limit themselves to magazines published in Canada's largest urban centres, and none of which consider periodicals published in the Maritime Provinces. Expanding the focus beyond Canada's metropoles within a translocal framework, however, invites consideration of the ways the periodical form itself counters a "geography of publishing where the center holds an almost unchallenged sway."[56] Studying those forms necessarily involves literary and discursive analysis, reading the "literary" in its broadest sense to encompass a range of genres published in modern periodicals: essays, editorials, open letters, and advertisements, as well as poetry and fiction. However, it also demands attention to the situatedness of texts within the material form of the periodical.

Understood as a distinct form, the periodical can be read to generate meanings among and across its diverse textual, visual, and material aspects. Those meanings are, in turn, shaped by the respective editorial programs of individual periodicals. Such editorializing often involved the conscious arrangement of materials and the creation of extradiegetic narratives through juxtaposition, annotation, and total structure. Accordingly, I argue that phenomena such as literary regionalism are best understood as the product of reciprocally related processes of authorial intent, editorial decision-making, and critical reception, and not qualities that inhere in individual literary texts. The centrality of editorial practice, in particular, is important not only for what it reveals about the circulation and reception of literature, but also for what it tells us about the capacity of periodicals to emphasize or conceal the inherently mobile character of their own production and distribution.

Finally, what the periodicals examined in this study all share is a remarkable degree of mobility, a quality with particular consequence for the study of place and identity in the modern period. If one hallmark of modernity is the profound transformation in the scale and momentum of movement and connectivity, then periodicals constitute the key records by which this transformation can be traced through the east coast. As a mobile form, the periodical – its circulation, diffuse contributors, and mobile readership – dramatizes the translocal networks of writers, editors, and readers that discursively produced place and identity in the early twentieth century. Recently, this inherent mobility of form has been noted in American and transatlantic-British studies. Heather Haveman argues that magazines not only trace "translocal and impersonal associative relations," but also work to "create the kinds of geographically dispersed *translocal* groups that characterize modern societies."[57] Similarly, in *British Settler Emigration in Print 1832–1877*, Jude Piesse argues that nineteenth-century transatlantic periodicals "not only reflected mobility, but were actively involved in producing it."[58] For Piesse, the periodical was "intertwined" with forces of mobility not only through its "investment in circulation" and its "transnational range," but also via its formal dynamics.[59] The form of the periodical itself, argues Piesse, bears "intrinsic associations with dynamics of motion, migration, and flow."[60]

Piesse's theorization of periodicals as both records and producers of mobilities offers a sound basis for the study of periodicals on Canada's east coast. The magazine itself was an eminently portable medium. Even a trenchantly regionalist magazine such as *Acadiensis* could attain surprisingly wide distribution, its editor David Russell Jack boasting of subscribers from "the Atlantic to the Pacific coasts, and from the Klondike to Southern California," with a small list of "European subscribers" to boot.[61] But editors and contributors themselves were also highly mobile and diffuse. To appreciate this mobility, one need only consider Theodore Goodridge Roberts, who, having left New York to cover the Spanish-American War in 1898, sailed by barkentine to Brazil, contracted malaria, returned to Fredericton to convalesce, and founded *Kit-Bag* before setting off for Barbados in 1903. And though mobility was always socially differentiated, always constrained by what Doreen Massey calls the "power-geometry of time-space compression," voluntary mobility was not strictly the privilege of the cosmopolitan elite.[62] Abraham Beverly Walker, too, was remarkably mobile. Walker left New Brunswick to study at Washington's National University and returned with his LLB to New Brunswick, where he was called to the bar in 1882. In 1889 he left again, intending to emigrate to Atlanta, Georgia. He toured the United States and lectured on "the Negro Problem" for two years, before returning to establish *Neith* in 1903. And no one is more representative of this incredible mobility than Michael Ambrose McInnes, a printer from Summerside, PEI, who founded the regionalist *Maple Leaf* in Oakland, California, in 1907. That magazine was integral to popularizing the "Maritimer" as a coherent identity position, an achievement facilitated by paid subscribers in seventeen American states and all Canadian provinces. Thus, even as magazines such as *Acadiensis* and *The Busy East* depended upon notions of stasis and fixity to define the regional community to which they appealed, periodical culture on the east coast was perpetually in motion.

Place and region, then, were consistently produced and inscribed through discursive processes that played out across sometimes vast translocal networks of people and print. Periodicals offer the primary records we have of those discursive processes, and those records are markedly more diverse and heterogeneous than has been acknowledged in print-culture histories of the region. This picture of diversity and heterogeneity, however, is incomplete. It is, in fact, one hazard of periodical studies that the periodical form comes to be seen as inherently inclusive. Accordingly, the periodical is sometimes discussed as almost utopian in its ability to draw people and groups from all strata into an imagined, all-inclusive public sphere. Thus, Beetham argues that even the "most homogeneous" periodicals "were and are characterized by diversity of voice and authorial attribution."[63] More recently, Haveman celebrates the form's accessibility, contending that, "[as] long as printers have unused capacity, any individual or group with information to disseminate, a point of view to promulgate, a community to build, or a cause to promote can arrange to publish a magazine."[64] We might question, however, the extent to which magazines were available across all "strata" of society "as tools of communication and community building."[65] In fact, the periodical is not a universally accessible, democratic form. Much as periodicals on the east coast speak to diversity and dissension, they also provided the means to consolidate remarkably restrictive and homogenous conceptions of regional and national identity; these were identities that were linguistically English, optically white, and ethnically European. And invariably, conceptions of place and identity in the pages of east-coast periodicals depended upon settler-colonial epistemologies of space. Before turning to the chapters and periodicals of this study, then, it is worth registering the significant limits set by a focus on Anglophone print periodicals.

MI'KMAW PLACE-BASED MODERNITY AND THE LIMITS OF PERIODICAL FORM

History is coded and we can't escape her.
There are no honours or monuments to honour our dead.
There is a coal-firing power plant instead.
Three smokestacks to honour our plight,
perfect metaphor brought to life.

Rebecca Thomas, "Remember Turtle Grove"

Any iteration of settler-colonial geography, Thomas's elegy for Turtle Grove suggests, inevitably contains the traces of what it has displaced. When Gersham Tufts arrived in Dartmouth, Nova Scotia, from Boston in the 1760s, he could not have known that the small cove in which he settled would be home to a power-generating station bearing his name. Nor could he have known that the image of the Tufts Cove Generating Station and its three five-hundred-foot smokestacks would come to symbolize a gritty, blue-collar identity that residents of Dartmouth would cling to when the province merged the city with Halifax in 1996. That amalgamation became a point of unbounded resentment for many Dartmouth residents who readily believed it would destroy their sense of community and belonging. Dartmouth's MLA Marilyn More publicly lamented this "loss of identity" and, quoting Joseph Howe, condemned the "treachery and connivance" by which the people of Dartmouth came to be "governed by strangers."[66] A decade later, the image of Tufts Cove took on new resonance. Plastered across hoodies, coffee mugs, and dish towels in the wake of rapid gentrification, the image became symbolic of an edgier urban character as national news media dubbed Dartmouth "Halifax's Brooklyn" and Canada's "hippest neighbourhood."[67] Thus would the image of Tufts Cove become a shifting signifier in the negotiation of place identity across the microgeography of modern conurbation. Gersham Tufts, of course, would know none of this.

What he did know was that the thousand acres he was granted in Dartmouth Township in 1790 included the eleven-acre community of Kebeceque, whose Mi'kmaq residents suddenly found themselves living on disputed lands.[68] For Tufts, his descendants, and generations of neighbours who followed, the Mi'kmaq presence at Tufts Cove, known as Turtle Grove by others, was unacceptable. Several failed attempts were thus made to expel the Kebeceque Mi'kmaq throughout the nineteenth century.[69] Then, in January 1917, white landowner and petroleum dealer Vincent Farrell wrote to Duncan Campbell Scott at the Department of Indian Affairs that he could "not tolerate any longer this treatment or the continual annoyance from the Indians."[70] He later sent notice to the Mi'kmaq that they would be removed by December of that year. The department was at a loss over how to handle the situation. It was tasked with resolving such disputes, but, like the neighbours at Tufts Cove, could not conceive of the transient lifestyle of the Kebeceque Mi'kmaq as being compatible with land rights and property ownership. The government, as Andrew Parnaby observes, "viewed the Mi'kmaq not as an ally or even an enemy, but as a problem," and an inscrutable one at that.[71] Mi'kmaw seasonal migration and resource procurement, which continued alongside modern forms of occupational pluralism in urban areas such as Dartmouth, remained incomprehensible to white settlers and to the settler state.

Yet it was precisely this unknowability that had helped constitute migratory movement as a strategy of anticolonial practice. As Jacob Remes observes, the "complex networks and migration rendered [the Mi'kmaq Kebeceque] illegible to the white, colonial state, and it was exactly this illegibility and transience that were their best tools for resistance."[72] This "illegibility," the inability of the state to "read" or know societies or individuals, should not be taken to imply an absence of textuality. In the 1910s, resistance to the dispossession of Kebeceque land and colonial domination was led by Jerry Lonecloud. Lonecloud's leadership, like that of other Mi'kmaq and Wolastoqiyik leaders, depended upon his ability to strategically translate Wabanaki "ways of knowing" to the non-Indigenous in varied forms, including letters, petitions, and written testimony.[73] Thus, when Lonecloud wrote to the department in November 1917, he combined Mi'kmaw oral testimony with an appeal to the colonial legal tradition. Pointing to the oral testimony of elder residents, Lonecloud argued that the Mi'kmaq had camped at Tufts Cove "since time out of mind," and that Farrell's "claim" to the land could not annul the Mi'kmaw "right" to the land, "even if it be regarded only in the light of what is termed squatter's rights."[74] The effectiveness of Lonecloud's arguments in this and several other petitions cannot be known; just weeks after he sent the letter, the Halifax Explosion obliterated the community of Kebeceque, effectively granting Farrell's demands. What the letters reveal, however, is the extent to which, even during what Passamaquoddy historian Donald Soctomah calls the "invisible years," Mi'kmaw land-based resistance took textual *as well as* oral and material forms.[75]

These textual forms – innumerable letters, petitions, court testimonies, and documented oral histories – are almost entirely absent from the pages of periodicals in the modern period. Important exceptions exist. Arthur Huff Fauset's "Folklore from the Half-Breeds in Nova Scotia," a series of tales collected from mixed Black and Mi'kmaq storytellers at Lequile during his 1923 sojourn, was presented without critical commentary in

The Journal of American Folklore in 1925. It was one of several collections of Mi'kmaw and Wolastoqey stories published in the journal in the 1920s. And yet, when Mi'kmaq voices appeared in the pages of scholarly journals or local newspapers, they were invariably appropriated and mediated by settler anthropologists, folklorists, or journalists. The result is that a focus on periodicals as the primary records of modern place and identity is necessarily incomplete, unable to account for the range and diversity of expression that helped constitute Indigenous modernities on the east coast in the early twentieth century. Accordingly, a significant qualification to the foregoing is the failure to address what Kirby Brown calls New Modernist Studies' "Indian Problem": its failure to consider Indigenous literature and culture in any substantive way even as it works to expand the temporal-geographic scope and socio-cultural contexts of modernism. Indigenous Peoples, writes Brown, "are conspicuous not in their recovered presence made possible by these democratizing critical shifts but in their ongoing absence from these conversations."[76] That absence is also conspicuous in the present study, which does not explore how such expressions as Lonecloud's, what Remes calls "folk legalism that sought to use the government's logic of law and property against it,"[77] might themselves constitute an innovative modern form, a significant instance of Mi'kmaw place-based modernity. And this failure does not result simply from the constraints of the periodical's textuality, which necessarily exclude nonalphabetic and other material forms, though those constraints are significant. As Lonecloud's example and innumerable others attest, Wabanaki leaders, activists, and writers *did* produce textual forms during the period. The periodical, however, was not the medium in which those forms were realized.

What the foregoing makes clear is that the negotiation of place and identity in modern Anglophone periodicals, for all its conflictual heterogeneity, necessarily partakes of the superimposition of settler-colonial geographies onto Indigenous territory, what Bryant calls "a transatlantic imposition laid atop Indigenous place-worlds."[78] This long history of occupation and imposition, of course, did not figure into the pre- and post-amalgamation political debates of the 1990s. The obvious irony subtending those debates is that residents of Dartmouth, unlike those of Kebeceque a century earlier, were never "governed by strangers" in any profound sense. Nevertheless, and despite the assault wrought by settler-colonial occupation and dominance on Wabanaki communities, the surviving Mi'kmaq of Kebeceque continued to deploy transience and textuality alike to thwart the centralization policies through which the state sought to control Wabanaki mobility and culture.[79] And inasmuch as Tufts Cove continues to circulate as a symbol of oppositional urban identity-formation, it necessarily bears the inscription of this earlier and ongoing history. Thus, any study of discursive modernity, regionality, or place in Anglophone periodicals must reckon with the fact that "beneath the heavy inscriptions of dominance exists an animate cultural and geographic Indigenous region that is … continuously reinscribing itself."[80] The first chapter of this study is concerned, in part, with how settler-colonial regionalism was predicated on such "inscriptions of dominance": narratives of cultural succession, inheritance, and self-indigenization that sought to dispossess Wabanaki Peoples of their lands. However, engaging earnestly and thoroughly with Indigenous modernities necessarily demands attention to forms other than the periodical, a project that goes beyond the scope of this study.

THE PERIODICALS

This book is organized into two parts roughly divided by the First World War. The first part, encompassing chapters 1 and 2, covers the period from 1895 to 1910. The second part, comprising the remaining three chapters, covers the period 1916 to 1933, with a particular focus on the 1920s. The first chapter deals directly with the discursive production of region and regionalism in *fin-de-siècle* magazines. In addition to briefly surveying seven magazines of the period, the first chapter establishes the historical context of the long *fin-de-siècle*[81] (1880s–1910s) on the east coast and articulates what is at stake in the historicization of the region as a contingent, constructed space. Contrary to much recent scholarship on regions, I argue that regionalization and regionalism in Canada must be understood as rooted in interrelated spatializing and identity-forming responses to twentieth-century modernity. Focusing on the regionalist magazine *Acadiensis* (Saint John, 1901–08) and the small literary magazine *Kit-Bag* (1902–03), I argue that the production of the "Maritime" region as an organic, homogeneous cultural space depended upon the juxtaposition of history, cartography, and literature in the pages of regional periodicals.

The second chapter focusses on Abraham Beverley Walker's *Neith: A Magazine of Literature, Science, Art, Philosophy, Jurisprudence, Criticism* (Saint John, 1903–04). Providing a forum for Black writers on and beyond the east coast, *Neith* advanced a Black separatist program that challenged the dominant discourses of post-race and Canadian exceptionalism. In so doing, Walker developed an Afromodernist political and literary aesthetic that fused Afrocentric neoclassicism with the prophetic tradition to renovate traditions of Afro-Protestantism and Black historiography. By reading this important magazine as an expression of Afromodernism, I counter Canadian modernist criticism's failure to adequately address Blackness as distinct from "race," as irreducible to one among various sites of marginalization and exclusion. Underpinning this chapter, then, is a recognition of the ways in which modernist studies have contributed to the obliteration of Blackness as they imagine Canada and Canadian modernity in the twentieth century.

The third chapter serves as a bridge between the first part and the second, introducing the next section. Here, I provide historical context for the socio-economic crisis that devastated local economies along the east coast in the 1920s, and I examine the effects of that crisis on shifting conceptions of collective identity and cultural politics in the interwar period. By contrasting the liberal-populist *The Busy East of Canada* (Saint John and Sackville, 1910–33) with the socialist *The Maritime Labor Herald* (Glace Bay, 1921–26), I argue that periodical literature in the 1920s helped to foster the affective investment necessary to constitute divergent political identities. In so doing, I outline and deconstruct a long tradition of analysis that has figured the Maritime Provinces in the early twentieth century as a premodern society whose literature and culture were uniformly defined by a conservative, apolitical antimodernism. Contemporary criticism of the east coast, I argue, must move beyond McKay's influential "folk paradigm" not only for a more accurate and fuller appreciation of cultural production on the east coast, but also to disrupt the tendency to chart interwar culture through a binary opposition between modernism and antimodernism. I conclude the chapter with a survey of transitional literature and criticism in *The Dalhousie Review* (1921–), a quarterly magazine that reveals the inadequacy of this binary to the study of interwar literature in Canada.

In the fourth chapter, I examine the general-interest magazine *The Busy East* as the vehicle for the Maritime Rights Movement, a regional protest movement that took root in the aftermath of the First World War. Contrary to older scholarship on regional protest of the 1920s, I argue that the Maritime Rights Movement is best understood as grounded in a form of populist-liberalism that helped construct the "Maritime People" as a collective political and cultural identity. The cultural correlative to this political program found expression in the popular war fiction of Will R. Bird, whose stories were published in almost every other issue of the magazine between 1927 and 1933. Bird's war fiction, I argue, offered readers a liberal fantasy through which affective investment in the liberal project was reproduced as common sense. It is thus exemplary of both the passing of the First World War into popular fiction and the centrality of fiction to the liberal political imaginary. Ultimately, the incredible success of regional protest, *The Busy East*, and Bird's fiction helped usher in a post-political era in which liberal hegemony went effectively unchallenged after the 1920s.

Before the late 1920s, however, the liberal hegemony seemed hardly assured. The fifth and final chapter registers the militant opposition to liberal capitalism advanced in the ultra-radical communist paper *The Maritime Labor Herald*. The *Herald* pioneered a leftist journalism that figured local and regional class struggles as the proximal manifestations of global working-class revolt. Accordingly, I argue that the poetry appearing in the paper helped to mediate between the local and the global, accruing popular sentiment to a collective class identity. Though all of this poetry is definably modern, key examples, represented by the poems of Joe Wallace and Becky Buhay, dispense with traditional poetics to achieve an effective modernism that predates the intersection of the literary left and modernism in the 1930s. This and the journal's role as a leading forum for socialist feminism in the early 1920s mark the paper's most significant contributions to interwar culture. The demise of the *Herald* coincided with the local left's spectacular collapse in 1926, but the legacies of radical labour action championed in the journal would continue to influence new liberalism after the consolidation of the liberal order and the ascendency of antimodernist cultural politics in the 1930s.

The year 1933 marks the end of the period covered by this study. It is also the year that *The Busy East of Canada* was renamed *The Maritime Advocate and Busy East*. The change in name signalled the completion of the magazine's decade-long evolution from a business magazine concerned primarily with political economy to a mainstream general-interest magazine. As *The Maritime Advocate* and finally *The Atlantic Advocate*, it would go on to become the longest-running and widest-circulating magazine published on the east coast, ceasing its eighty-two-year run in 1992. Yet the 1933 name seems to signal something more: namely, the triumph of a regional project that had begun at the turn of the century when the region and regional identity were as yet nascent, their existence unassured. Only after the 1920s would antimodernism form the cultural core of the newly consolidated liberal order, working to expunge the contested, unstable, and fraught ascendence of place and region as common-sense loci of personal and collective identity. Thus, one decade after his formative trip to Nova Scotia, what Fauset had failed to find there – an isolated, primitive folk society free of the trappings of the modern world – was taking shape in popular narratives of the region. As those narratives assumed the status of truth, the once-obvious contingency of the nascent region would all but pass from collective memory, and along with it went recollections of the dissent and resistance that had found expression in modern periodicals. It is tempting, then, to read these periodicals as artifacts of a lost era, aberrations in the *longue durée* of Maritime conservatism. Yet when a decidedly modernist cultural formation took shape in mid-century New Brunswick, fostering a new vocabulary of place and identity, it looked back to those formations that had preceded it. However effective the ideological workings of the antimodernist hegemony after 1933, it was never complete and never unchallenged.

1

The Construction of Region in *Fin-de-Siècle* Magazines

In the winter of 1885, the province of Nova Scotia was beset with discontent. Amid mass out-migration, a minor depression, declining primary industries, and feelings of political subordination within Confederation, there was now talk of the province's secession from the dominion. Led by Premier W.S. Fielding, the Liberal government motioned to petition the federal government to repeal the act of Confederation, even as members of Fielding's own party assailed him for exhuming "the putrid carcass of repeal."[1] Lines were drawn, and the party was split between secessionists and unionists.[2] It was in the midst of this turmoil, on 1 January 1886, that Halifax's Tory paper, *The Morning Herald*, published a special New Year's supplement intent on charting the future of Nova Scotia. Crowning the list of contributions was an essay titled "The Outlook for Literature: Acadia's Field for Poetry, History and Romance" by the literary *ne plus ultra* of Canadian nationalism, Charles G.D. Roberts. Asked to prognosticate on the "future of literature in Nova Scotia," Roberts instead insists that no literature is Nova Scotian that is not first Canadian:

> It is the future of Canadian nationality with which every son of Canada is most concerned; and our literature will be false to its trust, will fail of that very service for which young nations have ever relied upon their literature, if it does not show itself the nurse of all patriotic enthusiasms, and the bane of provincial jealousies.[3]

Articulating a nationalist argument against cultural parochialism, and in favour of a "patriotic" literature capable of quashing "provincial jealousies," Roberts's article reads as an apt companion piece to the unionist arguments alongside which it was published. When Roberts does set out to answer the question posed, he reframes it as "the part likely to be played by Nova Scotia talent in the making of our national literature."[4]

Oft-cited as a foundational document of Canadian literature, Roberts's "Outlook for Literature" has been variously interpreted as evidence of his belief in the "essentially regional nature ... of cultural practice,"[5] and as a testament to the way in which nationalism "attempts to subsume the local and the regional to the larger purposes of national unity and national aspiration."[6] In light of this critical concern with the relationship between the "regional" and the "national," readers might expect to find some articulation of regionalism in the essay itself, some regional sentiment or rejection thereof, perhaps some reference to the "Maritimes," the "Maritime Provinces," or a "Maritime literature." To the contrary, the region, in its contemporary guise, remains entirely absent. Only Roberts's deployment of the poetic "Acadia" in the title suggests any vision of a regional scale. Far from expressing the sort of "barnyard regionalism" later modernist critics would charge him with,[7] Roberts's paper, when situated at its original site of publication within the context of Nova Scotian secessionism, functions as an attack on Liberal secessionists' attachment of political and cultural feeling to the delimited, geopolitical entity of the province. The attachment of such feeling to "the region," the formulation of a regional identity, or a "regional consciousness," would have seemed improbable: "the term 'Maritimes,'" writes social historian Judith Fingard, "no more reflected a collective sense of identity within the region in the 1880s than it had ever done."[8] "The moulders of public opinion," among whom Roberts can be safely numbered, "gave precedence to almost any identity other than a regional one, whether it be community, province, nation, continent, or empire."[9]

What Roberts's article and Fingard's comments gesture toward is a more fundamental absence: that of the region itself. It was not simply the lack of a regional identity "within the region" that governed discourse in the three easternmost provinces; it was the absence of any cohesive community that could intelligibly be called a region. The region, not simply as an agglomeration of three provinces, but as a coherent geographic totality and as a locus for place-based identification, did not exist. And yet, two decades later, writing from Oakland, California, Michael Ambrose McInnis could dedicate his magazine *The Maple Leaf* (Oakland, 1907–49) to the "sons and daughters of the Maritime Provinces," and address himself intelligibly to an entirely new category of persons: "Maritimers."[10] What changed in the two decades between Roberts's nationalist address and McInnis's regionalist monthly? What spurred this new representation of space, and how had this new region come to be understood as coterminous with cultural identity? Was McInnis at once interpellating his readers as members of a regional community and producing the region with which they were to identify? In fact, McInnis's publication is the culmination of a much larger spatial process of territorialization and regionalization at the turn of the century, one that saw the production of the region and of regional identity, both of which were discursively produced in the pages of *fin-de-siècle* magazines. This chapter is a study of that specific process of regionalization as it played out in magazines in the Maritime Provinces between 1890 and 1910. But what that process reveals about the discursive formation of regionality, regional culture, and literary regionalism offers a corrective to conventional narratives that fail to adequately account for the history of Canadian regionalism as a political, social, and cultural, as well as literary, phenomenon.

Focusing on the magazines that served as the vehicles for discursive constructions of the region, this chapter challenges several assumptions that continue to inform critical discussions of regionalism today. The first of these, suggested in the foregoing, is that modern regions existed prior to the development of regionalism as an ideological, political, and cultural phenomenon.[11] The second assumption is that regions in Canada necessarily exist, or once existed, within a scalar hierarchy of region, nation, and globe, whereby subnational regions form one spatial scale that exists on the periphery, margin, or *hinterland* of the nation-state within a centre-periphery model. Finally, and closely connected to the first two assumptions, but existing more as an ambiguity in extant scholarship than as a fundamental assumption, is that literary regionalism is a quality that inheres in literary texts – which are then said to give expression to the cultural, geographic, and social particularity of the region – and that it exists independently of editorial and critical processes of cultural selection.

Contrary to these assumptions, an analysis of regionalism in *fin-de-siècle* magazines reveals that the region, the "Maritimes," was, first of all, the product of social processes and the discursive construction of regional identity, both of which were inseparable from broader spatializing processes during the transition to industrial modernity. Second, attention to the translocal networks and plural public sphere that constituted magazine producers, contributors, and readerships reveals that regions themselves are produced and negotiated translocally. As such, a hierarchical scalar logic is unable to account for the multidirectional flow of global cultural exchanges that have not only always penetrated regional space, but also fundamentally shaped and encouraged the discursive construction of the "Maritimes," both in the pages of regional magazines and beyond. And third, investigating the adjacency of regionalism and literary culture in the pages of magazines suggests that literary regionalism at the beginning of the twentieth century was as much a function of editorial practice and critical reception as it was a quality of literary texts themselves, involving a process of cultural selection that sublated descriptions of local setting and phenomenological expressions of place into a constructed regional (and regionalist) canon.[12] Accordingly, situating regionalism in the Maritime Provinces within the socio-historical context of the *fin-de-siècle* reveals at once the implication of identity, politico-cultural feeling, and territoriality in *any iteration* of "regionalism," and, further, the location of "literary regionalism" in editorial and critical practice. What is at stake in the recuperation of *fin-de-siècle* magazines is not merely the recovery of critically neglected literary cultures (many of which gained greater recognition through publication outside the region), but a richer understanding of how the region was discursively produced within the context of late modernity.

REGIONAL MAGAZINES IN THE MARITIME PROVINCES DURING THE LONG *FIN-DE-SIÈCLE*

It bears reiterating the importance of print media to the processes of territorialization and identity-formation in the era preceding the rise of radio, television, and other mass telecommunications media. The relationship between print culture and nation-building has been well studied, with many scholars working from Benedict Anderson's influential *Imagined Communities* to examine the convergence of nationalism and the rise of mass print technologies. The nation, however, is not the only geographic scale at which space and identity are produced. And though the integral role played by magazines and newspapers in the construction of the

Canadian nation-state and national identity has been well documented, the crucial relationship between regionalism and periodical culture remains unexamined. Investigating regional periodicals, then, offers insight into the textual, editorial, and discursive processes of region-building that are both similar to *and* dissimilar from those performed by national magazines. Dissimilar, because the "region" was constructed as a natural fact of culture and geography, represented as a geographic primitive distinct from the bureaucratic, administrative, and ideological nation-state and from its provincial counterparts. At the same time, a survey of *fin-de-siècle* magazines reveals sharp distinctions that expose the heterogeneity, competing interests, and internal communal, ethnic, and sectarian division that regionalism sought to contain and conceal. Indeed, the genre of the magazine was particularly conducive for containing and concealing internal difference.

A closer analysis of magazines suggests that the magazine as a genre was particularly well-suited to the discursive construction of regional identity and literary regionalism. Magazines afforded degrees of editorial control that allowed for the recontextualization of literary texts within the textual and visual field of the magazine, imposing a regionalist orientation onto texts, and constraining and conditioning the possible meanings generated from their juxtaposition. This production of extradiegetic and extratextual narratives of regionality repositioned literary texts as the essential expression of collective cultural identity. The resulting regional canon obliterated the deterritorialized or cosmopolitan literary spaces of some texts, while emptying others of highly localized (and not definably regional) content. In turn, the cultural identity these texts were supposed to express was geographically encoded through the use of maps, historical cartography, and explicit critical statements. Thus, at the same time that these magazines helped sustain local literary cultures, they also sublated them into a regionalism not necessarily attested to in literary texts themselves. Emerging in what Linda and N. Merrill Distad term the "golden age" of "periodical publishing as the primary instrument and medium of public discourse," *fin-de-siècle* magazines in the Maritime Provinces were not only the primary vehicles for regionalism, they were also the medium in which the region was produced and negotiated.[13]

The emergence of the region as a locus for place-based identity coincided with a sudden proliferation of periodicals in the three provinces during the long *fin-de-siècle*. In addition to numerous special-interest magazines, this period saw the creation of six general-interest magazines in less than six years between 1895 and 1901: *The Nova Scotia Illustrated* (Halifax, 1895), *The New Brunswick Magazine* (Saint John, 1898–99; 1904–05), *Prince Edward Island Magazine* (Charlottetown, 1899–1905), *The International* (Saint John, 1901–02), *Cape Breton and Nova Scotia Magazine* (Sydney, 1901–02), and *Acadiensis* (Saint John, 1901–08). *Kit-Bag* (Fredericton, 1902–03), the only magazine of this period devoted strictly to poetry and fiction, appeared a year later. These magazines contributed to the emergent regionalism, but they also varied in their specific communal commitment, scope, intended readership, and duration. Taken together, they suggest diversity and division within and across the three provinces as much as they do homogeneity and cohesion. They reveal a divided field of disparate places and spaces even as they engage in the discursive construction of the region, wedding an intense interest in local history to Romantic attestations to the historicity and cultural distinctiveness of the emergent region. A new regional historiography was thus complemented by a critical interest in promoting a "regional" literature which could be abstracted and recontextualized as both expressive and constitutive of the region's culture.

This regionalizing process operated both within and outside the three provinces, and it was not only the result of symbolic constructions in cultural magazines, but also a function of the political and economic transformation of the Maritime Provinces in the final decades of the nineteenth century. The broader contexts of these transformations were at once national, conditioned by the consolidation of the Canadian Confederation, and transnational, thoroughly implicated in expanding transatlantic networks of people, ideas, information, goods, and culture. But magazines were not merely conduits for an emergent regionalism that had its origins elsewhere, origins independent of meanings generated through textual iterations of regionality and regional identity. Though the cultural producers of emergent regionalism were heavily invested in conceptions of the region as a geographic primitive, an already-constituted totality with pre-historical depth and a distinct culture, those very concepts were the consequences, not the source, of new territorial understandings.

Any thoroughgoing account of regional magazine culture on the east coast, then, must also account for its context: the transition of the three provinces to industrial modernity. But though that transition produced commonalities – patterns of uneven development and industrialization, urbanization, and out-migration – that cut across provincial and various group identities (class, race, gender, localisms, etc.), the regionalist discourse expressed in *fin-de-siècle* magazines supplemented those commonalities with a far more drastic attempt to use history, geography, and literature to construct a homogenous, monolithic regional community. In short, magazines provided the principal medium for the discursive construction of the region as the organic, originary site of a collective cultural identity. This production of a bounded, coherent, and cohesive regional space was both capacious and exclusionary: capacious in that the region exceeded both the boundaries of its three constitutive provinces and those of the Canadian nation-state, and exclusionary in that it was predicated on assumptions and representations of cultural and racial uniformity, variously effacing and policing cultural and racial difference.

Two key magazines, *Acadiensis* and *Kit-Bag*, reveal the integral function performed by periodicals in the period spanning the turn of the century. Nowhere was the regionalist project more consciously and aggressively advanced than in *Acadiensis*, a quarterly magazine based in Saint John and "devoted to the interests of the Maritime Provinces of Canada."[14] Its editor, David Russell Jack, was committed both to fostering a sense of shared culture and history, and to achieving the political unification of the three Maritime Provinces. The longest-running of the *fin-de-siècle* magazines, *Acadiensis* provides the most salient example of an editor and contributors actively engaged in constructing the region. None of the other *fin-de-siècle* magazines were as unequivocally regionalist as *Acadiensis*. Nevertheless, a comparison of *Acadiensis* with those magazines that were seemingly provincial in scope, such as *Prince Edward Island Magazine*, *The New Brunswick Magazine*, and *Cape Breton and Nova Scotia Magazine*, reveals shared assumptions about place, region, and identity. Often featuring contributions from the same writers, these magazines deployed local history and cultural criticism in support of a new territorial perspective, one that represented an homology between region and culture, even as divergent representations of the region betrayed a contested space wrought by provincial, communal, and sectarian division.

To the extent that they offered literary and cultural criticism while providing space for the publication of poetry, fiction, and *belles-lettres*, regional magazines, and their editors and contributors, attempted to formulate the basis for a distinct regional literature. They constructed a regional canon not by encouraging literary regionalism, but rather by producing it at the level of editorial practice. In fact, the literature published in *fin-de-siècle* regional magazines was not disconnected from popular national and international literary trends. Amateur attempts at "local colour" fiction and poetry anticipated the spectacular popularity of L.M. Montgomery and Stephen Leacock, although they generally lacked the satire, social critique, and humour of those authors' works. And much as the publication of appropriated Mi'kmaw and Wolastoqey oral stories represented an attempt to "self-indigenize" at the regional level, so too did white authors' appropriation of Indigenous themes, subjects, and imagery cater to the popular demand for exoticized stereotypes displayed by bourgeois audiences across Canada. At the national level, Pauline Johnson, despite her determination to challenge received stereotypes, represented for white Canadians an acceptably "safe" expression of Indigeneity;[15] at the regional level, figures like Gabe Acquin, the Wolastoqiyik guide, interpreter, and showman, were similarly romanticized and "idolized" as commendably colonial subjects.[16] Nationalism and imperialism were also prominent themes of the poetry and fiction published in *fin-de-siècle* regional magazines; and the containment of those themes within localist frameworks mirrored the reception of works such as Sara Jeannette Duncan's *The Imperialist*, dubbed in *Saturday Night* to be "photographic in its fidelity to local conditions and types."[17] It was ultimately the Victorian Romanticism of the Confederation poets, however, that had the greatest influence on regional magazines and the amateur authors published there. And like Bliss Carman and Roberts, local writers were cast as the agents of a distinct regional literature.

Committed to publishing "regional" literature, *fin-de-siècle* magazines provided a forum for local writers to publish poetry and fiction, thereby helping to sustain local literary cultures. However, the prioritization of regional history and the inability to compensate authors limited the number of literary works editors were willing to publish in any given issue. Of the six general-interest magazines listed above, only the fleeting *Cape Breton and Nova Scotia Magazine* appears to have paid contributors, and even then, only for a small number of solicited contributions. The result was that general-interest magazines attracted few original contributions from professional writers. In contrast, *Kit-Bag*, a little magazine devoted strictly to poetry and fiction, offered the only significant outlet for original and experimental writing. Edited by Theodore Goodridge Roberts, the magazine lasted only three issues. Its primary significance derives from its role as one of only a few non-commercial literary magazines in early-twentieth-century Canada, and as an antecedent to little magazines in the second quarter of the twentieth century. But it is also notable for its eschewal of any regionalist ideology. Positioning itself as a "chap book" opposed to mass-market periodicals, *Kit-Bag* typifies the way in which literary texts representing highly localized spaces were sublated into a regional canon via their reception and critical positioning in regionalist discourse. Again, *Acadiensis* provides a case in point, inducting *Kit-Bag* into "the realm of Acadian literature," a literature that *Acadiensis* aimed to impart as the cultural manifestation of regional identity.[18]

By the end of the first decade of the twentieth century, the emergent regionalism fostered in *fin-de-siècle* magazines had coalesced in the regional and national imaginary. Publications within and beyond the three provinces readily spoke of and addressed "Maritimers" and the "Maritimes" whence they came. Arriving at the end of the long *fin-de-siècle*, in 1907, and published some 5,000 km away from the three Maritime Provinces, *The Maple Leaf* appears as an affirmation of the regional identity that had taken shape over the preceding decade. But it also exposes what had remained largely concealed in the pages of general-interest magazines published within the three provinces: namely, that the region had never existed as a bounded, impermeable space, but was always constituted and produced by distanciated networks of people, many of whom – editors included and writers especially – did not live within the conventionally prescribed boundaries of the fledgling region. The most prominent contributors to regional magazines throughout the period were highly mobile, and several were absent from the region they worked to produce. Hence, in the final analysis, regionalism itself must be understood as a translocal phenomenon, as much the product of nostalgic yearnings from away as the desire for a coherent community within. What *The Maple Leaf* shares with its regionally resident counterparts is a conviction in the essential belonging of a people to a place. As such, it subscribes to many of the same problematic exclusivities, racial, gendered, and class-oriented, that characterize the emergent regionalism advanced in *Acadiensis* and other *fin-de-siècle* magazines.

The foregoing suggests the extent to which the region and regionalism were the products of discursive construction in magazines. That process was not divorced from the social and economic climate in which those magazines were published. Regionalism was negotiated in relation to specific and complex local, national, and transnational circumstances: the conditions brought about by incomplete and uneven industrialization, the consolidation of the nation-state, and the both liberating and unsettling consequences of a rapidly expanding transatlantic world. These conditions encouraged new representations of place and the projection of a thoroughly modern process of regionalization back in time, lending ideological coherence to a space that was in actuality heterogenous, internally divided, and contingent.

INDUSTRIAL MODERNITY IN THE EAST

The literary cultures and territorial politics developed in *fin-de-siècle* magazines were not merely a secondary expression, an epiphenomenon, of changing economic and social substructures. Taken as "an active consciousness and assertiveness of particular regions, *vis-a-vis* other regions, as territorial and social enclosures," regionalism, and its discursive formation in print culture, was very much part of the socio-cultural processes involved in the transition to industrial modernity at the end of the nineteenth century.[19] According to Herb Wyile, the end of the twentieth century saw a resurgence of regionalism bound up in a "profound transformation," one marked by "demographic decline, increasing out-migration (especially from rural areas), major shifts in the resource industries, and intensified debate about the region's place in the rest of the country."[20] For Wyile, this transformation bore a complex relationship to concurrent "regional redefinition and cultural vitality," their coincidence indicative of the correlation between political, social, and economic crisis and cultural ferment.[21] But the very dynamics of that "charged milieu," in which "mobility is a watchword and stability a thing of the past," were also defining features of the region's transition from an Atlantic mercantile economy to industrial modernity nearly a century earlier.[22] This key period of socio-economic transition, effectively ignored in recent studies of Canadian regionalism, bears further examination, for the rapid growth of *fin-de-siècle* periodical culture was thoroughly implicated in the equally rapid social and economic transformations across the Maritime Provinces. Most importantly, these transformations encouraged the new understanding of space and territoriality in which magazine editors were invested. However, they also effectively shaped literary and print-cultural developments in the region, facilitating the adoption of new technologies of print. At the same time, uneven industrialization created an economic situation that forced professional writers to seek larger audiences and greater remuneration elsewhere, a situation that compelled the editors of regionalist magazines to "claim" these authors for a regional canon.

Characterized by rural depopulation, urbanization, out-migration, pockets of growth, and general decline, the period spanning 1890–1910 saw the expansion of the "new industrialism" as variable economic growth and urban expansion "masked the deeper weakness" in the economies of each of the three provinces.[23] Between 1880 and 1911, the rural population of the Maritime Provinces declined while the total urban population doubled in size.[24] Meanwhile, the 1890s alone saw nearly a hundred thousand people emigrate from the three provinces; population-growth rates dropped accordingly, to 2 per cent in Nova Scotia, 0.2 per cent in Prince Edward Island, and 0.01 per cent in New Brunswick.[25] Growth in the provinces' manufacturing sectors through 1880–1910 was substantial but unequally distributed, "centred not so much on areas or sub-regions as upon widely scattered communities."[26] The economic and demographic rivalry between Halifax and Saint John weakened both cities and effectively negated either's claim to be the regional capital. Lacking a single, strong regional metropolis, industries throughout the three provinces were left vulnerable to takeover by foreign and central-Canadian enterprise. By 1895, "only confectionary and manufacturing related to iron, steel, and local staples remained under regional control."[27] The introduction of mass-marketing and mass-production techniques through the spread of branch businesses similarly inhibited economic growth. Wholesaling and retailing manufactured products, branch businesses severely impeded the development of secondary manufacturing in the three provinces, prefiguring greater national centralization and differential integration into the global market.[28]

The effects of these broad trends appear to suggest a shared "regional" experience of industrial modernity. Certainly, representations of such shared regional experience were central to the cultural historical narratives developed in *fin-de-siècle* magazines. In fact, no single narrative effectively captures the economic vicissitudes experienced by different communities throughout Nova Scotia, New Brunswick, and Prince Edward Island during this period. Even the mass out-migration that seemed to distinguish the three provinces from the rest of Canada was experienced differently in different localities. While many communities saw drastically declining growth rates relative to the rest of Canada, the port cities of Halifax and Saint John, mill towns such as St Stephen and New Glasgow, and the new railroad centres of Moncton and Amherst all experienced rapid population growth as they transitioned to modern industrial centres.[29] Immigration continued to bring newcomers to cities, while coal-mining and industrial work brought labourers from Great Britain, continental Europe, and the West Indies to industrial centres. Sizeable Jewish and Lebanese communities also emerged in Saint John, Halifax, and Sydney during the period.[30] Notably, while regionalist magazines celebrated the growth of certain population centres, racialized and minority groups were entirely absent from their pages.

Moreover, minority groups, and racialized communities in particular, experienced few benefits from industrial expansion and burgeoning reform movements. The turn of the century saw increased job and housing discrimination against Black Nova Scotians and Black New Brunswickers, and most Black-owned businesses in Saint John and many in Halifax either closed or sold out to whites because of the difficulty of obtaining capital. Mi'kmaq and Wolastoqiyik populations were, "for all practical purposes, barred from industrial ventures by local prejudice, lack of capital, and the rigid provisions of the Indian Act."[31] In urban centres, the emergence of progressivist and social reform movements encouraged support for an interventionist government, more effective public-health systems, education reform, demands for universal suffrage, and "various forms of social regeneration, from temperance to child welfare, to physical culture, recreation, and sport."[32] Fiscal deficiencies and a highly partisan political order, however, largely hindered the development of interventionist provincial states and the uniform spread of progressive reform beyond urban areas.[33] Unsurprisingly, regional magazines were concentrated in these urban areas and were thus shaped not only by the progressivist impulse, but also by the globalizing flows that accompanied industrialization.

In effect, the shift to industrial modernity produced an uneven social and economic geography. According to Larry McCann, "the Maritime Provinces in the 1890s comprised a region that was diversified, separated – that is, fragmented – geographically, culturally, economically, and politically."[34] But the consequence of the new industrialism in the three provinces was not merely the fragmentation of an already constituted geographic whole. Rather, the transformations wrought by the new industrialism and accompanying social and political shifts precipitated a re-evaluation of space, for a concurrent transformation of spatial understanding that saw the creation of the region. T.W. Acheson effectively captures the nineteenth-century situation in his analysis of post-Confederation industrialization in the Maritime Provinces when he writes, "the Maritimes had never been a single integrated organic unit; it was, in fact, not a 'region' at all, but a number of British communities clustered on the Atlantic fringe, each with its separate lines of communication and its several metropolises."[35] As the three provinces transitioned from an Atlantic economy to a continental one, however, the increasing political and economic influence of central Canada recast the metropolitan-hinterland arrangement. The resulting loss of political and economic power in the Maritime Provinces clearly influenced the emergence of regionalist magazines and the anticentrism they espoused.

Regionalist magazines can be read, in part, as a response to Canadian federalism and the growing economic and cultural dominance of central Canada. Underdevelopment in the Maritime Provinces was directly related to internal structural inadequacies and poorly implemented federal policy. These factors laid the foundations for deindustrialization and economic decline in the twentieth century. For most people living in the Maritime Provinces, however, the consequences of underdevelopment and incomplete industrialization, profound economic and social decline, would not be fully experienced until well into the second and third decades of the twentieth century. That acute sense of socio-economic crisis is addressed in the third chapter of this book. In the first decade of the twentieth century, though, "few had realized the weaknesses of the region's economy in relation to central Canada."[36] As Ian McKay observes, Nova Scotians in the 1890s had "a sense of living in a rapidly expanding province" and "before the 1920s there was remarkably little sense of economic crisis."[37] However, the economic confidence, general optimism, and progressivism that marked Victorian-era Canada could not entirely attenuate the perception that the three Maritime Provinces were quickly becoming appendages to a larger, politically dominant central Canada, or the realization that they increasingly constituted a cultural and political hinterland. According to Colin Howell, the provinces' declining political importance "coincided with a diminished role in their own economy," resulting in a general belief that the three provinces, if not yet facing an economic crisis, were nevertheless becoming politically weaker and economically poorer as a result of marginalization within the Canadian federation.[38] There was a strong sense in each of the Maritime Provinces that their "influence on Confederation was rapidly declining," a fact that "was driven home by the losses in representation in the House of Commons which followed each census after 1881."[39]

Thus, the emergence of the region and its discursive construction in regional magazines must, on one level, be understood within the context of an expanding Canadian state and accompanying intensification of Canadian nationalism. The Maritime Provinces were at once swept up in this resurgent nationalism and alienated from it. Ian McKay argues that, in response to the interwar crisis, regional cultural producers "felt called upon to develop a new, more distinctive vocabulary of identity," but that "Canadian nationalism, fixated on central Canadian symbolic landscapes and historical myths, left little room for Maritimers."[40] Certainly, that alienation would inform radical responses to the social climate of the interwar period, the subject of the final three chapters of this book. But the development of such a vocabulary of identity had begun much earlier, providing the impetus for emergent regionalism and facilitating the invention of the "Maritimers" to whom McKay refers. As David Frank observes, the "1890s marked a new stage in the process of Canadianization, when technologies of integration such as the railways enabled the reconstructed empire of the St Lawrence to extend its hegemony over the Dominion by developing national markets in goods, labour and capital."[41] Regionalism was, in part, a response to this consolidation of the nation state. Accordingly, a hyperawareness of shifting centre-periphery relations helped shape the regionalist project launched in the pages of *fin-de-siècle* magazines, and that awareness surfaced in discussions of out-migration, economic development, transportation policy, and cultural history. On a subtler level, however, the region was cast as the natural container of culture, and magazine editors were compelled to posit the region as an authentic, organic space, not only in contrast with the inherently political, abstract, and consciously engineered nation-state, but also within the broader context of an expanding transnational world.

Constructions of the region were thoroughly implicated in the globalizing processes of modernity – of expanding transnational networks of people and the everyday transnational flow of ideas, information, people, money, goods, and culture – that shaped modern industrial society. In a basic sense, this speaks broadly to the ways in which "Canadian culture has always been situated within the complexities of larger international contexts."[42] More than that, though, Canadians in the decades preceding and following the turn of the century witnessed the profound transformation of spaces both proximate and distant: rapid westward expansion and settlement, the creation of Alberta and Saskatchewan, the navigation of the Northwest Passage, exploration and surveying expeditions to the far north, new imperialism, and the South African War. As elsewhere in Canada, to live in the Maritime Provinces at this time was to have an acute sense that new spaces were literally appearing beyond the horizon. Though this sense of an expanding world encouraged a new spatial imagination, it did not express itself as such; instead, it found expression in what was *represented as* the resuscitation of old categories of place, categories that reinforced a sense of us and them, here and elsewhere. At the same time, there was an awareness that the Maritime Provinces themselves were becoming increasingly permeable to transnational flows.

Magazine cultures in the three provinces, and, in turn, the regionalism they advanced, did not simply "respond" to, were not simply "reactions against," the globalizing processes of late-nineteenth-century modernity. Rather, they were the products of geographical mobility, multidirectional transcultural flows, and distanciated networks of people, including writers and editors. While a more globalized sense of place frequently surfaces in the pages of *fin-de-siècle* magazines, whether in discussions of imperial federation, international affairs, or European literature, the emergent regionalism was more frequently expressed in localist terms. This localist impulse, and the desire to establish a community of regional sentiment, conceals the degree to which print media is inherently mobile, and the degree to which editors and cultural producers constructing and representing the region were themselves itinerant. In effect, regionalism itself masks the fact that, as Ash Amin maintains, "the plural public sphere involved in the making of a region is spatially diffuse and geographically mobile."[43] Attention to such relationships – to the region as a process of territorialization that was a part of industrial modernity, the product of a mobile public sphere – avoids what Ansi Paasi sees as the tendency to "conceptualize phenomena and processes occurring *in* and *between* regions" rather than "theorizing over regions as parts of these processes."[44]

None of this is to suggest that the editors and cultural producers of *fin-de-siècle* magazines were aware of and deliberately obscured the inherently mobile, transnational nature of the regionalist project. Nor should one claim that they were conscious of producing something, a region, that was not already "there." Rather, regionalization was premised on much more deeply engrained notions of space "as (necessarily, by its very nature) divided/regionalised."[45] The basic assumptions of the regionalist project were undergirded by what Doreen Massey sees as "a particular hegemonic understanding of the nature of space itself, and of the relation between space and society."[46] One aspect of this understanding of space, writes Massey, "was an assumption of isomorphism between space/place on the one hand and society/culture on the other. Local communities had their localities, cultures had their regions and, of course, nations had their nation-states."[47] For editors such as Jack, the region was a natural fact with pre-historical depth; it did not need to be created, only recovered and clarified. *Acadiensis* was Jack's attempt to recover and clarify.

ACADIENSIS AND EMERGENT REGIONALISM

Regarded as "one of the most important periodicals of its kind produced during the era,"[48] *Acadiensis* pioneered the professionalization of history in the region while articulating the foundations for regionalism in the Maritime Provinces. Moreover, understood as a crucial document in the history of Canadian regionalism more broadly, *Acadiensis* can be seen to both affirm and challenge conventional assumptions about regionalism in Canada. Though it certainly articulates the "anticentric" opposition to "civic and cultural nationalism" that Wyile ascribes to regionalism,[49] *Acadiensis* also reveals the extent to which regionalism often colludes with, rather than contests, nationalism and settler-colonialism in its attempt to indigenize itself, to cast the region as an originary community with pre-historical depth. Contrary to Frank Davey's contention that regionalism necessarily precludes "other grounds for identity and individual subjectivity than those of geography," the regionalism advanced in *Acadiensis* was predicated on race and class, encoded geographically through an appeal to cartography.[50] The collective cultural identity advanced as "regional" was thus grounded in a cultural genealogy that served particular (white, Loyalist settler-colonial) race and class interests, buttressed by a cartographic impulse that emplaced literary and historical narratives within a legible geography. This regionalism was neither explicitly reactionary nor "deeply conservative,"[51] but was couched, no less problematically, in the progressivist, liberal rhetoric of inclusion. This involved circumscribing and containing difference as well as effacing it, deploying historical and literary narratives to establish a criterion for regional identity.

Furthermore, though geography, politics, and history are often understood to form the core of any regionalism, an analysis of *Acadiensis* helps resituate the literary at the centre of territorial politics and identity formation, revealing how editorial practice and critical reception constructed literary texts as the cultural correlative of overtly political regionalist polemics, casting the literary as expressive of a collective regional identity. *Acadiensis* thus demonstrates the function of magazines as vehicles for territorial and cultural politics. As a material medium and genre, the magazine afforded degrees of editorial control that effectively shaped the reception of texts, literary and otherwise, and the construction of a regional canon. The editorial deployment of apposition and juxtaposition generated meanings not contained in individual literary, historical, scientific, and cartographic texts alone, drawing together disparate discourses to create extradiegetic and extratextual narratives of regionality and regional identity. Literary texts were recontextualized within this regional framework, sublated into a powerful representation of geographic determinism, socio-cultural homogeneity, cultural succession, and racial hierarchy that was rendered coherent within the textual field of the magazine. Thus, in *Acadiensis*, the mythic, "poetical," essentially literary space of "Acadia" was reified, wedded to geology, cartography, and history to produce an ostensibly coherent and concrete cultural-geographic region. This union was accomplished within and enabled by the discursive context of the magazine itself.

Since the resurgence of regional studies in the late 1990s, criticism on literary regionalism has almost entirely neglected the historical relationship between periodical culture and regionalism; David Russell Jack, however, was keenly aware of it. Two years after *Acadiensis* first appeared, on 9 May 1903, Jack delivered an address to the Royal Society of Canada titled "Acadian Magazines." In it, Jack forgoes an introduction, promptly describing the first "Acadian" magazine, John Howe's *The Nova Scotia Magazine* (1789–92). He proceeds to describe thirty magazines published in "Acadia" over the course of the late eighteenth and nineteenth centuries up to the publication of *Acadiensis*. Jack's conclusion, however, marks an abrupt shift. Challenging Ontario's "[claim] to be the literary centre of Canada," Jack provides a dramatic argument, couched in the rhetoric of Empire, for a union of the Maritime Provinces under the banner of Acadia: "Putting aside all differences, standing shoulder to shoulder, and presenting a united front, there is no reason why the brightest diadem in the crown of the fairest daughter of the greatest Empire that has been, should not be known to the world as the Province of Acadia."[52]

Ostensibly a straightforward, evaluative history of magazine publishing in the Maritime Provinces, the address attempts to project a collective regional identity onto the past century while mobilizing that history in service of a new regionalist politics. John Howe's *Nova Scotia and Illustrated Monthly* becomes "the earliest Acadian magazine of which there is any record"; the articles of Moses Perley in *The Amaranth* "have not been equalled and certainly not excelled by any other Acadian magazine writer"; and the end of the nineteenth century marks but a "new era in Acadian magazine literature."[53] Beyond cataloguing magazines published in the Maritime Provinces, Jack traces the contours of an emergent regionalism, one he had been championing in the pages of *Acadiensis* for the past two years. Jack implies a certain logic connecting magazine publishing to regionalism, one that figures the proliferation of *fin-de-siècle* magazines as an efflorescence of a regional, "Acadian" literature. That most of the magazines he describes were either principally colonial, provincial, or national mattered little; the address is less concerned with the past than it is with the future. In *Acadiensis*, the recovery of the past for a (regionalist) politics of the present would be the guiding editorial principle. "The time is now ripe," writes Jack in the opening editorial, "for a still closer amalgamation of the people of Acadia, this land of our fathers, into one great Province." "It shall be our constant effort," he continues, "to endeavor, by the interchange of thoughts and ideas, by the study of the past, and taking thought for the future, to pave the way for such a movement."[54] Though this regionalism was white, settler-colonial, predominantly Anglo-Protestant and United Empire Loyalist, it did not efface racial and cultural difference so much as subsume cultural particularities into a teleological narrative of historical continuity and cultural succession. Thus, the United Empire Loyalists are framed not only as the successors to the region's Mi'kmaq, Wolastoqiyik, and Acadian inhabitants, but also the inheritors of selected cultural practices and traditions, all of which could be contained under the catch-all "Acadia."

Jack's use of "Acadia" in relation to the Maritime Provinces had much precedent. In 1855, the geologist and paleontologist Sir William Dawson had titled his geological survey of Nova Scotia *Acadian Geology*, explaining that Acadia was the "old and beautiful name ... by which Nova Scotia, New Brunswick, and the neighbouring islands were known to the early French colonists."[55] The name was retained, writes Dawson, as a "poetical appellation."[56] As a "poetical appellation," "Acadia" was in vogue. In the first book-length poem by a settler author in what would become Canada, *The Rising Village* (London, 1825; Saint John, 1834), Oliver Goldsmith anticipated this infatuation: "Then blest Acadia! ever may thy name, / Like hers, be graven on the rolls of fame."[57] In "Canada" (1886), Charles G.D. Roberts wrote of "Acadia's chainless tides,"[58] and in "Low Tide on Grand Pré" (1887), Bliss Carman's speaker imagined a beloved "so long from home and Acadie."[59] Countless other poems, novels, and dramatic works adopted the formula for churning the expulsion of the Acadians into saleable historical romance. What is more, Acadia was a place one could visit. As the English author Douglas Sladen recalled after touring Grand Pré with Bliss Carman and Charles G.D. Roberts, "the meadow itself, like all Acadian meadows, is deep with hay, aromatic with clover, and glowing with wild flowers."[60] Of course, the immense cultural cachet attached to the name was directly traceable to Henry Wadsworth Longfellow's *Evangeline, A Tale of Acadie*. The myriad influences of what Ian McKay and Robin Bates term "the Evangeline Phenomena" thoroughly saturated literary and cultural production in nineteenth-century Nova Scotia.[61] Edward E. Rice's Broadway musical extravaganza *Evangeline; or, The Belle of Acadia* (1874), Charles G.D. Roberts's novel

A Sister to Evangeline (1898), and A.L. Hardy's photobook *The Evangeline Land* (1902) are but a few successful works to cash in on the popularity of Longfellow's poem. Nevertheless, though the fanatical usage of "Acadia" suggests a halcyon past of pastoral innocence unperturbed by provincial boundaries, it should not be taken as indicative of nineteenth-century regionalism. If, in the nineteenth century, Acadia, that "pseudo-European Arcadia, bathed in a warm pastoral glow and a suitable setting for one of Grimm's fairy tales," had been rendered identical with nineteenth-century public perceptions of Nova Scotia, it could only ever gesture vaguely toward a community of regional scale.[62]

All this seems relatively detached from the allegedly more pragmatic usage invoked by Jack. For Jack, Acadia is "a title now recognized by the scientific world as applying to the territory embraced within the area of the Maritime Provinces, including a small portion of the Province of Quebec and the State of Maine."[63] Far from being an unadorned, commonsensical, "scientific" title, however, Jack's Acadia signals an altogether new usage; it conveys associations more cultural than the geological region articulated by Dawson, more scientific than the structuring mythology of *Evangeline* and its numberless progeny. Jack's "Acadia" did not shed these various other associations: its sometimes vague, indiscriminate application to Nova Scotia, the Arcadian pastoralism of its literary usage, its evocation of a premodern antiquity, and its connection to nineteenth-century geological science. Rather, those meanings are folded into one as "Acadia" is redeployed in service of Jack's regionalism. To temper the romantic excess of the Evangeline Phenomena, however, it was necessary to affect a greater air of scientificity. Thus, when Jack, with the support of the New Brunswick Historical Society, agreed to publish a new journal of history, science, and literature, "Acadiensis" was chosen for the title.

Appearing in January of 1901, "by the light of the dawn of a new century," *Acadiensis: A Quarterly Devoted to the Interests of the Maritime Provinces of Canada* was published in Saint John and financed jointly by the New Brunswick Historical Society and the New Brunswick Loyalist Society.[64] Its production and financing speak to cultural conditions in Saint John at the turn of the century. "[Drawn] primarily from the ranks of the city's extensive professional and business community," members of both societies were, in the late nineteenth century, looking to the city's Loyalist past as a source of stability in the face of profound "economic reorientation," the consequences of Saint John's rapid industrialization.[65] What D.G. Bell calls the "Saint John School" of historians and late-Victorian literati was thus concerned first with local and provincial history, and only secondarily with regional historiography.[66] Nevertheless, after the demise of *The New Brunswick Magazine* in 1899, both societies were eager to throw their support behind a new journal, and they guaranteed financial support when Jack pitched *Acadiensis* in 1900.

Jack himself was, in fact, a typical member of both societies. A descendent of United Empire Loyalists, a prominent businessman, vice-consul for Spain, and a civic booster, Jack was an amateur historian of local repute and a "painstaking antiquarian of the old school."[67] Now thirty-seven years of age, Jack was well-positioned to edit and publish the new journal, an endeavour that would consume much of his time, energy, and money over the next eight years. Yet, Jack's aspirations for the journal were also more ambitious than those of his confreres. Jack intended for the journal to "deal largely with matters historical," but its scope was to be categorically regional.[68] Equally as welcome as historical essays were "descriptive, scientific or philosophical contributions" and "contributions in verse, as well as short stories, in which the principal scene is laid in Acadia, or which are the production of Acadian writers."[69] In fact, the "scene" was rarely "laid in Acadia," but, as the ensuing will show, Jack took great pains to position texts and their authors as the product of the "Acadian" environment. The magazine was printed on antique laid paper. Its covers, printed on matte cover stock of varying earth-tone colours, were subdued and featured the title and subtitle surrounded by a low-key floral motif (fig. 1.1). It was generously illustrated, featuring paintings and photographs of rural landscapes, cityscapes, portraits, historical objects and artifacts, and maps, which were occasionally printed on foldouts. Advertisements, which were generally for local businesses, were kept to a minimum, averaging two to four pages per issue. Over the course of its eight-year run, the length of each issue remained generally consistent at just under one hundred pages. Annual subscriptions cost $1.00 until 1903, when the price was raised to $1.50.

Combining the scientism of the Latin "-ensis" ("pertaining to" or "originating in") with the idyllic romanticism of "Acadia," his chosen title, "Acadiensis," prefigures the tensions that appear at the core of the

Figure 1.1 The cover of *Acadiensis* 5, no. 4, October 1905. The cover remained unchanged through the magazine's eight-year run.

magazine: between rigorous, scientific historiography, cartography, and natural science, and the promotion of a "regional" literature that was predominantly Romantic and cast as representative of a distinct, Acadian/Arcadian regional environment. This tension is typified by *Acadiensis*'s two most distinguished contributors (incidentally, also brothers-in-law): W.F. Ganong, a botanist, historian, cartographer, and professor at Smith College, Massachusetts; and Bliss Carman, the most internationally famous of the Confederation Group of poets. Over the course of the magazine's eight-year run, Ganong would contribute an article to nearly every issue. His contributions in historical geography are generally deemed to have the greatest scholarly value of those published in *Acadiensis*, but they also reveal the cartographic impulse that complemented the magazine's literary representations of space. Within *Acadiensis*, Ganong's cartography provided an encoded and thus credible space in which readers could locate historical and literary narratives. In contrast, Carman contributed only a handful of poems, most of which had been previously published elsewhere. The influence of his late-Victorian Romanticism (if not his mystical transcendentalism), however, is at evidence in much of the poetry contributed by lesser-known and amateur authors. More importantly, Jack's critical positioning of Carman's poems, as well as those of Carman's cousin, Theodore Goodridge Roberts, is exemplary of the way literary regionalism becomes a function of editorial practice. Together, then, Ganong and Carman offer two forms of representing place and space, both of which were deployed to great effect in the pages of *Acadiensis*.

For Ganong, "maps are the graphic records of the influence which geography has exerted upon the course of history," and it is "hence natural that from all sides their scientific study should be viewed with much approbation."[70] Trained as a botanist in Munich, Ganong was influenced by the natural philosophy of Alexander von Humboldt and the anthropogeography of Friedrich Ratzel.[71] The strain of geographical determinism Ganong embraced was grounded foremost in the application of Darwinian evolution. Not merely approximate representations of space, maps "of any region taken collectively offer a fascinating study in evolution."[72] As Graeme Wynn records, "so strongly did Ganong feel these similarities [between evolutionary science and cartography] that he contemplated the classification of early maps into families, genre, and species."[73] He similarly insisted that geographers and historians be "trained rigidly in the modern scientific spirit of inquiry."[74] "Comprehensive, methodical, and exact," Ganong's scientific and ostensibly impartial approach to cartography and historiography placed him among a generation of Canadian historians who, according to Martin Taylor, brought about a "new era" in the professionalization of history in Canada.[75] Moreover, the publication of Ganong's historical geography exerted a strong influence over representations of space in *Acadiensis* and provided a "scientific" basis for a distinct regional identity.

Though Ganong authored general articles on regional historiography and cartography for *Acadiensis*, the bulk of his contributions comprise a series of articles detailing the history of toponymy and cartography in various localities in Nova Scotia and New Brunswick. As such, they do not so much expound a general theory of geography and geographical determinism as practise it, tracing the "evolution" of specific locales, their boundaries, settlement, and toponymy, to their "origins" (usually found in the linguistic traces of Mi'kmaw and Wolastoqey place names). His series in historical cartography titled "Origins of Place Names" locates a comprehensive explanation for history in the cartography and geographical evolution of place.[76] For Ganong, New Brunswick and the other Maritime Provinces were a *terra incognita* awaiting scientific clarification.

Ganong's desire to map the region carefully and meticulously might be understood as a form of what Joe Painter calls "cartographic anxiety": not only a "desire to make geographic space legible" through "visualization," but also the need to "bring elements of the unknown inside the fortress to be dissected and exhibited, and thereby made knowable."[77] Ganong expresses as much in *Acadiensis*, proclaiming his desire to study the region and "make known its geography, resources, and scientific phenomena down to their minutest features."[78] But another recurrent aspect of cartographic anxiety, argues Painter, is the tendency to treat regions as "relatively homogeneous bounded territorial entities,"[79] a tendency born out of the "goals of systematization, boundedness and totalization."[80] Accordingly, Ganong, writing of the cartographer's motivation, lays stress on "boundaries" as the apogee of cartographic work: "it is a matter of extreme interest to follow the gradual crystallizing out of a given region from the great homogeneous undifferentiated mass of which at first it is an unrecognizable part, and to trace, in the light of its causes, the gradual unfolding of its outlines and the definition of its boundaries."[81]

Nevertheless, while Ganong certainly espoused a geography that saw regions as bounded, fixed spaces, he did not entirely ascribe to the notions of regional identity being promulgated in *Acadiensis* via the veneration of Loyalist settlement. In fact, he strongly condemned historiography driven by "local pride or the natural desire to make prominent those heroic or other stirring events which appeal to the healthy human imagination or which magnify the merits or glories of one's own people."[82] The same scientific principles that guided Ganong's approach to regional geography led him largely to reject "the symbolic and spiritual conceptions of earlier romantic historians," and "romantic values were subordinated to the scientific spirit."[83] Ganong truly believed scientific and literary-romantic

Figure 1.2 William Francis Ganong surveying Long Lake, Victoria County, New Brunswick, 1901.

writers were "well nigh mutually exclusive," but that exclusivity did not appear as a contradiction in the pages of *Acadiensis*.[84] It was not in spite of the tension between the romantic and scientific, but in part through it, that Jack was able to impose ideological coherence over contrasting representations of space. He did so at the level of editorial practice, juxtaposing the literary and the cartographic to produce a legible space in which readers could locate a cultural identity of which the literary was understood to be fundamentally expressive.

The issue for April 1902 is exemplary of the way in which under Jack's editorial direction the magazine's textual and bibliographic codes operate to produce representations of regionality and regional identity. Featuring historiography, poetry, Mi'kmaw lore, potamology, and an historical sketch of seventeenth-century *Acadie*, the issue showcases the constitutive elements of *Acadiensis*'s particular regionalism: a literary regionalism marked by the preponderance of an "Acadian" natural environment; the assertion of Indigeneity via the appropriation of Mi'kmaw and Wolastoqey oral stories (supplemented with accompanying ethnographic material); the assertion of the region's historicity via *Acadien* history; the scientific description of local and regional geography; and polemical arguments for the study and preservation of local history and culture. Not all of the contributions are, in themselves, regionalist. Most of the poetry and the Mi'kmaw legend, for instance, eschew any commitment to a place-based politics. Rather, the combination of juxtaposition, annotation, and total structure creates an extradiegetic and extratextual narrative of regionality that draws the evidently non-regional into alignment with the explicitly regional.

The issue is prefaced by Carman's "A Supplication," an original contribution later collected in Carman's *From the Green Book of Bards* (1903), the second in his five-volume series *Pipes of Pan* (1902–06). A three-stanza incantatory prayer for the return of April, the poem is in the same vein as Carman's several songs of spring. The poem thus proclaims the restorative potential of communion with nature, a potential that comes close to being realized in the final stanza as the metre finally falls into more regular iambic pentameter:

> Behold, across the borders of the world,
> We wait the reappearance with the flowers,
> Disconsolate, dispirited, forlorn,
> Our only childish and perpetual prayer,
> "Return, return!"[85]

"A Supplication," like many of Carman's poems in the *Pipes of Pan* series, is centrally concerned with "the therapeutic powers of the natural world."[86] Also like those poems, it is informed by Carman's spiritualism and interest in "occult ('secret,' 'magical') knowledge."[87] Taking the form of a supplication, presenting a "perpetual prayer," and structured on an incantatory rhythm, the poem implies the apotheosis of "mother" April as deity; spiritual communion with nature thus figures as religious ritual. At the same time, the poem gestures toward the "tonic" qualities that Bentley, Hodd, and others have identified with Carman's "Delsartean or unitrinian system of mind-body-spirit harmonization."[88]

What the poem is not concerned with is an articulation of local or regional setting. In fact, the poem is detached from any localized space and, as James Cappon observes of Carman's nature poems generally, it "serves less as scenic description than as a suggestion of a mystical penumbral environment of life."[89] In fact, the poem explicitly aspires toward the decontextualized, universal space of nature, encompassing the collective "our" diffused "across the scattered borders of the world."[90] Nor does its position at the beginning of the issue necessarily suggest a strong regional connotation; rather, it simply seems fitting that the April issue of *Acadiensis* should be prefaced with a prayer to "Mother April." Nevertheless, the meanings the poem generates are conditioned by the texts that follow, suggesting intertextual connections that situate the poem spatially and historically. This is achieved most saliently through its juxtaposition with Montague Chamberlain's article "Primitive Life of the Wapanaki Women," an ethnographic article that attempts to document the social and cultural lives of pre-contact Wabanaki women. At the centre of the article is a discussion of Wabanaki spirituality that conspicuously parallels Carman's pantheistic spiritualism in "A Supplication."

According to Chamberlain, "nature had taught [the Wabanaki] that in the unseen world there was a power far greater than their own ... which revealed itself in all physical phenomena."[91] The prime deity Chamberlain identifies with Wabanaki spirituality, who "dwelt in the sun, was, in their minds, the mother of life." As if echoing (or historically prefiguring) Carman's poetic genuflection toward "Mother April," Chamberlain describes the morning prayers of a Wabanaki woman: "As the shining orb rose into view the woman knelt on the ground, and, holding her babe toward the sun, implored the spirit to look with pity upon her helpless child."[92] Concluding with a description of an old, dying Wabanaki woman, and thus evoking the well-worn "vanishing Indian" trope, Chamberlain's article does not just offer a superficial parallel with Carman's poem; rather, the juxtaposition of the two pieces constructs an extradiegetic narrative of cultural succession. If Chamberlain's Wabanaki are not yet "vanished," they are surely no longer the bearers of their own cultural and spiritual heritage. Carman assumes the mantle, figuratively subsuming Indigenous spiritual practices into his transcendentalist-mysticism.

It is important to qualify the apparent parallels between Carman's poem and Chamberlain's article. It is unlikely either author had any knowledge of the work of the other. The subtext that is born out of their juxtaposition is a function of editorial, and not authorial, decision-making. Yet the meanings generated through the adjacency of the texts are multiple and consequential. In terms of regionality, the texts offer a representation of space that conflates modern constructions of the region, Jack's "Acadia," with Wabanahkik: the territory of the Wabanaki roughly coextensive with the French colony of Acadia, and "precisely the ground" *Acadiensis* was "to cover."[93] This spatial logic entails a concomitant historical narrative, one that constructs white-settler, English cultural producers as the inheritors of Indigenous culture (and thus Indigeneity itself) and imparts greater historicity (in effect, pre-historical depth) to modern constructions of the region. Paradoxically, this narrative depends upon representing both the extinction and survival of the Wabanaki: the assimilation of Wabanahkik into "Acadia" depends upon their extinction (or, at the very least, their subjection and assimilation), while their survival is necessary to cast the Wabanaki as the living, premodern foil against which regional progress and white-settler modernity can be defined. Thus, Chamberlain's Wabanaki "are not of a plastic nature, and the Indian of today differs but little from the Indians of three centuries ago."[94]

This powerful narrative of cultural succession is sustained in vol. 2, no. 2 through the piece that follows Chamberlain's article, a translation of "Glooskap" by Jeremiah S. Clarke. Clarke figures Glooskap, the hero and trickster figure of many Mi'kmaw and Wolastoqey tales, as "the first Acadian exile," thus projecting contemporary constructions of Acadia into a pre-colonial past.[95] This "desire for indigenous or originary grounding" is a characteristic that Frank Davey argues all regionalisms share with colonialism.[96] Accordingly, the co-option of Indigenous culture – what Terry Goldie has termed "indigenization," the process through which "the 'settler' population attempts to become as though indigenous, as though 'born' of the land" – was central to the cultural dimensions of the regionalism developed in *Acadiensis*. In his "Aesthetic Attributes of Acadia," printed in the second issue, Isaac Allen Jack devises a criterion for a regionalist literature and art predicated on notions of geographical determinism. Concluding that a distinct poetry and art depend upon "historical and traditional associations and climatic and typographical [topographical] conditions," he asks "to what extent Acadia possesses these requirements for aesthetic culture."[97] The first source, argues Jack, is to be found in the "peculiar beauties" of the "archives of the Algonquin race." In a rhetorical sleight of hand, Jack at once co-opts Indigenous history for Acadian history, and denigrates it, lamenting that "the Indian period of our history" cannot finally provide "the nuclei for our most noble, intellectual fabrics."[98] In his article on Acadian literature, "On Certain Literary Possibilities," A.B. De Mille, son of novelist James De Mille and professor of English and history at King's College, similarly comments, "there is enough wild life in Nova Scotia to catch the attention of the literary stroller. Most important in this regard are the Indians – what is left of them."[99] Figuring the Mi'kmaq inhabitants of Nova Scotia as a near-extinct aspect of regional geography, indistinguishable from "wild life," De Mille warns the would-be collector of Indigenous oral stories to keep any writerly intentions hidden, for the Mi'kmaq keep their stories "jealously guarded."[100]

These critical articles, manifestoes even, serve as a key to the production of literary regionalism in *Acadiensis*. Far from articulating a regional literary program in opposition to Canadian romantic nationalism, they reveal key intersections between the two, exposing the way in which regional spaces are often produced in collusion with the broader discourses of nationalism. They exhibit a regional iteration of what Jennifer Blair et al. identify as one dimension of the "politics of recollection": the default identification of cultural products as fundamentally national. This process, they argue, "risks falsely projecting a fixed concept of the Canadian nation-state back in time, which lends it an additional antiquity or authenticity not to be found in its actual history of sporadic and contested conquest."[101] The projection of the modern region into a pre-historical Indigenous (and French-colonial, Acadian) past is rehearsed again and again in the pages of *Acadiensis*. It is epitomized by such erroneous studies as D.R. Jack's inquiry into "the origin of the Abenaki and their *extension into Acadia*,"[102] and suggested through the publication of such poems as N. McAdam's "The Indian Mound" in which the bones of Champlain's party mingle with "the dust of braves" who "So long have left their place, / Not even tradition keeps / Their name or tongue or race."[103]

Though backward projection served to marshal historicity and authenticity in service of the regionalist project, the discursive construction of a timeless, immutable region did not operate exclusively through the co-option of Indigeneity from Indigenous Peoples of Wabanahkik. Nor did the production of literary regionalism always involve the appropriation of Indigenous oral culture. More frequently, poems appear to have been published on the basis that they celebrated that portion of the population (white-settler, Anglican, Loyalist) that was deemed to be archetypical of a regional identity. Such poems as H.A. Cody's[104] "Loyalists's Reception" and F.A. Wightman's "To the Memory of the Brave Loyalists" were thus held to be self-evidently regional. Other poems and stories were rendered expressive of regionality by way of an appeal to the basic assumptions of geographic determinism. Accordingly, poems describing highly localized spaces or particular geographical features were deemed "regional" insofar as the distinction between place and region could be elided.[105]

Similar assumptions of geographic determinism allowed poetry set in undefined spaces to be understood as the expressions of a homogenous regional space. Again, editorial decisions conditioned the reception of the literary as fundamentally regional, and the conscious organization of texts in any given issue coupled the imaginary space of the literary with the quantifiable, legible space of cartography, history, and earth science. Thus, Herbert Brewster's "The Days That Are Not" with its "wayward wending stream" appears opposite Joseph Whitman Bailey's potamological study "Some Features of the Rivers of New Brunswick."[106] In another issue, Bliss Carman's "Song of the Four Worlds," in which the "northward" people "are loyal to the glory of their past," is juxtaposed with a photograph of the crumbling house of La Salle, an eighteenth-century voyageur of the "primeval forest" (an obvious reference to Longfellow's "forest primeval").[107]

This is not to suggest that the poets who published in the pages of *Acadiensis* objected to their poems being incorporated into a canon of "Acadian literature," nor that they did not share Jack's regionalist ideology. What is more, an analysis of much of the poetry in *Acadiensis* clearly benefits (as does *Acadiensis* itself) from contextualization within the geographically situated socio-economic and intellectual milieu in which it was composed and published. Rather, what is at issue is the process through which the literary was absorbed into a particularly powerful representation of regional homogeneity, one buttressed by geographic determinism and a narrative of cultural succession. The cartographic and historiographic work of contributors such as Ganong and Chamberlain offered a credible, scientific, and often visualized space to locate cultural expression. And geographic determinism – in Ganong's more specific, evolutionary formulation, and in the most basic sense, as a belief that geography and environment shape social and cultural identity – provided the animating link between region and regional identity.

By wedding a conception of the region as a geographic primitive to a narrative of cultural succession, *Acadiensis* could present a kind of cultural genealogy that saw white, Anglican, Loyalist culture as the natural successor to those cultures that historically preceded it. This did not result in the effacement of racial and cultural difference so much as it did the policing of difference. Jack's liberal regionalism did not entail a reactionary exclusivity, but it did work to circumscribe and contain difference. The marginalization of non-Loyalist cultural groups was couched in a liberal rhetoric of inclusion. Nominally, the French *Acadiens* were invited to "join hand in hand" with the United Empire Loyalists "in a political union, embracing what is now known as the Maritime Provinces."[108] *Acadiensis*'s publication of articles by such prominent *Acadien* writers as Pascal Poirier seemed to legitimate this claim. Rhetorical appeals to "laying aside all differences of politics, race, and religion" did little, however, to mitigate the triumphalism that characterized the magazine's United Empire Loyalist history.[109] The vast body of Loyalist history produced in the pages of *Acadiensis*, from the major events of Loyalist settlement to the tedious minutiae of Loyalist genealogy, established a hierarchy of regional identity, one which firmly established the hegemony of white, Anglican, Loyalist history and culture. This is not to invalidate the real and substantial contributions the magazine made to documenting Loyalist history in Canada, a history that Jack and others perceived to be threatened, soon to "be irrecoverably lost."[110] Rather, it is to suggest that in developing a hegemonic narrative of the region dominated by Loyalist history, a parallel criterion for *regional identity* was developed. Long, serialized lists of Loyalist genealogy comprised a staggering portion of the magazine's contents over its eight-year run, and these impressed upon the reader that, to truly be a constitutive member of the modern "Acadia," one must locate one's name on those lists.

For all the cogency and authenticity that literary, historical, and cartographic representations of space and identity could lend the construction of a homogenous, coherent regional community, Jack's commitment to the unification of the three Maritime Provinces as "Acadia" still required more direct polemical arguments. This came in the form of a series of articles by Reginald Harris in 1906 and 1908, under the title "Union of the Maritime Provinces." Harris's basic argument was the same as that of the Maritime Board of Trade, insofar as he argued that three provinces would benefit economically and politically from an administrative and legislative union. Harris does not explicitly position the proposed union in opposition to the nation-state or "nationality," but his militant language, figuring the provinces as "fighting shoulder to shoulder" for "what they are justly entitled to," reveals the sense of grievance that such a union was intended to address. Just as Jack sought to counter cultural and literary centralism, so Harris aimed to oppose the political and economic marginalization of the three provinces. But utilitarian arguments of economics and political exigency appear to have been inadequate to the task of marshalling political feeling, and thus Harris finally predicates his argument on social and cultural uniformity, adopting a vocabulary of identity: "there is no diversity of nationality. No particular province is markedly peculiar in its institutions and laws. The language of all is English. There is no recognition of particular religious institutions to divide one province from another. All are homogenous."[111] As he put it in the final issue of *Acadiensis*, "our interests ... are identical."[112]

ACADIENSIS AND *FIN-DE-SIÈCLE* REGIONAL MAGAZINES

That the unionist aspirations of Jack and Harris never came to fruition – never, in fact, gained widespread public support – was of little consequence to the magazine's lasting significance. In the final analysis, it was the consolidation of an idea, the representation of the region as an historical, geographical, and cultural fact, that was the magazine's most consequential contribution to regionalism in the Maritime Provinces. As David Frank writes, while Jack's "idealistic agenda" for the political union of the provinces "turned out to be less prophetic than expected in 1901," the magazine's effort to generate "regional awareness" left a significant legacy: "the existence of a regional identity cannot be denied and discussions of Maritime Union have remained a staple theme in regional politics for much of the 20th century."[113] It is more difficult to determine the magazine's immediate impact – that is, the extent to which it shaped public opinion and fostered a broad-based identification with the region during its eight-year run. *Acadiensis* was frequently cited in regional magazines and local newspapers and was regularly reviewed in national magazines such as *Canadian Magazine*, *The Canadian Home Journal*, *The Canada Educational Monthly*, and *Bulletin des recherches historiques*. The *Review of Historical Publications Relating to Canada* dedicated a three-page review to *Acadiensis* in 1902, and later described it as having "no rival among similar periodicals in its scholarly articles, artistic appearance and profuse illustrations."[114] According to Peter Laroque, *Acadiensis* was "extremely ambitious, and professional by contemporary standards" and "the magazine is considered one of the most important periodicals of its kind produced during the era."[115]

But, like most magazines in turn-of-the-century Canada, it was never a financial success. Jack and other members of the Acadian society frequently subsidized its publication. Jack covered deficits out of his pocket. Having serialized J.W. Lawrence's *Judges of New Brunswick and Their Times* in volume eight "at great cost," Jack decided to suspend publication with the October 1908 issue.[116] Subscriptions and advertisements never fully covered the cost of publication and postage. For a magazine of regional scope, it does appear to have achieved a considerable circulation both within and beyond the region,[117] but nothing that could approximate the impact of either larger national magazines or local newspapers, "the primary instrument and medium of public discourse" in the late nineteenth and early twentieth centuries.[118] On the other hand, the republication of material from *Acadiensis* in local papers – Reginald Harris's 1906 article on Maritime Union, for instance, reappeared in the *Halifax Herald* and several other dailies throughout Nova Scotia and New Brunswick – indicates the larger, more indirect public reception of Jack's regionalist program. More revealing still is the broader efflorescence of magazine publishing of which *Acadiensis* was a part.

Fin-de-siècle magazines in the Maritime Provinces were the effort of a nexus of public intellectuals, many of whom were, like Jack, concerned with representations of territorial identity. Writers such as Ganong, W.O. Raymond, C.W. Vernon, Jeremiah S. Clark, Montague Chamberlain, J.F. Herbin, W.P. Dole, and Charles Campbell frequently contributed to two or more general-interest magazines. *The Prince Edward Island Magazine*, *The New Brunswick Magazine*, and *Acadiensis* all regularly featured the same authors. At times, each of these magazines also reprinted articles originally published in another, such as the articles of Jonas Howe, originally published in *Acadiensis* in 1901 and republished in *Prince Edward Island Magazine* later the same year. Many of these writers, including Jack, were also regular contributors to daily newspapers; while others, such as Archibald Irwin, the editor of *Prince Edward Island Magazine* and publisher of the Charlottetown *Examiner*, were also involved in newspaper publishing. This confluence of writers and editors is indicative of the substantial public influence of a small, interconnected group.

Nevertheless, the publication of common contributors did not necessarily translate into shared interests, and no shared criterion of regional identity can be traced across the seven general-interest magazines of the period. Contrary to what Harris called the "identical" interests of the three Maritime Provinces, regional magazines reveal a high degree of variation in scope, content, and communal commitment. Most of the magazines were nominally provincial. Moreover, they generally articulated the interests of an educated elite who spoke on behalf of a dominant cultural group. Though those groups were invariably white and English-speaking, each magazine exhibited different communal and sectarian commitments. Thus, in contrast to the Anglican-Loyalist *Acadiensis*, both *Cape Breton Magazine* and *Prince Edward Island Magazine* showed a preoccupation with Scottish genealogy and history; and both were more balanced in their coverage of Catholic and Protestant subjects. J.S. Bowles's *The International*, on the other hand, was directed at expatriates and aimed to foster "an intercurrent bond between Canadian-Americans and American-Canadians."[119]

Nevertheless, most *fin-de-siècle* magazines began to show a tendency toward regionalism during the period. W.K. Reynold's *New Brunswick Magazine*, for instance, situated itself within a lineage "of magazines in the Maritime Provinces" from the outset, and cautioned that the title "does not imply that only New Brunswick interests are to be considered." "Its special field," wrote Reynolds, "is the Maritime Provinces," and "the scope of the magazine is a broad one."[120] Publishing articles on a range of historical and scientific topics, Reynolds frequently reiterated this commitment to regionalism in his book reviews section, insisting that "the Maritime Provinces occupy no mean place in the fields of science and literature."[121] Even *The Cape Breton and Nova Scotia Magazine* demonstrated a movement toward regionalism, changing its name in the fourth and final issue from *Cape Breton Magazine* "with a view to extending the field and enlarging and improving the publication generally."[122] What is more, all of the magazines exhibited an intense interest in local history, and all deployed common tropes in their particular construction of regionality, advancing the same narratives of cultural succession and English hegemony that were to be more fully developed in the pages of *Acadiensis*.

Thus, while *Acadiensis* was alone in propounding an explicitly regionalist polemic, it was nevertheless at the centre of a broader discourse carried out in regional magazines, all of which were devoted to advancing shared assumptions of cultural distinctiveness, geographic determinism, and cultural succession. And these shared assumptions eventually eclipsed the internal division and diversity which the magazines themselves exhibited. Though they did not formulate a common criterion for regional identity, they shared a more general sense that the region existed as the organic container of a relatively homogeneous culture. This culture was purportedly manifest in a literature that was perceived to be born out of common experience, shared history, and geography itself.

Fin-de-siècle general-interest magazines contributed to the production of a literary regionalism through the publication of poetry and fiction that was deemed to be either sufficiently "regional" or written by local or "regional" authors. In so doing, they provided a forum for aspiring and amateur writers, helping to sustain local literary cultures in the wake of mass out-migration of writers from the three provinces. Though most poems and stories were either amateur efforts or reprints of well-established authors such as Carman, Charles G.D. Roberts, and Theodore Roberts, there were notable exceptions. The early poetry of Hiram Alfred Cody appeared in *Acadiensis*. Cody would go on to become a bestselling author of popular fiction. The Acadian activist and poet J.F. Herbin regularly published in regional magazines, contributing verse and historical sketches to *Acadiensis* and *New Brunswick Magazine*. *Prince Edward Island Magazine* is marked for having provided space to several notable women authors. Elizabeth Lee Owen's historical sketches first appeared there in 1900, offering "an early example of social history" that was "both vivid and revealing,"[123] and exemplary, writes Carole Gerson, of the "general effort to establish identity by recording the past."[124] When journalist, author, and political activist Katherine Hughes left teaching to undertake "literary work" in 1902, "she had already established a modest reputation as a writer" after having published articles and stories in *PEI Magazine*.[125] And Jessie Gourlie Hogg published her first short stories there in 1899 before founding a literary annual, *Christmas Chimes*, in Charlottetown in 1901; the annual ran for eight years.

However, with the exception of the fleeting *Cape Breton and Nova Scotia Magazine*, none of the general-interest magazines paid for contributions. They were thus incapable of financially supporting professional writers within the region. The result was that the most prominent "regional" writers to appear in these magazines – writers such as Bliss Carman and Charles G.D. Roberts – were not writing from within the region at all. Yet it was these writers, more than the amateur writers whose verse often emulated the Confederation Group, that magazine editors like Jack raised up as representative of a distinct, regional "Maritime" or "Acadian" literature. These writers did frequently adopt distinctly local themes and settings, but the canonization of such texts as "regional" depended upon the elision of the local and the regional; rarely were the texts unequivocally suggestive of a shared culture at the regional scale. Rather, it was their critical reception in regional periodicals that positioned them as the agents of a distinct regional idiom and a collective cultural identity.

KIT-BAG AND LITERARY REGIONALISM-AS-RECEPTION

Just as literary regionalism within *Acadiensis* became a function of editorial practice, so too did the reception of literature published in books and other magazines operate to establish and dictate a regional canon. *Kit-Bag*, the only strictly literary magazine to emerge during this period in the Maritime Provinces, is illustrative of the process whereby thoroughly cosmopolitan literary efforts were reclaimed as the products of regional culture. Like *Acadiensis*, *Kit-Bag* has received almost no critical attention outside a few passing references in Canadian literary and print-cultural histories. Yet it is perhaps the only *fin-de-siècle* magazine in the Maritime Provinces worthy of recovery on the basis of literary value alone, constituting one of two aesthetically noteworthy little magazines in Canada at the turn of the century, the other being Toronto's *Tarot* (1896).[126] In effect, *Kit-Bag* eschewed the localism and nationalism of earlier Confederation poets while retaining their cosmopolitanism, developing a markedly more modern sensibility within the strictures of late-Victorian Romanticism and envisioning a recognizably transatlantic literary space. *Kit-Bag* thus offers a sharp contrast to *Acadiensis* and other *fin-de-siècle* magazines, indicative as it is of a vibrant local literature that celebrated, rather than concealed, transatlantic mobility and culture. Critical reception of the magazine, however, obscured its thematic transatlanticism by recontextualizing its contents and constructing it as fundamentally localist and regionalist. Ultimately, that reception not only constructed a regional literary canon from identifiably cosmopolitan poetry and fiction, but also concealed the fact that the writers and producers of that canon were thoroughly cosmopolitan subjects.

Theodore Goodridge Roberts was exemplary of such transnational cultural production. In 1901, Roberts contracted malaria and returned for his convalescence from Barbados to Fredericton, where he established *Kit-Bag*. It was the product of a small group of dedicated writers and survived for only three issues. It was also committed to maintaining high aesthetic standards: "the KIT-BAG is not a Scrap-Basket. It is a Chap Book, published by a few Free-Lancers and Adventurers, and is a printed sign of the survival of the fittest – their fittest."[127] Roberts explicitly positioned *Kit-Bag* in opposition to mass-market magazines catering to "The Million": "What is The Million? It is something Great and Rude, that frightens the Editors. It would read of Automobiles, and Kings of Commerce. It makes the Venture pay. In verse it knows not what it wants."[128] And *Kit-Bag* was fundamentally cosmopolitan: "Of Everywhere and Nowhere, of the Centres of Civilization and the Ends-o-the-Earth, are the inspiration and the dream."[129] Many of the magazine's contributors, including Roberts and the magazine's managers J.A. Winslow and John Bodkin, were from Fredericton. In fact, roughly a quarter of the writers to appear in its pages were of some relation to the Roberts and Carman families. Yet the magazine and its literature were neither localist nor regionalist. Nor were they avowedly nationalist.

Following D.M.R. Bentley, Tracy Ware has claimed that Canada's Confederation Group of poets are best described as "cosmopolitan" nationalists.[130] This cosmopolitan nationalism, writes Bentley, comprised an "enabling combination of the international and the local, the classical and the Canadian."[131] For Ware, it was cosmopolitanism that saved the Confederation poets from "uncritical nationalism." As Ware explains in

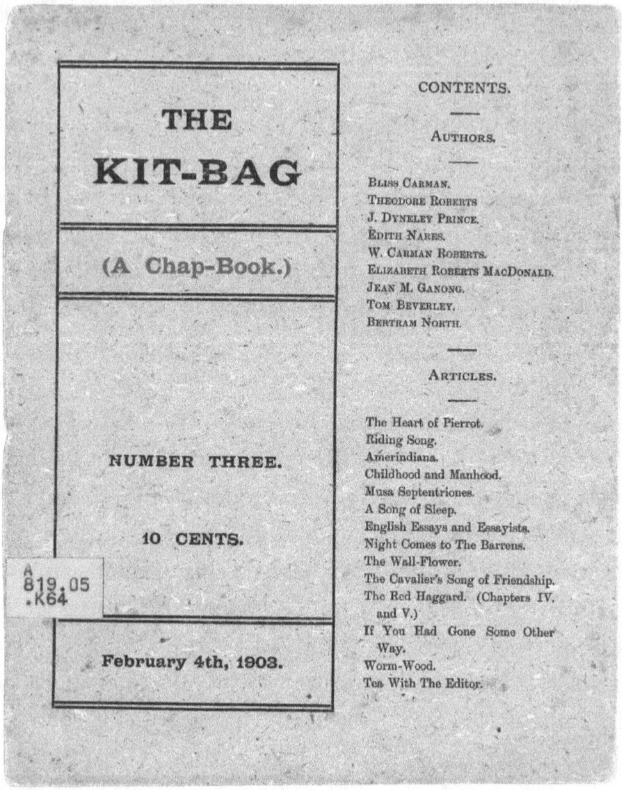
THE

KIT-BAG

(A Chap-Book.)

NUMBER THREE.

10 CENTS.

February 4th, 1903.

CONTENTS.

AUTHORS.

BLISS CARMAN.
THEODORE ROBERTS
J. DYNELEY PRINCE.
EDITH NARES.
W. CARMAN ROBERTS.
ELIZABETH ROBERTS MACDONALD.
JEAN M. GANONG.
TOM BEVERLEY.
BERTRAM NORTH.

ARTICLES.

The Heart of Pierrot.
Riding Song.
Amerindiana.
Childhood and Manhood.
Musa Septentriones.
A Song of Sleep.
English Essays and Essayists.
Night Comes to The Barrens.
The Wall-Flower.
The Cavalier's Song of Friendship.
The Red Haggard. (Chapters IV. and V.)
If You Had Gone Some Other Way.
Worm-Wood.
Tea With The Editor.

Figure 1.3 The cover of *The Kit-Bag* 1, no. 3, February 1903.

"Cosmopolitan Nationalism: Canadian Literature of the Confederation Period, 1867–1914," cosmopolitan nationalism consisted in the ready embrace of international literary influences, the recognition of cultural pluralism (or at least French-English biculturalism), and "respect" for "the regional diversity of Canada."[132] With respect to the latter, writes Ware, writers of the Confederation period "often [identified] their settings in detail" and, "unlike later regionalists, they showed little interest in defining themselves against the centre."[133] If such cosmopolitan nationalism defined literature of the period from 1867 to 1914 – a time when Canadian writers, "dependent as they were on journals, publishers, and audiences abroad," were "necessarily international"[134] – then *Kit-Bag* represents the local print instantiation of a more modern, more thoroughly transatlantic sensibility. It was, like many of its American *fin-de-siècle* counterparts, oriented toward "the vagabond lives of artists."[135] This was not a modern*ist* sensibility, but it was uncompromisingly cosmopolitan and never perceptibly nationalist, breaking beyond the discourses of localism and nationalism while retaining the cosmopolitan ethos of the early Confederation poets.

The production of *Kit-Bag* was local, and its prevailing aesthetic was late-Victorian, but the literary space envisioned in its pages was transatlantic, thematizing mobility through stories and poems of travel, adventure, seafaring, riding, and long-distance lovers. "Local colour" is subordinate to stories of international escapades, and in those texts that treat highly localized spaces, settings are generally nameless and deterritorialized. Of the eighteen poems and five stories that appear in the first issue, only four refer to specific places, one set on the coast of Labrador, another in England, one in Canada, and the last, Roberts's "The Sportsman's Limericks of Many Lands," mentioning Newfoundland, New Brunswick, Boston, and Brazil. Across the three issues, those stories that do explore specific places are often concerned with articulating the phenomenological experience of landscape, though they frequently use geography as a metaphor for psychological turmoil or a convenient setting for an exploration of (international) romantic longing and tragedy.

Roberts's "At a Place that Has No Name" is typical of the treatment of place and landscape as an abstract, *terra incognita*, void of "local colour." The story revolves around three travellers who venture off their ship, the *SS Glencoe*, to spend a few nights camping on an unnamed stretch of the coast of Labrador, north of "Battle Harbour." After swimming, eating, drinking, singing, and playfully brawling, the men converse against a "brown and lifeless barren," a backdrop almost entirely void of form: "here were only the sea and the rocks, the sky pricked thinly with stars, and the sand painted red by the fire."[136] On the surface, the story exploits this empty and austere landscape as a vehicle to explore character types: the adolescent poet-student O'Rourke, the big, aging Englishman Wadham, and the middle-aged explorer Harding. Each is plagued by romantic feelings: Wadham by loss, O'Rourke by unrequited love, and the newly engaged Harding by separation from his lover. None dwells psychologically in the place they now find themselves. O'Rourke dreams of "many distant places," Wadham reminisces of London, and Harding looks toward an unnamed "greener and cleaner land."[137] They are in a liminal space, between destinations, and the emptiness of this space figures metaphorically as the temporal "space" between meaningful life events.

The climax of the story, however, would appear to mark a shift. The sudden drowning of Harding, the explorer and a Fellow of the Royal Geographical Society, offers an easy metaphor for the process by which "empty" or formless places are inscribed with meaning. Yet it is distance and isolation from society, and not the weight of Harding's death, that finally imbue the nameless place with meaning. Sailing past the spot years later and recalling Harding's death, O'Rourke turns to a woman beside him who asks, "did you really think you would never find me again?"[138] In the concluding lines, O'Rourke realizes that that thought "seemed the most awful thing connected with the place that has no name."[139] It remains a liminal space, defined not by Harding's death, but by the feelings of hopelessness, isolation, and loneliness with which it was connected for all three characters. The "place that has no name" thus finally figures as the "elsewhere" that the characters wished not to be.

In itself, the story appears as a romantic tragedy that uses a remote, isolated, and barren setting to stage a sentimental tale of separation and loss followed by romantic union. Interposed as it is between poems and stories of travel and adventure, however, the story can be seen to align with a larger aesthetic celebration of mobility. In the same issue, Roberts's poems "Gentleman and Adventurers" and "In the Hand of the Wind," Tom Beverly's poem "When the Hill-Tops Call Me Away," Bertram North's story "To a Shipmate," Ralph Howard's poem "His Watch Below," R.K.'s sketch "The Jester," J.G.'s poem "Juliana Horatio Ewing," and the unsigned "Sportsman's Limericks of Many Lands" all celebrate travel. Still others lament separation from distant lovers. The few that do mention identifiable places (in Canada, the United States, Europe, and South America) help to situate the literary space of the magazine within a transatlantic world, a world defined, as in Roberts's artistic meditation "The Story-Writer," by "unceasing converse" on the "grey North Atlantic."[140] At the same time, the issue produces a sense of movement that is only offset by several (generally parodic) historical romances of knights and their exploits. To be sure, the first issue of *Kit-Bag* demonstrates formal and thematic variety, and the whole cannot be reduced to stories and poems of travel. But situated within the broader literary milieu dominated by local-colour writing and nationalism, the preponderance of peripatetic themes in *Kit-Bag* appears not only conspicuous, but tantamount to an editorial aesthetic. The two subsequent issues exhibit less emphasis on mobility and themes of itinerancy, but no greater prominence is given to bounded territorial spaces (i.e. the nation, the region). Nor are the authors championed as being of local origin. The magazine clearly aspired to reach an international readership and rarely are authors identified as being "of" any particular place.

However, despite the deterritorialized, transatlantic literary space developed within the magazine, local and regional periodicals generally cast *The Kit-Bag* as an autochthonous vehicle for regional literary culture. Typically, this involved simply emphasizing the magazine's purportedly local content and its local origins. Writing in Fredericton's *The Daily Gleaner*, one reviewer of *Kit-Bag* commented on the "unusual spirit" of the poetry and fiction it contained and claimed that "the production of a publication of this kind in Fredericton shows that the land that produces the workers is also able to turn out the finished product."[141] *The Educational Review* of Saint John was less direct, praising *Kit-Bag* as an "attractive magazine in make and contents" containing "poems and original matter of local interest."[142] Unsurprisingly, it was in *Acadiensis* that the magazine was most clearly positioned as a channel for literary regionalism.

Jack's review of *Kit-Bag* in the January 1903 issue of *Acadiensis* is relatively superficial and generally avoids commenting upon individual works. In "make up," *Kit-Bag* is "neat and attractive," and the reader will find "much in it that is likely to win their favour and imagination."[143] Jack does go to pains, however, to stress the magazine's "Acadianness." He begins his review of *Kit-Bag* by declaring it "the latest addition to the magazine literature of Acadia."[144] Twice more in the two-page review he welcomes the magazine and its editors to "the realm of Acadian literature."[145] "May our new contemporary," writes Jack, "be a co-worker with us in endeavouring to create in the people of Acadia a greater liking for all that is good and true in art and literature."[146] Nevertheless, however much Jack wished to drive home to the reader that *Kit-Bag* was an "Acadian magazine" containing "Acadian literature," the review is not as effective at stressing the regionalist character of *Kit-Bag* as are more subtle editorial cues. It is the arrangement of the issue, the implied connections between its literary, artistic, historical, and cartographic contents, and the re-publication of poems from *Kit-Bag*'s first issue that ultimately impose a regionalist orientation onto *Kit-Bag*.

The review itself follows an article on the American poet Charles Gamage Eastman, who, Jack claims, "was born within the limits of Old Acadia" and whose poetry shows that "he loved his native land and the common things of nature which it contained."[147] Eastman's "Snowstorm" prefaces the issue, and another poem, "The Dirge," appears before a history of St Andrews Church in Saint John. Entirely disconnected from *Kit-Bag*, these texts nevertheless establish the context for material reprinted from the magazine. Roberts's poem "My Comrade" appears before W.P. Dole's "Some Fine Art": a study of the artist John C. Miles, "a native of Saint John," "the grandson of staunch Loyalist ancestors," and a painter of "the most imposing and romantic places in all of Acadia."[148] Miles had been living in Boston, and Dole welcomes his return, concluding that he will "probably spend the remainder of his life in his native land."[149] Incidentally, Roberts himself had just returned to "his native land" (though he would not stay long). Less incidental is the juxtaposition of Dole's essay with Roberts's "My Comrade," in which the speaker wonders after a lost comrade: "Maybe he fights! Maybe he paints! / … / My comrade out of many lands."[150] The poem does not express desire for return, but revels in worldly companionship; the speaker exults in his ability to "hold [his comrade's] hands" "all 'round the world."[151] However, placed adjacent to Dole's study of (the recently returned) Miles, the speaker of Roberts's poem appears to desire his comrade-cum-painter's repatriation. Thus, paradoxically, the poem appears in *Acadiensis* as an affirmation of regionalist sentiment and nativist longing.

In the same issue, Elizabeth Roberts MacDonald's "The Inlander," reprinted from the first issue of *Kit-Bag*, appears opposite W.F. Ganong's "The Origin of Place-Names in Inglewood Manor." "The Inlander" is a short, unrhymed poem in which the speaker sees stars as "a thousand harbour lights beckoning" her and concludes, "far inland drifts the thunder of the sea."[152] Altogether divorced from any identifiable place, the poem's imagined space obtains specificity and credibility via apposition. Ganong's article, which includes a detailed map of the area along the border of King's and Saint John counties, New Brunswick (fig. 1.4), offers an encoded and thus legible space in which to situate MacDonald's speaker: namely, within the "inland" area along the border that was increasingly home to the suburbs of the port city of Saint John. In contrast, at its original site of publication, the poem shares the page with

Figure 1.4 W.F. Ganong's *Map of King's and Saint John Counties*, New Brunswick, in *Acadiensis* 3, no. 1, January 1903.

Roberts's "Gentleman Adventurers" and reads as an expression of confinement and longing. The speaker who sleeps "far inland" is beckoned by a sea which, in the final two lines, is "unchanged, yet throbbing with a note of change."[153] The speaker is thus beckoned not only by harbour lights, but also by the potential to break from the unchanging enclosure of "inland" space. So, in the final line (which appears, erroneously, as the penultimate line in *Acadiensis*), the sea is "fraught with dreams to stir me in my sleep."[154] The poem thus participates in the celebration of travel developed throughout the first issue of *Kit-Bag*; in the pages of *Acadiensis*, however, this context is exchanged for one of regional affirmation.

Ultimately, the sense of transatlantic mobility developed in *Kit-Bag* would seem antithetical to the organic, bounded, and relatively impermeable regional space constructed in *Acadiensis*. The reception of *Kit-Bag* as a "regionalist" literary magazine, however, worked to obscure the imaginative and thematic transatlanticism of its poetry and fiction. Certainly, the critical positioning of *Kit-Bag* had a less detrimental effect on its overall reception (and consequent obscurity) than did its ephemerality. Having recovered from malaria and married his nurse, Roberts returned to Barbados in 1903, ceasing publication of *Kit-Bag* after just three issues. But the regional designation (along with the broader nationalist dictates of Canadian criticism) still curtailed a deeper engagement with the magazine's cosmopolitan character. Short-lived though it was, *Kit-Bag* had marked an important moment in the local literary culture of Fredericton; but its significance derived largely from its engagement with, not a retreat from, the wider, transnational currents of *fin-de-siècle* literary cultre.

And *Kit-Bag* was, after all, the product of thoroughly cosmopolitan, transnational writers. Roberts spent his formative years in Fredericton, but his stay there in 1902 was but a brief interlude in a career that saw him travel almost constantly, living in New York, Cuba, Newfoundland, Brazil, Barbados, France, England, and across Canada. Roberts was not alone; most of the magazine's contributors were living, had lived, or were soon to live outside the Maritime Provinces. New York, in particular, was home to many of its foremost contributors, including Tom Beverly, Bliss Carman, and William Carman Roberts, each of whom were part of the mass "Canadian literary emigration" that has been documented by Nick Mount in *When Canadian Literature Moved to New York*.[155] But *Kit-Bag* was not the only magazine whose production involved transnational connections. *Acadiensis*, too, was marked for its publication of international writers. Its most prominent contributors, Bliss Carman and W.F. Ganong, both resided in the United States. And Jack himself was an avid traveller. The Canadian vice-consul to Spain and an agent to the North British and Mercantile Insurance Company, Jack frequently contributed travel articles to the Montreal *Star* and the Brooklyn *Eagle*. His travels abroad also inspired many of his civic activities; he struck and chaired the committee to bring electric street lights to Saint John, helped design the city's first concrete buildings, owned and operated one of the first motion picture theatres there, and opened a resort on the outskirts of the city.[156] Far from "intensely conservative," Jack was a modern liberal reformer whose urban community was being transformed, in part, by the importation of international culture and technology, and by its integration into an industrial economy.

BELONGING AND EXCLUSION: REGIONALISM AS A TRANSLOCAL PHENOMENON

What emerges from a closer examination of the lives and activities of these cultural producers is an image of rapid change, mobility, and progressivism, an image inconsistent with the static, fixed, and bounded spatial figurations produced by regionalism. Regionalism was not, in fact, incongruent with twentieth-century industrial modernity, a regressive holdover from a premodern past in which space was fixed, place was coherent, and identity was stable. To the contrary, regionalism was an integral part of the spatial and cultural dynamics involved in the uneven transition to industrial society. Moreover, it was a part of processes – economic, political, social, cultural – that exceeded regional and national boundaries. In terms of *fin-de-siècle* magazines, this involved myriad transnational and translocal cultural exchanges; and in terms of the region itself, it involved distanciated networks of groups and individuals who not only identified with the emergent regional community, but actively contributed to its construction.

Regionalism, then, cannot be understood exclusively, as Davey contends, as "a concern or phenomenon of nation states, a potential part of its intranational power negotiations."[157] Nor is the global context of regionalism a recent development, an aspect of the "increasingly dominant neo-liberal sensibility and the broader trend of economic globalization" of the past three decades.[158] Regionalism has always been a translocal phenomenon, one that posits the region as a point of orientation, identification, and belonging within both national and transnational contexts. This is not to deny the significance of centre-periphery relations to the production and mobilization of regions and regionalisms, but it is to suggest that the rigid overemphasis on centre-periphery models has been inadequate to the task of encompassing the multiple ties and connections that exceed the prescribed boundaries of both the region and the nation, as well as the problematic exclusivities that so often attach to regionalisms. In *fin-de-siècle* magazines, translocalism was obscured by the isomorphism between region and culture posited by the regionalism they advanced. But there were exceptions, the most salient of which, *The Maple Leaf*, appeared at the end of the period, on the other side of the continent.

On 13 March 1910, *The San Francisco Call* ran a story on "the Sons and Daughters of the Maritime Provinces." The organization, whose San Francisco branch's membership alone numbered "more than 400," was hosting its fourth annual ball.[159] The organization had been founded six years earlier in nearby Oakland, then an emerging urban centre poised to become a dominant industrial hub in the Pacific Southwest. The west coast terminus for three transcontinental rail lines, Oakland had roughly sixteen hundred trains pass through it each day.[160] Between 1900 and 1910, the population of Oakland more than doubled as the city annexed surrounding areas and as the city's growing manufacturing sector, construction projects, processing plants, and coastal trade economy drew thousands of migrants.[161] Among those who migrated to Oakland and the San Francisco Bay Area at the turn of the twentieth century were hundreds of Canadian expatriates from the Maritime Provinces, provinces that, by demographic and economic metrics, seemed Oakland's polar opposite. That group of immigrants included the founder and president of "the Sons and Daughters of the Maritime Provinces," Michael Ambrose McInnes.

A printer from Summerside, PEI, McInnes left his $8-a-week job at *The Summerside Journal* on 5 September 1889. One week after arriving in San Francisco, he found a printing job at the starting rate of $25/week.[162] A few years later, McInnes had enough money to set up his own printing shop with another former Summerside resident, Walter Harrington.[163] In 1906, the pair constructed a three-story building in downtown Oakland which was to house their printing shop and the office for a new magazine, *The Maple Leaf.* A monthly magazine "devoted to the interests" of "Maritimers" at home and abroad, *The Maple Leaf* published articles on current affairs in the Maritime Provinces, popular history, articles about expatriate "Maritimers," and poetry. It also served as the official organ of the Sons and Daughters of the Maritime Provinces, whose meetings, "free to every Maritimer in the cities around the bay," were recorded in every fourth issue.[164] But it was not restricted to expatriates, and every issue featured contributions and letters by both current and former residents of towns and cities throughout PEI, Nova Scotia, and New Brunswick. Within two years the magazine had subscribers in seventeen states, the territory of Hawaii, Mexico, and all Canadian provinces.[165]

The incredible success of *The Maple Leaf* – it would be published continuously for forty years until McInnes's death in 1947 – stands in contrast to the attrition and failure that characterized magazine publishing on the east coast. By 1907, *Acadiensis* was the only *fin-de-siècle* magazine there still in print. 1905 had seen the demise of both *Prince Edward Island Magazine* and *The New Brunswick Magazine*, while others – *Nova Scotia Illustrated*, *Cape Breton and Nova Scotia Magazine*, *The International*, and *Kit-Bag* – had barely survived two years. Other general-interest magazines would follow intermittently. *The New Brunswicker*, for instance, published for three years between 1907 and 1910. Regional magazines, and *Acadiensis*, in particular, had effectively defined the emergent regionalism, and *The Maple Leaf* appears as an affirmation of the regionalist project. But general-interest magazines within the three provinces were ultimately unable to sustain themselves without an effective economy of scale. Certainly, none could match the extensive reach and duration of *The Maple Leaf*, which actively targeted a large, geographically diffuse readership.

Publishing news, articles, poems, and letters contributed by both "Maritimers" abroad and those in "the old home," *The Maple Leaf* fostered a network of translocal exchange, making visible the mobile plural public sphere in which the region was produced. Unlike the regionalist politics of Jack and Harris, who often articulated regionality as a resistance to increasing cultural and economic centralism, the regionalism articulated in *The Maple Leaf* expressed itself primarily as a form of transnational longing. Nostalgia for the places left behind was coupled with "an intense and self-conscious boosterism of the new home."[166] Yet these different expressions of regionality were both fundamental components in the broader production of regional space. Moreover, both were the products of geographically diffuse, translocal networks. These translocal connections – existing between specific, distanciated localities, crossing provincial, state, and international boundaries – constituted a form of cross-border exchange that was as much a part of global dynamics, of communications, transportation, trade, and labour migrancy, as a response to the consolidation of the nation-state.

What remained relatively concealed in magazines such as *Acadiensis* was laid bare in *The Maple Leaf.* The latter clearly involved the production of a space that would form a nucleus for identification within and *beyond* the specific geographical territory deemed to constitute the region. To be sure, the criterion for regional identity, that which constituted a "Maritimer," was still dependent upon notions of territoriality, of an always already regionalized world. Both expressions of regionalism were premised on the assumption of the essential belonging of a particular people to a particular place, and they both depended upon notions of a positive, fixed, and territorialized community that could form the locus for a coherent cultural identity. However, regional identity could never be comfortably contained within a prescribed territory, and such identification necessarily exceeded the boundaries of the region and the nation-state to encompass the staggering proportion of "Maritimers" who, by the first decade of the twentieth century, lived abroad. The region was not merely a middle term between the highly localized specificities of place and the more discernibly political, ideological, and generally abstract nation-state, though it was often positioned as such by those opposed to centralism. Rather, it consisted in and was defined through the networks of geographically diffuse groups who identified with and helped to produce a community of regional sentiment.

In reality, the "region" never existed as a bounded, fixed space, much less as the container of a homogenous culture. *Fin-de-siècle* regionalism must finally be understood as a fundamentally translocal phenomenon rooted in the desire to fashion a space of belonging within a broader transnational world. Crucial to the ascendance of the region as a locus for identification was the "naturalized narrative" of a homology between region and culture.[167] Literary regionalism, the (apparent) expression of regionality in literature, thus served the need for an "authentic" collective cultural identity.

While there were some authors who consciously cultivated a regional literary space, and many more who explored highly localized places within the conventional boundaries of the region, literary regionalism was more a function of editorial and critical practice than it was the result of authorial intent. Moreover, literature, arts, and historiography were all deployed in service of particular, narrow conceptions of what constituted modern regional identity.

The regionalism developed in the pages of *fin-de-siècle* magazines was neither uniquely regressive nor uniquely reactionary. The exclusivities that emerged simultaneously with efforts to articulate regional identity were the contingent products of broader social, historical, and political discourses of which regional magazines were a part, and not a problematic inherent to place-based identification itself. Contingent, because the region need not necessarily be conceived of as exclusive of other forms of identification. But forging a sense of rootedness and belonging via the creation of territorially bounded spaces does create an inside and an outside; and any regional community predicated on the homology between a prescribed territory and cultural particularity must of necessity involve inclusions and exclusions. However fundamental the need for belonging was to the spatial imagination of *fin-de-siècle* modernity, the definition of a distinct, homogenous cultural identity tethered to place involves a concomitant determination of who and what does and does not belong.

And both within and outside the region, the formulation of regional identity at the turn of the century was predicated on exclusions: not only on spatial criteria such as boundedness, proximity, and distance, but also on concepts of cultural and racial difference. Despite efforts to (nominally) represent French-Acadian and Indigenous Peoples, narratives of cultural succession, inheritance, and hierarchy combined with notions of geographical determinism to shape a powerfully exclusionary representation of region and regional identity. Other groups, most notably the sizable Black populations in Nova Scotia and New Brunswick, were almost entirely effaced from regionalist discourses. Whether it be the Anglican-Loyalists in *Acadiensis* and *New Brunswick Magazine*, or Catholic and Protestant Scots in *PEI Magazine* and *The Maple Leaf*, *fin-de-siècle* magazines almost invariably conflated regional identity with a particular cultural and racial group. In this, regionalism was aligned with, rather than opposed to, nationalism and imperialism: for all the historicity and authenticity that a co-opted Acadian and Wabanaki history could lend regional identity, that identity was ultimately defined as white and predominantly Anglophone; Jack's Acadia was not the French *Acadie*, much less Wabanahkik. While the comparison of *fin-de-siècle* magazines reveals internal division, cultural plurality, and heterogeneity, representations of homogeneity generally succeeded in masking contradictions internal to the regionalist project. But opposition did exist, and occasionally, it found expression in periodicals of protest and reform. Generally, these publications sought broader arenas in which to challenge dominant discourses. Abraham Beverly Walker's Black-nationalist magazine *Neith* is exemplary of those publications that challenged, often indirectly and through the rejection of regionalism as a legitimate vehicle for identity politics, the hegemonic discourse of emergent regionalism during the long *fin-de-siècle*.

2

Post-Race, Afromodernism, and Abraham Beverly Walker's *Neith*

On the evening of 23 February 1903, members of Saint John's *haut monde* crowded into the York Theatre for what promised to be an evening of "great delight."[1] For the past month the city's papers had been advertising a new musical production of *Uncle Tom's Cabin* and opening night had arrived. Though it was not the first "Tom show" to have been staged in Saint John, this one was special: a five-act musical dramatized by Charles Townsend and performed by the Saint John City Cornet Band, this was to be the first *local* production and would feature a "grand Southern Plantation scene" with "several new spectations."[2] The show did not disappoint. When the curtains went up at 8:00 pm, wrote one reviewer in the *Saint John Globe*, "there was a round of hearty hand clapping for the very effective stage setting."[3] The ensuing scene, in which "the darkeys [who] were seen picking cotton ... gave a short concert" was, similarly, "greatly enjoyed and heartily applauded." In short, the "immense audience" was thoroughly delighted.[4] In the reviewer's words, why wouldn't they be pleased with "Stowe's sympathetic and ever popular story of the South"?[5]

For the white members of the audience, Saint John was emphatically *not* the "South," but an iteration of "the New Jerusalem," the "land of Canaan."[6] Stowe's story served to define Canada and its oldest incorporated city, Saint John, *against* the bigoted, intolerant United States. As one contributor to the local Catholic paper would write several weeks later in a letter titled "Race Distinction": "in this great Dominion of ours," the central issue was not "the colour line as it is in the United States," but "the religious line."[7] For most white Canadians, racial prejudice was a non-issue and the so-called "Negro problem" was a distinctly American one. And so, Saint John concertgoers enjoyed *Uncle Tom's Cabin* with clear consciences and light hearts, perhaps already looking forward to the next sensation, the Carleton Cornet Band's minstrel show to be held on 10 March, "a first-class burnt-cork show … one of the old kind."[8]

Saint John's "Tom show" of 1903 and its production and reception are illustrative of a particular problem faced by Black writers and editors in Canada at the turn of the century. Those who sought to foster a dialogue around race and racism in Canada in the post-bellum period were confronted with a trenchant narrative of liberal tolerance, buttressed by what Winfried Siemerling calls "popular assumptions and complacencies about early Canada as a haven for blacks mistreated south of the border."[9] "The moral capital earned through Canada's role in the Underground Railroad has been happily pocketed in this perspective," Siemerling contends, "while continuing black Canadian life has been cast as somehow exterior to the nation."[10] This obliteration of Blackness occurred at the regional level just as it did at the national level; the regionalism advanced in the pages of *Acadiensis*, *Prince Edward Island Magazine*, and *Cape Breton Magazine* was no more and no less inclusive of racial diversity than the Canadian nationalism to which it responded. Both were predicated on assumptions of uniform racial identity. Emergent regionalism thus had the effect of excluding Blackness via the same nationalist processes by which whiteness was continually rendered synonymous with "Canadian" identity, a process effected, in part, through "centuries of erasure of people of colour from Canadian media."[11] For Black writers seeking to address and combat anti-Black racism in Canada, the problem was twofold: the "colour line" and de facto segregation created near-insurmountable barriers for Black writers, editors, and publishers, while a mainstream denial of that same "colour line" meant that appeals to the general, predominantly white, Canadian public fell on deaf ears.

It was into this milieu – a city, a region, and a nation, all secure in the myth of Canadian tolerance and diversity – that Black barrister and journalist Abraham Beverley Walker launched *Neith: A Magazine of Literature, Science, Art, Philosophy, Jurisprudence, History, Reform, Economics* (1903–04). The first issue received notice, alongside reviews of *Uncle Tom's Cabin* and news of the impending general election, in nearly all of Saint John's eight newspapers. But conspicuously missing from all but one of those papers was any mention of *Neith*'s central role as a vehicle for Walker's Black nationalism, his numerous articles on racial equality and Black rights, and his own radical solution to "The Negro Problem." The situation is telling: as an impressively produced periodical that published essays and poetry by Saint John's leading intellectuals, *Neith* was lauded as a welcome addition to regional print culture. However, as a magazine dedicated to providing "a forum" for "those who are bleeding under the heel of despotism and caste,"[12] *Neith* seems to have been regarded as somewhat of an anachronism.

Over its short run of just five issues, *Neith* thus reveals the precarity of a magazine that sought to articulate a radical Black politics at a time when periodicals in the Maritime Provinces were trenchantly regionalist and when periodicals outside the region were obsessively preoccupied with Canadian nationalism. In effect, *Neith* appeared when no similar vehicle for anti-racist discourse existed north of the 49th parallel. The once-vibrant intellectual tradition sustained in Black newspapers such as Henry and Mary Bibb's *The Voice of the Fugitive* (Canada West and Ontario, 1851–53) and Mary Ann Shadd's *The Provincial Freeman* (Ontario, 1853–60?) had all but ceased, and similar journalistic efforts would not appear until the late 1910s and 1920s. In this austere publishing climate, anti-racist print and positive articulations of Blackness were confined to church-sponsored booklets, pamphlets, petitions, and other ephemera. It was not in spite of this precarity, but, in part, because of it, that Walker engaged in a polemic that at once assimilates and transcends the matrices of nationalist and imperialist discourses into which *Neith* was launched. Situated at the intersection of competing discourses – emergent regionalism, Canadian nationalism, North American Black nationalism, pan-Africanism, and British imperialism – *Neith* sought to be international in scope and significance, even as it was rooted in and shaped by its specific local, regional, and national contexts. The result was short-lived but significant. At once providing a forum for Black intellectuals within the Maritime Provinces and committed to a pan-African Black nationalism, *Neith* challenged the homogenous and exclusionary regional identities then being constructed in the region's cultural-historical magazines. In effect, by rejecting regionalism as a legitimate vehicle for identity politics and social criticism, *Neith* challenged the notion of a racially and culturally homogenous region.

But the significance of *Neith* as a literary-cultural magazine goes beyond its having contested monolithic, homogenous constructions of region and nation within the limiting discursive context of *fin-de-siècle* Canada. As one of the few Black periodicals published in Canada during this pivotal period, *Neith* offers an especially productive ground for examining the relationship between Black expressive culture and modernism in Canada. Notwithstanding the magazine's innovative visual aspect, this Afro-modernist aesthetic is not immediately apparent from the magazine's literary content. While modernist affinities can be sighted in the range of authors Walker cites and celebrates in *Neith*, it is his own critical approach, the philosophy of art and politics developed over *Neith*'s five issues, that ultimately underpins his politico-cultural modernism. This modernism is political in that it begins by contemplating the modern Black polity at the particular historical conjuncture of the turn of the century. This was a moment marked by the failure of Reconstruction and the intensification of racial violence within a reformed, ostensibly progressive liberal order. Through a transnational engagement with Afro-modernist thought in America, Walker responds to this moment by developing a program committed to the imbrication of the aesthetic and the political. The cultural and aesthetic dimension of this program hinges, in turn, on a discursive strategy that fuses Afrocentric classicism with the prophetic tradition. Far from being divorced from Walker's political program, this discursive strategy renovates cultural traditions grounded in Ethiopianism, Afrocentric historiography, and Afro-Protestantism in order to envision emancipatory futures for Africa and the Black diaspora. *Neith* thus provided the vehicle for this Afro-modernist vision.

Neith first appeared in February 1903. It was printed by Paterson Publishing & Co. in super octavo format on medium-weight printing paper with a matte finish for covers and a gloss finish for images. Ranging from fifty-four pages (no. 5) to seventy-six pages (no. 3), and averaging sixty pages per issue, the magazine was an expensively produced, illustrated monthly. Its stated purpose, expressed in the first issue's editorial, was "to set people thinking, to extirpate erroneous ideas, to advance the spirit of freedom, to stir up a feeling of brothership among all men, and to spread Christian civilization throughout Africa."[13] The first issue of *Neith* is exemplary of Walker's editorial direction: running to seventy-two pages, the issue consisted of prefatory remarks followed by eleven unsigned short essays, five medium-length essays (including the first part of Walker's serialized "The Negro Problem, and How to Solve It"), four signed longer essays, three poems, literary notes (comprising brief essays, commentary, and reviews), and editorial announcements. In addition to Walker, six contributors are identified in the first issue. The topics of the essays vary widely, but nearly all contribute to the Afrocentric, imperialist ideology to which Walker was committed, and nearly three-quarters of the first issue concerns subjects directly related to African American, Black Canadian, or pan-African issues, politics, and initiatives. For Walker, *Neith* was to be a vehicle for change and racial advancement, and at the core of his editorial program was a conviction that civil discourse coupled with creative expression could effect social reform. And yet, four issues later and already behind on its publication schedule, *Neith* published its final issue in January 1904.

Situating *Neith* in its local, national, and international publishing contexts, this chapter begins by locating within *Neith* the same radical politics – pan-African, nationalist, and imperialist – that scholars have previously identified in Walker's other published works. That political project, however, cannot be adequately understood without attending to the form of political and cultural modernism Walker developed in *Neith*. Thus, the second part of this chapter turns to consider *Neith* and Walker at the juncture of Afro-modernity, modernism, and Black expressive culture in Canada. Such an attempt to locate early-twentieth-century Black writers like Walker under the rubric of modernism presents its own set of difficulties. These difficulties are connected, on the one hand, to the failure of Canadian modernist criticism to consider Black writing, and, on the other, to the constitutive tension between modernity and Blackness identified by theorists and critics of Black cultures in Canada and elsewhere.

Nevertheless, modernism remains a valuable frame through which to read Walker and *Neith*, not simply for challenging an exclusionary modernist tradition, or for a politics of representation, but also for registering Walker's key engagements with the global intellectual movements that defined the modernist moment. These engagements reveal an intellectual genealogy that includes such major figures of Afro-modernism in America as Booker T. Washington and W.E.B. Du Bois, as well as lesser-known members of the Caribbean diaspora, including AME pastor and classicist

H.A.S. Hartley. Walker's own aporetic response to a reconfigured modernity at once intersects with and diverges from these contemporaries. By paying attention to Walker's own discursive strategies, his oratorical prose and his deployment of classicism and the Afro-Protestant prophetic tradition, we can begin to trace the contours of his unique modernism across his dozens of essays in *Neith*.

Ultimately, Walker's modernism was constrained by the limited discursive space afforded Black writers in a nation so frequently cast as "post-racial."[14] That the publication of *Neith* also coincided with the intensification of what Barrington Walker and others have termed "Jim Crow Canada" simultaneously lent Walker's project greater urgency and severely restricted the scope of action available to him. By examining both representative contributions from white Canadian writers and the magazine's reception in regional papers, the third and final part of this chapter examines the limits and pressures exerted on *Neith* and Walker's editorial polemics by the predominantly white-settler society in which it was published, and which constituted its base readership. Walker's modernism and his attempts to negotiate the cultural terrain of post-race finally suggest the failure of regionalism to account for the range of identifications advanced by writers and editors during the *fin-de-siècle*. This situation does not imply that regionalism held no currency for Black writers in the period, but rather that the need to mediate between local, regional, national, and transnational contexts, without lapsing into either homogenizing deterritorializations or narrow particularisms, was as much at issue in early Black Canadian writing and print culture as it is today. Short-lived though it was, *Neith* nevertheless provides an entry point into these discussions of racial, aesthetic, and territorial politics while also constituting one of the most fascinating periodicals produced in *fin-de-siècle* Canada.

While there exists no sustained critical treatment of *Neith*, Walker's career as a lawyer, journalist, and civil rights activist has received variable attention in several studies, most notably W.A. Spray's *The Blacks of New Brunswick*, Robin Winks's "Negroes in the Maritimes: An Introductory Survey" and *The Blacks in Canada*, Barry Cahill's "First Things in Africadia; Or, the Trauma of Being a Black Lawyer in Late Victorian Saint John," and George Elliott Clarke's "Winking at Winks" in *Directions Home: Approaches to African-Canadian Literature*. Spray, though significant for providing one of the earliest histories to reference Walker, gives only a cursory description of Walker and *Neith*. In contrast, Cahill's article provides the most comprehensive biography of Walker. Cahill details the systemic and bureaucratic racism Walker confronted as the first Canadian-born Black barrister, as well as the politics and "white-chauvinist" culture that prevented Walker from maintaining a successful law practice in Saint John. Cahill, though acknowledging *Neith* "merits a study in itself," is squarely focussed on Walker's career in law.[15] On the other hand, Winks's chapter "Source of Strength? – The Press" in *The Blacks in Canada* offers the most extensive treatment of *Neith*, but Winks's approach is marred by his refusal to deeply engage with the form and content of the magazine beyond cursory and superficial description. Nor does Winks treat Walker and his writing as a legitimate subject for critical analysis, opting instead to position Walker as a hopelessly naïve aberration in the history of African-Canadian print culture, albeit one of "considerable talent."[16]

Clarke, rejecting Winks's "usual professional sneering," provides the most sustained examination of Walker's social, political, and philosophical thought.[17] Clarke submits Walker's 1905 treatise *Message to the Public* to close analysis while situating Walker within the broader fields of North American and pan-African political-cultural thought. He identifies Walker as an Afrocentric "neo-British imperialist," whose *Message to the Public* "weds New World African imperialism to the globalist white supremacy articulated by backers of an 'Anglo-Saxon union' between Great Britain and the United States."[18] In *Neith* the contradiction that arises from these apparently disparate ideologies appears not only within Walker's thought, but between articles. The same "African diasporic imperialism" and "precocious fascism" that Clarke sees operating in *Message to the Public* are in evidence in the pages of *Neith*, though Walker had not yet conceived of the African Civilization Movement of which he writes in the former.[19]

Neith can thus be seen as a sort of proving ground wherein Walker introduced, developed, and amended his positions on a range of political and cultural subjects, critical stances he would later consolidate in his *Message to the Public*. Accordingly, the political-cultural touchstones that Clarke stresses in his discussion of Walker – Booker T. Washington's "Atlanta Compromise" (1895) and *Up from Slavery* (1901), W.E.B. Du Bois's *The Souls of Black Folk* (1903) – are also central to many of the

Figure 2.1 Photograph of Abraham Beverley Walker from *A Message to the Public by Dr. A.B. Walker, President and Promoter of the African Civilization Movement*, 1905.

articles published in *Neith*. Yet *Neith* also provides insight into additional key figures not covered by Clarke, most notably the classicist Rev. Henry Alexander Saturnin Hartley and Rev. Henry McNeil Turner, former bishop of the African Methodist Episcopal Church and editor of the newspaper *The Voice of the People* (1901–05). In *Neith*, Turner is both listed as a contributor and cited by Walker as an ally in the cause for emigration to Africa. Finally, *Neith*, more than Walker's other publications, must be read in relation to "the nexus of African-Canadian intellectuals in the Maritimes" in which Clarke locates Walker.[20] In fact, many of those

"Africadian" intellectuals whom Clarke suspects Walker to have been familiar with, including Rev. John Clay Coleman, Rev. Adam S. Green, and James Robinson Johnston, are listed as contributors to *Neith*. Such inclusions not only confirm Walker's familiarity with leading Black or Africadian intellectuals, but also suggest that the direction of influence may have been reciprocal.

Hence, while the critical-theoretical framework developed by Clarke informs much of the foregoing analysis of *Neith*, it is also important to recognize the way in which the magazine differs from Walker's other publications. The form of *Neith* – the periodical and the monthly magazine as a genre – shaped the individual texts it contained. The total signification of each issue derives not from any individual text, but from the textual and bibliographic aggregate. Articles on the Canadian economy, the threat of irreligiosity, and English factory legislation; conventional Victorian-Romantic verse expressing melancholic nostalgia and saccharine rural idylls; literary essays extolling the genius of Emile Zola and Henrik Ibsen; reviews of the latest chapbooks of Charles G.D. Roberts and Bliss Carman: all are interposed between Walker's forceful polemics on racial advancement and Black nationalism. The nature of the medium, then, demands that Walker's work be both read in relation to and parsed from the articles, essays, and poems from other contributors to the magazine, as well as in relation to his subscribers and the reading public to whom the magazine was addressed.

And just as Walker's *Message to the Public* must be placed in conversation with the works of Washington and Du Bois, so *Neith* finds analogues among twentieth-century African-American magazines. These include magazines that resemble *Neith* in form and content, magazines such as Walter Wallace's Washington-friendly and accommodationist-oriented *Coloured American Magazine* (Atlanta, 1900–09); J. Max Barber's increasingly anti-accommodationist *Voice of the Negro* (Atlanta, 1904–05); and W.E.B. Du Bois's short-lived *The Moon Illustrated* (Memphis, 1905–06) and much longer-lasting *The Crisis* (Baltimore, 1910–). These magazines, not exclusively Black, but focussing primarily on African-American concerns, were political and cultural periodicals with a strong literary focus, "involved first in political and social occurrences and then in black literature."[21] In scope and content, *Neith* most resembles these early-twentieth-century American magazines: while committed to an explicit Black-nationalist politics, *Neith* comprised essays and poems on a range of topics. To an extent, Walker also aligned *Neith*'s literary criticism with its politics, even if the poetry published within was generally divorced from the immediate political message Walker intended to communicate.

As for the specific political enterprise to which *Neith* was committed, it finds its closest analogues in newspapers such as Henry McNeal Turner's *The Voice of the People* (Atlanta, 1901–04) and, over a decade later, Marcus Garvey's *Negro World* (New York, 1918–33). Both of these periodicals served as vehicles for the promotion of their editors' respective back-to-Africa schemes: Turner's International Migration Society and the Black Star Line operated by Garvey's Universal Negro Improvement Association. Insofar as emigration to Africa and "spread[ing] Christian civilization throughout Africa" formed two key objectives of Walker's editorial agenda, McNeal's and Garvey's periodicals were united in purpose with *Neith*. These publications, however, were weekly papers, their format and scope dissimilar to that of *Neith*. In contrast, *Neith*, in basic physical format and the range of titles it includes, appears to align as much with conventional British and Canadian miscellanies as with the activist Black magazines then emerging south of the border. Nevertheless, while *Neith* does share similarities with some of Canada's literary and general-interest magazines of the period, such as *Saturday Night* (1887–2005) and *Canadian Magazine of Politics, Science, Art and Literature* (1893–1939), those similarities are largely superficial. Any likeness derives from organization, generic structure, and the subjects of select articles, but *Neith* and comparable Canadian periodicals are entirely distinct in their specific iconography, visual aesthetic, polemics, and political commitments. A closer examination of the first issue dispels any illusion that *Neith* was a conventional Victorian periodical.

A glance at the cover of *Neith* no. 1 would likely serve to alert the reader to the novelty of the magazine (fig. 2.2). Printed in dark blue, the cover features an illustration of Neith, "an Ethiopic divinity," holding a scepter in her left hand and grasping a bolt of lightning in her right. These bolts emanate from the title, centred just above, which is drawn in capitalized sans-serif font. Surrounding this image is a trefoil arch featuring an image of the Great Sphinx in the upper left and of the Great Pyramids in the upper right. At top-centre is an inverted pentagram. Along the bottom, at the base of the columns that frame either side, is the Latin inscription *Ecripuit cælo fulmen sceptrumque tyrannis*, "he/she snatched the lightning from heaven and the sceptre from tyrants." The entire image occupies all but the top and bottom margins. In the top margin appear the volume number, date, and issue number. Written in the bottom margin is the frequency of appearance, cost of subscription, and city of publication: "issued monthly: $1.00 a year: 10c. a single copy. ST. JOHN, N.B. CANADA." Much can be gleaned, or at least conjectured, from this imposing image, but Walker leaves no need for speculation. The "Editorial Announcements" inform the reader that "Neith was an Ethiopic divinity, and was worshipped in Meroe, Egypt, and Carthage. She stood for Liberty, Wisdom, and Eternal Justice, and presided over the thunder and the tempest."[22] The phrase inscribed on the cover, writes Walker, was adopted "as being more attributable to [Neith] – a splendid myth, a sacred fiction, imagined and adored by the greatest and noblest people of all antiquity – than to the one that it was originally fabricated to flatter."[23] The same design, in varying colours, would appear on the cover of all five issues.

Notably, this visual aesthetic aligns *Neith* with African-American magazines in two ways. First, it reflects an editorial commitment to encouraging visual arts with African themes and iconography, paralleling what Du Bois described as his own attempt to "encourage graphic arts" both through "magazine covers with negro themes and faces" and by "portray[ing] the faces and features of colored folk."[24] Second, the choice of Neith as the magazine's governing icon engages the Ethiopianism embraced, albeit in sharply distinct ways, by Walker's leading African-American contemporaries, including Du Bois, Paul Laurence Dunbar, and, later, Marcus Garvey. Du Bois, for instance, incorporated representations of Neith into his own "African-centred ideology" concerning Black femininity. Gary Lemons explains that, for Du Bois, "motherhood embodied the essence of Black womanhood which he idealized in the form of the mythological African goddess Neith, his universal symbol of maternality."[25] Though Walker did not explicitly connect Neith to a women's liberationist philosophy as did Du Bois, he clearly draws on an Ethiopianist aesthetic to contribute to a form of cultural nationalism that was, like Du Bois's, "rooted in African mythology popularized in the early 1900s."[26]

Thus, in addition to anticipating the visual aesthetic and iconography employed by African-American magazines such as *The Crisis*, the cover, imagery, and physical form of the magazine all serve an aesthetic function

Figure 2.2 The cover of *Neith* 1, no. 2, March 1903.

that parallels the magazine's textual content. When taken in conjunction with Walker's explanatory note, the iconography and symbolism incorporated in the cover are suggestive of key conceptual orientations with which Walker engages within the magazine: Afrocentrism, Ethiopianism, classicism, the veneration of African antiquity, racial equality, imperialism, and even anti-Americanism (suggested by his not-so-subtle contempt toward the slave-owning Benjamin Franklin, "the one [the motto] was originally fabricated to flatter"[27]). The first issue thus provides a paradigm for the symbolic force of what Jerome McGann calls "the deployment of a double helix of perceptual codes: the linguistic codes, on one hand, and the bibliographical codes on the other."[28] This interplay between content and form, or linguistic and bibliographical codes, continued between the covers of the first issue through the frequent use of bold, italicized Latin quotations, with occasional illustrations of biblical and ancient figures, photographs of British royalty, and photographs of Black contributors, interposed among the two-column text blocks. The effect is a field of visual and textual signifiers that suggest coherence, even as the range of its textual contents seems to produce marked contradictions. The visual aesthetic of the first issue thus anticipates, complements, and deepens the interplay of its varied articles, essays, and poems.

The contents of the first issue of *Neith* can be roughly divided into two parts. The first and more substantial part contains short and medium-length essays by Walker on a range of topics, primarily concerning racial politics, civil rights, and British-colonial affairs. The second half includes articles, poems, and reviews by several other contributors on varied subjects. None of these short articles are signed, but the similarity of focus and the forceful, oratorical prose in which they are written suggest they are the product of Walker's pen. Across these sixteen brief and medium-length essays, one can trace the contours of Walker's Black nationalist program, characterized by a pan-African perspective, an Afrocentric appeal to antiquity and Ethiopianism, neo-British imperialism, and a condemnation of the irremediable racial intolerance by which Walker defines the United States. The geographic scope of Walker's analyses is extensive, encompassing North America, the Caribbean, and Africa; and this broad-ranging analysis is crucial to Walker's politics, for it is through an articulation of pan-African unity in the struggle against racism, and against repressive, racist regimes, that Walker formulates his nationalist project.

BLACK NATIONALISM, PAN-AFRICANISM, AND IMPERIALISM

For Walker, the "Negro Problem" is a national problem, even if the Black nationalism he articulates frequently involves the sublimation of British-imperial values. To that end, Walker often appears less concerned with locating a distinct Black cultural identity than with combatting the libel of racial inferiority on a global scale. So it is that in "Negrophobes Should Be Kept out of Africa," Walker does not oppose British colonialism and cultural imperialism in Africa per se, but rather the racial intolerance and inequality that is, for Walker, the *contingent* consequence of colonialism: "England's African policy should be to preserve, as far as possible, African territory for the Negroes and a class of white people who are manifestly and professedly friendly to the Negroes."[29] For Walker, racism is manifest not in the system of British imperialism itself, but in the impediments to racial equality in the colonies, in any "opposition to the development and civilization of the negroes."[30] This is not to suggest Walker did not value national sovereignty. In "Hayti and Its Enemies," Walker addresses the political instability that characterized Haiti at the turn of the century, indicting the "negrophobes" who are "constantly finding fault with Hayti." "These outbreaks of insurrection," he continues, "are not puzzling or surprising. In countries where the rulers possess all the learning and the masses all the illiteracy, the government is generally cruel and corrupt."[31] Here, Walker swiftly transitions from discussing the specific geopolitical situation in Haiti to broader reflections on pan-African sovereignty, defending Haiti as a model of Black self-determination. In contrast to Walker's professed allegiance to British imperialism elsewhere, such anti-colonial tracts underwrite a pan-Africanist approach to nationalism predicated on national sovereignty.

In the first issue of *Neith*, Walker's pan-African nationalism is best gleaned from his articles on Africa and the African diaspora outside the United States. However, it is the articles treating post-Reconstruction America, Jim Crow, and African-American politics that exhibit Walker's fiercest polemics against racial intolerance, on one hand, and his deepest engagement with African-American intellectual currents, on the other. Walker's assessment of the situation in the United States is clearest in his article "Tillmanism, or Mob Rule in the South." There, Walker specifically targets the southern United States, but the threat to African-American freedoms, rights, and their continuing existence as a people, is not confined to the south. For Walker, the beginning of the twentieth century marked an escalation of racial hatred that threatened the existence of African-heritage people within and beyond the United States, "East, West, North, and South."[32] Walker thus rejected any solution to American race relations that did not involve emigration: "Negroes have one trump card left ... The trump card I mean is emigration: emigration to Africa, the land of their forefathers, where the destiny of their race must be worked out and eventually settled."[33]

Nevertheless, while Walker's "Tillmanism, or Mob Rule in the South" and its complement "The Negro Problem, and How to Solve It" ultimately propose emigration as the only solution to "the Negro problem," they also represent Walker's deepest engagement with Washington and Du Bois in the pages of *Neith*. Contrary to Winks's account, Walker's attitude toward Booker T. Washington was neither straightforward nor entirely condemnatory. According to Winks, Walker held that Washington was "a deluded man," incapable and unwilling to lead African America in the struggle for civil rights and racial advancement.[34] Yet Walker does not "[oppose] the industrial training program advocated by Booker T. Washington" *tout court*, as Winks suggests.[35] To the contrary, when Walker turns his gaze toward Africa, Washington-style vocational education provides the model for his own imperialist program. However, Walker does deploy Du Boisian terms to denounce Washington's accommodationist reforms in the United States. In particular, Walker is critical of the submission of African-Americans to white political rule and the relinquishment of civil rights and higher education.

In contrast with Walker's discussion of industrial schools in Africa, "Tillmanism, or Mob Rule in the South" considers Washington and his accommodationist agenda within the context of American race relations. Walker begins, not by calling Washington a "deluded man," but by lauding him as "a distinguished Negro, and one of the greatest men of his age."[36] Distinguished, great, but misguided. For Walker, Washington's willingness to forsake higher education for African-Americans was his cardinal failure: "Mr. Washington took the opponents to giving the Negroes, except in very few cases, an academic education, at their word. That is, he reduced their logic and special pleading to practice." The result, Walker maintains, is that Washington "supplied the market with ... black men and black women who can hew wood and draw water with a graceful and pleasing and studious smack."[37] Accommodation, then, was well-intentioned but ineffective. Moreover, the consequences of relinquishing political rights deprived African-Americans not only of the potential for social betterment, but also of the possibility for individual subjectivity: "The very moment that the Negro's name is erased from the voters' list, he is an abject, defenceless, hopeless slave; nay even worse than an abject, defenceless, hopeless slave: a downright, miserable, cringing outlaw; a target for scorn and contempt and violence."[38] In effect, the deprivation of civil liberties and rights, which defined the modern moment to which Walker responded, was tantamount to genocide: "It would be far better for every Negro in the South to commit suicide, or be slain, or assassinated, or massacred, than to attempt to live there after he is denuded of his political and civil rights."[39]

This existential crisis would prove crucial to Walker's modernism and his critique of the modern liberal state, but Walker does not suggest that disenfranchisement is the direct result of Washington's program. Rather, Walker's severest criticism is directed towards Washington's conciliatory approach to southern whites, a contributing factor, but not a sufficient cause:

> In fact, Mr. Washington has been, from start to finish, ready and willing to do anything, or go anywhere, or make any kind of compromise, in order to appease the gaping wrath of his people's foes ... All that the oily-tongued, two-faced wiseacres have had to do has been to command him to dig and sweat and bleed, and he has immediately lifted his hat and made an obeisance, and, without even a sigh or a frown, set to digging and sweating and bleeding.[40]

It is easy to read too far into these apparently damning criticisms without bearing in mind the context in which they appear. While Walker entirely rejects accommodation as a viable solution to American race relations, he does not place primary blame on Washington. Despite his outmoded and ineffectual program, Washington remains for Walker a "magnificent" and "unparalleled [hero]," tragically deceived and thwarted by "the obdurate Southerner."[41]

Walker thus agreed with Du Bois's assessment that, though the disenfranchisement of African-Americans was not the "direct result of Mr. Washington's teachings ... [Washington's] propaganda [had], without a shadow of a doubt, helped [its] speedier accomplishment."[42] And Walker's agreement with Du Bois goes beyond support for the political franchise. Walker is also in agreement with Du Bois on the need for higher education, which is central to Walker's back-to-Africa colonization scheme, what he would later call the African Civilization Movement. In the first instalment of "The Negro Problem, and How to Solve It," Walker places "academic" education at the centre of his imperial enterprise: "To cultivate the whole human family up to the highest possible standard or degree in everything that makes for righteousness is doubtless the final cause of education, nay, more, the ultimate object of religion, the *summum bonum* of human possibility."[43] Walker is thus committed to higher learning for all, regardless of race or class; but academic education is also requisite to his proposed solution for reasons other than universal education.

Walker believed academic education was necessary to foster a leadership class of Black elites who could realize his imperialist project, "whereby the continent of Africa may be colonized, civilized, and Christianized, and the Negro race made the most useful and important force in the world."[44] This leadership class would comprise "20,000" of "the best and most intelligent types of the Negroes of Canada, and of the Negroes of the British West Indies, and of the Negroes of the United States."[45] For Clarke, the "precocious fascism" that is apparent in Walker's Afrocentric imperialism finds a corresponding "attitude" in Du Bois's *Souls of Black Folk*.[46] The clearest formulation of this inclination toward nationalist authoritarianism, though, is given at the outset of Du Bois's essay "The Talented Tenth": "The problem of education ... among Negroes must first of all deal with the Talented Tenth; it is the problem of developing the Best of this race that they may guide the Mass away from the contamination and death of the Worst."[47] Walker's leadership class is, on one level, the double of Du Bois's "talented tenth" dressed in British-imperial garb.

What separates Walker from both Washington and Du Bois is the precise solution to the "Negro problem" that he proposes. Favouring emigration would appear to put Walker at odds with the dominant currents of African-American thought at the beginning of the twentieth century. However, there were those, such as Henry McNeal Turner, who advocated similar schemes, and Walker goes as far as possible to align such programs with his own. In "Tillmanism, or Mob Rule in the South," Walker claims that "Bishop Turner's idea is the correct one; the Negroes must get up and leave the United States altogether or be exterminated."[48] In the fourth installment of "The Negro Problem, and How to Solve It," Walker expands upon Turner's International Migration Society in order to suggest the viability of his own stratagem: "The Rt. Rev. Henry M. Turner, of Atlanta, Georgia, Senior Bishop of the African Methodist Episcopal Church, and editor and publisher of *The Voice of the People*, is a firm and resolute believer in African colonization, and has been instrumental in bringing about, in the South, an organization to that end."[49] Walker was not alone, then, in advocating emigration to Africa. Moreover, in addition to echoing the emigration plan advocated by Turner, Walker's "African colonization" plan anticipated the back-to-Africa scheme advocated by Marcus Garvey through his Universal Negro Improvement Association nearly two decades later. In effect, Walker's position did not neatly align with any of the specific programs being advanced by Washington, Du Bois, or Turner. Rather, it is best understood as one position in a constellation of approaches that included accommodation, integration, civil rights, and emigration, with Washington's *Up from Slavery*, Du Bois's *The Souls of Black Folk*, Turner's *Voice of the People*, and H.A.S. Hartley's *Classical Translations* (1889) forming key coordinates for Walker's cultural-political thought.

Both this intellectual genealogy and the print-cultural analogues *Neith* finds in African-American magazines alert the reader to Walker's transnational engagements with contemporary Black intellectual currents while cutting through some of the rhetoric Walker himself deploys in an appeal to white-Canadian nationalism and British imperialism. More importantly, though, they invite an analysis of *Neith* that situates it in relation to Afro-modernist thought in America. If *Neith* was, as Clarke maintains, a "little magazine" – a genre always closely associated with the production and dissemination of modern and, finally, modern*ist* literature – we might ask whether it was also a vehicle for modernism.[50] More to the point, if Walker's "touchstones" – Washington's *Up From Slavery* and Du Bois's *The Souls of Black Folk* – are those that have long been associated with the origins of Afro-modernism in America, then it may prove productive to locate *Neith* at the intersection of Black expressive culture and modernism. To date, this is an encounter that has been almost entirely neglected in Canadian modernist studies.

AFRO-MODERNITY, MODERNISM, AND BLACK EXPRESSIVE CULTURE IN CANADA

Situating Walker in relation to a range of writers and thinkers, from Washington and Du Bois to the lesser-known classicist H.A.S. Hartley, provides a productive basis for reading Walker's essays and journalism as a form of political and cultural modernism connected to the origins of

Afro-modernism in America. This modernism involves, first, a commitment to the interdependence of politics and art at the level of critical and editorial practice and a neoteric response to a reconfiguration of modernity; and second, at the level of discursive practice, it involves the fusion of Afro-Protestantism and classicism into a distinct political aesthetic. I am concerned here with the specific modernist sensibility developed in *Neith*, but I want to suggest, by extension, that the recuperation of early-twentieth-century Black print culture might offer a basis for theorizing the relationship between modernism(s) and Black expressive culture in Canada more broadly. Such an approach is complicated, however, by the fact that there is little critical precedent for reading modernism in Black Canadian writing. In fact, any attempt to broach the idea of "Black modernism" in Canada must begin by addressing both the critical supposition of its non-existence and the potential problems such a framework might introduce.

The beginning of the twentieth century is generally considered a period in which there was a dearth of Black writing in Canada. In *The Black Atlantic Reconsidered*, Winfried Siemerling summarizes the critical consensus when he observes that, "after the outpouring in the nineteenth century, a resurgence of black Canadian writing occurred only after the increase of Caribbean immigration policy in the 1950s on."[51] Though Siemerling acknowledges the publication of Black writing in the range of ephemera produced in the period spanning 1900–60, he nevertheless concludes that "[a] renewed, more substantial literary output would have to wait until the latter third of the twentieth century."[52] Accordingly, Siemerling leaves unexamined those texts produced by Black writers and editors during the period. What are the consequences of this relative dearth? More particularly, given Siemerling's decision to omit the period spanning 1900–50, what are the consequences of curtailing an investigation into early-twentieth-century Black writing in Canada on the basis of relative paucity? These questions carry considerable weight for what they suggest not only about the relationship between Black cultural expression and Canadian modernism, but also about the possibility of recuperating any textual records of twentieth-century Afro-modernity in Canada prior to the 1960s.

It is fair to say that the extant body of Canadian modernist criticism suggests that there are no textual records of Black Canada's engagements with the global intellectual movements of modernism. To be sure, most book-length studies of modernism in Canada in the past two decades involve some recognition of the role of race and racism in modern Canadian literature. In *Unreal Country* (2002), Glenn Willmott highlights the "encoding of racial difference" in Canada's modern literature and explores its relationship to imperialist ideologies in the fourth chapter of that book.[53] Willmott points to Terrance Craig's *Racial Attitudes in English-Canadian Fiction, 1905–1980* (1987) as the pre-eminent work on race and racism in English-Canadian fiction, but neither Willmott nor Craig offers discussion of Black writing.

More frequent are appeals for closer examinations of racial politics in Canadian modernism, and acknowledgment of modernist criticism's failure to adequately address race, which is in turn positioned as one among various sites of marginalization. In his introduction to *The Canadian Modernists Meet* (2005), Irvine asserted the need to examine "co-emergent modernisms" to account for the diversity of modernist practices in Canada and to interrogate the canon's "centres and peripheries."[54] Since then, both *Wider Boundaries of Daring* (2009) and *Making Canada New: Editing Modernity in Canada* (2017) have challenged the "masculinist genealogy" of Canadian modernism, advocating an expanded canon inclusive of women in order to "augment existing histories of the modernist period."[55] "Issues of race, gender, and sexuality," write the editors of *Making Canada New*, "have notoriously been elided by masculinist, white narratives of Anglo-American modernism."[56] Such elision, they argue, has been challenged by both the many "revisionary studies" of Canadian modernism over the past two decades and by the "renovatory activity" of editorial scholarship.[57] Similarly, in his conclusion to *Translocated Modernisms* (2016), Kit Dobson recognizes the need to question received histories to recognize those marginalized by "the dominant conceptions of modernism, those that are gendered, racialized, classed, and beyond."[58] These critical interventions have all helped to revise the conventional narrative of Canadian modernism and the received canon; none, however, refer to Black writing in Canada or to the possibility that Black writing in Canada may bear some relationship to literary, cultural, and political modernism. This marks a substantial critical oversight, for while there may exist no large, untapped repository of Black Canadian modernist writing, a sustained engagement with early-twentieth-century Black writing and print culture renders untenable the belief that Black writers here were disconnected from Afro-modernist thought elsewhere.

Of course, substantial work *has* been done outside of modernist studies to recover early Black writing in Canada. George Elliott Clarke, Winfried Siemerling, Wayde Compton, and Karina Vernon are but a few of the most prominent scholars to have expanded the archive of Black Canadian literature backward to include writing produced prior to the 1960s. Notwithstanding Clarke's reading of Anna Minerva Henderson's *Citadel* (1967), however, extant studies of early-twentieth-century Black Canadian writing demonstrate a critical reticence to locate Black writers within the framework of literary modernism, a reticence that may point to deeper reservations about the viability of "modernism" as a critical category for Black writing.

Reading Walker as a modernist, by situating him in relation to Afromodernism in America or by otherwise postulating Black modernisms in Canada, presents several difficulties connected to modernism in particular, as well as to the relationship between Blackness and the idea of "modernity." This involves recognizing that it may be neither desirable nor productive to bring early-twentieth-century Black writers such as Walker under the rubric of Canadian modernism. This is especially true insofar as that critical endeavour entails the evaluation of Black writing according to the pre-established modernist dicta that have so long guided Canadian modernist criticism. The value of *Neith* and Walker's essays does not derive from their alignment with "modernism," nor is their aesthetic worth coextensive with how far they can be shown to conform to Anglo-American aesthetic values. At the same time, a critical reading of Walker's "modernism," understood in its broadest sense as an intellectual response to a particular historical conjuncture, to modernization, and to twentieth-century modernity, confronts a more fundamental problem, one that has been addressed in recent theorizations of modernity by such scholars as Michel-Rolph Trouillot and Richard Iton.

Taken together, Iton and Trouillot suggest that the very idea of "Black modernism" involves a tension not easily resolved within the conventional narrative of Western modernity. For Iton, "any simplistic reconciliation of the modern and the black" is suspect: "in the language game staked out by the modern, blacks are uniquely locked into a relationship that allows few possibilities for agency, autonomy, or substantive negotiation."[59] Iton suggests that it is not merely the dominant scripts of modernity that cast Blackness as other, but that the exclusion of Blackness is contained in the idea of the modern. Iton thus follows Trouillot's assertion that modernity "requires an alterity, a referent outside itself – a pre- or nonmodern in relation to which the modern takes its full meaning."[60] This formulation, that claims to modernity are at once historical and geographical claims, intelligible only insofar as there is a pre- or non-modern other against which the modern is defined, has significant implications for theorizing "Afro-modernity" and "Black modernism" in North America. Accordingly, the response of leading critics has been to theorize alternative modernities, including but not limited to Paul Gilroy's "black Atlantic" as, necessarily, a "counterculture" of modernity;[61] Trouillot's "Other from within, the otherwise modern";[62] and Michael Hardt and Antonio Negri's "altermodernity" as a "decisive break" with modernity.[63]

This critical response to modernity's failures, its inadequacy to account for the complexity of Black culture and Black polities, has informed the work of Canadian critics such as Siemerling, who sees the "different time-spaces" of Black Canadian writing as "[contributing] to the countermodernity that Gilroy has evoked in *The Black Atlantic*."[64] A similar need to challenge "triumphalist"[65] narratives of progress (though not specifically in terms of their relationship to Black culture) has likewise informed a tendency in Canadian modernist criticism toward "altermodernities." Accordingly, Kit Dobson maintains that "possible routes into these altermodernities can be sighted in modernism, [and] the entangled webs of aesthetics and politics."[66] These critics provide an important precedent for locating *Neith* within the "relational practices" of "black Canadian writing," practices that "generate new time-spaces and genealogies, as well as other possible futures of modernity."[67] Yet such a "sighting" of routes cannot merely celebrate the end of modernity; it must involve a concomitant effort to examine how dominant discourses of Canadian modernity have historically marginalized Black expressive culture.

Rather than jettisoning the term "modernism," then, I suggest that it retains value as a critical paradigm and aesthetic category in the context of Black Canada. Deployment of the category, however, requires substantial qualification. This involves not only a recognition of what Iton calls the "constitutive tension" that exists between the terms "black" and "modernism,"[68] but also a resistance to absorbing early-twentieth-century Black writing into the received canon of Canadian modernism and a recognition of the ways in which modernist studies have contributed to the obliteration of Blackness as they imagine Canada and Canadian modernity in the twentieth century. By thus shifting the critical terrain, we can begin to approach *Neith*, and Walker's writing in particular, with a view to sounding for a modernism that unsettles as much as it buttresses many of the features deemed to have defined modernist literature in Canada.

SOUNDING FOR MODERNISM

Walker's modernism emerges in his own polemical essays, in his specific response to modernity and his distinct discursive strategies, but it is connected to a broader aesthetic philosophy expressed in *Neith*. What is apparent from even a cursory survey of the magazine, however, is that the poetry featured in each issue, penned almost entirely by white members of Saint John's literary set, offers little if any variation on the prevailing Victorian Romantic modes that dominated the pages of most *fin-de-siècle* national and regional magazines in Canada. Moreover, the magazine's verse, save for the single poem "Neith," frequently bears so little relation to Walker's polemical journalism as to produce noticeable inconsistencies. Such poems as Charles Campbell's "Museum Shell" with its melancholic longing for the "misty memory of vanished years"[69] jar against Walker's preceding assessment of racial politics, his concern with futurity, and his predictions that "in time, the Negro race will overtake [the British Empire] – *tempus omnia revelat*."[70] Attention to common tropes does reveal an editorial preference for classicism, an orientation that underpins Walker's own political aesthetic, as well as his alignment with the Afrocentric philosophy of history being developed by contemporary African American thinkers such as Du Bois. But none of the verse published in *Neith* resembles the sort of literature called for in the first issue when Walker, quoting socialist writer and critic Abraham Cahan on the Russian realists, declares that "the present struggle for popular institutions will give birth ... to a new great literature, one which will mirror the new era."[71] In effect, the poetry Walker published in *Neith* served to obscure the racial aesthetics of Walker's writing rather than augmenting his modernism.

More telling than the verse he chose to publish is Walker's own literary criticism and that of his son, George Gilbert Walker. On the surface, modernist predilections can be detected in the range of writers acclaimed in the pages of *Neith*: naturalists Emile Zola and Thomas Hardy, realists

Leo Tolstoy, Vladimir Korolenko, and Maxim Gorky, the symbolist Dmitry Merezhkovsky, and the transitional figures Henrik Ibsen and Henry James. Zola, in particular, is given special attention in articles by both Walker and George Gilbert Walker. In "Realism in Fiction," the younger Walker celebrates the realist novel for its ability to present "both the psychic and physical in their highest form of delineation," and he celebrates Zola as its foremost practitioner.[72] Zola's willingness to explore social taboos is deemed a decisive mark of his craft: "Zola shows you sinks and cesspools of squalor and filth, morally and physically, and makes you feel that you are in the midst of it."[73] Notably, what Walker extols here as Zola's foremost achievement are those aspects of his naturalism that also helped shape modernist fiction in Canada.

The influence of figures such as Zola, Ibsen, and Hardy on the development of modernism in Canada has been well-documented. As Colin Hill notes, "critics have identified a naturalist strain in the *oeuvres*" of many of Canada's leading modernist novelists.[74] As a "hybrid genre," explains Hill, modern realism in Canada was shaped by the influence of "European and American realisms and naturalisms, and various modernist movements."[75] In the Canadian context, it is difficult to overstate the importance of this literary genealogy and the realist genres it influenced; Glenn Willmott goes so far as to suggest that "realism is a descent into Canadian national particularity" and that the postcolonial Bildungsroman, as a genre of modern realism, offers a key to "the structures of feeling and interest in Canadian modernity."[76] Accordingly, when Walker celebrates realism and naturalism, proclaiming Ibsen "one of the most imposing literary personages in the world," it is tempting to locate him within a critical tradition that anticipated the emergence of a specifically Canadian modernism.[77]

And yet the national paradigm is more likely to limit than to expand an understanding of the intellectual tradition of which Walker was a part. Rather, Walker's familiarity with and penchant for contemporary international literary movements is best interpreted as one aspect of his transatlanticism. Moreover, the writers Walker celebrates do not form a coherent and consistent aesthetic tradition from which he might be said to have drawn in his own writing, which was never conventionally "literary." Nearly as important to Walker as European and American naturalists and realists were figures such as Harriet Beecher Stowe and

Paul Laurence Dunbar, whose works had a more direct bearing on *Neith*'s anti-racist agenda. Thus, while a particular focus on Zola and references to Hardy, James, and Ibsen may indicate lines of influence that parallel those of major writers of modern fiction in Canada, writers such as Frederick Philip Grove or Morley Callaghan, these are not as significant as the particular orientation toward literature and politics that was developed in Walker's critical essays about those authors.

For Walker, the importance of figures such as Zola and Ibsen derives from the power of naturalism to provide a vehicle for social critique. In his article "Emile Zola," for instance, Walker interprets Zola's *oeuvre* as an assault on modern society, which "presented the aspect of a huge, dissolute, leprous monster, appeasing its diseased and abnormal appetite on vanity, wretchedness, and despair." Zola, argues Walker, "was not afraid to speak of society as he saw it, or snatch from its face its mask, and thus expose all its ugliness and foul sores."[78] The critique Walker identifies in Zola's work is similarly interpreted by George Walker as a crucial function of Zola's naturalism, in which the reader "[sees] shame by looking upon the society of the great metropolis."[79] According to Walker, naturalism is as much a political enterprise as it is an aesthetic one; Zola's stories are not merely artistic works, but "great philippics against vice and sham."[80] More importantly, Walker connects this social critique to the politics of race. It is Zola the author of "*J'Accuse…!*" rather than of the Rougon-Macquart cycle that Walker ultimately deems "a prophet." Zola's role in the Dreyfus affair and his condemnation of the French state's antisemitism made him an enemy of those "hateful perjurers" Walker elsewhere identifies with racist regimes of power.[81]

Worth noting in Walker's discussion of Zola are traces of Walker's own rhetorical strategies: the pathologization of racism in a "diseased" society, the politicization of classicism in the form of modern "philippics," and the identification of a prophetic tradition of apocalyptic or jeremiadic social criticism. What Walker appreciates in Zola's fiction is the imbrication of the political and the aesthetic that underpins his own essays. A "champion of the oppressed," Zola represents for Walker the ideal of the politicized author expounding "the broadest and deepest and highest doctrines of truth and equity – doctrines which benefit all alike, regardless of kindred or color."[82] Notably, Walker's claim to the universality of Zola's writing here does not mitigate the significance of Zola's social critique in relation to the politics of race. Rather, it makes explicit what Walker implies throughout: that politicized works can be mobilized toward all forms of social criticism, including the anti-racist objectives of his own program.

This rejection of art as a purely aesthetic practice distances Walker from traditionally conceived notions of high-modernist aesthetic detachment. At the same time, it aligns Walker more closely with contemporary thinkers such as Du Bois, whose aesthetic philosophy would eventually propound a necessary connection between politics and art. In his 1926 article "Criteria of Negro Art" published in *The Crisis*, Du Bois provided his most explicit statement of the relationship between art and political commitment: "Art is propaganda and ever must be ... I stand in utter shamelessness and say that whatever art I have for writing has been used always for propaganda for gaining the right of black folk to love and enjoy."[83] Walker never made statements as unequivocal as Du Bois did in the 1920s, nor did *Neith* provide a forum for Black poets as did Du Bois's *The Crisis* during the Harlem Renaissance. But Walker did invariably wed "beauty" as an aesthetic ideal to "truth and equity,"[84] anticipating Du Bois's insistence that "the apostle of Beauty ... becomes the apostle of Truth and Right not by choice but by inner and outer compulsion."[85] As it is with the literature Walker celebrates, so it is with his own essays; the particular aesthetic philosophy that begins to emerge in such essays as "Realism in Fiction" and "Emile Zola" invites an analysis of Walker's essays attentive to what Iton refers to as the "aesthetic grammars" of political discourse.[86] It is by shifting the focus from the conventionally literary to the aesthetic and rhetorical dimensions of Walker's essays, to the "poetics of the political,"[87] that *Neith* emerges as an important vehicle for Black modernism.

What Iton refers to as the aesthetic grammars – the "signs, styles and performances"[88] – of Black political communication have been a subject of American modernist criticism for several decades. As K. Miranda Simmons and James Crank observe, "the subversion of traditional formalism and a repositioning of aesthetics in relation to discursive performance and political action" was part of the "pivotal" scholarship initiated in the 1980s by such critics as Houston Baker and Henry Louis Gates Jr.[89] Baker's classic study *Modernism and the Harlem Renaissance* (1987) and his later *Turning South Again: Re-Thinking Modernism / Re-Reading Booker T.* (2001) are particularly germane to the analysis of Walker's writing. Baker effectively delineates "a different timeline of modernist work and sensibilities," one bookended by "cultural moments of both political and creative forms."[90] Combined with his assertion that Afro-modernism cannot be "confined to a traditionally defined belle lettres or to Literature with a capital and capitalist *L*," Baker's analysis provides both a starting point for reading modernism in *Neith* and a basis for locating Walker (however obliquely, given Baker's national framework) as a dissident voice within the "discursive constellation that marks a change in Afro-American nature on or about September 18th 1895."[91]

If, as Baker argues, Washington was "the quintessential herald of modernism in black expressive culture," we might analyze Walker's oratorical prose with a critical eye for the "culturally specific and canny rhetorical appropriation" that Baker terms "the mastery of form."[92] We might also position Walker's writing in relation to what Paul Gilroy interprets as Du Bois's "aporetic responses to American modernity," a genre of modernism, Gilroy argues, that was "inaugurated in Du Bois's *The Souls of Black Folk*."[93] Such comparisons are not only productive, but necessary to adequately appreciate the depth and contemporaneity of Walker's writing and his particular response to the consequences of a reconfigured modernity.

WALKER'S APORETIC RESPONSE TO MODERNITY

The historical juncture to which Walker responds in *Neith* is not a sudden rupture, but the particular reconfiguration of modernity marked by the failure of Reconstruction and the subsequent failure of Washington's politics of accommodation. Walker's critique of accommodation was central to his program of racial advancement, but his cultural and political modernism aimed to make sense of a more profound set of circumstances of which accommodation was only a part, one emanating from the American South but reverberating globally. This set of circumstances corresponds to what Saidiya Hartman terms "the double bind of equality and exclusion that distinguishes modern state racism from its antebellum predecessor."[94] Here it is necessary to return to Walker's "Tillmanism and Mob Rule in the South" to register a particular moment of aporia. This aporia, if not analogous to Du Bois's "aporetic responses to modernity," nevertheless arises out of the same crisis and the perceived impossibility of language to address effectively the disenfranchisement and violent subjection of Blacks in America.

For Walker, this apparent impasse begins with the challenge of bearing witness to racial violence in the American South: "The history of the South is a record of a series of crimes; awful crimes; crimes against God and man and religion; crimes so brutal, so heinous, so revolting, that it would be an unpardonable sin to express them in words."[95] In this instance, the ethical consequences of bearing witness, rather than the failure of language itself, temporarily suspend Walker's analysis; and this initial refusal to bear witness to the "crimes" of the South anticipates his subsequent reluctance to reproduce the scene of a lynching, "the most execrable freak of insanity that has ever afflicted or cursed human society."[96] One might read this momentary reticence as a refusal on Walker's part to summon what Saidiya Hartman terms the "terrible spectacle" of racial violence, scenes of violence that invoke "the spectacular character of black suffering."[97] Yet Walker goes on to invoke just such a scene, deploying precisely the sort of "theatrical language" that Hartman contends is "usually resorted to in describing these instances [of black suffering]."[98] It is not the unrepresentability of such scenes that produces Walker's aporia, then, but the futility of representing forms of violence that are effectively sanctioned by the modern, post-Reconstruction state.

What initiates Walker's aporia is his recognition, at the very moment he reproduces the violent scene of a lynching, that this bearing witness is futile. Walker demurs that neither the pathos the scene is intended to evoke nor reasoned argument can appeal to the American majority. To the contrary, such "loathsome, deplorable" scenes have "ruined the temper of the nation" and "argument, or logic, or reason, has no more effect upon [the majority], especially when it is friendly to the Negro, than it would upon some incurable Bedlamite."[99] Moreover, racial violence itself precludes remonstration. Black Americans "dare not, in either public or private, discuss their situation for fear of being lynched," "the Negro press is gagged and muzzled both in the south and in the north," and "there is no retribution in the courts."[100] It is the fact that such racial violence is permitted, even enabled, by the progressive, democratic liberal state that finally renders this crisis inexorable.

Thus, the impasse Walker confronts in "Tillmanism" is, in effect, "subjection in the context of freedom" – what Hartman describes as "the corporeal anxieties of the liberal order" and their consequence, "the wedding of equality and exclusion in the liberal state."[101] For Walker, this state-sanctioned violence is not inimical to democracy; it does not exist in spite of it; rather, it is facilitated by

> [the] malevolence and prejudice of the rude multitude, the majority; i.e., the invincible, irresistible, irrevocable power, in the United States, both North and South, which makes for evil, disorder, oppression, and the reign of terror; and the very power that can never be coaxed, persuaded, or coerced into giving the Negroes their due.[102]

Without the political franchise, Walker suggests, African-Americans have no hope of combatting the racism of the white majority; and yet the same political powerlessness makes them targets of racial violence should they attempt to gain suffrage. Hence, the failure of accommodation was the failure of Black America to understand that "to disfranchise them simply means to ruin them and blight them as freemen."[103] And yet Walker holds little hope for the civil rights reforms of Du Bois, suggesting instead that the near future will see "the utter disarmament of the Negroes of the ballot."[104] Protest, social criticism, and public debate, Walker suggests here, have no currency in a fundamentally unjust society.

Of course, Walker mobilized social criticism and public discourse toward racial uplift despite his apparent doubts as to their efficacy. In fact, "Tillmanism and Mob Rule in the South" is atypical of Walker's essays insofar as it expresses a profound scepticism about the possibility of racial uplift, a skepticism that Walker overcomes in the conclusion by appealing to Black separatism. Elsewhere in *Neith*, Walker responds differently to the terror of democratically endorsed and legally sanctioned racism. In "Lynching in the South" he advocates armed resistance (though he explicitly disavows violent insurrection against the state), declaring that "a thousand Negroes are fit to flog fifteen hundred crackers; that is, if the Negroes are armed like the crackers with Winchester rifles."[105] Conversely, in "A Reasonable Protest," Walker endorses the "lawful" civil protest of the National Afro-American Press Association in their struggle for "civil and political rights."[106] And, of course, in "The Negro Problem and How to Solve It," Walker outlines his own solution to the "problem of the colour line": emigration to Africa. Each of these approaches emphasizes very different aspects of Walker's program, from radical forms of militant resistance to comparatively conciliatory forms of lawful protest. Nevertheless, the essays in which these various proposals are articulated rely on common rhetorical patterns and discursive strategies. Rarely, as in "Lynching in the South," such strategies bordered on sedition; more commonly, they involved forms of social criticism that incorporated psychoanalysis, classicism, and a prophetic rhetoric grounded in Afro-Protestantism.

H.A.S. HARTLEY, CLASSICISM, AND THE DISCURSIVE STRATEGIES OF WALKER'S MODERNISM

Throughout *Neith* and his separately published works, Walker engages a range of discursive strategies to advance his analyses of and proposed solutions to race relations in a transnational context. Some of these, such as his rhetorical appeals to British imperialism and Canadian nationalism, appear as heuristic devices designed to gain support for Black separatism among the white Canadian public. Others, however, are more fundamental to Walker's project. Of these discursive practices that are constitutive of Walker's political aesthetic, a uniquely Afrocentric classicism and prophetic rhetoric are perhaps the most salient, linking Walker broadly with figures such as Henry McNeal Turner and directly to other neglected figures such as AME preacher and classicist H.A.S. Hartley. But the rhetoric of pathology also marks an important tool deployed by Walker, one worth noting before turning to the prophetic and classicist models.

Again, "Tillmanism" offers a productive example. There, Walker deploys the rhetoric of psychopathology to characterize racial intolerance and violence in the United States, using a discursive strategy similar to the "canny rhetorical appropriation" that Baker describes as foundational to African-American modernism. The state-sanctioned and hence democratically endorsed "prejudice," "disorder, and oppression" that Walker terms "Tillmanism" is the manifestation of an endemic racism that Walker, to give it a "definite form in pathology and nomenclature," terms "misethioposis."[107] He further deems lynching a "freak of insanity" and characterizes the white American majority as "Bedlamites" infected with "a veritable disease" and "abnormal emotion."[108] Walker's appeal to psychopathology in his analysis of race relations is not unique. According to Fred Moten, "[the] cultural and political discourse on black pathology has been so pervasive that it could be said to constitute the background against which all representations of blacks, blackness, or (the colour) black take place."[109] Walker, however, self-consciously co-opts the vocabulary of Black pathology in order to analyze white racism, a phenomenon he claims is so pervasive as to render America irremediably hostile to Blackness and, hence, uninhabitable.

Walker's analysis in "Tillmanism" places him in a tradition of Black writing that deploys psychopathology toward anti-racist and anti-colonial resistance, again inviting comparisons that place him in dialogue with thinkers from Du Bois to Frantz Fanon. Nevertheless, though Walker's commitment to Black nationalism and separatism signals affinities with later figures such as Garvey, Fanon, and Malcolm X, his discursive strategies generally align him more closely with contemporaries Du Bois and Washington. They also reveal other lines of transatlantic influence from outside the United States, influences that helped shape the fusion of Afro-Protestantism and classicism that defines Walker's political aesthetic. Of these influences, the Trinidadian pastor, physician, and classicist Rev. Henry Alexander Saturnin Hartley had perhaps the most formative effect on Walker's classical orientation. This important connection has been overlooked in extant discussions of both Walker and Hartley and it bears further examination.

Hartley was only in New Brunswick and Nova Scotia for a few years, but during that time he published the two books that constitute his oeuvre. On 15 November 1889, about one year after Hartley arrived in Saint John, a notice appeared in the *Saint John Daily Sun* announcing the publication of his first book, *Classical Translations*. Divided into a preface and five sections, the collection contains twenty-nine poems from Martial, Catullus, Horace, Propertius, Ovid, and Tibullus; selections from Cicero's *Pro Archia*; excerpts from Ovid's *Fasti*, *Epistulae ex Ponto*, *Heroides*, and *Amores*; selections from Aesop's fables; and a few concluding passages from the French Romantics: Alfred de Vigny, Jean Reboul, and André Chénier. Published by one of the largest and most distinguished firms in nineteenth-century Canada, J. & A. McMillan, the book was nevertheless overshadowed by Wilfred Campbell's *Lake Lyrics and Other Poems* (1889), published by McMillan that same year.[110] It has since been almost entirely forgotten. Only recently has Hartley received scholarly attention as a significant classicist with the publication of Michele Ronnick's chapter

Figure 2.3 Photograph of Henry Alexander Saturnin Hartley from *Physicians and Surgeons of America: A Collection of Biographical Sketches of the Regular Medical Profession*, 1896.

in *Classicisms in the Black Atlantic* (2020). Ronnick identifies Hartley's *Translations* as "a singular achievement" and "the first book of translations from the literature of ancient Greece and Rome made and published by a person of African descent in the western hemisphere."[111] Ronnick's article is invaluable for having helped rescue Hartley from almost total obscurity and for highlighting his pioneering contributions to Black classicism. Yet a closer examination of Hartley's life and work in Saint John also reveals the significant influence he had on Black intellectuals in Saint John, most notably Walker.[112]

In fact, Walker was among those community leaders who sought an educated clergyman to lead the congregation at St Philip's African Methodist Episcopal Church in the late 1880s.[113] Consequently, Hartley, a native of Port of Spain, Trinidad, was brought to Saint John from Ontario in 1888. When Bishop Benjamin Tanner visited Saint John for Hartley's installation in August of that year, Walker gave the address at his reception. In it, Walker spoke of the need for higher education among Black citizens, for "a skilful and learned class of men": "we are producing just such a class of men … [yet] we should not forget that it is our duty to keep producing them." Such a leadership class, declared Walker, "must first learn to be honest sceptics," must be schooled in "modern thought," and must preach a Christianity devoid of "barbarous fanaticism, or the intoxicated fancies of supercilious bigots."[114] Educated, urbane, and fluent in five languages, Hartley was exemplary of this "new class" of Black intellectuals. Evidently, Walker and Hartley came to know one another well, founding a fraternal order together in November of 1888.[115]

Politically and philosophically, however, they differed. As Judith Fingard observes, Hartley was an integrationist.[116] At the celebrations for the 101st anniversary of the AME Church, Hartley "prayed for the day when … separate organizations would not be needed" for Blacks and whites and declared that "[he] did not believe in race churches."[117] In 1890, Hartley addressed the Methodist conference in Fredericton, "expressing the hope that the time was not far distant when the coloured line would be abolished and there would no longer be any need for a separate Church communion."[118] And in an address at Saint John later that year Hartley called for an end to segregation in churches and schools.[119] Whether or not Walker agreed with Hartley's stance on integration in the 1880s is unclear. What is clear is that he entirely rejected integration in favour of separatism by the time *Neith* appeared in 1903. This fundamental difference is important for understanding the divergent ways in which Walker and Hartley deployed classicism in their work. While both adopt the classical model, and while Walker was almost certainly influenced by Hartley's *Classical Translations*, their political differences inform their particular orientations toward the classical tradition. For Hartley, classicism offers a vision of universal humanity that corresponds to his integrationist approach. By contrast, Walker, though amenable to Hartley's classical humanism, also sees in classicism a rhetorical tool that can be used in service of, even integrated into, an Afrocentric and Black nationalist political program.

Though it is clear that Walker shares Hartley's investment in humanism, his engagement with the classical tradition is premised on an Afrocentric rendering of classical antiquity. In short, Walker rejects a Eurocentric understanding of classicism, positing that "Greece was civilized … by Phoenicians and Egyptians" and that all "Ethiopians, Egyptians, Libyans, and Phoenicians were Negroes – black people."[120] In effect, Walker constructed an historiographical account of Africa and the African diaspora that not only paralleled the classical origins of Western humanism, but which also theorized the African origins of the classical tradition. Walker thus adopts and radically expands the central tenets of the aforementioned Ethiopianist tradition, "the Afro-Atlantic literary-religious tradition" that took inspiration from Psalms 68:31: "Princes shall come out of Egypt; Ethiopia shall stretch out her hands toward God."[121] Interpreting the verse as a prophecy of African redemption and resurgence, Ethiopianism, as Saheed Adejumobi explains, "linked Africa historically to the ancient classical era, challenging the then prevailing idea that the continent had no history before the arrival of European colonizers in the mid-nineteenth century."[122] In "The Negro Problem and How to Solve It" Walker expanded upon such interpretations, offering scriptural readings in order to formulate a complex history of African and African-diasporic descent. This account included the claim that figures such as "Homer, Plato, Archimedes and Euclid" were of mixed race.[123] Thus, Walker's engagement with the classical tradition is underpinned by a radical Afrocentrism that necessarily conditions his quotations of and allusions to Greek and Roman texts. Accordingly, Walker does not intend to exclude the role classics might play in seeking redemption when he writes that "it must be on their African blood that [Africans] ultimately win the goal and regain their ancient prestige and power."[124] For Walker, Afrocentric classicism constitutes an act of reclamation and thus becomes an affirmation of Black cultural nationalism.

Though more radical than many of his predecessors and contemporaries, Walker's Afrocentric historiography expands upon the "new epistemological approach" that Maghan Keita claims was forged by Black intellectuals throughout the nineteenth and early twentieth centuries.[125] To accept this new "epistemology of blackness," argues Keita, was "to think of blackness as constituting a way, or a number of ways, of knowing the world."[126] What is important here is not the factual accuracy of the relative Blackness or whiteness of ancient Egypt, Phoenicia, Greece, or Rome, but the critique that is embedded in the Afrocentric challenge to conventional history. As Keita explains, "new historiographies" emerge from this epistemology and these historiographies "challenge the existing paradigm – a paradigm of white supremacy."[127] Hence, Walker's Afrocentric history constitutes an incisive critique in and of itself.

Moreover, the epistemological foundations of Walker's historiographical and political thought clearly distinguish his deployment of classicism from Hartley's, pointing to the ways in which Black classicism is implicated in identity politics, and the "strategies – rhetorical and otherwise – for affirming a particular historical and cultural legacy."[128] Both authors express their commitment to humanism through classicism, but by rejecting the Eurocentric premise of classical scholarship Walker goes beyond affirming humanist principles. As Patrice Rankine observes in *Ulysses in Black*, "[given] its broader cultural implications, Black classicism might imply to some a conciliatory, integrationist stance, which is advocated with a degree of condescension."[129] Neither Hartley nor Walker should be read as condescendingly conciliatory; however, whereas the affirmation of Black intellectuality and humanity appears to be the principal aim of Hartley's classicism, Walker offers a more radical appropriation of the classical model, one that mobilizes what Rankine terms the "counter-hegemonic strand" of Greek and Roman thought, a strand which "included resistance to power on multiple fronts."[130] This counterhegemonic strand of classical thought is frequently at evidence in *Neith*.

The first article to appear in *Neith* illustrates the often-subtle ways Walker engaged classical counterhegemony, offering two instances of classical quotation in the context of class struggle. Titled "The Late Coal Strike," the article discusses the 1902 anthracite coal strike in Pennsylvania by the United Mine Workers of America. Referring to "organized labour" as "one of the greatest powers today," Walker celebrates the potential for trade unionism to "affect the order and trend and basis of civilized society."[131] Indicting unfettered capitalism, Walker quotes Book 6 of Virgil's *Aeneid* to caution against the failure of the state to prioritize the interests of labour over capital: "*Fascilis descensus averni; / Sed revocare gradum superasque evader ad auras / Hic labor, hoc opus est*" ("the road down to

Avernus / Is easy. Black Dis' door gapes night and day. / The work, the effort, is to walk back up / Into the open air").[132] Drawing an analogy between the Katabasis of Virgil's *Aeneid* and the excesses of *laissez-faire* economics, Walker uses Virgil here to make a progressive but relatively moderate argument for economic interventionism. Walker's subsequent quotation from Cicero's *De Legibus*, however, suggests the possibility of a more insurgent meaning. Insisting that "the people" are greater than "any trust, or any syndicate, or any monopoly," Walker refers to Cicero's "immutable, eternal rule": "*salus populi suprema lex esto*" ("let the safety of the people be the highest law").[133] Again, given Cicero's conservative republicanism, the famous quote is hardly expressive of counterhegemony in itself.[134] However, the juxtaposition of the *Aeneid*, the founding myth of Rome, with Cicero's dialogue, composed in the final years of the Roman Republic, injects Walker's analysis with an apocalyptic current. Walker's invocation of *De Legibus*, composed just three years before Caesar crossed the Rubicon and plunged Rome into civil war, should be read to suggest the impending fall of the American republic, attaching greater urgency to Walker's warning in the same article that capitalism, if left unchecked, would result in "civil war."[135]

Considered in isolation from Walker's discussions elsewhere, this counterhegemonic reading of the quotations from Virgil and Cicero may appear somewhat tenuous. It is borne out, however, in Walker's more explicit critiques, in articles such as "The Philosophy of Society" and "The United States." In the former, Walker condemns the decadence of America's economic elite, which "reminds one of the frightful conditions of society in the latter days of ancient Rome." "It would seem," writes Walker, "that history is repeating itself."[136] Walker further alludes to the impending fall of the United States by stating that "[t]he same laws which punished the passions, excesses, and vices of Sodom and Babylon are still in force," and he sustains this threefold analogy by alluding to the destruction of Croesus's empire at the hands of Cyrus of Persia, a defeat Walker attributes to acquisitiveness and sacrilege.[137] Similarly, in "The United States," Walker invokes Nero and the fall of the Julian-Claudian dynasty as an analogy for contemporary America, claiming that the "United States is a fair repetition, to-day, of the Roman Empire in the reign of Nero."[138] And in "Tillmanism," Walker warns of "the clouds and mists … beginning to forbode a dreadful storm," likening Black accommodationists to the citizens of "Herculaeneum and Pompeii" before "Mount Vesuvius overwhelmed them with lava," and concludes with a quote from Luke 17:1, "it is impossible but that offences will come."[139] Invariably, these fusions of biblical and classical allusion take on a prophetic form in which Walker finds the discursive means to overcome the aporia produced by the double binds of equality and exclusion, freedom and racial violence.

THE PROPHETIC TRADITION, AFRO-PROTESTANTISM, AND THE GEOGRAPHY OF WALKER'S MODERNISM

The sense of inexorability that Walker attaches to racism in the United States, as well as the flights of rhetoric with which he proclaims the imminent demise of white America, can be productively read in relation to what Cornel West describes as the "prophetic tradition in Afro-America."[140] Specifically, Walker's writings, and his critiques of America, in particular, exhibit the "aggressive pessimism" that characterizes "Black prophetic practices."[141] For West, this pessimism "regarding the possibilities of fundamental transformation of American societies and culture" emerges because "[the] odds seem so overwhelming, the incorporative strategies of the status quo so effective – and the racism so deeply entrenched in American life."[142] The fit between West's comments and Walker's pessimism in "Tillmanism" is striking, but a similar sense of pessimism animates the interwoven rhetorics of apocalypse and classicism that permeate all of Walker's polemical essays. More to the point, West's characterization of this aggressive pessimism as "sobering rather than disabling, a stumbling block rather than a dead end, a challenge to meet rather than a conclusion to accept" helps to reconcile Walker's apocalyptic rhetoric with the optimism he expresses toward Black futurity. It is the coupling of pessimism with a projected vision of Black resurgence that allows Walker to move from an apocalyptic vision of existential crisis – the vision of Black America being "blotted out, extinguished, annihilated"[143] – to the conviction that the twentieth century might yet see the emancipation of Africa and the African diaspora from the enduring bondage of the modern liberal state.

The prophetic mode Walker adopts in his analyses of race relations, and into which he integrates biblical and classical allusion, is decidedly religious. As such, it runs contrary to the literary-intellectual secularism conventionally understood to define much of the modernist moment. As Josef Sorett observes in his recent study *Spirit in the Dark*, "orthodoxy has enshrined secularism as the appropriate, shared ideology of modern racial subjects and as the assumed substance of black literature." "In short," Sorett argues, "Afro-modernity is imagined as secular."[144] This dichotomy between sacred and secular, however, is inadequate to account for the range of practices developed by writers such as Walker in response to the reconfiguration of modernity at the turn of the twentieth century. In fact, this presumed dichotomy has tended to obscure the fact that in the twentieth century "religion persisted as a powerful presence in literary visions of modern black subjectivity and social life."[145] If Walker's writing constitutes a neoteric response to modernity, then, it is not because it rejects expressive traditions grounded in Afro-Protestantism, but because it redirects and enlarges traditional models of classicism and Black Christian discourse as it imagines alternative futures for Black diasporic peoples. Rather than distinguishing Walker from his contemporaries, this Afrocentric rendering of classical and Afro-Protestant thought highlights key connections between Walker's writing and modern Black intellectual currents elsewhere, particularly those that constituted the "discursive constellation" of Afro-modernism in America,[146] but also those stretching beyond North America to the Black Atlantic and, conceptually, the "black Aegean."[147]

For Du Bois, "the problem of the twentieth century is the problem of the color-line."[148] Walker agrees with the problem, but his solution differs from Du Bois's. In "The Negro Problem and How to Solve It," Walker proclaimed the twentieth century "the beginning of a great epoch, a great era; the beginning of a great inspiration, the inspiration of a purer humanity … a brand-new dispensation of Liberty, Justice, and Right."[149] For Walker, however, only emigration to Africa could usher in this new era. Walker's separatism does closely correspond to the solutions advocated by Henry McNeal Turner and, later, Garvey, but unlike those figures, Walker's analysis of the problem and his proposed solution were also shaped by the geopolitical and discursive contexts of Canada. Walker's Afrocentric nationalism is modelled on a form of neo-British imperialism and his proposed solution is not merely emigration to Africa, but the colonization of "some propitious part of British Africa" by educated, Christian, Anglophone members of the African diaspora.[150] Hence, while it is necessary to locate Walker within the transatlantic, diasporic culture of the Black Atlantic in order to appreciate the lines of influence that helped shape his modernism, it is also necessary to recognize the limits and pressures confronted by Walker in a specifically Canadian context. This was a context in which Canada's comparatively small Black population and *Neith*'s reliance on a predominantly white-Canadian readership meant that Walker had to articulate his politics through the interstices of Canadian nationalist and British imperialist discourse.

NEGOTIATING THE DISCURSIVE TERRAIN OF POST-RACE

Attention to Walker's Afrocentric, prophetic- and classicist-inflected response to modernity provides a critical basis for reading Walker's Afromodernism against the Canadian nationalism and British imperialism that frequently surface in the pages of *Neith*. However, though Walker's modernism aligns him with Afro-modernists like Washington and Du Bois, his racial politics, informed as they were by an adaptation of neo-British imperialism and Anglo-Christian cultural values, are often disconnected from those of his American confreres. In the pages of *Neith*, this disconnection figures as a dissonance between Walker's radical Black politics and the often-uncritical Canadian nationalism expressed by the magazine's white contributors. Moreover, this dissonance never surfaces as an outright contradiction; the incompatibility of Walker's struggle against racial intolerance and white Anglo-Canadian nationalism is resolved via the rhetorical construction of Canada as tolerant, egalitarian, and peaceable. In effect, Walker's editorial strategy had to negotiate a discursive context in which Canada was almost invariably represented as "post-racial." That is, "post-racial" in one specific sense articulated by David Chariandy, namely, "as a site beyond the evils of racism specifically directed toward Blacks."[151] The support Walker variously expresses for Canadian nationalism and the British Empire, then, must be read against a dominant national discourse that functioned to exclude Blackness as fundamentally constitutive of the modern nation-state. Attempting to negotiate the terrain of post-race, Walker frequently lent credence to the idea that Canada was, if not free of racism, nevertheless morally superior to the fundamentally and legislatively racist United States.

Of course, Walker understood racism stopped neither at the Mason-Dixon Line nor at the 49th parallel; yet both within the first issue and across *Neith*'s five-issue run, Canadian exceptionalism prevails. In fact, Walker rarely directs criticism toward either Canada or Britain, and when he does, it lacks the oratorical potency of his invectives against white America. Thus, when Walker criticizes the racist undertones in articles about Haiti to be found in the Canadian press, he displaces blame onto the United States: "the news in Canada concerning Haiti is specially prepared to mislead the reader. It comes through United States agencies, and through the hands of correspondents who are bitterly hostile to the Negro race."[152] Similarly, when Walker critiques Alfred Milner's education policy in South Africa, he does so indirectly. The British-colonial policy, which was intended to Anglicize Afrikaner children, brought forty teachers from Canada to teach in "camp schools" in the wake of the Boer War.[153] In "Treat Boer and Black Alike," Walker suggests that "the experiment should not stop with the Boers. It should also extend to the Negro Natives." Walker stops short, however, of accusing Milner of maintaining a prejudicial policy, finally restating that "the Negroes of British South Africa are as much entitled to the kindly consideration of British Statesmen as the Boers."[154] The education of white Afrikaner children was by no means a benevolent gesture. Rather, it was intended to denationalize Afrikaner children and consolidate British control over South Africa.[155] For Walker, however, the injustice lay not with Britain's linguistic and ideological imperialism, but in the neglect of South Africa's Black indigenous population. That the latter was the inevitable result of the former – the result of a system of colonial education predicated on racist assumptions of white superiority – is an inference Walker never explicitly draws. Thus, Walker's criticism of Canadian society, in the rare instances it appears at all, is invariably veiled. In short, compelled to address an intensely nationalist white-Canadian audience, Walker was denied the language necessary to formulate a dialogue of racial equality and empowerment that specifically targeted the nature of national and regional racisms within Canada.

Neith thus demonstrates Walker's modernism and his socio-political and ideological commitments while engaging the competing discourses of British imperialism, pan-Africanism, and Black nationalism. At the same time, the magazine reveals the way in which a hegemonic discourse of Canadian exceptionalism exerted pressures and limits on Walker's

Black-nationalist project. The total effect is to at once put forward a radical Black politics while affirming and consolidating the myth of Canadian tolerance and racial equality. The first issue exhibits how Walker's editorial practice used the magazine's structure, its bibliographic code, to resolve these seemingly contradictory purposes. At the crux of this resolution is W.O. Raymond's article "The Negro in New Brunswick," the first article in the issue not penned by Walker.

"The Negro in New Brunswick" is a detailed and comprehensive work of investigative history. In fact, the article, which was republished in *The New Brunswick Magazine*, remains the basis of much scholarship on early Black Canadian history today (via Spray and Winks). In it, Raymond documents the earliest arrival of enslaved and free Blacks in the former colony of Nova Scotia and traces the history of slavery and Black immigration up to the nineteenth century. Though marked by a strong tone of paternalism, the article provides a relatively straightforward and rigorously documented history. Within the pages of *Neith*, however, the article performs more crucial bibliographic and conceptual functions: it serves as a bridge between the first part of the issue, containing Walker's articles on race, and the second part. This second part contains two articles on Canadian political economy and nationalism (Robert Wilson's "The Canadian Outlook"; H.A. McKeown's "The Progress of Canada"), an essay of literary theory (George Walker's "Pleasures of the Imagination"), two poems (Charles Campbell's "The Museum Shell"; W.P. Dole's "Fedei Responsa"), and brief literary commentaries and reviews. Structurally, then, Raymond's article provides the reader with an effective transition between the two parts.

Conceptually, however, it reconciles Walker's Black nationalism with the Canadian nationalism of Wilson and McKeown. Bringing the historical narrative up to the 1833 *Slavery Abolition Act* and its aftermath, Raymond concludes:

> After the passing away of slavery in the Maritime Provinces, slaves from the United States frequently crossed the international boundary, and having 'shook the lion's paw' entered upon a life of freedom. Despite the obstacles that have hampered the development of our brothers in this Province, their progress in education and refinement has been marked, and the outlook for the future has never been brighter than it is today.[156]

By documenting slavery, anti-Black racial violence, and discrimination in New Brunswick, only to relegate them to the past, "The Negro in New Brunswick" reinforces the myth of Canadian exceptionalism. In effect, it demarcates a boundary between a dark past and a "bright" today; between Black illiteracy and "education"; between Black incivility and "refinement"; and between American slavery and Canadian "freedom." Raymond acknowledges the "obstacles" Black Canadians have faced in Canada, but the final chord he strikes is one of Canadian progressiveness. This superimposition of a temporal scheme, according to which Canada progressed toward and achieved racial equality in the nineteenth century, anticipates the articles by McKeown and Wilson and renders the first issue of *Neith* coherent, even as it mitigates the strength of Walker's modernism.

The coherence of the first issue does not result from complete uniformity of subject or opinion. Rather, this coherence is a logical one, deriving from the dissolution of apparent contradictions between Walker's condemnation of racial intolerance, his promotion of Black nationalism, and other contributors' white-Canadian nationalism. There were internal differences of opinion within *Neith*; Wilson's and McKeown's articles concerning Canadian national development and identity, for instance, do not merely extol Canada's virtues. Rather, they offer two contrasting arguments regarding Canada's political and economic independence. Wilson argues in favour of imperial federation, while McKeown advocates closer economic and commercial ties to the United States. Such contests reflect broader national debates around Canada's relationship to the United States and Britain, debates that only intensified during the ongoing Alaskan Boundary Dispute of 1903. However, both lines of argument were predicated on what McKeown referred to as "the calm and settled conviction of the greatness which the coming years will yield to [Canada]"[157] and what Wilson considered Canada's superior "civil and religious liberty."[158]

Again, the bibliographic context of *Neith* sheds light on Walker's political orientation. Walker's endorsement of British imperialism may seem to run contrary to his own Afrocentric imperialism, but it also allowed Walker to appeal to Canadian Imperialist Federationists.[159] The juxtaposition of Walker's "The Negro Problem and How to Solve It" and Wilson's "The Canadian Outlook," divided only by a poem and Raymond's article, seems to confirm such an appeal. Here, proximity and a shared imperialist ideology overwrite any conflict between Walker's call for Black Canadians to emigrate to Africa and Wilson's claim that the "phenomenal progress" of Canada has led "immigrants by the thousands [to seek] homes within her borders."[160] Such alignments contribute to a sense of consistency that effaces more profound incongruities. So it is that Walker applauds immigration to the Canadian north-west the same month local papers announced the doubling of the Chinese Head Tax to $500;[161] and he extols the "Canadian principles of Liberty and Equity"[162] when Canada's unofficial immigration policy actively discouraged the immigration of African-Americans to Canada on the basis of racial inferiority.[163] The result is not just a rhetorical appeal to Imperial Federationists and Canadian nationalists, but an attempt to advance an anti-racist discourse in Canada while keeping *Neith* palatable to a white-Canadian audience.

RECEPTION, RACISM, AND REJOINDERS

Ultimately, Canadian readers did find *Neith* palatable, but not with the broad taste Walker had hoped. Rather than showing sympathy for Walker's racial program, reviewers generally ignored it in favour of the articles submitted by white contributors. Acclaim for *Neith* was selective. The reviewer in the *Saint John Star* called *Neith* a "handsome magazine of sixty pages," noting that "the book is well printed on fine paper."[164] Saint John's *The Educational Review* praised the magazine's "elegant design" and the "candid and thoughtful style" of its contents.[165] And *The Guardian* of Charlottetown observed that "the list of contributors for the coming year includes a large proportion of the best writers and leaders of thought in the Maritime Provinces."[166] These reviews, however, make no mention of the themes of Black nationalism, racial advancement, and Afrocentrism that dominate each issue, never mind the polemical modernism through which Walker articulated those themes. While *The Educational Review* alludes to "editorial discussion of various social and literary questions,"[167] the *Saint John Star* effectively glosses over the magazine's central polemic: "Besides the editorial work of Dr. Walker, there are very interesting contributions by Rev. Dr. Raymond, Hon. H.A. McKeown, Rev. Dr. Wilson and George Walker, with poems by Charles Campbell and W.P. Dole."[168]

Three months after the appearance of *Neith*'s first number, David Russell Jack, regionalist *par excellence* and editor of the cultural-historical magazine *Acadiensis*, discussed in the first chapter, summed up local reception of *Neith* in an address to The Royal Society of Canada:

> The first issue was dated February 1903, and its advent had been looked for with much curiosity by the literary coterie of St. John [*sic*]. In fact it may be stated that honours were easy as between *Neith* and the Local Election for the House of Assembly. The coming of each was anticipated for some time and the public curiosity having now been satisfied as to both issues, the people of that city are seeking a new sensation.[169]

A significant but passing novelty seems to be what many reviewers considered *Neith*; no discussion of subsequent issues of the magazine appears to have been published in local papers. Unlike most reviewers, Jack does acknowledge *Neith*'s racial focus, noting that the magazine is "chiefly devoted to the Negro race, and its *alleged* wrongs."[170] Taken in conjunction with his comment that Walker's son George is the "*alleged* author" of the article "The Pleasures of the Imagination,"[171] Jack's estimation of the magazine evinces a marked degree of racist condescension.

If selective acclaim describes the most favourable reviews of *Neith*, and curious condescension the middle ground, then overtly racist hostility marks the other extreme. Such was the tenor of the final and longest review of *Neith* published in local papers, which appeared in the 7 March issue of *The New Freeman*. In it, the reviewer commends Paterson & Co. for the high production quality and A.J. Charlton for the cover image. He also acknowledges Raymond, Wilson, and McKeown, whose contributions are deemed "fully up to the excellent standards of each of them." As the reviewer turns to Walker's articles, his tone shifts: "The editor, who deals with many subjects, has all the proneness of his race for exaggerated thought and extravagant language." The reviewer goes on to attack Walker for his article on Emile Zola, writing that his "fulsome adulation of Zola is simply disgusting, and impresses the reader that the writer did not know what he was writing about or that his literary olfactory faculties are so impaired as to be unable to distinguish a cess pool from a flower bed." The review concludes on a facetious note that drives home the editors' fundamental objection to *Neith*: "out of deference to people (ourselves among the number) whose higher education is somewhat limited, the editor might condescend to use fewer quotation from the classics ... they never have the strength and vigor of good, honest, anglo-celtic words."[172] The hypocrisy of a pre–Vatican II Catholic writer critiquing Walker's use of Latin quotations is less significant here than the reactionary racism that pitted Walker's Afrocentric classicism against the "strength and vigour" the reviewer identifies with "anglo-celtic" culture. In the end, Walker's Afro-modernism was perceived to threaten the primacy of British values in Canada and Canada's essential whiteness, and that was sufficient incitement to censure. Just as the editors of *The New Freeman* saw Walker's Black nationalism as a specific threat to Irish-Catholic interests, white Canadian readers considered Walker's Afrocentrism a threat to national interests, interests that were culturally British and optically white. Insofar as Blackness was cast by white Canada as fundamentally incompatible with Anglo-Saxon British values, Walker's professed allegiance to "British institutions" was inconsequential.[173]

Walker's attempt to negotiate the discursive terrain of post-race, including his responses to critics, involved nominal expressions of support for Canadian nationalism, but his rejoinder to the *New Freeman* review was not simply diplomatic. Referring to the reviewer as "some ignorant, prejudiced, bigoted scribbler," Walker offers a figurative threat:

> [Our] assailant is like the ass that a good-natured lion tried to be demonstrably neighborly with, and which mistook the lion's kindness and grace for a lack of courage and strength, and one day furiously jumped on the lion when he least expected it; of course, at the end of the fray there was a dead ass.[174]

By offering a variation on Aesop's fable, Walker's response turns the classicism derided by the anonymous reviewer back on *The New Freeman* to humorous but pointed effect. By positioning *The New Freeman* as the allegorical ass, Walker may intend to align *Neith* with the Protestant majority of Saint John while drawing attention to *The New Freeman*'s Irish-Catholicism, but Walker finally dismisses the paper as anachronistic and inimical to the Canadian context: "We live in Canada and not Mississippi, and we are not going to fondle or flatter a thing whose open envy we are perfectly satisfied will be more profitable to us than its sugar-coated deceit."[175] Contrary to Winks's claim that the Canada-Mississippi distinction is "somewhat irrelevant,"[176] Walker's calculated response plays upon the tendency for white-Canada to define itself vis-à-vis American violence and intolerance. However, Walker was not simply conceding the myth of Canadian exceptionalism; his particular point is that *Neith* will not be "gagged and muzzled" as he felt the Black press was in the American south.[177] Walker's argument is as much a statement of resolve as it is a concession to Canadian audiences.

According to Winks, "Walker did not stand firm" in advancing that editorial mission. Winks cites increased space for advertisements, fewer editorials, and reduced "Negro material" as evidence of Walker's resignation.[178] Walker did increase the number of advertisements from six to eleven in the second issue, but this initial increase was clearly not the result of any lack of resolution in the face of criticism. In fact, the number of advertisements decreased to ten in the third issue, which came immediately after Walker's polemical response to critics. What the bibliographic trajectory of the magazine reveals is not a story of abating political engagement and attrition, but of increasing financial difficulty and decline. Tellingly, while the proportion of material dealing with racial politics remained constant, the issues consistently shrank, with the fourth and fifth issues numbering only fifty-six and fifty-two pages, respectively. Finally, the fourth and fifth issues were printed on cheaper, light-weight pulp paper and contained fewer photographs. All of these changes are indicative of financial trouble. The indigence and transience of *Neith* were typical of Canadian magazines generally. At the turn of the century, Canadian magazine publishing was a financially risky undertaking and Canadian magazines "could boast of few long-lived examples."[179] That Walker sustained *Neith* for over a year is a testament not only to Walker's skill as an editor, but also to his remarkable struggle to satisfy the magazine's readership without sacrificing his program of racial advancement.

The third issue appeared three months behind schedule and five months elapsed between the fourth and fifth issues. The fifth issue would be the last, but it is fitting that *Neith* ended the way it began, restating the magazine's pledge to "offer all opposition within our capacity to every form of evil or oppression."[180] To the end, *Neith* provided a forum in which Walker strove to articulate an Afrocentric, Black-nationalist program that transcended its local, regional, and national contexts. To promote that program to a Canadian readership, however, Walker had first to engage an anti-racist dialogue in a city and nation where such discourse had been rendered all but invisible, "obliterated from the Canadian psyche in general."[181] This was a context in which white-Canadian antipathy precluded the very critique – transnational in scope but directly targeting local, regional, and national racisms – that might have made Walker's politics more proximately operative for Black communities in Saint John, the Maritime Provinces, and Canada. The geopolitics of Walker's Pan-African project, however, did not necessarily represent a deterritorialization of racial politics.

BLACK GEOGRAPHIES AND REGIONAL IDENTITIES

Walker's modernist vision of Black futurity was fundamentally a spatial project, one that theorized separatism as the only solution to racial oppression in white-dominated Western states, and that posited the continent of Africa as the eventual site of belonging for all African and African diasporic peoples. But though that separatism might be taken to imply a disconnection from the localized or regionalized realities of long-resident Black subjects in the Maritime Provinces, it was in fact integrally tied to activist traditions at the local and regional levels. Most immediately, Walker was part of a much longer tradition of activism in Saint John centred on St Philip's African Methodist Episcopal Church. That tradition included the integration politics of Hartley and subsequent civil rights organizations such as the British Negro Protective Association. Though Walker's African colonization scheme, unlike Hartley's integrationism, failed to win substantial support in the city before Walker's sudden death in 1909, there is good reason to reject Winks's claim that *Neith* "sank without a trace."[182] *Neith* introduced Black separatist politics to Saint John and very likely made Saint John residents responsive to similar such movements. When Marcus Garvey's UNIA held a meeting at St Philip's in May of 1922, it was "well attended," the audience sat with "rapt attention," and a Saint John chapter was formed that evening.[183] It is difficult to determine with certainty whether Walker's separatism decisively influenced the community toward Garveyism, but given the remarkable similarity between Walker's program and that of Garvey, Walker's close ties to St Philip's, and his role as community leader, activist, and public intellectual, it is highly probable that it did.

Similarly, on a regional level, *Neith* provided a forum and a focal point for Black intellectuals in the Maritime Provinces, including the aforementioned Halifax-based lawyer and activist James Robinson Johnston; Rev. John Clay Coleman, author of *The Jim Crow Car; or Denouncement of Injustice Meted Out to the Black Race* (1898); and Rev. Adam S. Green, author of *The Future of the Canadian Negro* (1904). Notably, the final issue of *Neith* featured Green's "The Present Demands for an Educated Negro Ministry," in which he argued for higher education among the Black church leaders in the region, a need made more acute by the globalizing influences of new media, "the daily press, the telegraph, the telephone, the ocean cable, the Marconigram, railways, steamships, and a thousand-and-one other devices of diffusing knowledge."[184] Green's demand for Black education was a response to the contemporary moment of expanding transatlantic networks, and like Walker's aporetic response to modernity, Green's analysis takes aim at the double bind of equality and exclusion in the modern liberal state. What these intersections reveal is not a magazine that was divorced from localized sites of production, dissemination, and Black social and political struggle, but one that connected urgent issues faced by local and regional Black cultures to the global struggle for racial justice and Black liberation. Yet the situatedness of local and regional Black cultures within and across the concrete geography of the Maritime Provinces is not easily reconciled with emergent regionalisms that effectively obliterated Blackness from hegemonic constructions of the region.

Like those *fin-de-siècle* regionalist magazines examined in chapter 1, *Neith* was the product of translocal cultural exchanges. Unlike the editors of those magazines, however, Walker rejected regionalism as a legitimate vehicle for identity politics and social criticism, opting to foreground rather than to obscure the translocal and transnational linkages that constituted the region and its Black communities. As a Black nationalist magazine, *Neith* repudiated the exclusionary whiteness of *fin-de-siècle* regionalisms by the very fact of its existence, but it also rejected the region as a primary locus of identification. Insofar as *Neith* offers coherent geopolitics across its diverse articles, it might be understood to point to the ways in which "black geographic narratives … reconfigure classificatory spatial practices."[185] Certainly, Walker's Black-nationalist modernism upset regional classifications predicated on cultural and racial uniformity and insularity. For Katherine McKittrick and Clyde Woods, "the lives of [Black diasporic] subjects demonstrate that the 'common-sense' workings of modernity and citizenship are worked out, and normalized, through geographies of exclusion."[186] For Walker, the region might be understood as one manifestation of such geographies of exclusion. Perceiving white domination and racial intolerance to be so pervasive as to render North America irremediably hostile to Blackness, Walker rejects the Maritime region, the Canadian nation, and the North American continent as potential sites of belonging.

Of course, Walker's position was one among many adopted by Black writers, editors, and leaders in the Maritime Provinces. When *The Atlantic Advocate*, the first Black newspaper in the region, appeared in Halifax in 1915, the paper aimed to be "the voice of coloured people in the Maritime Provinces," and was devoted to "the interests of coloured people in the Dominion generally, but more particularly to those in the Maritime Provinces."[187] Placing particular emphasis on "the need for unity" at the regional level and committing itself to recording local and regional Black history, the paper imagined the region as a principal space of belonging and the appropriate scale at which to engage the struggle for racial equality and civil rights. Read in relation to the politics of place, as articulating "different desires for home,"[188] *Neith* and *The Atlantic Advocate* do not resolve tensions between transatlantic, diasporic, regional, and national frameworks. They do, however, suggest that these tensions were as much a part of the heterogenous discourses informing early Black Canadian writing as they are an animating feature of contemporary critical discussions. And both periodicals contested the whiteness that had been wedded to regional identity at the turn of the century, a union that was not merely symbolic but rooted in concrete geographies of exclusion.

When Saint John theatregoers took in the city's first local production of *Uncle Tom's Cabin* in February 1903, they were likely unaware that, far from a haven for fugitive slaves and Black Loyalists, Saint John had been founded upon the exclusion of Blackness. The 1785 Saint John royal charter at once established the oldest city in British North America and constituted what is perhaps the first legislative act of racial discrimination against Blacks in present-day Canada, granting only "unto the American and European *white* inhabitants … the liberties, privileges and pre-eminences of freemen."[189] By the time the charter was amended in 1849 to allow "any black person or person of colour" to "become a free citizen of, and be admitted to the freedom of the said City,"[190] structural violence, inequality, and racism were firmly embedded in the urban geography of Saint John. The city itself thus attests to the perpetual precarity produced by racialized geographies that exclude people of colour from conceptions of citizenship and subjecthood. Within this context, *Neith* emerges as the dissident voice of a disappeared community, a forum for people conceived of as non-citizens within the dominant white order. In this way, the project Walker articulated in *Neith* transcended, even as it was forced to engage with, the regionalist, nationalist, and imperialist discourses of its time, achieving an effective modernism relevant to Black cultures within and across local, regional, and transatlantic geographies.

3

Culture in a Crisis

Cultural History and East Coast Literature Between the Wars

In the final year of the First World War, Samuel Henry Prince, like hundreds of thousands before and after him, left Nova Scotia for the United States. The task he set himself that spring was to explain the very nature of social change. The default condition of any body politic, argued Prince, was "conservatism, immobility, and 'determined resistance to change'"; rapid social transformation required "the shattering of the matrix of custom by catastrophe."[1] The Halifax Explosion, reasoned Prince, was just such a disaster. *Catastrophe and Social Change: Based Upon a Sociological Study of the Halifax Disaster* (1920), the first "systematic study of disaster,"[2] appeared less than three years after the explosion decimated the city of Halifax on 6 December 1917. In Prince's study, post-disaster Halifax figures as a modernist nightmare where "human phenomena which many knew of only as hidden away in books, stood out so clearly that he who ran might read."[3] In the midst of this anomie, the "utter and complete … social disintegration" into which Halifax descended in the immediate aftermath of the explosion, Prince found the seeds of social progress: "The catastrophe smashed through strong walls like cobwebs, but it also smashed through fixed traditions, social divisions and old standards, making a rent which would not easily repair."[4] For Prince, the explosion enabled and expedited a process of progressive social, economic, and civic modernization that promised nothing short of deliverance from an obsolete pre-war social order.

Ground-breaking, dated, and largely forgotten, Prince's study remains remarkable for the extent to which it anticipated the circulation of the explosion as a symbol of Canadian modernity in a national fantasy that was and is sustained by a veritable industry of popular history, fiction, and film. In fact, by the time Prince embarked on his PhD in sociology at Columbia University, the explosion had already entered popular fiction with the publication of Frank McKelvey Bell's *A Romance of the Halifax Disaster* (1918). Centred on the love affair between Tom Welsford, a young soldier fighting in France, and Vera Warrington, a young nurse stationed in Halifax, the narrative reaches its climax when the explosion reunites the young couple and kills Vera's aging fiancé, freeing her to accept Tom's proposal. As absurd as it is saccharine, Bell's novella might be best forgotten but that it is the first in a long tradition of popular fiction to represent the disaster within a romantic formula, binding the desire for a reconciled and regenerated community to the personal, erotic desire of its protagonists. Twenty-five years later, Hugh MacLennan brought this formula to its apotheosis with the publication of his incredibly successful *Barometer Rising* (1941). The entrance of that novel's protagonist, Neil Macrae, into "the future" is Canada's becoming "the central arch which united this new order";[5] it is the advent of a national and nationalist modernity. What is key here is not a discrepancy between Prince's donnish sociology and the romantic desire that drives the fiction of Bell and MacLennan, between the official and the popular, but, rather, the ease with which technocratic modernization, embodied in Prince's study by the Halifax Relief Commission and urban redevelopment, passes into the symbolic framework of the nation as the sign of beneficent liberal progress.

Easily lost in such a survey are the historical and symbolic consequences of the explosion and subsequent reconstruction effort at spatial scales other than the national, scales obviated by the particular claim to modernity imagined in these texts. If the explosion represented interwar national becoming, what could it mean for the local and transnational contexts that precipitated the disaster, that would shape the experience of those who did and did not benefit from relief efforts? At the local level, the relief commission and urban redevelopment were not beneficent for all. The exclusion of Black families from Canada's first public housing project, the Hydrostone, and the exclusion of Africville from the commission's rehabilitation plan, the systematic indifference and skepticism displayed by the commission toward Black claimants, and the permanent obliteration of the Mi'kmaw settlement of Turtle Grove, the only remaining Indigenous settlement in the Halifax area, demonstrate how racism operates to retrench and solidify geographies of exclusion in moments of crisis.[6] This production of uneven geographies was not symptomatic of the incomplete arrival of modernity in the urban space of Halifax and its environs; it was, rather, the operation of modern urban planning across pre-existing fault lines of race and class. Moreover, both the disaster and reconstruction were inextricably tied to transnational forces that bear little resemblance to the official national metanarrative of "Canadian unity and resourcefulness."[7] This involved not only the feel-good story of international relief and Canadian-American reciprocity, but also the basic fact that the disaster resulted from the strategic position of Halifax within a futile war of European imperialism.

What could this fantasy of national modernity mean for a region on the edge of crisis? As an international symbol of Canadian modernity, the explosion was severed from the particularities of place. The future it heralded was not for the city it had devastated. Halifax was not to be, as MacLennan would later describe it, "an unfailing barometer for the social health and prosperity for the whole country,"[8] but an index of profound regional conservatism. There is, then, a contradiction between what the explosion symbolized for the nation and what it failed to symbolize for the region. Yet it is precisely the capacity of the symbol to persist in the face of historical contradiction – between social progress and exclusion, between liberal optimism and historical trauma, between regional decline and national becoming – that makes it so durable. A survey of canonical literature by interwar "regional" writers hardly contests this general picture of staid regional conservatism. To the contrary, the antimodernism that has become synonymous with "Maritime" writing in literary-cultural histories only serves to cement complementary notions of national progress and regional inertia. Thus, the leading writers identified with the region during this period – L.M. Montgomery, Frank Parker Day, Charles Bruce, Thomas Raddall, and even MacLennan[9] – are invoked as proof that the Maritimes remained a bastion of political conservatism, literary traditionalism, and cultural antimodernism. And this reading is entirely compatible with notions of a dynamic western Canadian progressivism. If the Halifax Explosion necessitated change, so this reading goes, it was not to be found on the east coast of Canada, associated as that area was with the very "conservatism, immobility, and 'determined resistance to change'" that the explosion and the First World War had ostensibly shattered elsewhere.[10]

But there is an alternative route into this past to be found in the periodical literature of the 1920s. A comparison of two overlooked periodicals of the period, *The Busy East of Canada* (Saint John and Sackville, 1910–33) and *The Maritime Labor Herald* (Glace Bay, 1921–26), offers a history of interwar cultural politics drastically different from that which juxtaposes the national fantasy of progressive modernity with a uniformly conservative regional culture. In what Benedict Anderson has termed Canada's "era of high capitalist nationalism,"[11] these periodicals advanced divergent political responses to the region's social and economic crisis of the 1920s, helping to forge broad political identities in defiance of a Canadian nationalism that many within the region deemed largely responsible for deindustrialization and decline. For the communist and ultra-radical *Maritime Labor Herald*, this meant militant opposition to liberal capitalism, of which petit-bourgeois nationalism was an instrument. The relationship between *The Busy East of Canada* and nationalism was far more ambiguous; deploying populist rhetoric in conjunction with an overriding commitment to economic liberalism and liberal individualism, *The Busy East* championed a form of regional protest that remained invested in the liberal state even as it assailed the failure of Canadian federalism to ensure regional parity.

Though focused specifically on two periodicals and the literature they published from about 1921 to 1931, chapters 4 and 5 can be read as conceptually anchored in the year 1926, a watershed in the history of class conflict and regional protest in the Maritime Provinces, as well as a key turning point in Canadian constitutional history. In July 1926, the British Empire Steel Corporation, the largest employer in the region and one of the largest employers in Canada in 1920, declared bankruptcy and went into receivership.[12] In January of that year, the province's Royal Commission Respecting the Coal Mines of the Province of Nova Scotia, headed by Sir Andrew Rae Duncan, released its report on the Nova Scotian coal industry, marking the end of the most intensive period of labour revolt in the region's history.[13] The same month, in response to regional protest led by the Maritime Rights Movement, Mackenzie King's minority government announced the Royal Commission on Maritime Claims, also headed by Duncan and popularly known as the Duncan Commission. Though it did little to resolve the region's economic woes, that commission would fundamentally alter the tenor of regional protest, anticipating the more comprehensive changes to distributive federalism enacted after the Second World War.[14]

Both of those reports were born of the catastrophic collapse of regional manufacturing and the broader social and economic crisis that gripped the region in the 1920s; yet they were also closely connected to significant national and international developments. The 1925 federal election, in which King's Liberals won only six of twenty-nine seats in the Maritime Provinces, forced King to address regional protest, but it also led to a period of political and constitutional instability, culminating in the 1926 King-Byng Affair.[15] That constitutional crisis helped shape discussions at the 1926 imperial conference that resulted in the Balfour Declaration of 1926 and, eventually, the establishment of Canada as a self-governing dominion under the Statute of Westminster in 1931. In short, 1926 witnessed profound changes to what constituted citizenship in the region and the nation, changes that would help shape conceptions of personal and political identity in modern Canada.

It is in the midst of these transformations that *The Busy East* and *The Labor Herald* emerge as key documents in the formation of collective identity at the regional scale. The integral role these periodicals played in class conflict and regional protest in the 1920s demands that they and the literature they published be read within that turbulent socio-political milieu. As in the preceding chapters of this study, chapters 4 and 5 examine the literary and cultural forms of these two periodicals as intimately bound to their editorial polemics and ideological commitments. Accordingly, this chapter frames Part 2 by discussing persistent notions of regional conservatism, premodernity, and cultural latency, arguing that these periodicals are best understood as diverging from the modernist/antimodernist dichotomy often invoked to chart opposing forms of interwar Canadian culture. The chapter concludes with a survey of another magazine, *The Dalhousie Review* (1921–), which reveals the inadequacy of this dichotomy to theorizing the intermediate and transitional aesthetics of interwar literature. Though the *Review* never committed itself to literary modernism, the journal's publication of modernist criticism and free verse clearly attests to the gradual acceptance of modernism among the province's intellectual elite. As the only lasting quarterly established in interwar Nova Scotia, the *Review* thus provides an important starting point from which to challenge the prevailing picture of an uncontested antimodernist hegemony in the

Maritime Provinces. Chapter 4 focusses on *The Busy East*, from its inception in 1910 through to 1933 when it was renamed *The Maritime Advocate and Busy East*. The chapter is most concerned with the 1920s, tracing the magazine's role as a vehicle for the Maritime Rights Movement and populist-liberalism before analyzing Will R. Bird's war stories, which began appearing after 1926, in relation to liberal fantasy. Finally, chapter 5 registers the radical left's opposition to regionalism, nationalism, and liberal ideology in *The Labor Herald* between 1921 and 1926. Focusing on the journal's social-political critique and the poetry that complemented that critique, I argue that the journal mediated between the local space of concrete political action and the transnational space of the global left.

Though it is necessary to explore the broader political movements of which these two latter periodicals were a part, it was the discursive sequences through which these magazines advanced their respective political movements that constituted their contribution to the cultural politics of the interwar period. And though neither periodical ever formulated a clear or definitive position on the relationship between the aesthetic and the political, both *The Labor Herald* and, eventually, *The Busy East* dedicated ample space to the publication of literary writing. The forms and genres appearing in each periodical were distinct. *The Labor Herald*, a labour paper that declared itself a "journal" of working-class resistance, published poetry – proletarian and thus overtly political – by a range of authors, including Nova Scotian poets Joe Wallace and Dawn Fraser, and Ontario communist leader and socialist-feminist Becky Buhay. In contrast, *The Busy East*, a commercial general-interest magazine, published short fiction, most notably the war stories of Will R. Bird, which on the surface bore no clear relation to the magazine's regionalist mandate. Unlike such magazines as *Acadiensis* and *Neith*, neither *The Busy East* nor *The Labor Herald* ever offered a substantial, coherent position on the social function of literature and art. As such, the extent to which editors intended literary content to reflect the periodicals' ideological objectives must be gleaned from the literature itself.

Both chapters 4 and 5 argue that the literature published in these periodicals not only complemented their respective polemics, but also helped foster the affective investments necessary to constitute viable political identities. In the case of *The Labor Herald* and radical leftism, this political identity was, in one sense, a given: the proletariat or working class.

But it is one thing to adopt the discursive antagonism of "revolutionary" struggle in order to frame or analyze Nova Scotia's local labour disputes; it is quite another to galvanize working-class identity in relation to a global movement of anti-capitalist resistance. It is beyond the scope of chapter 4 to examine whether *The Labor Herald* finally succeeded in its attempt to gain support for a global class struggle, though, as we shall see, there were signs that it was at least partially successful. Rather, what is at issue is the role that poetry played in that attempt. By mediating between the specificities of Cape Breton's violent labour wars and a vision of international working-class solidarity, the poetry that appeared in *The Labor Herald* each week suggested to its thousands of working-class readers that their own local struggles were implicated in, and constitutive of, a transnational proletarian culture. In short, poetry generated the affective dimension necessary to connect the local to the global. At the same time, the resonance between the journal's poetry and polemical essays extended this affective dynamic to other critical issues, most notably gender politics and socialist feminism.

In a broad sense, this argument might be framed in relation to Raymond Williams's "structures of feeling," insofar as the literary content of both of these periodicals is understood to contribute to the "affective infrastructure" that inflected readers toward affiliation and identification with a particular political position or group.[16] Unlike the poetry of *The Labor Herald*, Bird's fiction bears no immediate resemblance to what might be termed, following Williams, "formally held and systematic beliefs."[17] Taking my cue from Lauren Berlant's theorization of "fantasy" and Ian McKay's analysis of Bird's liberalism, I argue that Bird's war stories can be understood to advance a liberal fantasy that corresponds to the liberal-populism of the Maritime Rights Movement of which *The Busy East* was the "official organ."[18] And yet, even as this liberal fantasy yoked affect to the more prosaic economism of the movement, it also fostered ideological investment in the liberal nation-state, undermining the "regionalist" foundation that had formed the locus of the movement's political identity, the "Maritime people" at the beginning of the decade. And this, finally, suggests one way to read the politics of concession and accommodation that ultimately ended this critical cultural and political moment. Rather than interpreting this terminal date as signalling the complete failure of the Maritime Rights Movement or the total collapse of the radical left, I suggest that it marks a move toward the post-political that anticipated the political and social consensus that was to emerge in Canada and elsewhere at the close of the Second World War.

However we interpret the end of this period, these periodicals evidence a divided and contested cultural terrain that was far more dynamic than has been heretofore recognized in literary and cultural histories. No less than the *fin-de-siècle* regional magazines that preceded them, these periodicals speak to cultural-political division. As such, the chapters that follow challenge a critical flattening of regional culture in Canadian criticism, whereby the conservative antimodernism of the 1930s is deemed to have already achieved an effective cultural hegemony by the 1920s, if not prior to that decade. No work has been as influential in this regard as Ian McKay's *Quest of the Folk: Antimodernism and Cultural Selection in Twentieth-Century Nova Scotia* (1994). Returning to that study in order to delineate its precise temporal and geographic scope, I suggest that McKay's work has been read, erroneously, as a comprehensive explanation of regional culture in the first half of the twentieth century. By recovering periodicals and literature from the 1920s that do not fit comfortably within McKay's paradigm of "the Folk," the second part of this book offers a corrective to contemporary regional scholarship that collapses this decade of crisis into the 1930s and extends McKay's analysis to the regional scale with little qualification. In effect, *The Dalhousie Review*, *The Busy East*, *The Labor Herald*, and the literature they published necessitate a reconsideration of the sometimes confused and contradictory ways "antimodernism" has been taken up and deployed in Canadian criticism.

This line of argument builds upon a robust body of scholarship in the fields of political, economic, and labour history that has challenged regional stereotypes. It would be wrong to suggest that this scholarship has not informed treatments of the region in general histories of early-twentieth-century Canada. What is striking, however, is the absence of any comparable attempt within literary and cultural scholarship to perform similar recovery work, to complicate an historical narrative that casts the culture of the Maritime Provinces in the early twentieth century as uniformly conservative, belated, and antimodern. More than deconstructing stereotypes, however, contesting that historical narrative requires us to move beyond McKay's "paradigm of the folk" in the study of early-twentieth-century literary and print culture in the Maritime Provinces.

BEYOND PREMODERNITY, CONSERVATIVISM, AND ANTIMODERNISM

Since the 1990s, most scholarship on "Maritime" or "Atlantic-Canadian" culture has had to engage with McKay's influential paradigm of the folk. Generally, this scholarship has conceded the hegemony of cultural antimodernism in the first half of the twentieth century in order to demonstrate how contemporary writers challenge that paradigm, just as they are seen to challenge the constructions of a homogenous, organic region discussed in the first chapter of this study. Regional scholarship in this vein often reflects the same ambiguity around the concept of antimodernism that can be detected in Canadian modernist criticism generally. Moreover, it has almost invariably ignored periodical literature; *The Dalhousie Review*, *The Busy East*, and *The Labor Herald*, like *Acadiensis*, *Kit-Bag*, and *Neith*, have received no attention from literary critics and cultural historians. But before turning to critical discussions of antimodernism, and the role periodicals like *The Dalhousie Review* might play in complicating the antimodernist/modernist dichotomy, it is necessary to register how regional stereotypes have evolved from explicit charges of "conservatism" and "backwardness" to more nuanced claims about the region's belated modernization and its paradoxical experience of modernity.

The tradition of analysis that aims to complicate and deepen the historiography of the Maritime Provinces and repudiate stereotypes of the region is not new. Since at least the 1970s, the preoccupation of regional historians with defending the region against disparaging generalizations has been so prevalent that it has sometimes been seen to constitute an almost-gratuitous complaint. As Peter Thompson observed of "folk stereotypes" in his 2012 review essay of recent Atlantic-Canadian literary criticism, "there is a seemingly unquestioned assumption that people in central Canada or elsewhere want Atlantic Canada to be quaint and backwards, but little evidence [is] employed to back up this claim."[19] Though Thompson is right to suggest that stereotyping is now presupposed by most regional critics (and therefore less apt to be supported by specific examples), we might query whether there has ever been a dearth of evidence for these suppositions.

Tired and reductive ideas – that the region was untouched by modernity, modernized well after the rest of Canada, and saw no progressive movements in the first half of the twentieth century – are not hard to find, and they have a long history. In 1901, responding to regional demands for more equitable political representation, John A. Cooper, the editor of one of the leading national magazines at the time, *Canadian Magazine*, reasoned that, though "Ontario and the West realised some years ago that the building up of Canada was not any easy task … it can hardly be said that the Maritime Provinces have come to a like realization."[20] The result, declared Cooper, was "turpitude, inactivity, dissatisfaction," and a regional culture "tinged with pettiness and narrowness."[21] Subsequent commentators echoed Cooper's assessment, and his emphasis on apathy and parochialism, in particular. Writing in *MacLean's* in 1926, Harold Cunningham offered a laundry list of the region's "psychological ills": "Lack of confidence and creative imagination; a disposition to scorn private initiative and depend upon governments for everything; a pessimistic outlook that is purely mental and a suspicion of all things Maritime that has no foundation whatsoever."[22] Already by mid-century, a general picture of unchanging regional malaise had been established.

In the latter half of the century, the same narrative of regional conservatism continued to circulate, particularly among historians of the Canadian left. Frank Underhill was merely summarizing prevailing popular wisdom in his 1963 Massey lecture when he made the oft-cited quip that, "[a]s for the Maritime provinces, nothing, of course, ever happens down there."[23] It is unsurprising, then, that ten years later historian H. Clare Pentland should charge eastern-Canadian labour in the early twentieth century with a tendency toward "cheerful, unimaginative, rather childlike accommodation,"[24] a disposition historian David Bercuson would subsequently attribute to "conservative religious attitudes," "the influence of conservative metropolitan centres such as Halifax and Antigonish," and "an essentially conservative community."[25] In this mainstream brand of national history, focussed as it was on celebrating western-Canadian progressivism against the backdrop of the stable, stolid east, any contradictory evidence could be framed as an anomaly and dismissed as unrepresentative. The resurgence of regionalist history in the 1970s culminated in several major works, including David Alexander's *Atlantic Canada in Confederation* (1983) and Ernest Forbes's *Challenging the Regional Stereotype* (1989), that effectively exploded the stereotype of Maritime conservativism. Yet these studies had limited influence at the national scale, and the same assumptions of regional conservatism continue to inform perceptions of the region today. Thus, more than a century after John Cooper, political scientist Barry Cooper states, "as a matter of fact," that "[the Maritimes'] stagnation and decadence remain the most prominent features of pre-modern communal life to have survived into the present."[26] The latter Cooper's claim is atypical; few academics have been willing to state so bluntly the assumptions that often subtend discussions of the region in national histories.

Nevertheless, the connection Cooper draws between the well-worn trope of "stagnation" and ideas of premodernity reflects a shift in how claims of innate regional conservatism continue to circulate in contemporary scholarship, including cultural history and literary criticism. We can take as one example Glenn Willmott's observation, from his otherwise discerning *Unreal Country*, that "the rural regions of the Maritimes (like those of Quebec) modernized much later than those of Ontario or the Prairie provinces."[27] Willmott's remarks are not only more measured than those of earlier commentators, they are also largely correct. However, it is the process whereby "modernization" and "modern economic development" are conflated with the experience of "modernity" per se that allows Willmott to move, later in the book but rather seamlessly, to the claim that, "[f]rom the turn of the twentieth century forward, the Maritimes had a retarded postcolonial development in Canada, and a more persistent social ideology of traditional community."[28] Willmott is not making a specific claim about deindustrialization, underdevelopment, or industrial modernization; he is advancing the paradoxical claim that the "modern Maritimes" were defined by the persistence of premodern social structures.

However inconsequential the material conditions of rural modernity in the region might be to Willmott's reading of Nova Scotian fiction, his interpretation of the region's economic history places him in line with commentators like Cooper. For Willmott, the "nostalgia for a premodern society" that he detects in Ernest Buckler's *The Mountain and the Valley* (1952) is not a yearning for an invented pastoral past, but actually "conform[s] well to the economic history of the region."[29] Such generalization does not generally diminish the perceptiveness of Willmott's analysis of modern Nova Scotian novels; however, it does imply a blurring between the historical, material conditions of modernity in the region, how those conditions have been portrayed in a regional canon, and how regional fiction has been interpreted by critics to mimetically reflect social reality. Of course, the stable, harmonious premodern society remembered by Buckler's protagonist David Canaan had not simply ceased to exist by the interwar period: it had never existed. In effect, analyses such as Willmott's confuse more legitimate claims – that antimodernism and literary traditionalism remained more prominent in the Maritimes than they did elsewhere in Canada, that nostalgia pervaded mid-century regional fiction, and that deindustrialization and decline led to economic crisis and uneven development – with the profoundly mistaken view that in the twentieth century there existed (exists, even now) a static premodern society on the east coast of Canada – as critic W.H. New once put it, "everyone's half-forgotten past and no-one's future."[30]

It is this gap between a society riven by the consequences of modernity and the image of a stable, unchanging, premodern "folk" society that is the starting point for McKay's *Quest of the Folk*. Contrary to commentators like Cooper and Willmott, McKay insists that the history of twentieth-century Nova Scotia "is not the history of a settled, ordered Folk society, but of a region that experienced many of the contradictions of capitalist modernity."[31] Increasingly in the 1930s, however, this social reality was obscured by a powerful antimodernist mythomoteur. McKay terms this brand of antimodernism "Innocence," referring to the "elaborated myths" that represented the province as "essentially innocent from the complications and anxieties of modernity."[32] And at the core of this Innocence, existing as its essential embodiment, was "the Folk": an unsophisticated, quaint people isolated from modernity and epitomized by (though not limited to) the image of the simple, rural fisherman. This was not a distantly remembered past glimpsed in the remnants of a collapsing industry, it was the invention of bourgeois cultural producers.

Far from evidencing the persistence of tradition and the survival of premodern social structures, then, the antimodernism that dominated cultural production in Nova Scotia from the mid-1930s through the 1950s was itself a product of modern capitalist development. This antimodernism was thoroughly commercial, "structured by the very modern capitalism from which it seemed to provide a momentary and partial escape."[33] And it was also classed, developed by a "loose network" of urban, bourgeois cultural producers who, through their writing, art, handicrafts, photographs, and radio broadcasts, helped to reify the "pre-modern 'Otherness'" of Nova Scotia.[34] The paradox, of course, is that this antimodernism simultaneously depended upon and concealed its own commercial reproduction. As Herb Wyile explains, the process of cultural selection that rendered Nova Scotia synonymous with premodern simplicity "masks the degree to which the region was and is industrialized and how thoroughly it is bound up in an increasingly global, modern, capitalist economy (including the very tourist industry promoting such a stereotype)."[35] By at least the 1930s, the Folk paradigm, aggressively promoted by a rapidly expanding provincial tourism industry and attested to in a vast body of antimodernist literature and art, was ubiquitous in Nova Scotia.

The influence of McKay's work on subsequent studies of regional culture has been immense. In 2012, Thompson argued that one of the most significant theoretical developments in twenty-first-century Atlantic Canadian criticism had been "the systematic way it has incorporated" the insights of McKay's *Quest of the Folk*.[36] Nearly a decade later in *Nights below Foord Street* (2020), Thompson observes that "the influence of McKay's work is pervasive to the point where the folk paradigm ... has come to stand as a baseline measure for what counts as local culture."[37] It is unsurprising then that Wyile's *Anne of Tim Hortons*, arguably the most influential work of regional criticism since *Quest*, is especially indebted to McKay. Wyile positions the contemporary writers he examines in opposition to the "prevailing impression of culture in the Maritimes and Newfoundland" as "pre-modern, rural, and small-m maritime."[38] Similarly, David Creelman's *Setting in the East: Maritime Realist Fiction* (2003) connects tensions in regional realism to a "persistent sense of longing and nostalgia in Maritime society," which is, in turn, reflected in the paradigm of the folk and the "image of the Maritimes as an old fashioned land, steeped in a myth of innocence."[39] Though not without reservations, these critics demonstrate that there is much explanatory power to be derived from McKay's study of twentieth-century Nova Scotia and its application at the regional scale. Few studies,[40] however, have probed the limits of McKay's paradigm as an explanation of cultural production in the twentieth century.

McKay's *Quest of the Folk* is not a comprehensive explanation of interwar regional culture *tout court*; it is, rather, a more specific investigation of Nova Scotian antimodernism and the folk paradigm that achieved cultural hegemony only after the 1920s. Certainly, the conditions that provided the "impetus" for antimodernism in Nova Scotia – the rapid development of the tourism economy, the weakening of radical labour, and the "erosion of left-wing ideologies"[41] – are traceable to the "profound" economic and social crisis of the 1920s.[42] But tourism became a state function "after that decade," and the ideological space occupied by the new conservative antimodernism became vacant only with the changed dynamics of class struggle "after the late 1920s."[43] This more precise timeline is especially important for understanding the cultural milieu of *The Dalhousie Review*, *The Busy East*, and *The Labor Herald*, all of which began publishing literature prior to the 1930s. As we shall see, the gradual acceptance of modernism in the pages of the *Review* runs counter to the ascendance of folk-oriented antimodernism in the 1930s. Moreover, though the war fiction of *The Busy East* can be seen to anticipate the imminent rise of antimodernist tropes, it hardly conforms to anything like McKay's folk paradigm, while the proletarian poetry of *The Labor Herald* is antithetical to the depoliticized nostalgia so typical of folk-centred antimodernism.

McKay's analysis of twentieth-century Nova Scotian culture has not been immune to critique. Among the earliest critics to question the viability of the folk paradigm as an explanation for regional literary culture was Gwendolyn Davies. Examining the "home place" in the region's modern literature, Davies argues that "to dismiss this literature as static, merely a product of middle class romanticization, is to ignore the elements of realism, irony, and economic cynicism permeating much of it."[44] Creelman, too, takes issue with McKay's critical valuations of the region's novelists. Examining realism in modern fiction, Creelman finds conflicting threads of liberalism and conservatism that suggest much greater ideological complexity than McKay concedes in *Quest*. As such, Creelman rejects McKay's assessment that writers such as Frank Parker Day were "of a piece with the entire Quest of the Folk,"[45] "and thereby party to the conservative and antimodernist politics of that project."[46] And Herb Wyile, though primarily concerned with subversive threads in contemporary literature, takes issue with McKay's "tendency to make out those activities associated with the Folk … to be naive or disingenuous, ironic or even cynical, leaving little space for a more genuine engagement with the place of such activities in life on the East Coast."[47] Together, Davies, Creelman, and

Wyile suggest the problems that arise when the folk paradigm is extended, without reservation, to the region's canonical literature.

If a general picture of absolute and uncontested antimodernist hegemony has been allowed to stand in for a more nuanced examination of cultural production in the interwar period, then, it has not resulted simply from the failure of recent critics to mount incisive critiques. Most often, however, those critiques emerge from engagements with literature produced after the 1960s, in which an ostensibly more sophisticated postmodern sensibility has finally supplanted folk-centred antimodernism. By contrast, those studying literature and culture between the wars have either to concede the inescapable influence of antimodernism or else to position their subjects as isolated exceptions. Indeed, McKay's own assessment of regional culture admits few exceptions. Though McKay draws on Antonio Gramsci's theorization of hegemony to highlight contingency and to explicitly position his work against "economistic and culturalist reductionisms," he frequently gives the impression that the paradigm of the folk was all-encompassing, inexorable, and absolute.[48] As such, McKay sometimes inducts writers into his antimodernist canon without sufficient justification, suggesting that *all* cultural producers were "susceptible to the appeal of antimodernism and the folk."[49] Finally, though McKay's antimodernism was almost invariably socially conservative and economically liberal, it was also fundamentally devoid of a conscious, critical politics.

If, elsewhere, antimodernism represented an "ideologically mobile force," in Nova Scotia it was "much more one-sidedly reactionary" and the identity to which it contributed "much less politically definable."[50] It is this absence of critique, the lack of political consciousness, that most distinguishes the antimodernism McKay theorizes from that of T. Jackson Lears in *No Place of Grace: Antimodernism and the Transformation of American Culture, 1880–1920* (1981). For Lears, whose work remains foundational to discussions of the concept in Canadian criticism, twentieth-century American antimodernism formulated a radical critique of modern liberal capitalism. Lears's focus on a critique rooted in "profound conservatism," however, has been largely jettisoned from the work of subsequent critics, including McKay. But McKay's debt to Lears is greater than his scattered references would suggest. In fact, most of the central concepts through which McKay theorizes Nova Scotian antimodernism in *Quest* and with Robin Bates in *In the Province of History* – the preponderance of the folk and folk culture, the crucial role played by urban bourgeois cultural producers, the emphasis on innocence, history, and tourism as "therapeutic," and the "antimodern impulse" itself – as well as the Gramscian framework of those studies, are to be found in Lears's earlier text. Missing from McKay's study of Nova Scotian antimodernism, however, is the "cultural critique" that Lears's celebrates in its American counterpart.[51] For McKay, Nova Scotian antimodernism never mounted any incisive critique, conservative or otherwise.

And this, finally, is where the key stakes lie in the re-examination of interwar culture in the Maritime Provinces. Following McKay by rejecting reductive and now-myopic interpretations of the region as "premodern" and essentially conservative, critics are still left to contend with a narrative of regional culture that sees the antimodernist folk paradigm as having been the only mode available to those writing in or about the region between the wars. However crucial McKay's folk paradigm is for making sense of the past, critics must move beyond that paradigm as the only explanation for cultural production in the interwar period. This does not mean rejecting its insights, nor avoiding discussions of antimodernism; rather, it involves taking a different approach to meeting the "daunting task" that McKay himself describes elsewhere: "to reconstruct the more subtle politics of cultural selection and to understand the ways in which partial and contingent readings attain the status of obvious truths."[52] Approaching this problem must go beyond celebrating contemporary literature's postmodern suspicion of tradition; it must also attempt to recover modes of cultural practice that did not conform to, and often rejected, the antimodernist impulse.

The recovery of critically neglected periodicals such as *The Busy East* and *The Labor Herald* is only a small part of that broader project. But it is an important part, not only revealing counterexamples to mainstream antimodernism, but also disrupting a totalizing narrative that casts Nova Scotia – and, via subsequent critics, the cultural space identified with the region generally – as unproductive and void of any politically conscious, critical culture in the second quarter of the twentieth century. The consequences of adhering to that narrative extend beyond the misrecognition of important points of cultural-political divergence; they also reinforce an historical apperception that projects mid-century antimodernism further into the past, overlaying internal difference with "an east-coast

Celtic ethnicity that is Old World, racially white and homogeneous."[53] This refraction of the analytical gaze, then, not only skews how we interpret "regional" culture between the wars. It also reinforces the illegibility of key anti-racist, anti-regionalist, and/or anti-nationalist voices that rejected the prioritization of regional and Canadian-national affiliations in the constitution of personal and political identities, including *Neith*, as we saw in the second chapter, and *The Labor Herald*, the subject of the fourth. Excepting the recent work of modernist critics such as Tony Tremblay, this historical recovery work is a task that most critics of regional culture have rejected in favour of reading examples of contemporary literature that have more obviously moved beyond the folk paradigm.

In fact, the literature in *The Busy East* and *The Labor Herald* offers important historical precedent for contemporary literary trends, if only because it renders modern subjects and themes that are irreducible to antimodernist tropes and figures of the folk. But it is also literature that responds to, rather than retreats from, its historical moment. Its authors were attempting not to deny, but rather to make sense of the conditions and catastrophes of twentieth-century modernity: the cataclysm of the First World War, and the devastating effects of a collapsing economy and capitalist underdevelopment. True, the strategies adopted by the writers and editors of these periodicals only rarely incorporated the "make it new" doxa of modernist formalism, and never the avant-garde's quest for experimental compositional forms that could adequately communicate the fragmented, alienated subjectivity of the modern individual. But neither did they involve the sort of "recoil" from modern existence so distinctive of antimodernism.[54]

And *The Busy East* and *The Labor Herald* were not the only interwar periodicals in the Maritime Provinces that complicate the modernist/antimodernist dichotomy. Established in Halifax the same year that *The Labor Herald* made its debut, *The Dalhousie Review* (1921–) was far more subdued in its politics than either the *Herald* or *The Busy East*. Like those periodicals, however, it deserves closer scrutiny for its publication of literature and criticism, particularly by women, that advanced and promoted an intermediate, transitional poetics and a critical sensibility that was neither definably modernist nor unequivocally antimodernist. An exhaustive examination of the *Review* is beyond the scope of this chapter. However, given the journal's longevity – it remains the longest-running quarterly in Atlantic Canada – and its publication in Halifax, ground zero for the bourgeois cultural producers driving "the antimodernist Quest of the Folk,"[55] it is worth considering the *Review*'s role as a vehicle for transitional modernism in the interwar period. Coinciding as it did with the ascendence of the folk paradigm, the journal's gradual acceptance of literary modernism in the 1930s seriously troubles the notion of an uncontested antimodernist hegemony in interwar Nova Scotia.

TRANSITIONAL MODERNISM AND *THE DALHOUSIE REVIEW*

On the morning of 6 December 1917, Archibald McKellar MacMechan was seated on his dining-room sofa reading the newspaper when "two terrific explosions" blew in the windows of his house.[56] In the confusion that followed, MacMechan gathered his family, ran into the street, and quickly ascertained the cause of the explosion from neighbours. Ignoring warnings of further explosions and instructions from authorities to gather in a nearby park, MacMechan set off for the library at Dalhousie University. By noon, MacMechan was sifting through a debris of toppled shelves and broken glass, carefully moving the scattered volumes out from under the shattered Palladian windows and into the corners of the library "where rain and snow could not reach them."[57] The image that emerges from MacMechan's account, carefully documented in his private journal and history of the explosion, offers a stark contrast with that described by Prince in his study of the disaster. Far from "social disintegration" and the obliteration of "fixed traditions" witnessed by Prince,[58] MacMechan's is an account of order restored and tradition preserved. MacMechan never shies away from describing the horrors he witnessed, nor does he deny the "vast turmoil" into which the city descended in the days that followed.[59] Yet his is a tale of heroism triumphant, history "touched with the quality of myth."[60] There is, moreover, something especially compelling in the image of MacMechan toiling in the wake of the explosion, rescuing from the elements the modest collection of books he had helped to amass.

In short, if one were to try to distil in a single scene the effort to salvage tradition from the wreckage of the war, one could do worse than that of MacMechan in the library. The scene seems to convey something essential, too, about MacMechan's legacy as a late-Victorian antimodernist. His Romantic-nationalist criticism, his nostalgia-laden histories of Nova Scotia, his mentorship of such pre-eminent antimodernists as Helen Creighton, "*the* Maritime folklorist" and archetypal purveyor of the folk paradigm[61] – all would seem to position MacMechan as a stalwart bastion of tradition trenchantly opposed to the modern. Working against this assessment, however, are MacMechan's positive reviews of such modernists as Virginia Woolf and his influence on writers as diverse as Lucy Maud Montgomery, Ernest Buckler, and Kenneth Leslie, the latter of whom would "turn increasingly to modernist experimentation as to the left" in the late 1920s and 1930s.[62] In short, MacMechan was a critical antimodernist: cosmopolitan and thoroughly in tune with contemporary literary trends, but one who "sought accommodation rather than espousing a break with past traditions."[63] McKay never discusses MacMechan in *Quest*, referring only in passing to "the influential Nova Scotian essayist and academic,"[64] and then only to register MacMechan's early support for Creighton and his defense of Frank Parker Day's *Rockbound*.[65] Nor does McKay ever discuss *The Dalhousie Review*, the journal MacMechan helped found in 1921 and the only lasting literary periodical established in interwar Nova Scotia. Given that omission and the emphasis MacMechan himself placed on "the importance of Canadian periodicals"[66] to the growth of national literature – it was half of his thesis in his most important work, *Headwaters of Canadian Literature* (1924) – it is worth surveying *The Dalhousie Review* for what it might reveal about the tension between traditionalism and innovation, literary antimodernism and modernism, in interwar Nova Scotia.

Though he helped establish the *Review* and was a frequent contributor of articles and reviews until his death in 1933, MacMechan was never a member of its editorial board. The magazine did, however, reflect the brand of critical antimodernism MacMechan championed, and, like MacMechan, it cannot be comfortably inducted into the canon of acritical antimodernism described by McKay. Founded in 1921, the *Review* aimed to fill a middle ground between "technical learned journals" and magazines of "literary entertainment."[67] Its editor from 1921 to 1947 was Herbert Leslie Stewart, a Dalhousie professor and philosopher who, in his opening editorial, identified a need for periodicals like the *Review* in Canada, "where tradition is less firmly consolidated, and where the hitherto untried experiment is being more frequently ventured."[68] It was hardly a manifesto, but Stewart's picture of a milieu unencumbered by "tradition" and ripe for "untried experiment" appeared to open the journal to innovative verse and contemporary thought, if not literary modernism.

A survey of the journal's interwar contributors appears to confirm that openness. Throughout the period, the journal published contributions by several canonical Canadian modernists. E.J. Pratt, A.M. Klein, and Leo Kennedy contributed poems. A.J.M. Smith, Raymond Knister, and Frederick Philip Grove contributed essays and sketches. Scholarly contributions came from such modernist-inclined figures as critic Douglas Bush, painters Arthur Lismer and Barker Fairley, and rising media theorist Marshall McLuhan. A closer examination of their contributions, however, dispels any notion that the journal served primarily as an incubator for these writers' modernism. In essays, Knister wrote on "The Poetry of Archibald Lampman," Fairley on "Goethe the Poet," and McLuhan on the mysticism of G.K. Chesterton. These writers did find in their subjects opportunity to celebrate modern aesthetics. Thus, Douglas Bush identifies in the work of Matthew Arnold and Thomas Hardy a strain of pessimism that runs into such "signposts" of twentieth-century literature as "*Ulysses* and *The Waste Land*,"[69] and Fairley finds a "great exemplar in Goethe" for the "modernist tendency" toward "the poetry of metaphor."[70] Moreover, by the 1930s, adulation for modernists in articles such as W. Harvey-Jellie's "T.S. Eliot Among the Prophets" and C.I. Glicksberg's "Poetry and Social Revolution" became more common. That such articles were appearing in the province's most prestigious journal in the 1930s constitutes a glaring exception to the apparent hegemony of folk-centred antimodernism in that decade. But on the whole, the journal's analytical gaze, especially in its first decade, remained firmly set on the past, its primary subjects drawn from previous generations.

A similar tendency toward traditionalism characterized the poetry contributed by writers such as Pratt, Klein, and Kennedy. Published in the January 1925 issue, Pratt's "The Dear Illusion," a nostalgic plaint in rhyming quatrains, is the work of Pratt the Romantic lyricist, not the transitional poet who mounted a "modernist revolt against a delayed Victorianism."[71] Such transitional modernism can be detected in Pratt's later contributions, such as his allusive and densely symbolic "The Highway," but in this poem from 1932, the form remains traditional.

Appearing in the same year, Kennedy's "Exile" is not only a conventional Shakespearean sonnet, but also anticipates, with its "wheeling gulls" and "dories in the cove," the pastoral imagery of the mid-century folk paradigm.[72] In the next issue, Klein's "Seasons," a series of four Petrarchan sonnets, is more indicative of a modernist sensibility, straining against its conventional form in its evocation of a desolate and violent natural world. Combining such idiosyncratic juxtapositions as "jaundiced leaf" and "solar slaughter" with slant rhymes, "frost" / "dust," "thrust" / "holocaust,"[73] Klein conspicuously extends T.S. Eliot's "cruellest month" to a Canadian environment of climatic extremes.[74] If not modernist, the poem certainly complicates the pastoralism associated with interwar antimodernism. Klein's wasteland, however, remains structured in a highly conventional form, and in this it evidences Stewart's editorial resistance to free verse. Indeed, despite what his opening salutation might suggest, Stewart was not very amenable to modernism and remained a staunch traditionalist throughout his tenure. Thus, writing to contributor Frances Starr in 1933, Stewart expressed his unequivocal disdain for formal experiment: "I am not much of a critic of free verse, and as a rule I don't like it. We never use it in the *Review*."[75] Whatever openness to modernism the journal's content might suggest, then, it was not the result of Stewart's editorial direction.

But the *Review* did "use" free verse, and Stewart was not the only member of the editorial board. More than MacMechan and even Stewart, it was Eliza Ritchie whose contributions shaped the literary outlook of the journal during its first decade. A Cornell-educated philosopher and prominent Halifax suffragist, Ritchie was a founding member of the editorial board, a position she would hold until her death in 1933. During that time, she also contributed well over one hundred reviews and several articles to the journal, making her by far the single most prolific contributor of literary criticism. As Carole Gerson observes, the influence of Ritchie, a "well-known feminist," on the editorial board "likely both attracted other women to the *Review* and justified their presence."[76] It is unclear whether or not Ritchie was responsible for soliciting the "overtly feminist articles" that Gerson points to in her discussion of the *Review*. She did, however, regularly review and promote the work of emerging women writers. Often, Ritchie reviewed lesser-known writers alongside established British and American authors, as when her review of W.B. Yeats's

The Tower (1928) preceded a no less laudatory review of Nova Scotian Jennie N. Smith's collection *Isles of Paisley* (1928). Like Smith, many of the women whose works Ritchie reviewed have long been forgotten. Many, too, catered to a conservative Canadian readership still averse to modernism in poetry and prose.

But though Ritchie's preference for traditional verse is unmistakeable in her own poetry and her edited anthology *Songs of the Maritimes* (1931), her criticism in the *Review* reveals a far more nuanced reception of literary modernism. Ritchie's review of H.D.'s *Heliodora and Other Poems* (1924) in the October 1924 issue, for instance, reveals how Ritchie navigated popular aversion to modernist experiment without compromising her critical standards. Granting that the free verse of "ultra-modern" poets may prove "a stone of stumbling and rock of offence" to the "conservative reader," Ritchie celebrates H.D.'s collection as "a finished product of great beauty and charm."[77] Her point, one that critics like Stewart failed to appreciate, is that the "metrical methods" of modernists like H.D. may be free of rigid structure and rhyme, but not "'free' in the sense of a lawless disregard for technique."[78] Rather than offer polemics, Ritchie sought to educate her readers in an appreciation for modernist aesthetics. Moreover, Ritchie brought the same respect for experiment and innovation to her appraisals of Canadian literature. Her several reviews of Pratt's collections, for instance, are marked for lauding Pratt's "originality,"[79] his "distinction of style,"[80] and his "realistic treatment" of themes "with simplicity and directness, avoiding all obvious sentimentality."[81]

Still more revealing than her reception of H.D. and Pratt, however, is Ritchie's review of *Dream Tapestries* (1924), the second collection by pioneering imagist Louise Morey Bowman. There, Ritchie takes aim at the "curious conservatism" that plagues "literary appreciation in Canada": "we are shy of approving any mode of artistic expression other than the traditional – and the tradition must have come from the mother country."[82] The "we" to whom Ritchie attributes this "conservatism," in its antipathy to experiment if not its uncritical colonial mentality, might readily describe the criticism of reviewers like Stewart, but not that of Ritchie. Warning that such "prejudice" against experiment "may make us blind to what is of real and permanent value," Ritchie turns to the work of Bowman: "more than any other of our Canadian poets, she is endowed with the gift of a keen, true and far-reaching vision."[83] In

Figure 3.1 Eliza Ritchie, ca. 1887.

particular, Ritchie acclaims Bowman's "boldly and starkly realistic" portraits of urban life, and her "vivid pictures" and "impressionist study" of place.[84] What Ritchie appreciates in Bowman's work is, in a word, its modernism. Appearing in the April 1926 issue, the review is a key to Ritchie's influence over the *Review*. It is important not because Ritchie's criticism consistently betrays a modernist sensibility, but because it indicates the extent to which her promotion of modern women writers encouraged them to submit their work. That Ritchie was also receptive to literary modernism, however, may well explain the free verse that did appear in the journal.

In fact, formal experiments in the *Review* came not from the pens of modernist men, but from women writers. Between 1921 and 1940, the *Review* featured formally innovative poetry by at least eight women: Anne Marriott, Joyce Marshall, Floris Clarke McLaren, Frances Angus, Anne Margaret Angus, Louise Moulton, Florence Elizabeth Westacott, and Louise Morey Bowman. Though a few of these writers – namely Marriott, McLaren, and Bowman – have since been recognized as integral to the emergence of literary modernism in Canada, the others have been mostly forgotten. Some were local writers; many submitted work from across Canada. Few of their poems are unequivocally modernist in form and content, and most published traditional forms as well as free verse, but all of them put pressure on the literary traditionalism with which Stewart ostensibly sought to align the journal. Several more women regularly published in strictly traditional forms. Notable among the traditional poets were Nova Scotian Norma Ethel Smith and prominent Ontario poet Audrey Alexandra Brown, whose "five collections of brilliant Romantic poetry," writes Brian Trehearne, "satisfied the yearning for cultural continuity of Conservative Canadian readers."[85] The result is a considerable body of late-Victorian Romanticism that caters to conservative tastes, punctuated with transitional poetics that make a definite break towards modernism. For the most part, the women contributors to the *Review* elude easy categorization and occupy what Gerson, writing of mid-century modernity and Canadian women's fiction, identifies as "the middle ground between modernism and anti-modernism, two poles shaped by a small coterie of male academics, authors, and journalists."[86] Again, Bowman is significant. Contributing five poems between 1926 and 1934, Bowman published more poetry in the *Review* than any other single poet during the same period besides Pratt, who also contributed five poems.

Together, Bowman's poems demonstrate both thematic coherence and formal variety. Her first two poems, "Just Before Dawn" and "Dragon Orchard," are both long narrative poems in free verse. Their innovation results as much from their fragmented, stream-of-consciousness presentation as from the imagism for which Bowman is remembered. In both, the creative impulse is set against the threat of domesticity, what the speaker of "Dragon Orchard" calls "the woman's part": "grave grey days" and the "starved monotony / of pale and wan routine."[87] For the subject of "Dragon Orchard," the blossoming of the titular orchard and its subsequent rotting represent the foreclosed promise of redemption, mirroring her stifled expression. By contrast, it is the fear of neglect and obscurity that haunts the dying subject of "Just Before Dawn": "They published just one little slender book / Of her poems … Critics say they're very fine."[88] Read as a meditation on the artist figure, the ambiguity of the criticism – "very fine" suggesting, at most, underwhelming reception – may suggest a correspondence between mediocrity and convention. However, it is Bowman's most conventional poem in the *Review*, "Follow – Follow," a twenty-three-line poem loosely structured in ballad stanzas, that most clearly articulates the poet's ambivalent relation to the traditional and the modern. In it "the Old," "gloriously formed," come "streaming down the years" as "the New," "nebulous shapes of grey and green," come "seeking forms yet unseen."[89] The turn in the final stanza looks forward to the very collision that Bowman affects through her irregular ballad form: "Somewhere afar on the future's hill / Where every faith is crucified / The Old and the New shall meet."[90] In many respects, it is precisely this collision between the old and the new that characterizes the journal in which the poem appeared.

If we accept Wanda Campbell's argument that Bowman was "one of the initiators of the modernist movement in Canada,"[91] then the *Review*'s inclusion of her poetry in the 1920s and early 1930s testifies to a more eclectic literary policy than Stewart nominally allowed. And though Bowman's was the most unequivocally modern verse to appear before the late 1930s, she was not alone in advancing a modernist sensibility in poetry. A fidelity to imagism can be detected in poems such as Frances Angus's "Lagoon," while even conventional poems such as Louise Moulton's "Process" and "Our Aeroplane" take up decidedly modern themes as they play with the strictures of metred verse. Moreover, Ritchie was not the only critic in the *Review* who was receptive to modernism. An even more trenchant defense of literary modernism can be glimpsed in essays contributed by New Brunswick writer Grace Tomkinson. Writing in "Colonialism and Art" in 1931, Tomkinson echoed Ritchie's review of Bowman, indicting the "national inferiority complex" that impedes creative practice in former colonies such as Canada where "heavy respect for the traditions and opinions of [the] mother country" precipitates "mediocrity."[92] Four years later, in "The Watched Pot of Canadian

Poetry," Tomkinson called for "ruthless irreverent criticism" to counter the provincialism that had resulted from failing to apply "universal standards" in the assessment of Canadian literature.[93] For Tomkinson, "the new poetry in Canada should be more rugged, less romantic and cloyingly sweet," and she concluded optimistically that "[it] is bound to be more cosmopolitan."[94] Tomkinson's celebration of the "cosmopolitan" over the provincial anticipates A.J.M. Smith's distinction between the "cosmopolitan" and the "native" in his controversial introduction to *The Book of Canadian Poetry* (1943). Still, unlike Ritchie's criticism of the 1920s, Tomkinson's modernism of the 1930s is not so much prescient of impending changes in Canadian literature as it is representative of the gradual acceptance of literary modernism in Canadian criticism.

Largely the same can be said of the *Review* itself: it was never, in fact, a significant vehicle for modernist experiment, but neither was it uniformly antimodernist in any meaningful sense. True, Tomkinson's modernism jarred against the criticism of authors such as A.M. Stephen, whose invective against "the 'free verse' schools" of poetry appeared two issues after her "Colonialism and Art."[95] But it was precisely such critical debate that the journal aimed to foster. In short, the *Review* was always primarily an organ for liberal intellectualism and only secondarily a literary magazine. Its significance to interwar culture in Canada, then, derived less from the literature it published than from the diverse criticism it championed. But this critical and scholarly function never prevented the journal from publishing interesting literature. Be it Bowman's free verse or Audrey Alexandra Brown's sonnets, the literature in the *Review* reflected the divergent tastes of its editors, contributors, and readers. Ironically, by the time that folk-oriented antimodernism had achieved ascendency in 1930s Nova Scotia, those tastes were shifting toward literary modernism. Yet to characterize the contents of the *Review* as rigidly divided into two opposing camps, emergent modernism and reactionary antimodernism, is to miss the point, for it ignores the fundamentally transitional character of the journal.

In fact, the *Review* returns us to a particular problem hampering the study of interwar culture generally: namely, the false dichotomy between modernism and antimodernism that is invoked, often implicitly, to define modern culture in Canada. Almost invariably, critics of antimodernist literature appeal to Lears to define antimodernism as "the recoil from an 'overcivilised' modern existence to more intense forms of physical or spiritual existence"[96] but supplement that definition with a more limited concept of antimodernism as the perpetuation of traditional literary forms. This collapse of literary and cultural-historical definitions has resulted in a lack of clarity as to what the term is intended to denote. "Antimodernism" thus frequently functions as a mere byword for literary traditionalism, altogether eliding Lears's far more robust theorization of the concept in literary-critical assessments of writers – again, often women – who might otherwise be located in the "middle ground" identified by Gerson. The result is a binary that casts an invariably regressive, reactionary, and conservative antimodernism against a Canadian modernist tradition that is deemed progressive, cosmopolitan, and sophisticated.

Of course, such a framework cannot comfortably accommodate the transitional poetics of writers such as Bowman or Klein in the *Review*. Nor can it adequately account for figures such as MacMechan, whose antimodernism was at once critical and complex, or Ritchie, whose traditionalism never precluded her reception and promotion of modernism. This framework, then, presents a particularly acute problem for studies of interwar culture in the Maritime Provinces. If modern Canadian literature between the wars is to be read as essentially bifurcated, or otherwise charted between the poles of antimodernism and modernism, then it must necessarily exclude much of the periodical literature published in the region during that period. A more nuanced reading of interwar periodicals like the *Review*, *The Busy East*, and *The Labor Herald* is necessary, then, not only because it renders a more complex picture of the cultural politics before mid-century, but also because it helps unsettle received categories including "antimodernism" that have yet to be adequately theorized in the Canadian context.

TOWARD A CRITICAL CULTURAL POLITICS

Rather than confirming assumptions of a uniformly conservative antimodernism, the literature of both *The Busy East* and *The Labor Herald* demonstrates the critical role that literary culture played in accruing popular sentiment to opposing cultural-political projects that have heretofore been studied primarily in relation to electoral politics, economic policy, and unionism. This is perhaps more immediately evident from the cultural politics of *The Labor Herald*, which forms the focus of the fifth and final chapter. The poetry of *The Labor Herald*, formally conventional as it was, always underwrote the journal's commitment to "abolishing the capitalist system and establishing a brotherhood of communism," attempting to treat directly the "chaos in the rapidly approaching time when capitalism will have collapsed."[97] The ultra-radicalism of that journal was not only anathema to acritical antimodernism in the Maritime Provinces; it also levelled a critique of liberal common sense that was remarkable for its militancy in the early 1920s when radical labour across Canada was mostly in retreat.[98]

By contrast, the fiction in *The Busy East*, the subject of the fourth chapter, was never fundamentally in contention with folk-oriented antimodernism. Still, the early war stories of Will R. Bird, whose own later travel writing would constitute some of the most vociferous folk-oriented antimodernism, invariably express a basic faith in liberal individualism, progress, and modernization that cannot be reconciled with the static folk society imagined by later antimodernists, including Bird himself. Moreover, Bird's liberal fantasy can be read as tracing the affective contours of the populist-liberalism of the Maritime Rights Movement. Far more than the radical left, which was severely weakened after 1926, the Maritime Rights Movement would come to define regional politics, helping to consolidate the collective political identity of the "Maritime People." As the official voice of Maritime Rights and the Maritime Boards of Trade, *The Busy East* represents a key document in the regional protest of the 1920s, as well as the politics of concession and accommodation that would initiate the movement's gradual decline. Together, *The Busy East* and *The Labor Herald* demonstrate that, even in the comparatively austere and intensely nationalist publishing climate of the 1920s, periodicals continued to form crucial points of intersection between social, political, and cultural currents both within and beyond the region. More than this, they were constitutive of the discursive field in which political identities were constructed and negotiated at local, regional, and transnational scales.

4

Liberal Fantasy, Populist Appeal

Will R. Bird's War Fiction and The Busy East of Canada

It was *The Busy East*, more than any other magazine, that would help establish the tenor of regional protest in the 1920s as economic decline and deindustrialization plunged the region into a severe social and economic crisis. Devoted to regional boosterism throughout its long tenure, *The Busy East* is best characterized as a commercial and business magazine that gradually transitioned to a general-interest magazine in the latter half of the decade. Already by the 1920s, the magazine had gained a central place in the social life of the region by promoting the political program of the Maritime Rights Movement. This was a program that was both classically liberal and populist in its appeal to the broad, nebulous identity of the "Maritime people." Examining the magazine's emergence as the vehicle of Maritime Rights at the beginning of the decade thus reveals the rhetorical strategies that local elites deployed to politicize regional identity in the interests of modernization and the consolidation of a liberal political economy.

But it is the magazine's cultural content, specifically its short fiction, that attaches its more narrowly economic and commercial focus to a broader cultural politics. Attending to the magazine's increasing commitment to literary publishing after 1926 thus reveals a still more significant *cultural* function: namely, the role that popular fiction played in generating affective investment in the interwar liberal order. The immensely popular war fiction of Nova Scotian writer Will R. Bird, which appeared in nearly every second issue of the magazine between 1927 and 1933, is paradigmatic of this process. In this respect, *The Busy East* might be read against the editorial direction of earlier *fin-de-siècle* regional magazines. Rather than constructing an extradiegetic narrative that shaped the meanings of literary texts within the magazine, as Jack did in *Acadiensis*, the editors of *The Busy East* published short fiction with virtually no editorial commentary, only rarely providing anything by way of cultural criticism. The result is a more reciprocal relationship between the literary and the polemical. Accordingly, the magazine's popular fiction can be read as generating meanings that remain submerged beneath, or inarticulate within, the magazine's articles and editorial essays. To this end, the liberal fantasy expressed in Bird's war fiction provided the cultural correlative of the magazine's liberalism, dramatizing the transcendence of the liberal individual above conditions of crisis. In its basic endorsement of the liberal nation-state, however, the magazine also undermined its explicitly regionalist mandate. Ultimately, this same devotion to liberal modernization would facilitate the rise of commercial antimodernism and signal the turn toward a form of post-politics in the early 1930s.

NEW LIBERALISM AND THE MODERNIZATION IMPERATIVE

The long history of *The Busy East*, however, begins prior to the First World War, well before an acute sense of crisis and widespread discontent would ignite regional protest under the banner of Maritime Rights. In fact, when it first appeared in 1910, the magazine was welcomed in newspapers throughout the Maritime Provinces for encouraging the region's "booming manufacturing and commerce."[1] Featuring the slogan "Watch Us Grow," the first issue was profusely illustrated, running to twenty-eight numbered pages with five pages of advertisements. In its first decade, the magazine's policy was to dedicate every second issue to the industry, commerce, and development of a specific town or city in the region. This policy was largely abandoned by 1919 as the magazine began to offer more by way of political analysis, economics, and general-interest content. A typical issue featured several editorials followed by two or three articles on economics or industry, a short story or sketch reprinted from such American magazines as *Rod & Gun* or *Forest & Stream*, and three general-interest articles in science, regional history, and travel. Issues concluded with a news section titled "Random Maritime Notes" and a personal advice and biography column titled "Business Man's Corner."

In many respects, the magazine's format would remain unchanged during its first two decades. Published in Saint John by the H.M. McAlpine Directory Co. with W.T. Guest as its editor and manager, the magazine's stated aim was to "boost, advertise and put before the moneyed immigrant our great advantages for farming and investment in the most attractive form possible."[2] For the first several years of its existence, the magazine was certainly attractive, with glossy pages and abundant illustrations (fig. 4.1), but it was no more interesting than that initial description implies; as one reviewer in the *Saint John Standard* tactfully put it, it was "a very creditable production, well printed, with appropriate and striking illustrations."[3] Nevertheless, its paid-subscription circulation of 1,200 was already "rapidly growing" by its second year, aided by its popularity among the region's urban bourgeois elite, those the United States Bureau of Manufacturing deemed Saint John's "most progressive class."[4] It was a magazine of its time, partaking of the booster-mania that was endemic to progressive-era North America. As such, the magazine was a testament to a society as yet in the throes of industrializing zeal, a zeal reflected in the "fine spirit of optimism" that pervaded its "well got-up pages."[5]

The society reflected in *The Busy East* was one preoccupied with the challenges of urban and industrial life. Modern urban planning, tax regulation, public and technical education, and a broad-ranging agenda of progressive reform all were evidenced in the pages of *The Busy East*. Moreover, as Ernest Forbes observes, even in its early years the magazine was "conscious of the need to assert a regional perspective" in opposition to a powerful national myth of westward-moving progress.[6] In this respect, it was something of a successor to *Acadiensis*, which had ceased publication just two years before *The Busy East* made its debut. However, the latter magazine was, for at least its first decade, far more concerned with industry, commerce, and political economy than with regional history and culture, and it never benefited from the editorial prowess of someone like David Russell Jack. In fact, it went through the hands of several editors during the first six years of publication until coming under the direction of Clement Chandler Avard, a prominent newspaper publisher and politician who moved the magazine to Sackville, established the Busy East Press, and printed the magazine from his own Tribune Printing Co.[7]

From this modest and somewhat precarious start, the magazine would become the longest-running magazine ever published in the Maritime

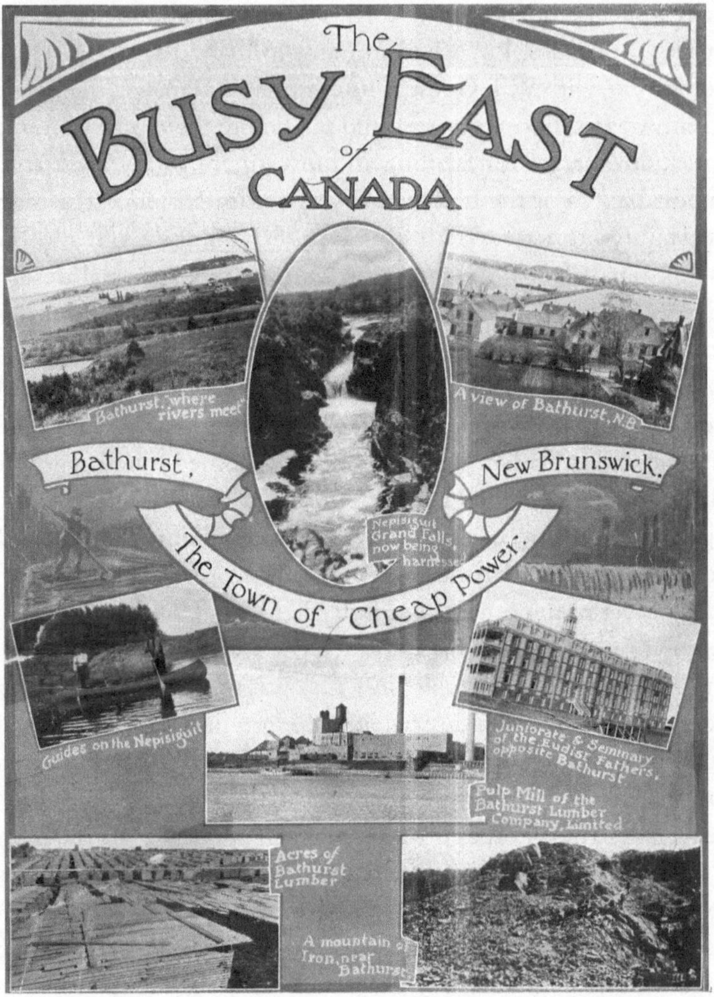

Figure 4.1 The cover of *The Busy East of Canada*, June 1920.

Provinces, first as *The Busy East of Canada* (1910–33), then as *The Maritime Advocate and Busy East* (1933–56), and finally as *The Atlantic Advocate* (1956–92). As *The Atlantic Advocate*, the magazine most approximated a mainstream general-interest magazine, with a growing circulation of about twenty thousand in 1959.[8] The significance of the magazine to the political and literary cultures of the Maritime Provinces, however, was never greater than it was between the wars, not only because the magazine became a vehicle for regional protest after the First World War, but also because the comparative dearth of publishing venues in the Maritime Provinces meant that magazines like *The Busy East* provided some of the only regular outlets for publishing there. As Sandrine Ferré-Rode explains, the "vitality" that characterized literary publishing in the Atlantic region in the nineteenth century had "faded by the First World War," after which time publishing was "largely confined to newspapers."[9] The strong literary focus of *The Dalhousie Review* (1921–) and the short-lived little magazines *The Song Fisherman's Song Sheets* (1928–30) and *Acadie* (1930) partially offset this picture of general decline. However, it is significant that Ferré-Rode identifies *The Busy East* as the one "notable exception" to the trend.[10]

The Busy East would not, in fact, emerge as a notable venue for literary publishing until the middle of the 1920s. Prior to 1924, most of the literary material it published was reprinted from American magazines. However, the magazine was noteworthy before that point for two reasons. First, it helped consolidate the vocabulary of regional identity that had been initiated in *fin-de-siècle* magazines such as *Acadiensis* and *The Maple Leaf*. This marked a deviation from the dominant discourse of popular and political nationalism generally, and from the default cultural nationalism of Canadian magazines, in particular. As Mary Vipond has shown, the 1920s were a difficult decade for magazine publishers across Canada. Faced with a deluge of American magazines, many Canadian magazine publishers attempted to capitalize on post-war nationalist sentiment in an attempt to secure more favourable postal rates and tariff protection.[11] According to the nationalist argument, "Canadian magazines were essential to the preservation and growth of Canadian literature and thus of a strong sense of Canadian unity and identity."[12] By contrast, *The Busy East* appealed to regional identity, taking up the cause of Maritime legislative union, and advocating united opposition to central- and western-Canadian political and economic interests.

Of course, this discourse was not entirely new; in many respects it was an extension and intensification of the regionalist discourse initiated in *fin-de-siècle* magazines. More than its *fin-de-siècle* antecedents, however, *The Busy East* politicized the identity of the "Maritimer" vis-à-vis pan-Canadian nationalism by deploying the logic of populism. As ex-Liberal parliamentarian and lawyer H.J. Logan put it in the May 1918 issue, "we are all Maritime people with distinct Maritime interests"; union, argued Logan, was necessary to counter central-Canadian dominance and the "growing influence of the west, whose interests and desires are often not in common with ours." [13] Elsewhere, Logan was less subtle, declaring to applause in Moncton in 1919 that "the upper provinces" had "stolen the heritage of the Maritime Provinces for fifty years."[14] It is important to recognize the extent to which this renewed discourse of regionalism, though never directly opposed to Canadian nationalism, was nevertheless agonistic in its attempt to construct the social field as fundamentally divided between the "Maritime people" and its Other, central- and western-Canadian business and political interests. This discursive manoeuvre – what can be called, following Ernesto Laclau, the "political logic" of populism – involved more than a particular perspective on Canadian federalism; it involved the construction of a collective political identity.

It is this discursive construction of popular identity that historians have intuited but none have investigated when referring to the "populism" of the Maritime Rights Movement. Thus, Charlotte Grey numbers the movement among those left-oriented "populist protests" that "had a profound impact on the national agenda,"[15] while historians McKay and Morton describe its "new conservatism, draped in right-wing populism."[16] But what is meant by the term 'populist' here? After all, the movement never had a particularly charismatic leader, nor any one identifiable leader for that matter, a condition frequently deemed necessary for the emergence of populism. Moreover, if we accept that the movement was fundamentally liberal – as I suggest, following Nerbas, we should – then it might appear to be anathema to populism, which many commentators consider to be contrary to modern liberalism, in theory as well as practice.[17] Understanding in what sense the movement was populist, then, requires the recognition, following Ernesto Laclau, that populism is "not a *type* of movement – identifiable with either a special social base or a particular ideological orientation – but a political logic."[18] In this respect, the analysis of historian Ernest Forbes is instructive.

In his book-length history *The Maritime Rights Movement*, Forbes never refers to populism, but he arguably goes much further by suggesting that its broad-based proponents actually constituted populist subjects. Forbes characterizes regional protest in the Maritime Provinces as the "spontaneous expression" of "the people."[19] According to this analysis, the Maritime Rights Movement "had its roots firmly grounded among the deepest concerns and aspirations of the people – aspirations of a political, economic, social, and cultural nature which were seriously threatened by the relative decline of the Maritime provinces in the Canadian Dominion."[20] This broad, heterogenous range of "aspirations," which correspond to the "rights" of "Maritime Rights," was fundamental to the constitution of political identity itself. It was, in effect, what Laclau describes as the "plurality of demands which, through their equivalential articulation, constitute a broader social subjectivity."[21] In short, it was this construction of the "Maritime people" as the embodiment of these heterogenous demands, as a popular *political* identity, that constituted the movement's populism. Thus, the accuracy of Forbes's characterization is not as important as is the political logic that underpins the analysis. Whether the specific objectives of the movement were rooted in the cross-class aspirations of the regional majority, or whether they represented the class-specific interests of the urban bourgeois elite, is inconsequential to the populist appeal of *The Busy East* and the movement it championed. What is key is the political identity generated by the movement's liberal-populism. And it is the intersection of classical liberalism and regional populism that makes the magazine's discursive appeal at once so unique in the context of interwar Canadian politics and so fundamental to modern political identity in the region.

The second reason *The Busy East* was remarkable before the middle of the decade has already been suggested: it was resolutely committed to the social, economic, and political modernization of the Maritime Provinces, providing a conspicuous counterexample to narratives of regional antimodernism. The magazine was central to what Greg Marquis sees as a "countervailing discourse of modernity" in the region, "as expressed through the media, business, politics, the arts and popular culture."[22] Marquis points to "the pages of the *Busy East*" as evidence that many in the region celebrated, rather than resisted, "economic and technological modernity."[23] And if there is anything that reflects the magazine's editorial direction between the wars, it is this pervasive representation of the Maritime Provinces as a modern industrial society. Countless articles and editorials extolled the "rapid and successful development of the Maritime Provinces,"[24] the need for a "broad vision with an ever-widening horizon,"[25] and the "industrial forward movement" of the "Eastern Provinces."[26] In 1919, R.V. Sharp proclaimed the limitless "growth" to be found in the region's "industrial future," a future "arriving daily" with the realization that "Maritimers … are not weary old pioneers" but "modern Canadians."[27] Images of textile and clothing factories, steel plants, concrete grain elevators, refineries, hydroelectric developments, residential and commercial urban development projects, ocean liners, and aeroplanes all saturated the pages of *The Busy East*. The editors never missed the chance to pair articles on regional subjects with images of industry, commerce, and urban development.

Even in the rare instances when imagery consistent with the folk paradigm appeared, it was always qualified by the magazine's overriding imperative to modernize. Thus, when Victoria Hayward's article "Sea Coast Homes of Our Maritime Provinces," was reprinted in *The Busy East* in 1921, replete with photographs of "fisher-folk" and fishing villages situated on rocky coasts, it appeared with a reassuring mouthful:

> The new roads, the autos, the modern builder, the agriculturalist, the large number of summer tourists, the shipbuilding, the improved methods of fishing, improved drinking water systems, direct and indirect foreign trade, library and lecture centres, expansion in railroads all radiating from and meeting again in Halifax – Queen of the Maritime cities – holding in her hand the fate, among other things, of these little homes, will all come soon.[28]

Nothing, it seemed, could stop the inexorable spread of progress to even the remotest villages of the east coast. And the beneficence of this onslaught of modernity was never questioned in *The Busy East*; even after severe recession triggered a socio-economic crisis in the summer of 1920, it was never suggested that the replacement of traditional society with modern capitalism could be anything but desirable.

It is remarkable, in fact, how unreservedly the magazine's editors endorsed this modernizing ethos, welcoming the "radical changes in industrial, social, and economic conditions" that would surely, they supposed, entail "new discoveries, new inventions, new devices for the benefit of people, new advances in art and literature, and the creation of a nobler world."[29] Obviously, this was not an outlook rooted in traditionalist conservatism. At the core of the magazine's vision for modern society was the liberal individual and the conviction that liberal-capitalist society would ensure opportunity and just rewards for those willing to toil and "pay the price of [their] best work."[30] If the diligent individual just used "his brains and common sense," the "rapid and wonderful changes of the new era" presented no threat, only opportunity.[31] As journalist H.S. Congdon succinctly put it in an article on transatlantic trade in 1923, "get busy and you get prosperity."[32] In this respect, *The Busy East* can be situated at the fore of what Jody Mason describes as the "slow and uneven installation of liberal common sense in Canada."[33] And here as elsewhere, an array of fantasies emanated from this liberal common sense: upward mobility, bootstrapping, and the incontrovertible justness of meritocracy were all prevalent themes. As Avard remarked in his article "Merit Is the Supreme Test," it was always "a great pleasure to chronicle the advancement of any man who has come up through the ranks, demonstrating his ability over heavy odds."[34] Accordingly, the belief that anyone who "devotes his life to one particular line of work" will "climb the ladder of success" underpinned many of the magazine's biographical articles, as well as the personal and business advice given in the editorial and "Business Man's Corner" columns, throughout the interwar period.[35]

Inasmuch as the philosophy of *The Busy East* expressed the increasingly commonplace values and beliefs of classical liberalism, however, it also evinced new liberalism's support for state intervention in the interests of social welfare. In his editorial "The New Spirit of the Age," Avard wrote of the new ethos of "getting together" that was transforming social and political life the world over, shaping everything from civic administration to international relations. Quoting Harvard professor William Bennett Munro, Avard acclaimed "the social revolution" taking place in the "hearts and minds" of the people: "the day of individualist and individual property rights has passed away forever in favor of the new ideal of community happiness and welfare."[36] It was up to the state to "step in and take over a great many economic and humanitarian enterprises hithertofore conducted privately or not at all."[37] This was not the classical liberalism of the previous century, with its narrow emphasis on negative rights, economic freedom, and individual liberty, nor even the non-state charity of progressive reform; this was the emergent sensibilities of modern, welfare-state liberalism.

This new liberalism would continue to inform the magazine's editorial outlook throughout its tenure, but the confidence with which it was expressed was not to last. When the brief post-war boom ended abruptly in the summer of 1920 and a severe recession set in, the magazine was forced to shift its focus from the expansion of social welfare to the management of crisis. In this radically transformed social and economic milieu, the magazine would never abandon its liberalism, but it would increasingly articulate that ideology through the logic of regional populism.

CRISIS AND THE POLITICS OF MARITIME RIGHTS

The precise cause of the region's economic decline after 1920 has long been a matter of scholarly debate. The problem perplexed renowned Canadian economist John Kenneth Galbraith, who pondered how "economic development skipped over" a region situated between the "world's leading economic hotspots – Western Europe and the eastern seaboard of the United States."[38] What is clear, however, is that 1920 marked the beginning of an economic crisis from which the region would never fully recover. "It is scarcely exaggeration," write historians Margaret Conrad and James Hiller, "that the Great Depression started nine years early in the Maritimes and Newfoundland."[39] Between 1920 and 1925, nearly half of all jobs in the region's manufacturing sector disappeared, and the decade witnessed the out-migration of roughly twenty percent of the region's population.[40]

The dominant political response to the economic crisis was the Maritime Rights Movement, a non-partisan regional protest and reform movement that aimed to remedy the economic plight of the Maritime Provinces by seeking redress from the federal government. It was led by politicians, businessmen, and professionals who organized around the Maritime Boards of Trade, but it gained widespread support amongst most occupational groups and across class divides.[41] Its leaders conducted a national campaign that involved frequent delegations to Ottawa, economic and political conventions, a strident propaganda and pamphlet literature, and national speaking tours.[42] It was promoted by newspapers throughout the region, but it was *The Busy East* that became the movement's "official organ" by resolution at the September 1920 meeting of the Maritime Board of Trade.[43] Despite this, the magazine's crucial role as the vehicle for regional protest has been entirely overlooked. Correcting that oversight not only reveals how the magazine's liberalism informed the ideology of the movement, it also illuminates how the magazine's popular literature helped interpret that liberal ethos to a reading public.

Scholars disagree as to where the Maritime Rights Movement should be situated on the political spectrum, with most historians accepting Ernest Forbes's interpretation that the movement was effectively without an ideological core. Historian Don Nerbas, however, has proposed a different interpretation. Pointing to the leadership role of Saint John's bourgeois elite beginning in the mid-1920s, Nerbas argues that the movement was shaped by significant "ideological and class biases" and fundamentally grounded in bourgeois liberalism. For Nerbas, the movement did not simply express the "deeply held concerns of ordinary Maritimers," as Forbes contends.[44] Rather, "enduring liberal notions surrounding the sanctity of the contract and the benefits of private enterprise structured [the] regionalist discourse" of the decade.[45] Nerbas's revisionist analysis of the movement's liberalism not only offers a corrective to studies that see the movement as ideologically empty, but also provides a framework in which the liberalism of *The Busy East* can be properly situated at the centre of this broader regionalist discourse. Accordingly, Nerbas points to a 1921 article that appeared in both *MacLean's* and *The Busy East* as an early example of regionalist arguments that were "deeply rooted in the logic of liberal capitalism."[46] Later, these arguments were taken up by the especially vocal Saint John merchant, and one-time Liberal politician, A.P. Paterson. For Nerbas, Paterson's case was premised on the "lynchpin of classical liberalism: the sanctity of the contract."[47] Paterson argued that more favourable freight rates, greater regional political representation, restructured transportation policy, federal subsidies, tariff protection, and the dismantling of interprovincial trade barriers did not involve federal charity. Rather, they were part of the federal government's contractual obligation under the terms of Confederation.

Paterson's liberal logic accorded well with the editorial politics of *The Busy East* and its modernizing, meritocratic ethos. His argument, which drew on the so-called "compact theory" of Confederation, was predicated on the "*laissez-faire* liberal assumption that capitalism was a progressive system, where the industrious prospered and the lazy floundered."[48] Moreover, Paterson repeatedly advanced these arguments in the pages of *The Busy East* itself. In the February 1929 issue, Paterson declared that the deindustrialization and decline of the Maritime Provinces resulted from the violation of the "covenant of confederation," "a treaty upon which the imperial act of union is based" and which guaranteed "protection of the Maritime Provinces from unjust burdens and handicaps."[49] Paterson thus deployed the vocabulary of negative rights alongside arguments for economic freedom, with "moral authority resting upon the classical liberal notion of contractual obligation."[50] Combined with the populist appeals to "the people" of the Maritime Provinces, Paterson effectively advanced an argument for increased integration into the liberal state under the guise of a quasi-nationalist regionalism. And this populist-liberalism was particularly well suited to *The Busy East*.

Over the course of the decade, *The Busy East* gradually began to target readers beyond the region's business community. It did so, in part, by expanding its literary and cultural content, and in part by making broad populist appeals that politicized regional identity. From at least 1919, Avard attempted to position the magazine as more than simply an instrument of the region's bourgeois commercial and political elite: it was to be the voice of the Maritime people. In fact, reasoned F.B. McCurdy in a sympathetic piece in the September 1919 issue, the two were not really so distinct, for the Maritime Board of Trade had "the people behind it."[51] McCurdy's coauthors agreed; the organization of the region's commercial and political leaders was the "only real force" for "waking the people up" to the necessity for unity, and through it, concluded N. Rattenbury, "our people" will "fight for the rights of the Maritime Provinces."[52] Ten years later, when his lengthy "Maritime Disabilities within Confederation" appeared in the February 1929 issue, Paterson argued that the "the people … had been doped and duped by education and propaganda into submitting to injustice to advance the interests of Central Canada."[53] Paterson began and ended that tract with the same admonition: "remember your breed – you are a Maritime people."[54] Such arguments discursively constructed "the people" in antagonism with an oligarchic other, identified variously with central-Canadian political elites and big business. As Nerbas explains, in the dominant regionalist discourse advanced by the proponents of Maritime Rights, "contesting the idea that Maritime decline resulted from central Canadian political machinations was indicative of regional disloyalty."[55] To be of the Maritime "people" was to identify the source of one's own sense of injustice not with something inherent in the political or economic system, the liberal order itself, nor with the nation-state, but with powerful political and economic groups who had, according to this narrative, abused and manipulated that system and violated the constitutional principles of Confederation.

These appeals were not merely rhetorical. As David Frank observes, the urban bourgeoisie, "more than any other social class … succeeded in identifying its interests with the larger cause of regional patriotism."[56] The "Maritime people" was constituted as the embodiment of the movement's heterogenous demands, as a common-sense popular identity that united the sometimes-contradictory claims the movement advanced. There can be no doubt that the proponents of Maritime Rights voiced legitimate grievances.[57] But popular identity cannot be constituted based on federal subsidies or freight rates alone; the sense of social and political injustice that gave unity to the "Maritime people" thus necessarily exceeded the totality of individual demands and grievances articulated by Maritime Rights. This sense of injustice was carried forward in the pages of *The Busy East* even after the 1926 report of the *Royal Commission on Maritime Claims* began to diffuse regional protest by disaggregating the movement's individual demands and making select concessions to regional interests. That report would quickly shift the direction of regionalist discourse from opposition to the inequitable structure of Canadian federalism to resolute support for the integration of the region into the liberal state.

The Busy East thus continued to appeal to "the Maritime people" even as it became evident that the Maritime Rights Movement was, increasingly, "not regionalist but nationalist in its ambitions."[58] Accordingly, the magazine's success at winning popular support to its political project hinged, in part, upon its ability to conceal the fact that the economic liberalism it endorsed had failed to prevent the collapse of the region's industries, resulting in widespread unemployment and precipitating an unprecedented socio-economic crisis. The idea that uneven development was in fact inherent to liberal capitalism, and thus at the root of the region's economic woes, never posed a threat to the liberal idealism of *The Busy East*. Rather than forming the core of a communitarian ideal, the regional subject that the magazine constructed vis-à-vis central-Canadian nationalism was imagined firmly within the framework of liberal citizenship.[59] In this way, the magazine coupled regionalism with individualism to sustain a vision of progress that stood in defiance of historical contradiction.

And this unfaltering faith in the beneficence of liberal progress, and the fantasies it provoked, would find its surest expression not in the magazine's polemical articles or its optimistic features on civic modernization, but in the popular war fiction it published after 1926.

THE LIBERAL FANTASY OF WILL R. BIRD

> Every human emotion ran its full gamut in that land of topsy turvy, and prolonged tensity of feeling wrought strange psychological changes which warped the soul itself … Unconsciously there were born faiths that carried men through critical moments, and tortured minds grasped fantasies that served in place of more solid creeds.
>
> Will R. Bird, *And We Go On*

In the June 1924 issue of *The Busy East*, a full-page advertisement announced the serialization of H.A. Cody's novel *The King's Arrow: A Tale of the United Empire Loyalists*. Cody's successful historical romance had appeared two years prior in 1922, but Avard's decision to purchase the exclusive rights to republish the novel signalled an important shift in the magazine's editorial policy. The appearance of the novel suggested not only Avard's desire to make the magazine more appealing to the general public through popular literature, but also a willingness to pay for literary contributions. No writer would take advantage of this new publishing venue as reliably as Will R. Bird, whose first contribution to *The Busy East*, "The Loyalty of Lieutenant Pringle," appeared in the April 1926 issue. This issue is particularly indicative of the magazine's aspirations to fulfill a literary as well as a political-economic role. In it, two articles of regional history and popular science counterbalance two articles on regional economy and industry in Nova Scotia; together, the literary contributions of Cody and Bird account for fourteen of the issue's thirty-two pages. It was in the following year, however, that Bird's association with the magazine began in earnest. In April of 1927, he published the first of his war stories there; he would subsequently publish a story in nearly every other issue for the next six years. By 1930, as one reviewer in Moncton's *The Daily Times* observed, Bird had become "a writer of note, well known [for] his contributions in *The Busy East*."[60]

So, for a period of more than five years, Bird's fiction comprised the vast majority of *The Busy East*'s literary content, injecting the prosaic and the polemical with the optimism of a fantasy born, paradoxically, of the cataclysmic horror of the First World War. His stories invariably avowed the rightness of the liberal common sense endorsed by the magazine and its contributors, but they added to those polemics an affective dimension that exceeded the sense of grievance and injustice attaching to Maritime Rights. In place of the limited regional subject conceived in antagonism, Bird's fiction offered readers the limitless potential of the liberal subject. From the wreckage and horrors of the First World War, Bird recovered an abiding faith in the promise of liberalism, "[salvaging] liberal individualism from the very war that others saw as its erasure."[61] While other veterans-turned-writers indicted the futility of the war, rendering dehumanization central to their narratives, Bird found within it the resources to assert a yet more resilient fidelity to notions of the coherent, sovereign self. Though he never shied away from vivid depictions of violence, Bird vigorously rejected the nihilism he detected in "sordid, sensation-seeking" anti-war novels such as Canadian veteran Charles Yale Harrison's *Generals Die in Bed* (1930) or Erich Maria Remarque's *All Quiet on the Western Front* (1929), the latter of which Bird reviled as "putrid with so-called 'realism.'"[62] Yet Bird's fiction was not, as his own invective suggests, free of "realism." In his best stories, moral and psychological conflict figure as an aesthetic tension between realism and romanticism, between realist depictions of depersonalizing violence and the romantic imperative to see the individual prevail intact and unvanquished. If brutality and violence threaten the integrity of the self, as they frequently do in Bird's stories, they never reduce the soldier to a "coarse-minded, profane creature."[63] It is this capacity of the individual subject to persevere and prevail – whole, integral, and spiritually, if not physically, inviolate – that constitutes the fantastic in Bird's stories.

By suggesting that Bird's fiction offers a liberal "fantasy," I mean first and foremost to draw on the sense of desperation that Bird himself attaches to fantasy in the context of war, those "fantasies" that were "grasped" by "tortured minds" and "served in place of more solid creeds."[64] In this sense, the fantastic implies individual agency and integrity in excess of what is plausible under the conditions he describes. To be sure, this implausibility generally detracts from the quality of Bird's popular stories, which almost invariably end in moments of disconcerting bathos. But within the formulae of Bird's fiction, this implausibility is not accidental; it is precisely the incredibility of his protagonists' personal triumphs that affirms the primacy of the transcendent liberal subject, the promise of upward mobility, and the potential for individual perfection. Thus, though Bird's fiction never offered an explicit, coherent theory of liberal individualism – or any explicit politics, for that matter – it did much to supplement the more prosaic polemics of Maritime Rights. Bird's fiction dramatized the fantasies through which affective investment in the liberal project was continually reproduced as common sense.

In this respect, Bird's war fiction partook of what Lauren Berlant describes as "the older state-liberal-capitalist fantasies" that continue to shape "adjustments to the structural pressures of crisis and loss."[65] For Berlant, such fantasies include not only social mobility, secure employment, and social and political equality, but also meritocracy and the assurance that liberal-capitalism will dependably provide individuals with economic security and opportunity to realize meaningful, fulfilling lives – in effect, many of the same promises on which the confidence and optimism of *The Busy East* were predicated.[66] If we understand fantasy, following Berlant, to entail the blending of the real and the imaginary through desire, the "harnessing [of] affect to political life," then Bird's war stories engage in precisely this sort of fantasy-work, expressing a Romantic-inflected desire for the individual to rise above the brutality and violence of war.[67] As I have suggested, this fantastical aspect of Bird's fiction is central to the cultural politics of interwar regionalism in *The Busy East*; yet it is also significant for what it reveals about the passing of the war into Canadian popular fiction, and the relationship of that fiction to the liberal political imaginary.

Though Bird has been mostly lost to the annals of Canadian literary history, he was arguably the most prolific Canadian chronicler of the Great War, and his influence on a generation of Canadian veterans was unparalleled. A veteran of the First World War who served with the Nova Scotia Highlanders and the Black Watch between 1915 and 1918, Bird produced five books, numerous non-fiction articles, and dozens of short stories about the war. As Thomas Hodd points out, "no Canadian author who served overseas has published more on the First World War than Will R. Bird."[68] More importantly, writes historian Jonathan Vance, Bird was the "unofficial bard" of the Canadian Expeditionary Force and his works enjoyed "immense popularity … among veterans."[69] But Bird's popularity was not confined to veterans. Between his war fiction and his tales of historical romance, Bird sold a staggering 552 short stories to magazines across Canada, the United States, and Europe. In the words of McKay and Robin Bates, "[there] was a time when, if the literary marketplace could speak, it might have sounded a lot like Will R. Bird."[70] More than a mere purveyor of liberalism, Bird was the prototypical agent of cultural entrepreneurship in Canada, a herald of what one writer in *The Busy East* proclaimed to be culture as commodity, "the industrial meeting of [a] new art consciousness."[71]

Since the 1990s, a revival of interest in Bird's writing has focused on his once-celebrated memoir *And We Go On* (1930), ""the 'lost classic'" of Canadian war literature.[72] Critics, however, have been split over how to interpret the politics of that writing. Bird's memoir figures prominently into Vance's argument in *Death So Noble: Meaning, Memory, and the First World War* (1997) that a conservative "war myth" was "central to Canada's memory of the Great War."[73] McKay and Robin Bates disagree, insisting that Bird "creates unavoidable difficulties for any dominant, homogenizing, organic, and conservative myth of Canada."[74] Bird's early war fiction tends to support the latter reading. Far from conservative, Bird's short stories affirm what McKay and Bates detect in Bird's oeuvre generally: a conviction in "the truth of liberalism – namely, the ontological and epistemological primacy of the individual."[75] Ignoring Bird's early war fiction, however, McKay and Bates overemphasize Bird's intentional "naivety" and "Innocence."[76] The result is that they take Bird at his word and stress his "active and self-aware resistance to … realism" without acknowledging the generic tension between realist and Romantic conventions in Bird's short stories of the 1920s.[77]

In fact, Bird's decision to write predominantly short fiction was itself a significant generic choice. In the introduction to his anthology of Bird's war stories, Hodd suggests that the short story form allowed Bird to create narratives more "diverse" in "perspective and outcome" than in his memoirs.[78] And elsewhere, Hodd suggests that Bird's stories are "especially deserving of critical attention" because they are "neither uniquely romantic nor realist."[79] Hodd is ultimately less concerned with the tension between realism and Romanticism than with the short story form itself, but his point about generic balance is an important one. At the same time, though Hodd acknowledges *The Busy East* and its successor, *The Maritime*

Figure 4.2 Members of the Royal Canadian Highlanders 42nd Battalion, with which Bird served in the First World War, in the Grand Place, Mons, on the morning of 11 November 1918.

Advocate, as significant venues, he singles out three pulp magazines as the "main outlets" for Bird's fiction.[80] In fact, Bird published in *The Busy East* more regularly than he did in any other single magazine. Though not all his contributions to the magazine were war stories, the war figured prominently in most of his stories of the 1920s, and many of the stories he would later publish in magazines such as *The Legionary* and *War Stories* first appeared in *The Busy East*. Such was the case with Bird's "His Deputy," which appeared there four months prior to being reprinted in *The Legionary* and which Hodd places at the fore of his collection. That story, with its ambivalent critique of authority and command hierarchy, its compromised realism, and its preoccupation with the self, offers a productive place to begin reading Bird's liberal fantasy.

"His Deputy" introduces settings, themes, and tropes to which Bird returns repeatedly in the pages of *The Busy East*. Some of these, such as the progressive degradation that accompanies incursions into no-man's-land, instill even his most sentimental war stories with a thread of realism, however bare. Though not always rescuing stories from shallow sentimentalism, this realist thread checks any purely romanticized depiction of war in Bird's fiction. The populist anti-authoritarian bent of nearly all Bird's protagonists similarly frustrates a uniformly favourable interpretation of the war experience. Meanwhile, other motifs, such as the frequency with which Bird's protagonists appear with noticeable disabilities – the protagonist of "His Deputy," for instance, is initially rejected from service because of a missing finger – are in fact grounded in Bird's own experience (Bird was twice prevented from enlisting for medical reasons). Any one of these tropes might offer a perspective from which to analyze Bird's representations of the war, but it is the relationship between naming and identity that forms the governing conceit in "His Deputy" and several other stories that would follow in *The Busy East*. In these stories, names function as ambivalent markers of personal identity – sometimes tokens clung to by soldiers amidst the homogenizing mass of the rank and file, at other times mere surface inscription, beneath which is to be found the moral and metaphysical core of the individual. In either capacity, names and naming offer not only an expedient means by which to individuate characters on a level deeper than surface appearances, but frequently also the plot devices around which stories are constructed.

Yet, as literary topoi, Bird's use of naming can appear almost aggressively contrived. Such is the case in "Priscilla's Private," in which the identical initials of two men underpin a romantic rebuff to hereditary privilege and a forthright celebration of rugged individualism. If "His Deputy" establishes key settings, motifs, and tropes through which Bird expresses his liberal fantasy, "Priscilla's Private" goes further by suggesting who qualified as "individuals" in Bird's fiction. The eponymous Priscilla is a young woman "anxious to divide herself from the common people," the "vulgarly materialist" "plebeian herd."[81] Accompanied by her as-yet-aptly-nicknamed companion Doggy, she travels from Toronto to Saint John in search of a soldier glimpsed on a platform at Union Station. She knows only his "aristocratic" name, Harold Roy Heathland, but she and Doggy manage to track him down. Alas, Harold is something of a deadbeat, not at all the man Priscilla remembered. Impending "catastrophe" is seemingly averted, however, as she begins to appreciate that the "faithful efficiency" of the "rugged and virile" Doggy eclipses the "ease, culture, travel, [and] privilege" she attached to Harold.[82] This crescendo reaches an absurd pitch when Priscilla has an epiphany: Doggy's true initials, H.R.H, are identical to Harold's. All along, it was loyal Doggy, a self-made man and "coming leader in insurance circles," for whom Priscilla had truly been searching.[83] Such pure contrivance is uncommon but not rare in Bird's war fiction. The manufactured moment with which "Priscilla's Private" concludes, however, is especially dissatisfying, denying agency to one of Bird's few women protagonists and reducing her judgment to the perception of a trite commonality. Obviously, it is Doggy, and not Priscilla, who emerges as the hero of the story; it is Priscilla's masculine sidekick, and not the protagonist herself, who proves himself an individual. In short, Bird's liberal fantasy is a male fantasy, conferring moral agency on subjects who are invariably white and masculine. Of course, this fact is not evident in most of Bird's war fiction; the front lines provide a setting from which women are conspicuously absent, and this makes "Priscilla's Private" somewhat exceptional.

Though "Priscilla's Private" is unique among Bird's war stories for taking as its protagonist a woman on the home front, the story is finally void of psychological depth, exhibiting none of the complexity that critics such as Williams and Vance find in Bird's memoirs. Instead, Bird substitutes sanguine, chauvinist romance for a more searching exploration of the moral complexities of wartime civilian life. Nevertheless, the story complements the remarkable optimism of the issue in which it appeared, an issue that proclaimed, just months after the 1929 stock market crash, that the economic depression was caused, "in a very real sense, by yielding to pessimism."[84] It was no matter that Nova Scotian industry had "struck rock bottom" or that the region faced not "the spectre but the fact of unemployment."[85] For Avard, hard work, determination, and optimism would "eventually see [the region] through the present crisis."[86] In fact, one suspects Bird of consciously pandering to *The Busy East*'s tireless assault on "defeatist pessimistic psychology"[87] when he has Doggy casually remark, as he gazes out the window of a train bound for Saint John, that it "looks prosperous down here."[88]

More to the point, Doggy becomes for readers of the magazine the embodiment of the "grit and determination and stick-at-it-ness" to which Avard refers on the page directly adjacent to Bird's story.[89] It matters little that millions are dying overseas, that the now-maligned Harold Heathland is a veteran living in squalor, or that Priscilla effectively curtails her aspirations of a more fulfilling existence to settle with Doggy; what matters is that Doggy's hard work, enterprise, and loyalty have won him affection and success. What Doggy shares with the protagonist of "His Deputy" – apart from a missing finger – is precisely this tenacity, this "stick-at-it-ness." More than mere character traits, these are the moral virtues that assure these men will prevail as individuals. And so, as Doggy and Priscilla motor off into a moonlit night, the reader is left with not only a happy ending, but also the promise of limitless potential, for "one could dream and make believe all they wanted to with [Doggy]."[90] However facile, "Priscilla's Private" translates the magazine's liberal ethos into the realm of fantasy, in which the objects of one's desire, Priscilla and prosperity, are yet attainable for the diligent and industrious (male) individual.

Not all of Bird's war stories in *The Busy East*, however, are dependent upon unequivocally romantic plots. More successful than either "His Deputy" or "Priscilla's Private" are those stories that evoke the severing of name and identity as the result of the war itself, or those that dispense with the naming motif altogether to register a more profound sense of self-estrangement. In such stories, the war is less a background against which to accentuate individuals than it is a real and imminent existential threat. The protagonist of "The Major's Prisoner," an "uneasy" and "stocky figure," goes unnamed until he tries to introduce himself to another man, only to be told that there is "'no use makin' acquaintance up here. They get killed off so fast you're just learnin' names for nothin.'"[91] He eventually distinguishes himself in an improbable, if not heroic, feat, but not before succumbing to misery and losing much of his "faith in human nature."[92] Appearing several months later in August 1930, "Umpty-Ump" further explores anonymity as an aspect of wartime experience. Passing through countless "war battered villages" to the monotonous "tramp, tramp of army boots in darkened streets," Private Tim Meeker's identity is reduced to an indefinitely long regimental number that no one cares to recite.[93] Plagued by visions of his name on "little white crosses," Meeker is finally told that his grave, should he die, will go unmarked; the sergeant responsible will "make no special crosses" to fit a ten-digit number.[94] These characters enter conflict with a sense of self already deadened by the indifference of those around them, and the recovery of selfhood becomes integral to the resolution of the story's conflict as well as the protagonists' survival. But it is Bird's attempts to convey the incomprehensible violence experienced in the Ypres Salient that raise parts of his fiction above mere formula, even as the romantic imperative works to accommodate realist representations to the conventions of the heroic quest.

The realism of Bird's war fiction is always a compromised realism, but it is no less fundamental to his representation of the war than the romantic framework in which it is deployed. For Hodd, Bird's war stories provided a "a form of psychological realism which his fellow veterans would have had little trouble relating to."[95] More than this, though, the realism that Bird intermittently evokes within the broader constraints of literary romance provides a generic precondition for his liberal fantasy. It is precisely the dehumanization that Bird describes in realist terms that imparts meaning and significance to the transcendence of the self. This realist dimension has been obscured, however, by the importance most critics attach to Bird's explicit rejection of "sordid" fiction and "so-called 'realism'" in his preface to *And We Go On*. A reading of Bird's fiction, however, might instead look to the preface of his novel of the same year, *Private Timothy Fergus Clancy* (1930), for insight into his generic sensibilities. There, Bird concedes rather than rejects realist representation, recognizing that "it is impossible to ever forget or omit the horror attendant on those old battlegrounds, the grimness of war, the sordid wretchedness of trench life in the Salient or on the Somme."[96] Far from refusing realistic depictions, then, Bird acknowledged their necessity to any serious representation of the war.

And yet, the incorporation of "horror" and "wretchedness" into Bird's romantic formula presents something of a representational challenge. For Bird, it was the circumstances into which soldiers were forced, and not the soldiers themselves, that constituted the horrific, the sordid, and the wretched. As a result, Bird frequently initiates his descriptions with explicit appeals to ineffability, implying a fissure between the soldier and an environment that exceeds intelligibility. In "His Deputy," Red enters the "unspeakable" Ypres Salient;[97] the protagonist of "Boots," Gerald Marrack, looks out over "an indescribable desolation";[98] and in "His Brother," Private Tim Meeker is overcome by "the indescribable wreak [*sic*] of blood" as he witnesses scenes that far surpass "the vivid horrors his imagination had wrought."[99] When Bird does move beyond the ineffable, it is to register the effects of this incomprehensible violence on individual psychology – the estrangement of individuals not only from their environment, but also from themselves.

In his attempt to accurately depict those experiences that threaten the psychological and moral sovereignty of the individual, Bird evokes an atmosphere pervaded by the uncanny. Descriptions that play upon light and shadow produce a chiaroscuro effect reminiscent of silent film.[100] The "fiery glare" of intermittent gunfire in "Boots" emits "flashes that [light] the trench walls with a bizarre effect, disclosing the rows of waiting men, whitening their bayonets."[101] Light is put to similar effect in "The Major's Prisoner," in which the protagonist's first glimpse of the battlefield reveals a spectral panorama: "Directly in front of him all was dark, but to his right the Hun flares rose and fell describing fleeting parabolas of brilliant light and casting strange shadows over a weird landscape."[102] Using vocabulary reminiscent of the opening passage in "His Deputy," Bird describes a landscape that is almost Gothic in its elicitation of horror, but which nevertheless remains credibly within the perceptual field of his protagonist.

The "strangeness" and "weirdness" of Bird's war-torn landscapes thus engender a menacing quality that comes into tension with the heroic plots of his romantic formulae. To be sure, this is not unadorned reportage; rather, the psychological realism Bird achieves in these descriptions is meant to register precisely the same "prolonged tensity of feeling" to which he refers in the preface to his memoir, an excess of affect that "wrought strange psychological changes."[103] In this atmosphere of sustained terror, protagonists experience visceral moments of defamiliarization as they attempt to comprehend scenes that cannot be assimilated to the realm of ordinary experience. Looking out over no-man's-land, Tim Meeker "saw barbed wire entanglements, and he noticed it did not have a semblance of the spaced perfection he saw at Bramshott. Flares were moving all the time, making weird, moving shadows in the wilderness beyond the wire, giving a ghastly sheen to its rubble heaps."[104] Difference elicits dread in this initial passage, but the familiarity of the setting in the next renders it nightmarish, as "ghostly, wavering light" illuminates a landscape "that [is] all the same, a wilderness of craters and rubble heaps."[105] This strange familiarity of the landscape, rather than its foreignness or its lack of "semblance," generates the anxiety Bird's protagonists struggle to dispel.

As characters are forced beyond the wire, entering the muddy, treeless territory between the trenches, the uncanny crystallizes into a feeling of anxiety that imperils the coherent identity of self and subject. As soldiers struggle to make sense of their surroundings, to return to the familiar, this anxiety manifests in a blurring of the horrific and the commonplace. Taking shelter in a crater, Tim Perkins is happened upon by a German soldier, but what he notices in the "revealing light" of a flare is not a weapon or some similar threat, but the man's "spectacles, huge, grotesque things."[106] As Gerald Marrack clambers out of a dugout, several men are instantly shot ahead of him, yet he can only contemplate why these men "pitch forward in a drunken sort of way."[107] When he is caught in an artillery barrage, it is not the "trembling" figures or "stark and cold" bodies of those around him on which Marrack fixates, but a haversack that falls over the parapet and bursts a few feet away: "He gazed stupidly at its contents: a pair of socks, a razor, a dirty towel."[108] In these moments, the protagonist's retreat to the commonplace intensifies rather than alleviates his terror as the familiar and mundane are rendered suddenly alien.

In those stories in which such psychological stress is prolonged, Bird's characters pass a breaking point, and instances of derealization give way to self-estrangement. As Perkins ventures beyond the front line, he becomes increasingly detached from the reality of his surroundings. The chaotic, "ear-splitting" sound of shell fire competes with cries that "penetrate the air with a peculiar pathos," introducing a discordance that mirrors Perkins's fracturing sense of self.[109] A succession of violent images – "corpses, their uniforms indefinite, rotten on broken parapets. A broken foot extended, the toe burst open. Shreds of torn khaki [flapping] eerily on wire strands" – gradually instils in Perkins "a fear that [verges] on insanity." For a brief period, this gradual accrual of dehumanizing experiences, the "culminative terror" of "unparalleled horrors," is coupled with the spectral presence of the dead – the return of the uncanny in the form of haunting doubles – and Perkins becomes totally self-estranged, "a stranger to himself."[110] Yet, Perkins's degraded psychological state is inevitably transitory. Convinced by an officer that his brother is holding the front line, Perkins recovers his mental faculties and resolves to fight. Injured, but now assured that his brother is not "up ahead," Perkins exults in "delirious triumph,"[111] which has nothing to do with patriotism, but rather with the consciousness of some "duty done" at the close of the story, a duty consisting in the recuperation of self-hood.

Perhaps unsurprisingly, when the monumental horror of the war, captured so viscerally in Bird's best stories, yields to the indefatigable will of the individual, the results are often bathetic. Having shot an unarmed prisoner and struggled through crushing nihilism, Private Parsons gathers his courage and captures two more German prisoners. Wounded in the effort, he resolves to go home and "go fishin'."[112] A similar fate awaits Private Marrack: having witnessed "horror unspeakable," he buries his inner conflict, dispels his fear, and saves his platoon from an ambush.[113] As he is carried out on a stretcher, he laconically remarks to the orderly, "see if you can't ship my boots along with me too … I've [just] got them broken in properly."[114] It would be easy to dismiss these conclusions as mawkish, even failed endings. But they are never misplaced. However aesthetically dissatisfying, the romantic imperative that Bird fulfills with unswerving fidelity is vital to the working out of his liberal fantasy. In Bird's fictive world of war, psychological trauma becomes prerequisite to the affirmation of the liberal subject. As realism gives way to romantic closure – merging fact and fiction, the real and the imaginary – fantasy is consummated in the figure of the pure, autonomous individual. For all the aesthetic potency and realist accuracy with which Bird renders his topological and psychological portraits, mimesis must ultimately yield to the imagination. And so, as surely as the nightmare of the Salient takes its toll on Bird's characters, those same characters recover the mental resources necessary to transcend their dehumanizing circumstances; Bird's characters do not merely survive, they emerge unbroken and exulted.

POST-POLITICS AND THE REGIONAL SUBJECT

Obviously, we are not to read Bird's popular war fiction as consciously and intentionally expressive of the specific liberal-regionalist project advanced in *The Busy East*. Bird's characters never commit themselves to any coherent, explicit politics, and their populist complaints are never tied to regional or national affiliations. More to the point, Bird did not see his war writing as 'political' at all. For Bird, these stories dramatized accurate, veritable memories of the war. They were episodes unearthed "from the dugouts of experience" to sharpen "edges of memory [already] beginning to wear thin."[115] In his memoir, argues Vance, "Bird made an explicit claim for the veracity of his own memory."[116] In his short stories, the claim to veracity is implicit, but still governs Bird's representation of war. As Hodd maintains, "the short story form afforded [Bird] the ability to depict the smaller events that made up the bulk of the real war experience."[117] Thus, Bird's fiction must be situated in oblique relation to Canadian novels of the Great War, a genre, argues Colin Hill, characterized by several "aesthetic and narratological challenges."[118] Certainly, we find at the core of Bird's war fiction some of the "tensions" being negotiated by Canada's modern realists, tensions "between romanticism and mimesis, subjectivity and objectivity, fact and fiction, traditional realism and experimentalism."[119] So too, Bird saw himself as giving an accurate, authentic, and therefore "true" depiction of the war, but in doing so, he never adopted the uncompromising realism of writers such as Charles Yale Harrison or Erich Maria Remarque.[120] Bird never abandoned the basic formulae of literary romanticism because his improbable romantic peripeteias conveyed what he took to be a more essential truth: the inviolable sovereignty of the individual.

Between 1926 and 1936, Bird published more than sixty-five stories in *The Busy East* and its successor, *The Maritime Advocate and Busy East*. These stories provided the cultural complement to a political discourse that was, by the mid-1920s, thoroughly liberal and often only nominally regionalist. What Bird's stories shared with the magazine's explicit politics was a common matrix of values and assumptions orbiting the free-standing individual. Both Bird and Avard were engaged in what McKay, in his influential essay "The Liberal Order Framework," describes as the "intensive process of subjectification, whereby liberal assumptions are internalized and normalized within the dominion's subjects."[121] Bird "normalized" liberal common sense not by denying the catastrophic fissure of the war or its psychic effects on soldiers, but by repeatedly imagining the transcendent liberal subject into being as an object of popular aspiration and desire. Thus, Bird never articulated a coherent politics, but his stories staged the fantasies – perfectionism, meliorism, and rugged individualism – upon which *The Busy East*'s liberalism depended for its legitimacy.

And it was with an affirmation of the individual, rather than the regional subject, that *The Busy East* concluded the decade in its January 1930 issue, the same issue in which Bird's story "Boots" appeared. Quoting from American writer and philosopher Elbert Hubbard, the cover featured "The Successful Man's Creed," assuring readers that "a man gets what he goes after" and that "there is something doing, somewhere, for every man ready to do it." Capping off a decade that witnessed the flight of nearly one-fifth of the region's total population, Hubbard's quote expresses a profound, albeit unintended, irony. In the lead editorial, Avard ruminated on what constitutes "a successful life."[122] Reasoning that "each individual has his own ideas of what constitutes success," Avard offered a series of fundamental principles to which any individual could adhere, among them "the value of time," "the success of perseverance," "the pleasure of working," "the worth of character," and "the wisdom of economy."[123] These were the principles – in effect, self-restraint, hard work, thrift, and character – that underwrote the magazine's faith in the future, not a conservative commitment to sustaining an organic regional community. And though the magazine's regional focus never abated, the articulation of regionalism through the politico-economic logic of liberal capitalism undermined the magazine's appeal to regional solidarity.

Whatever the apparent merits of this regenerated faith in individualism – the recovery of liberalism from the wreckage of the war, in defiance of severe socio-economic crisis – the regionalist discourse of *The Busy East* neither dispensed with earlier assumptions of regional cultural homogeneity, nor mounted any challenge to the exclusionary premises whereby the regional subject was imagined as Anglophone, European, white, and male. In fact, the magazine and Bird's fiction, in particular, are indicative of the extent to which interwar conceptions of the "individual" remained extremely limited, corresponding not to an abstract, universal entity, but to a racialized, gendered, socially specific, and historically situated ideal: the white, propertied, atomistic man. This was not the slow but sure advancement of liberal democracy toward multicultural egalitarianism, whereby "[more] and more people were brought aboard the good ship, and the unsightly detritus of the past vanished into the distance."[124] To the contrary, interwar liberalism and regionalism alike shared a racialized and masculinist ideal of subjecthood. Such attitudes were seamlessly accommodated to an emergent discourse of liberal citizenship. The region must avoid all "selfish insularity," wrote L.W. Simms in an article on progress in the June 1929 issue; immigration posed no threat, so long as it involved "a process of assimilation that conserves and elevates the high ideals in our native citizenship."[125] In short, individuality would be extended only to those whose race and gender qualified them for adequate liberalization.

In retrospect, it is easy to detect the contradictions submerged beneath the magazine's confident platitudes. The region's socio-economic crisis had quickly given way to the Great Depression, the devastating consequences of which were indisputable by 1930; and yet, the magazine continued to assure readers of the "revival of progress in the Maritimes."[126] Similarly, the relatively inconsequential concessions of the Duncan Commission on Maritime Claims, which tended to increase rather than alleviate the region's dependency on a centralized national economy, were welcomed in *The Busy East* as "herald[ing] the progress of the day."[127] It is with a profound irony that Avard declared in the January 1930 issue that "the beginning of better things can be said to date from the implementing of many of the sections of the Duncan Commission on Maritime *Rights*."[128] The distinction between "Rights" and "Claims" had not been lost on the commissioners as it was on Avard; as Frank notes, "the Duncan Report was a highly political document" and it "repudiated the Maritime Rights version of regional history" even as it acknowledged the need to provide a "sympathetic hearing for the region's pleas of incapacity."[129] The report did little, if anything, to remediate underdevelopment and deindustrialization in the region because it was never intended for that purpose. According to Donald Savoie, "King's objective in establishing the commission was to diffuse Maritime agitation and to engage in a policy of delay," and in this "[h]e succeeded."[130] It would be rash, however, to equate King's success with the failure of regional protest.

Whether one considers the Maritime Rights Movement to have failed or succeeded depends largely upon whose interests the movement is supposed to have served. If, as Forbes maintained, "the regional focus failed to yield expected results," it was not so for all social classes in the region.[131] To the contrary, the region's political and urban elite had much to gain from the wedding of liberal common sense to the cause of regional protest. Nerbas points out that in Saint John, "Maritime Rights represented an important political and ideological victory for a transformed local bourgeoisie."[132] According to this reading, the politics of regional protest – worked out and expounded in the pages of *The Busy East*, dramatized in the stories of Bird – were successful insofar as they facilitated the region's integration into Confederation and the Canadian liberal order.

The populist appeal through which the "Maritime people" came to be politicized in regional discourse never identified the region's ills with something inherent in the economic system. Instead, the regional subject was constructed and imagined via "an ideology that assumed the interests of capital and those of the community to be one and the same."[133] This is not to suggest that *The Busy East* and the movement it represented were never genuinely regionalist, but that the politics of accommodation and concession that this ideology expediated at the close of the decade foreclosed any substantive alternatives to the Canadian liberal order (an order that regionalism once claimed to have resisted), including the more radical communitarian critique posed by conservativism at the beginning of the decade. In effect, the success of Maritime Rights was to initiate a period of post-politics in which liberal hegemony prevailed largely uncontested. When a more conservative regionalism began to re-emerge at the end of the decade, it did not appear as a threat to liberal hegemony, but as an antimodernist cultural politics whose practitioners were "conservative in their social imagination (idealizing the permanence and stability of the rural social order) and liberal in their political economy."[134] This shift in *cultural* politics, epitomized by Bird's rather sudden turn toward antimodern historical romance and travel writing in the early 1930s,[135] was seamless. Ultimately, the modernizing ethos of *The Busy East* and the liberal fantasy of Will R. Bird formed but a small part of this broader move toward the post-political; yet, their heretofore unrecognized contributions to the discursive formation of interwar liberalism reveal much about the fraught history of modernity in the Maritime Provinces, and specifically its manifestation in the region's periodical culture. That history remains entirely inadequate, however, without registering the significant and vocal resistance to the liberal order mounted by the radical left. No periodical in the region – and, arguably, no contemporaneous periodical in Canada – was more militantly opposed to the emergent liberal common sense than *The Maritime Labor Herald*.

5

Left Transnationalism, Socialist Feminism, and *The Maritime Labor Herald*

Stepping into the Glace Bay office of *The Maritime Labor Herald* in 1924, *MacLean's* magazine reporter Norman Rein Reilly found a "bare,""dingy," L-shaped room with a few "rough wooden forms":

> The walls were dull red and held pictures; one of Karl Marx, three of Lenin, and a large colored lithograph from an Italian radical magazine. This picture, called *La Rivoluzione*, featured a long-haired, wild-eyed girl in scarlet, flanked by waving red flags, leading armed and frenzied workers along a road, against a lurid background of burning factories.[1]

The description of the room suggests a dreary existence of deprivation and despotism. But it is not intent on fearmongering; the image is, rather, a palliative. The radicalism here, the image suggests, is not a threat born of profound discontent, but merely marks the importation of foreign ideas read in foreign magazines. The workers here, for their part, had been duped – "inarticulate" and "impotent," they threw their support behind radical movements "for the gift of expression."[2] Even the *Herald*'s editor, James Bryson McLachlan, exhibited "plenty of hard, common logic beneath his communistic nonsense."[3] Unmentioned in the article is that the office of the *Herald* had been suspiciously set on fire during a protracted strike three months earlier, for the third time in three years, or that the paper's staff had been dragged from the office into the street and beaten three months before that.[4] Whatever Reilly thought of the paper's "fiery articles denouncing capital," there were many who deemed *The Labor Herald* a real and substantial threat to their interests and to the liberal order that sustained them.[5]

Entirely neglected beyond regional labour histories, *The Maritime Labor Herald* must be numbered among the most militant periodicals of the Canadian left during its five-year run from 1921 to 1926. A self-styled "journal of opinion,"[6] the *Herald* advanced a multifaceted program aimed at educating and organizing the working class toward the overthrow of capitalism. Appearing well before the 1930s, the height of proletarian print culture in Canada, the *Herald* helped initiate a new form of radical, avowedly communist journalism in which working-class resistance at local and regional scales was articulated as an aspect of proletarian internationalism. It was consciously translocal and transnational in scope. Nationalism and imperialism, deemed instruments of bourgeois capitalism, were subjected to frequent critique, while the region formed the practical scale at which global class conflict manifested as proximal, individual battles between labour and capital. It was in this regard that the literary helped mediate between the local and the global, conveying to the *Herald*'s readers that their own struggles were not only worthy of art, but also of a piece with a worldwide movement of working-class resistance. As the expression of a proletarian culture that was not limited to the space of region or nation, the poetry in the *Herald* helped consolidate shared meanings and common reference points. In this way, the *Herald* exploited the mass mediation of proletarian literature to foster and politicize a collective class identity that was not so much deterritorialized as it was translocal and transnational.

Of course, bound to the orthodoxies of the Old Left, this class consciousness did not incorporate a broad-based identity politics. Prioritizing class, the *Herald* largely ignored forms of identification that might complicate the universalist dogma of international socialism. The *Herald*'s stance on questions of race, in the rare instances it was mentioned at all, was contradictory: overt racism on issues of immigration coincided with support for anti-capitalist and anti-colonial struggles in Southeast Asia, or with denunciations of racial inequality in the justice system. The exception to this exclusive focus on an abstract (but tacitly white, Anglophone) working-class identity was the journal's attention to gender equality. To be sure, the paper consistently articulated a masculinist ideal of the working-class. The "worker," not unlike the liberal individual mentioned in the previous chapter, was rarely an unfractured, universal political category, but an historically specific and gendered ideal. However, the paper also dedicated ample space to prominent women on the left – many of whom were members of the Communist Party of Canada (CPC) – and instituted a women's column before anything similar appeared in the CPC's official paper, *The Worker*. Moreover, these writers – most notably Rose Henderson, Lucy Woodsworth, Becky Buhay, and Florence Custance – dealt directly with the "woman question," offering sophisticated analyses of the role of women in industrial capitalism and class conflict. In the final analysis, then, the *Herald* must be recognized as a significant vehicle for socialist feminism at mid-decade, even as the paper never moved beyond its preoccupation with working-class masculinity.

All of these discursive struggles played out in a paper that was, materially as well as ideologically, a collective effort. The *Herald* was published "by the workers for the workers" and the vast majority of its roughly 2,500 shares were owned by locals of Nova Scotia's District 26 of the United Mine Workers of America (UMWA).[7] Nearly all of those who took on leadership roles founding and producing the journal identified as socialists, and by 1922 most would be members of the CPC. McLachlan, who joined the CPC in 1922, was the driving force behind the paper's creation and was its proprietor from its inception, though he would not take on an official editorial role until 1924. J.S. Woodsworth initially accepted and then declined an invitation to edit the paper, and so the position was filled by William Ulrich Cotton, a lawyer and journalist from Cowansville, Quebec, who had edited the successful socialist paper *Cotton's Weekly* (1908–14).[8] Cotton edited the paper until spring 1923 when the position was taken over by Tom Bell, a prominent CPC organizer from Winnipeg. Printing expertise was supplied by Douglas Neil Brodie. A printer who had apprenticed in Halifax before moving to Glace Bay and setting up a printing firm there in 1900, Brodie was active in the Socialist Party of Canada, through which he met McLachlan. When the *Herald* was formed, McLachlan purchased Brodie's printing plant and Brodie agreed to serve as printer, publisher, and secretary-treasurer of the paper.[9] By 1922, the *Herald* had well over six thousand paid subscriptions, rivalling the circulation of many dailies.[10] It ran to eight pages, was published weekly, and featured at its core a "Voice of the Worker" column containing letters to the editor and resolutions from union locals.

Throughout its tenure, the *Herald* crusaded against two opponents: the British Empire Steel Corporation (Besco) headed by Roy Wolvin and the reactionary executive of the UMWA led by John L. Lewis. It is difficult

Figure 5.1 James Bryson McLachlan, 1933.

to overstate the significance of the *Herald* in spearheading the battles of District 26 against national and international corporate and labour leadership in the 1920s, but it is important to recognize these specific battles were always identified with – were, in fact, inherently implicated in – a broader transnational struggle against liberal capitalism. And though much of each issue was dedicated to local news and original political analyses, the *Herald* was also an early member of the Federated Press Service, which was formed in 1920 as "the first news service that provided affiliated papers with international reports of interest to the working class."[11] The journal also regularly published political analyses and directives by prominent figures of the Communist International (Comintern). And from its inception, but especially after 1922, the *Herald* dedicated space to original poetry. Its contents were thus wide-ranging and eclectic, and its arena of analysis far-reaching, even when the journal focussed its editorial energy on particular struggles of immediate concern to its shareholders.

The battles fought by District 26 in the 1920s have been well-documented in regional labour histories and in biographies of the communist union activist J.B. McLachlan.[12] But those histories, focussed as they are on the social movements of which the paper was a part, do not treat the *Herald* as an object of study in its own right, nor do they acknowledge the integral relationship between the literary and the political in the construction of working-class identity. As such, they fail to register the extent to which the *Herald* structured the discursive field of working-class culture in the region and pioneered a new, more radical journalism of the left in Canada, one that predates the "heyday of proletarian literature and arts beginning in the 1930s."[13] In fact, though Canadian leftist periodicals of the 1930s have received considerable attention in Canadian literary and print-cultural histories, studies of labour newspapers from all periods have been comparatively limited.

It is the Depression decade, rather than the 1920s, that is frequently deemed to have been the crucible of a renewed, if not new, proletarian culture in Canada. In particular, the publication of proletarian poetry – though only one facet of the complex literary culture developed in leftist periodicals – has been deemed integral to the expression of working-class identity during this period. Thus, following Cary Nelson, Dean Irvine argues that the "publication of poetry in working-class newspapers … marks the broader transformation of poetry's public and cultural function during the 1930s."[14] By emphasizing working-class consumption over production, argues Irvine, the "publication and reception of proletarian poetry in working-class newspapers assigns value to what Raymond Williams calls 'common' culture."[15] Irvine's comments here have particular relevance for the circulation of leftist periodicals at the national scale at a time when modernist poets were increasingly drawn to the left. But the "transformation" to which he refers was not inaugurated with the collapse of stock markets in 1929 and it did not strictly result from the intersection of leftist literary culture and literary modernism in the 1930s.

THE MARITIME LABOR HERALD
Our Books Open to the Advertisers
WEEKLY
Vol. 1 $2.00 PER YEAR. Glace Bay, Nova Scotia, Saturday, July 1, 1922 FIVE CENTS COPY No. 38

TRURO CONVENTION MARKS HISTORIC EPOCH

CRISIS COMING IN THE STATES

Social Democracy Will Be Won In Five Years

Continued on Page 4

Miners of District 26 Lead Canadian Labor Movement

Continued on Page 4

U. M. W. TAKE GREAT STAND

Nova Scotia Miners Draw Up Historic Document

Continued on Page 6

TWO EDUCATIONALISTS

Elliott Stands for Robbery, While Hadley Tells the Truth

Continued on Page 4

THE GAZETTE AND LABOR

Its Hostility Creates an Incentive Among the Workers to Be Radical

Continued on Page 8

WHAT THE MEMBERS ARE SAYING

The Rumblings of the Coming Revolution Echo Through Parliament

By J. S. WOODSWORTH

Continued on Page 5

Figure 5.2 The cover of *The Maritime Labor Herald*, 1 July 1922.

A more comprehensive historiography of proletarian literary culture in Canada must move beyond canonical modernists on the left and attend to those periodicals that predate the Depression. As Nelson points out, "[the] sense of rapid use – of poetry written to play an immediate role in public life – was not unique to the Depression."[16] Moreover, argues Nelson, "what distinguishes this phenomenon in the modern period" is, in part, "the means of circulation, the possibility of mass participation in the reading of poetry."[17] In the *Herald*, this potential for mass participation was augmented by the directions that accompanied poems, which instructed readers "to cut this out and save it with your pluck-me slips [pay stubs]" or to "cut out [these] poems and paste them in your scrap book."[18] Such instructions foreground the materiality of the text, demanding attention to the ways in which poetry became implicated in the everyday lives of working-class readers. Shorn of the aura attaching to the autonomous aesthetic object, the poetry in the *Herald* was at once positioned in reciprocal relation to the full range of the journal's contents and attained a life beyond the pages of the journal – through its preservation in a scrap book, or among pay slips, but also through its circulation via oral recitation and public display. At the same time, the literary significance of the *Herald* does not derive from its publication of poetry alone; its contribution to what Irvine calls a "'common' proletarian culture" depended rather upon the interplay of the literary, broadly construed, the polemical, the political, and the everyday within the mixed format of the newspaper.

The *Herald*, then, must be recognized as a significant antecedent to the more abundant leftist periodicals of the 1930s. As such, it provides a conspicuous and early example of how "literariness has been historically entwined with real labor struggles."[19] Nevertheless, it is important to recognize that the specific geosocial conditions out of which the *Herald* emerged were also exceptional in the 1920s, a period when "labour across Canada was in retreat following the defeat of the Winnipeg General Strike."[20] For Nelson, the cultural milieu of Depression-era America was shaped by a "general paradox": "hunger and unemployment and the many difficulties of everyday life went [hand in hand with] a sense of impending revolutionary change."[21] Several factors contributed to similar conditions in Cape Breton after the First World War, making it receptive to radical politics and uniquely productive of proletarian culture. A precondition for this was the creation of Besco, which became the largest industrial consortium in Canada after a merger of several firms in 1921.[22] By this time, the industrial communities in Cape Breton held one-fifth of Nova

Scotia's population, generated two-thirds of the province's revenue, and accounted for roughly half of Canada's entire coal production.[23] But the steel and coal industries were not isolated from the region's economic crisis of the 1920s and they did not prosper. Guided by an optimist corporate structure dependent upon unrealistic levels of market stability, "Besco was compelled to reduce its costs, [and] the reduction of workers' wages seemed to be the obvious strategy for corporate survival."[24]

For workers, this meant that their already-deplorable living and working conditions were steadily eroding at the beginning of the decade. In 1921, the infant mortality rate per 1,000 births in Sydney was 175.9 and in Glace Bay 305.9, compared to the national average of 88.9;[25] the average fatality rate for miners in Nova Scotia from 1908 to 1920 was an exceptional 3.75 per 1,000 men employed; and the wage rates paid in District 26 were considerably lower than those paid in Alberta's District 18.[26] Miners' families lived in company shacks that one writer in the *Sydney Post* described as "a positive disgrace to the most filthy parts of Constantinople ... little more than graveyards where humans are buried before they are dead."[27] Here were the severest effects of the region's socio-economic crisis, experienced by the region's most vulnerable class of waged workers. In the *Herald*, condemnations of these desperate conditions were coupled with an insurgent idealism, the acute sense of "impending revolutionary change" that Nelson deems characteristic of later Depression-era culture. Constantly fighting to improve their conditions and to block repeated wage reductions, the miners and steel workers of Nova Scotia conducted dozens of strikes, including three major strikes in 1922, 1923, and 1925 that would account for a staggering two million striker days.[28] This near-constant labour action, coupled with the workers' dehumanizing conditions, imbued the *Herald*'s revolutionary rhetoric with an immediate relevance.

From the outset, the *Herald* positioned itself in direct opposition to bourgeois liberalism and the mainstream press. Week in and week out, Cotton assailed the "kept press" of "capitalist pen flunkies who spill[ed] ink daily" trying to mollify the "growing, menacing, and threatening working-class."[29] But for the first several months of its existence, the paper stopped short of explicitly endorsing the radical left, adopting instead the reformist vocabulary of labourism.[30] This early reticence to declare, unambiguously, a communism-oriented editorial policy might suggest a pragmatic response to state repression in the wake of the Winnipeg General Strike. The normalization of wartime emergency laws through the enactment of Section 98 of the Criminal Code in 1919 – a broad statute that gave authorities in Canada the power to "target individuals or groups that expressed support for or advocated communism"[31] – meant that writers, editors, and intellectuals on the left had to negotiate a repressive legal and political climate. And yet, even in the earliest issues of the *Herald*, the journal's contributors barely concealed their ideological alignments. Thus, in an editorial in the 3 December 1921 issue, Cotton announced the paper would dedicate space to discussions of "transcendentalism and empiricism, of materialism and mysticism … of Bergsonian philosophy and its relation to the philosophy of Heraclitus, not to mention pragmatism, and a whole lot of other 'isms.'"[32] Of course, it was the 'isms' not mentioned in Cotton's tongue-in-cheek list – communism and Bolshevism – that subtended the magazine's critiques of liberal capitalism.

Increasingly, the *Herald* dispensed with the more subdued rhetoric of labourism in favour of an overtly militant discourse of revolutionary change. In the 17 June 1922 issue, Cotton clarified the role of the *Herald* as a medium of education, agitation, and organization. The "real function" of the *Herald*, wrote Cotton, was "to be a journal of opinion" and to "[devote] space rather to the interpretation of current happenings than to recording them."[33] Not unproblematically, Cotton drew on the discourse of slavery to justify the paper's mission.[34] The workers, wrote Cotton, "are supporting the Herald as an educative paper, to explain why and how the working class are in slavery, and how the working-class can overthrow the system that causes the slavery."[35] The journal's global perspective and pedagogical purpose were borne out in several articles in the same issue. Alongside local and international labour news appeared an explanatory article on historical materialism, an essay on liberalism and "freedom of contract," and an account of parliamentary activity by J.S. Woodsworth.[36] On the second page was a telegram from McLachlan to Vladimir Lenin regarding a proposed distress loan to Russia and a reply to McLachlan's telegram accepting the loan signed by Lenin's deputy, Alexei Rykov.[37] On the editorials page, an indictment of the Royal Canadian Mounted Police, "the gun-toting, strike breaking darlings of the capitalist class,"[38] appeared above an editorial comment on unemployed veterans warning that "ex-service men know how to hold a gun and they may not be content to starve in peace."[39] Inflammatory though it was, the issue charts several themes – notably pedagogy, transnationalism, and critique – that would define the paper for the duration of its existence.

Just as significant as the journal's editorializing, however, was the extent to which its militant rhetoric both reflected and shaped the politics of its readers: the workers who owned the paper. Two weeks after Cotton clarified the *Herald*'s role as a journal of education and agitation, the paper published a resolution from District 26, passed at its annual convention in Truro five days earlier, proposing to create a "united front of workers in Canada" and to affiliate with the Red International of Labour Unions (RILU). The resolution concluded with a declaration of rebellion: "we proclaim openly to the world that we are out for the complete overthrow of the capitalist system, peaceably if we may, forcibly if we must."[40] As John Manley observes, Tim Buck, who was then industrial director of the CPC and a speaker at the convention, was initially dismayed by the "slate of ferociously leftist resolutions," and worried that he would be held responsible by the party for the District's incaution.[41] Buck's worries were misplaced; in the recently established party paper *The Worker*, Maurice Spector deemed the document "inspirational."[42] This key document thus thrust the miners of Nova Scotia into the vanguard of the Canadian left, but it also revealed the extent to which the local and regional labour movement was envisioned and advanced as part of a global, anti-capitalist struggle. A remarkable feature of the document, argue Ian McKay and Suzanne Morton, is the way in which the "immediate problems of survival" are articulated in terms of "an urgent call for a global revolution."[43] The *Herald* had taken this balance between the local and the global as an organizing principle, anticipating – and, under the direction of McLachlan, influencing – the workers' commitment to the international left. In fact, the paper itself was not peripheral to the pivotal Truro declaration: the *Herald* was given a loan of $5,000 at the convention, and in the months following this decisive turn to the left, public discourse would centre on what McKay and Morton deem the journal's "ultra-radicalism" and its support for communist internationalism.[44]

From its inception to its demise in 1926, the *Herald* was targeted not only as a leading exponent of the left in Canada, but also as a conduit for an ostensibly dangerous form of political internationalism. In fact, leftism and internationalism were never treated as discrete facets of the *Herald*'s editorial program. As Patrizia Dogliana points out, the concept of "internationalism" itself was intimately linked to socialism: "In the political and public arena, the term 'internationalism' … long implied the idea and nature of 'socialism,' reflecting Marx and Engels' call to the working classes of the world to unite."[45] Accordingly, socialism was frequently positioned as a threat not only to liberal capitalism, but also to bourgeois nationalism. In the *Herald*, internationalism was cast as the necessary response to global capital: "international capitalism makes it necessary for all the workers of the world to present a united front to the capitalist class," wrote Cotton in July 1922, "so the class war is a far flung war that ranges wherever there is a capitalist and a wage worker."[46] This, the fundamental principle of proletarian internationalism, certainly shaped the *Herald*'s editorial program, but it never implied the denial of local circumstance or national particularity.

Discussions of the *Herald* in regional and national newspapers, among moderate labour, and in the political arena, however, consistently deployed notions of foreign influence and invasion. In June of 1922, the *Glace Bay Gazette* assailed the *Herald* as "an organ of international socialism" that had taken hold of the working-class to "impregnate their minds with revolutionary ideas, hostility to 'capitalism,' and class hatred."[47] A month later, Tom Moore, president of the Dominion Trades and Labor Congress, suggested that the "very real menace" posed by the *Herald* owed principally to the "teachings of Soviet Russia," the "mad creed of the Bolshevists," and "the dangerous policies of communism." According to Moore, the *Herald* advocated "revolutionary tactics" over "constitutional methods," not because the latter had consistently failed to redress the appalling conditions of life and work in the region, but because the paper was an instrument of a Soviet-directed communist movement.[48] In turn, the "extreme radical movement in Nova Scotia," as *The Globe and Mail* called it, could be imputed to the "Red doctrine" that the *Herald* "preached incessantly."[49] In these reports, the *Herald* was not the expression but the cause of working-class radicalism, simultaneously a product and an agent of international communism. As Besco official F.W. Gray put it to Nova Scotia Premier E.H. Armstrong, "[u]niformly provocative and seditious, [the *Herald*] persistently gathers together as part of one organized revolutionary movement every outbreak against constituted authority throughout the world."[50] However sensational, these characterizations rightly identify communist internationalism as a significant component of the journal's editorial politics. Misplaced, however, is the presumption of a unidirectional line of influence, according to which the *Herald* was the mere mouthpiece for a local, Soviet-controlled cabal.

In fact, internationalism alone is inadequate to account for either the local, material conditions of the *Herald*'s production or the paper's contribution to a leftist discourse that cut across national boundaries. This discourse was sustained by a transnational network of writers and journalists, few of whom were beholden to the directives of the CPC and the "Moscow line." However, the paper's devotion to the policies and leading figures of the Comintern and its enthusiastic support for the affiliation of District 26 with the RILU largely obscure its transnational character. Moreover, as McKay and Oleksa Drachewych argue in *Left Transnationalism*, the Comintern itself must be understood as not only an international body, but also a "transnational" movement, "in which intellectuals and activists developed networks that tied them together with others, without direct involvement of Moscow, and in which ideas and inspirations flowed over national borders without its central direction."[51] The *Herald*, which was never an official organ of the CPC and which, as a periodical, could not itself affiliate with the Comintern, was a vehicle for precisely this sort of transnational exchange. The paper entered into and circulated in what Bridgitte Studer describes as the transnational space of communism, "with its dense exchanges of persons and information," a space "extending beyond the national cultures that configure[d] it."[52] The *Herald*, then, is best understood as an intermediate between the local context of class struggle, in which only a minority of its readers were officially members of the CPC, and a transnational space of proletarian culture constituted as much by shared symbols, representations, and purpose as by affiliation with the Third International. This, what McKay and Drachewych term "left transnationalism," offers a far more useful framework in which to situate the *Herald* than the rigid, top-down model implied by communist internationalism alone.

The editors, writers, and readers of the *Herald* can thus be seen to have constituted a community not unlike that which Andrée Lévesque attributes to other organizations associated with the CPC, "a community that operated across borders," "that considered itself above the confines of nation, [and] one that shared a habitus."[53] By contributing to a sense of shared culture and community, the *Herald*, like the more formal communist organizations examined by Lévesque, helped to foster among its working-class readers a "collective class identity that was not limited to their factories or to their country."[54] Part of this process of transnational identity formation was pedagogical, part of it involved the dissemination of international news through the federated press, and part of it involved the promotion of common celebrations, commemorations, and symbols. The *Herald* drew on and emphasized such common symbols and celebrations, as when it reported on Glace Bay's May Day parade in 1923, when more than five thousand marched behind "the biggest red flag in Canada" emblazoned with "Long Live Communism,"[55] or when it announced the marriage of "comrades" Dan Smith and Mary Mollish, "married under the red flag" after a ceremony at St. Anne's Church in Glace Bay.[56] Such reportage provides some indication of how the symbolism, iconography, and vocabulary of the left had been integrated into the daily lives of many workers; but it also reveals the importance that the *Herald* attached to the symbolic dimension of a transnational proletarian culture.

As important as those shared symbols that circulated across borders were the transnational figures who served as special correspondents to the *Herald* – writers who could draw connections between distant class conflicts in Europe and Asia and working-class resistance in the coal fields and steel plants of Nova Scotia. Rose Henderson, an Irish Canadian journalist, social worker, and socialist feminist, served as special correspondent for the *Herald* from 1922 to its demise. From England, Scotland, and Ireland, Henderson contributed articles on topics ranging from "The Irish Question" and British parliamentary politics to "England's Surplus Women." In "Capital Internationalism," Henderson compared the situation of Welsh miners to that of miners in Nova Scotia, America, and Europe. She argued that miners everywhere had been "pitted" against one another and must become "as class conscious as their exploiters and recognize their international solidarity and interdependence."[57] Elsewhere, Henderson wrote extensively on the Irish Civil War. As Peter Campbell points out, in articles such as "Civil War in Ireland" Henderson offered direct analyses of the Irish situation, but "her real purpose was to use that situation to communicate ... international significance." Henderson drew on the "Canadian working-class reality of the unemployment of the postwar period," explains Campbell, to attack militarism and military spending in Canada and Ireland alike.[58] Henderson's journalism certainly drew parallels between Irish workers and their Canadian counterparts generally, but it is also important to recognize the urgency and relevance that Henderson's anti-militarism would have had in Nova Scotia when it appeared in the 16 September 1922 issue of the *Herald*. The article was published exactly one month after more than 1,200 soldiers – a quarter of Canada's standing army in 1922 – were sent to Glace Bay in response to a 100 percent strike by the miners of District 26. It was these sorts of direct, salient parallels that most effectively fostered a sense of transnational solidarity and identity. Writers such as Henderson thus interpreted to working-class readers the transnational linkages that not only brought the relevance of foreign class conflicts into focus, but also imbued local struggles with national and global significance.

And in addition to Canadian foreign correspondents like Henderson, the *Herald* featured local writers who described their travels abroad, particularly in Soviet Russia. Notable among these was Roscoe Fillmore, a Nova Scotian horticulturalist and socialist activist who travelled to the Kuzbas colony in Siberia in 1923 to work as a horticultural expert.[59] The *Herald* published a series of articles by Fillmore the same year. In "Peas, Potatoes, and the Proletariat in Kuzbas," Fillmore described his journey from Nova Scotia to Hamburg to Moscow to Siberia and assured readers that "the class conscious worker who travels over Russia and works in her industries knows in his bones that the revolution is a success."[60] In "Travelling in Russia" and "May Day in Petrograd," Fillmore continued his positive descriptions, lauding the hospitality of the Russian people, detailing the small successes won by his Russian comrades, and discussing the ravages of the "imperialist war."[61] Throughout, Fillmore maligns "Red Scare" caricatures of Russia as the product of "the distorted imaginations of various prostitute journalists writing for the capitalist press of Europe and America."[62] In retrospect, his rosy impressions of Soviet Russia appear ludicrous – his first meal in Russia is "roast goose" and he is adamant that state repression and "strict censorship … exist not in Russia."[63] Nevertheless, the direct, first-person form of his address, referring directly to the reader, and the trajectory of his narrative, which takes him from rural Nova Scotia to Siberia, help to create the perception of proximity and continuity, a perception that is reinforced by its juxtaposition with local and international news, letters, and advertisements.

In fact, the sense of a collective and transnational working-class identity that emerges from the mingling of local news, socialist symbolism, items of analysis, and travel narratives was dependent upon the mixed format of the newspaper. The juxtaposition of letters, ads, and articles on collage-like pages suggested the imbrication of the cultural, the political, and the everyday across spatial scales. In the *Herald*, this effect was heightened by a lack of clear divisions. Though the paper featured sections such as "Voice of the Worker," "The Editorial Page," and, after 1923, "The Women's Column," these sections were never discrete or self-contained. Fillmore's "Travelling in Russia," for instance, was published on the "Voice of the Worker" page, below a letter from a worker in New Aberdeen on housing conditions there and adjacent to another letter from Sydney Mines on dual unionism in Canada. These are accompanied by advertisements for Hinchey's bedding store in New Waterford, Tingley's Drug Store in Glace Bay, and several smaller ads for local and regional businesses. On the same page appears an unsigned article on the British Columbian lumber industry, which, in the wake of the Great Kantō Earthquake in Japan one month earlier, had raised the price of lumber to profit off the demand for coffins for the dead and homes for the homeless. The juxtaposition implicitly parallels Besco's refusal to replace "dilapidated shacks" in New Aberdeen with the exploitation of "a stricken people" in Japan.[64] The laconic conclusion to the latter article thus applies equally to both: "such is the way that human sympathy affects the bourgeoisie."[65] In every issue, the paper emphasized this impingement of transnational events, processes, and ideas on the everyday lives of workers, a relationship that was explicitly reinforced in analyses by writers such as Henderson, McLachlan, and Cotton. And it was in this respect that the proletarian poetry published in each issue helped to consolidate a sense of common culture and collective class identity.

POETRY AND PROLETARIAN TRANSNATIONALISM

Just as transnational exchanges of information and news allowed the global to enter the local on any given page, so too was local experience politicized and elevated through the poetry that appeared in each issue. This poetry was definably proletarian: aggressively political, dogmatically leftist, class-conscious, and often without aesthetic pretension or formalist aspiration. Within and across individual issues, however, a key difference emerges between those poems that tend toward a more abstract, symbolic representation of international class struggle and those that engage the highly localized space of political action through the depiction of specific lives and events. These divergent but mutually reinforcing tendencies toward abstraction and particularism helped define the spatial sensibilities according to which transnational proletarian culture was localized and local struggles sublated into a vision of global revolution. Both were integral to the articulation of collective class identity and helped constitute the affective dimension of the *Herald*'s cultural-political program. The poems of Dawn Fraser and Joe Wallace, the most frequent contributors of verse to the *Herald*, are representative of these divergent tendencies.

Fraser, a poet and journalist from Oxford, Nova Scotia, contributed thirty-four poems to the *Herald* from 1921 to 1926, more than any other single poet. His first poem for the *Herald* appeared in 1922 and from 1924 to 1926 his poems appeared almost biweekly. In *Progressive Heritage*, James Doyle effectively sums up the bulk of Fraser's poetry, suggesting that it "relies on straightforward, unambiguous statement, occasionally tinged with irony and sarcasm, but uncomplicated by ambiguity of tone or complexity of idea."[66] This conversational idiom and forthright tone of address were invariably structured in lines of flexible iambic pentameter or tetrameter following simple rhyme schemes. It is perhaps because of this formal, stylistic, and linguistic simplicity that other critics have stressed the historical content and contexts of Fraser's poems without attending to what they do *as poems* within the textual field of the paper. In fact, Doyle goes so far as to suggest that "Fraser's writing scarcely seems to qualify as poetry at all."[67] Accordingly, Richard MacKinnon, whose "Protest Songs and Verse in Cape Breton" is the only article-length study of verse in the *Herald*, forgoes analysis altogether and situates Fraser within the folk-song tradition, while Don MacGillivray and David Frank, in their introduction to Fraser's *Echoes from Labor's Wars* (1992 [1926]), focus strictly on the biographical and historical context of Fraser's poetry. The tendency of these critics to paraphrase and their reticence to analyze misses the significance the poems attain within their original site of publication, and they never attempt to determine the claim that poetry might have had on readers' attention. By contrast, Doyle goes some way toward correcting this critical oversight, arguing that Fraser's poems have "the potential strength of direct contact with human emotion" and are "strengthened not only by the emphasis on narrative, but also by the vivid impression that [the] narratives are true." For Doyle, Fraser "convinces the reader" that the suffering of workers in Cape Breton is real by communicating a certain affective intensity.[68]

But the thousands of readers who encountered Fraser's poems in the *Herald* each week did not need to be convinced of the veracity of their plight, nor was poetry likely to convert a reader to the radical left where essays had failed. The abundant analyses and polemics crammed into each issue had a much better claim to argument and persuasion. More revealing is Doyle's remark about narrative and affect. In the *Herald*, Fraser's poetry offered an affectively charged poetic that suggested to the paper's working-class readers not the truth of their experience, but its worthiness of art and posterity. In the most basic sense, Fraser's poems conveyed to readers that they were subjects in and of history. Narrating events as they unfolded, the poems integrated working-class experience into an historical narrative in which the collective figured as the agent of change. "The Case of Jim O'Coughlin," for instance, narrates the 1922 miners' strikes and the 1923 trial of J.B. McLachlan in 378 lines of heroic couplets. Though the poem celebrates the exploits of McLachlan, it is concerned rather with awakening political awareness than with individual triumph: McLachlan is of the "working mass," an agent of the "worker's cause" who sees "through the plan" of the "Capitalist Class."[69] The first installment of the poem also appeared just two months after McLachlan was convicted on charges of sedition and its final installment, with its injunction for workers to "fight on!," coincided with McLachlan's return to Glace Bay from Dorchester Penitentiary.[70] As such, Fraser's poetry often achieved an immediacy that was unmatched by the aesthetically superior poems alongside which it was published. In poems such as "The Crime of Johnny Kyle" and "The Case of Jim O'Coughlin," the defeats and victories of the miners became epic subjects. Unsophisticated and accessible, the poems succeeded in figuring the specific, detailed experiences of miners within a grand narrative of class struggle. The result was both an affirmation of the local, working-class cause and the integration of local figures such as J.B. McLachlan and "Red" Dan Livingston into the iconography of the radical left.

And despite their aesthetic limitations, Fraser's poems could deploy form and perspective to good effect. In his April 1924 poem "Cape Breton Miner and Besco," Fraser adopts the second-person perspective to situate the reader as the enslaved subject of the poem: "You will go into the mines, and toil all day / And work like a slave to keep hunger away. / You're slaving all day to provide us with coal: / But you don't get enough to keep body and soul."[71] Presented as a simple monologue, the poem obtains a sense of urgency through the use of future and present tenses, its second-person address, and its specific references to Besco, Cape Breton, and Newfoundland Prime Minister Richard Squires. Its conversational tone and rhymed couplets are accessible and forthright, and its referential scope is unambiguous: a miner reading Fraser's verse would know that they were to descend into Besco's mines the day after tomorrow, would know they were the subject of this poem. Thus, the poem does more than "[use] the quatrain format" to "[characterize] BESCO as an exploitative company," as MacKinnon tersely suggests;[72] it also interpellates and politicizes the working-class reader, transforming the reader into the subject of a class-conscious history that is at once local – manifest in the specific labour disputes and battles of industrial Nova Scotia – and global – of a piece with anti-capitalist struggles throughout the world. In this way, Fraser's poems communicated the history of Nova Scotia's working class to the very subjects of that history, providing narratives in which the expression of collective affect – shared frustration, sorrow, anger – was wedded to class consciousness. The frequency with which Fraser's poems appeared made this interpellation of working-class readers an important component of the paper's cultural appeal to a collective class identity.

In contrast to Fraser, Wallace offered a more sophisticated poetic sensibility, rendering modern subjects and social themes with a broader, international appeal. According to Doyle, Wallace was "the most successful, durable, and prolific of the writers associated with the Communist Party of Canada."[73] Though Wallace would later achieve widespread acclaim in the USSR and China, it was in the *Herald* that Wallace published much of his early proletarian poetry. Doyle is wrong to suppose that *The Worker* "introduced" Wallace to the reading public with its publication of "Awake!" in July 1923; the poem first appeared in the *Herald* in June of that year. In fact, all of the pre-1926 poems that Doyle refers to as "Wallace's *Worker* poems" – which, before 1926, "constituted the only distinguished literary contribution to the *Worker*"[74] – were first published in the *Herald*. This is significant, not for what it reveals about Wallace or his poetry per se, but for what it reveals about the function of poetry within the *Herald*. Read at its original site of publication, the "transcendent vision" Doyle identifies in "Awake!" complements the narrative poetry of Fraser, whose dramatic monologue "Tell My Friend, the Prison Warden, That I Hadn't Time to Call" appears directly below Wallace's poem. Whereas Fraser's poem recounts the particular – the attempted arrest of leading CPC member Malcolm Bruce in Glace Bay – Wallace's poem envisions solidarity among workers "in all lands" and "cities" across a "world locked in a struggle vast."[75] Together, the poems mediate between the proximate realities of radical labour in Nova Scotia and a deterritorialized ideal of revolutionary struggle, an ideal that defined transnational proletarian culture from the 1920s on.

Wallace's poetry thus provided a counterbalance to Fraser's localized narratives, a balance that was strengthened by the formal complexity of Wallace's verse. In his examination of literary modernism within *The Song Fishermen's Song Sheets* (Halifax, 1928–30), Bart Vautour positions Wallace in opposition to the Song Fishermen coterie's "bourgeois antimodernism." By using "conventional rhyming verse to develop alternative subjects in modernity," argues Vautour, Wallace's poetry "helps to open up the possibilities for modernism."[76] For Vautour, Wallace's poetry is modern not because it exhibits modernist formal experimentation, but because it rejects a romantic preoccupation with an imagined, nostalgia-laden past in favour of direct engagement with the conditions of modernity. Much of the poetry in the *Herald* is modern in this broad sense – modern in theme and subject even as it remains confined within the strictures of traditional form. Yet Wallace's poems in the *Herald* extend this engagement with modernity; though most of his poems are conventional, a few key texts break beyond traditionalism, demonstrating Wallace's willingness to affect a modern poetic sensibility in form as well as subject.

Representative of Wallace's efforts to experiment with form is his poem "The Rise of the Red River," which appeared in the 4 May 1924 issue of the *Herald*. The poem dramatizes the movement from the local to the global in twenty-one lines of free verse organized into stanzas of increasing length. The poem begins with a couplet that stresses the anonymity of the individual worker: "In an obscure spot, in a remote region, / An inconspicuous striker bites an indigestible bullet, doubles up, and dies." The couplet is followed by a single line, "A stain." The poem progresses accordingly, building toward an eschatological vision of communist utopia:

> The Red River, swollen with tributes from all times and countries,
> Bursts its banks and fertilizes the world
> With the bones of an extinct slavery,
> With the seeds of first born freedom,
> In the springtime, in the Red Dawn of the year.
> The ocean.[77]

Notably, the poem remains accessible and within the strictures of proletarian literature: its governing conceit, like its obvious political message, is uncomplicated. The accumulation of the water cycle parallels the organization of the working class; world communism, the poem suggests, is as inevitable as the running of rivers to the sea. But Wallace's rejection of rhyme and metre, his use of lineation to achieve a cumulative effect that underpins the poem's central metaphor, clearly marks a break beyond formal traditionalism. Moreover, "The Rise of the Red River" deploys formal experiment to communicate an epistemological shift similar to that which defined political poetry in the 1930s, namely the renunciation of individualism and the development of "a different kind of agency, one less self-absorbed and more directed toward the social text."[78] Agency in the poem is not achieved by the anonymous, individual workers, but by the collective. "The Rise of the Red River" stages the disavowal of what Nelson terms "expressive subjectivity"[79] in order to articulate a vision of international solidarity. The movement from the local to the global thus becomes coextensive with a progression from individual subjectivity to class consciousness. Ultimately, the formal experiment of "The Rise of the Red River," though present in other poems such as "Lenin Lies Asleep," was untypical of Wallace's verse. It was, rather, this radical epistemological shift – spatial as well as social – that marked Wallace's most significant contribution to the interplay of the literary and the political. And this interplay within the newspaper, the material form of the "social text," often entailed complementary rhetorical strategies, as with the juxtaposition of Wallace's and Fraser's verse, but it could also give rise to tension.

The poetry in the *Herald* did not merely lend affective weight to otherwise discrete items of analysis and news. Like articles, letters, and advertisements, poems were conditioned by their appearance within the discursive assemblage of the newspaper and, in turn, helped shape readers' engagements with the range of contents they encountered in any given issue. According to Nelson, political poetry of the 1930s "engaged in a continuing dialogue both with other poetry and with the other discourses and institutions of its day."[80] This dialogic was materially and textually manifest in the pages of newspapers like the *Herald*. In the most prosaic sense, the revolutionary poetics of Fraser and Wallace spoke to the same themes, issues, and topics that were articulated across various genres within the paper. All drew on a common rhetoric, vocabulary, and symbolism. More than this, though, poetry helped to interpret for readers the continuity between their own experiences and often-remote socialist movements elsewhere. Dramatizing the linkages that united geographically diffuse class struggles, poetry mediated between the local and the transnational, helping to foster affective investment in what was conceived of as a global proletarian culture.

But poetry could also shape meaning on the page in more direct ways. For Nelson, the identification of poetry with "transcendentalizing (or at least transhistorical) idealization" results in a "real tension" when it appears in the "transitory medium of newsprint."[81] Editors might attempt to resolve this tension by visually marking poetry's difference, separating it from surrounding content by placing it in boxes.[82] Such demarcation, however, rarely implied a disconnection, but rather called attention to points of intersection, especially when boxed poems appeared adjacent to boxed articles and advertisements. These intersections helped produce meanings in excess of the poems themselves. Thus, Wallace's short poem "Voice of the Worker" generates meaning not only in isolation, but also in tension with adjacent advertisements for grocery and department stores. For the titular worker – who must "count" every gulp of "pig's feet and tripe" and don a "dollar lid" and "shoddy suit"[83] – the 60c that P. Coady's was charging for a pound of tea would have been exorbitant; $14.00 for a satin-covered comforter at Hinchey's would have been out of reach entirely.[84] The poem alerts readers to a profound irony, one apparent on almost any single page: many of the goods and services advertised in the *Herald* were unaffordable for the paper's readers at a time when wages and working days were subject to repeated cuts.[85] More than giving humorous expression to a certain working-class desperation, then, Wallace's "Voice" produces meaning across the visually and textually fragmented newspaper page, inviting reflection on the medium of newsprint itself and its relation to commodity culture. In this way, poems could expose contradictions and connections, not only shedding their claims to "transhistorical" values, but also assimilating the non-literary to the affective field of poetry by making visible deprivations, inequities, and sites of resistance that were absolutely relatable to the everyday lives of working-class readers.

There was, however, a deeper tension that affected the reader and the subject being addressed – namely, who constituted the "working class readers" of the paper. The collective class identity constructed in the *Herald* depended upon a left discourse that championed social equality and challenged bourgeois chauvinism. But during the first two years of publication, the paper rarely addressed itself explicitly to issues of gender. In fact, for many contributors, the reader – the worker and the working class per se – was white and masculine by default. As Stephen Penfold observes, in working-class Cape Breton, and in the *Herald* in particular, the "worker" was crystallized in the image of the wage-earning man and "working-class grievances on a whole array of issues were defined in terms of the miner's concern for family and his role in it as sole breadwinner."[86] Such constructions of working-class masculinity appeared in every issue of the *Herald*. Titles like "'Papa, We're Hungry' Sobbed Little Children" stressed the male breadwinner ideal, while articles consistently connected class ideology to masculinity, as when, in early 1923, H.M. Bartholomew implored the "steel slaves of Sydney" to "remember you are MEN" who must "quit yourselves as men [and] FIGHT, DAMN IT, FIGHT!"[87] An editorial in the same issue warned that wives were a liability for radical leaders, vulnerable as they were to the enticements of "social events, dances, and exclusive affairs."[88] And the same misogyny surfaced in poetry, as in Fraser's "The Wearing of the Red," in which a miner's daughter "with ambitions / To shine in 'sassiety'" becomes the emblem of class collaboration and ungratefulness, a "poor, simple, little pin-head" and a "silly mental infant."[89] In these articles and poems, women were not only excluded from identification with the working class, but also a potential threat to its interests. Far from challenging existing gender relations and the tacit androcentrism of interwar liberalism, the discourse of the radical left appeared to be all the more invested in idealizing working-class masculinity and policing the boundaries of the political. In this context, the conclusion of Wallace's "Awake!" seems to suggest much more than the masculine generic: "Masters are nothing! Men are all."[90]

SOCIALIST FEMINISM AND MILITANT FEMININITY

But men did not represent "all" of the *Herald*'s readers and contributors. The development of a countervailing discourse of socialist feminism was in itself one of the paper's most notable achievements. The contributions of several prominent women – most notably Becky Buhay, Florence Custance, and Annie Buller – marked a critical intervention into the androcentric analyses that predominated during the paper's first year. One year after the publication of Wallace's "Awake!," as if in response to that poem, Becky Buhay's "Daughters Awake!" appeared in the *Herald*. In rhymed couplets, Buhay called on the "Daughters of the world" to "awake" and "demand the rights of humankind / The rights of body and of mind."[91] The poem advances a socialist vision of the world rebuilt, but it is as much a call for women to remake the program of the political left as it is an expression of anti-capitalism; gender is not imagined to be subsidiary to class, but works with it, the poem suggests, to produce distinct forms of oppression. Too long "the thralls of men / In kitchen, factory, and den," the women of the poem have been excluded from multiple publics: "without a voice," the absence of women from "history's page" implies both their exclusion from the broader bourgeois public sphere and their illegibility within the masculinist discourses of the left. Within the *Herald*, the poem reads as an incisive critique of the paper itself, a call to the paper's women readers to "demand the right to have your say."[92] Increasingly, women *were* demanding to have a say in the *Herald*; in May 1924, the first women's column appeared, featuring contributions from both local women and prominent women on the left from across the country. Two months later, the paper announced a series of articles to be written by "Comrade" Buhay,[93] a communist labour organizer from London, England, who had emigrated with her family to Montreal in 1912. These contributions marked a decisive shift toward more inclusive gender politics in the paper. And yet, it is important to recognize that, despite the paper's early masculinist rhetoric and often misogynist tenor, women had played key roles in the paper from its inception, roles that have been ignored in subsequent assessments of the *Herald*.

In fact, women had been involved with the paper from the beginning. Prominent feminist politician and social reformer Rose Henderson was among the leading contributors of signed articles throughout the paper's run, and social feminist Lucy Woodsworth was a regular contributor of articles on parliamentary politics and women's issues from 1921 onward. From 1921–22, American journalist and communist Anna Louise Strong, whose poems the paper obtained through the Federated Press, provided one of the most prominent poetic voices in the paper. And Florence Custance, whom Joan Sangster identifies as "the driving force behind the organization of the Communist women's movement," began contributing articles to the *Herald* in 1923.[94] The organization of Women's Labour Leagues (WLL) also appears to have been a decisive factor in the creation of the *Herald*'s women's column. As early as October 1923, Custance proclaimed to the *Herald*'s readers that if "women are to take their stand as co-workers with the men on equal footing – then they must organize."[95] A WLL was formed soon thereafter in New Aberdeen, and in March 1924 another was formed in Sydney under the direction of Custance.[96] The *Herald* reported faithfully on the organization and activities of these leagues, and in an article in the 15 March 1924 issue, Custance declared that "all true revolutionary workers" would support the mobilization of women who were being "confronted with a condition of extreme exploitation."[97] Custance thus made workers' support for gender equality a measure of their commitment to the revolutionary cause, a measure by which workers in Cape Breton apparently fared well. "In the recent struggles in Nova Scotia," asked Custance, "has the spirit of struggle been found wanting in the women of the working class? Indeed not."[98] For Custance, at least, the organization of working-class women was not peripheral to the objectives of radical left in Nova Scotia, but central to the "elementary struggles in light of preparation for final victory."[99] Ultimately, the contributions of women intellectuals such as Custance to the *Herald* prior to 1924 and the growing participation of local working-class women must be recognized as determining factors in the institution of a women's column.

Figure 5.3 From left to right: Florence Custance, Bea Colle, Becky Buhay, and Annie Buller, ca. 1926.

The first "Women's Column" appeared in the 23 May 1924 issue. To put this development into perspective, it is important to consider that the 1920s was a period of relative decline for the feminist movement in Canada. As Sangster points out, in the wake of the successes won by suffrage, "even feminists like Nellie McClung bemoaned the dearth of interest in the 'old' feminist issues of the pre-war days."[100] The work of the women's department of the CPC, Sangster maintains, was an exception, albeit an influential one. It is of no small significance, then, that the *Herald*'s women's column appeared more than a year before anything similar was instituted in the CPC's official organ, *The Worker*, which only "sporadically carried news of the women's department."[101] For a short time in 1924 and early 1925, the *Herald* served as the primary forum for socialist-feminist intellectuals associated with the CPC. Their contributions were not confined to the women's column, but it was there that the "woman question" was analyzed and debated at length. This was not to be a column for the discussion of fashion, beauty, relationship advice, or homemaking – content that was identified with bourgeois femininity and an emergent consumer culture. Rather, as Mrs McKinnon of Glace Bay put it in the inaugural column, "politically it [is] now just as important that the women should be organized" in order to expose "the real meaning" of class conflict and "take an active part in working for working-class control."[102] Maternalist rhetoric remained a common point of entry for many local contributors, but an acute awareness of the need for public and political action was the overriding theme of the column.

A month after the first women's column appeared, Becky Buhay's "Women and Capitalism" outlined the conditions necessitating women's involvement in labour militancy. Buhay insisted that recognition of the multiple oppressions of women was prerequisite to an effective communist politics, for "[the] woman of the working class feels even more keenly than the working man the struggles and trials of modern capitalism; for the proletarian woman is doubly cursed, she is a slave of a slave!"[103] For Buhay, opposing this double marginalization required the destruction of traditional and bourgeois feminine ideals, a project coextensive with the Marxist assault on false consciousness:

> The old picture of woman the gentle, sweet, modest creature (a creature halfway between an idiot and an angel) drawn so ably by the old-school novelists and even present day upholders of the corrupt social system, is fast fading in spite of all efforts of these gentlemen to keep the fantasy alive.[104]

Against such constructions, Buhay called for a modern form of militant femininity, women who could "*hate* as well as love." The system she indicts is at once capitalist and patriarchal, and its overthrow would follow the "awakening" of political consciousness among proletarian women: "The bloody crimes of the system call for a spirit of revolt that must be created within the hearts and minds of the proletarian sisterhood."[105] But such an awakening was not inevitable, and Buhay's analyses were consistently pedagogical as well as polemical. Only through an understanding of the social transformations wrought by changes in the productive forces of society could proletarian women be liberated from the conditions of slavery and the confines of bourgeois morality. "History," argued Buhay, "gives to our accepted ideas and codes a rude awakening."[106] Accordingly, over the next year, Buhay composed a series of eight articles specially for the *Herald* on "Women's Place in History," in which she offered an historical perspective on the inextricability of gender oppression and class exploitation.

Buhay's analysis in "Women's Place in History" offered a sweeping history of gender relations from "primitive communism" in "the earliest times," through ancient Rome, the Middle Ages, and the Reformation, up to the rise of industrial capitalism.[107] Her final three articles dealt with marriage, the social roles of women, and working women under the conditions of modern capitalism. To develop her analysis, Buhay drew on foundational Marxist texts. She referred in passing to Friedrich Engels's *Condition of the Working Class* (1845) and *Origins of the Family, Private Property and the State* (1884), as well as to August Bebel's *Woman and Socialism* (1910; orig. *Frau und der Sozialismus* 1883). In her attempt to synthesize Marxism and feminism into a coherent historical narrative and an actionable political program, Buhay accepted wholesale the economic determinism of Marxist orthodoxy. In so doing, however, she validated gender as a legitimate subject of left analysis, and as an axis of oppression that required special attention. More than this, her revisionist appeal to matriarchal prehistory situated feminism as the necessary counterpart to anti-capitalism. Beyond its obvious materialist approach to the history of gender and familial relations, Buhay's analysis takes as its starting point the "matriarchy myth," articulated by Engels in *Origins of the Family* and expanded upon by Bebel and other key communists such as Clara Zetkin.[108] Following Engels, Buhay argued that the rise of class society and private property entailed a shift from primarily matrilineal and matrilocal forms of social organization, in which gender oppression was non-existent, to a patriarchy under which women were excluded from social production.[109] For Buhay, there was much to be gained from Engels's argument that "the first class oppression [coincided] with that of the female sex by the male,"[110] but the focus on matriarchal prehistory – which Buhay, following Bebel, refers to as the "matriarchate"[111] – was less significant for its historical veracity than as a model for future emancipation. In this, Bahay's matriarchal prehistory echoes Abraham Beverly Walker's Afrocentric interpretation of classical antiquity in *Neith*: both looked to the past to develop a radical politics for the present. For Buhay, the matriarchal myth was proof that gender oppression was neither timeless nor unchangeable, and that women's liberation was not only possible but strictly necessary within the broader context of class struggle.

In the pages of the *Herald*, Buhay provided the paper's most sustained and sophisticated socialist-feminist analyses. Her articles would appear there until the paper's demise in 1926. But Buhay's were not the only contributions from prominent women in the CPC. Florence Custance continued to contribute articles on such topics as "The Women's Argument" and "International Women's Day." Meanwhile, Annie Buller offered cultural commentary on "Working Class Movies" and, in "Women and War," called on women to "become fighter[s]" in the "only war" that "women should and must support ... the final war for the liberation of the working class from capitalism."[112] In addition to these avowedly communist writers were more moderate voices on the left. Lucy Woodsworth continued to report on parliamentary activities and women's issues, and Agnes McPhail contributed a "Report of Women's National League" on the 1924 Congress of the Women's National League for Peace and Freedom – an organization whose liberal-humanist pacifism was subsequently criticized and rejected by the CPC.[113] And alongside these original contributions were articles by a range of American writers. From Boston, there appeared articles by physician and Marxist activist Antoinette Konikow advocating access to birth control and the organization of housekeepers.[114] Similar articles obtained through the Federated Press were authored by Mary Anderson, the first director of the United States Women's Bureau; Anna Mae Brady, a teacher and communist organizer from Chicago; and Helen Kaplan, also active in the Chicago Communist movement.[115]

And then there were articles and letters from local women. In "Anti-Lenin Lies," Blanche Carter assailed public schools for inculcating children in liberal ideology – "can you blame the present generation," she asked, "if they prefer yellow to Red, after such teaching?"[116] Carter's communist zeal matched that of any other contributor to the paper and she concluded her letter by summoning the spirit of Lenin, whose immortality was her "most earnest prayer."[117] In "Women Should Organize," Bert Boone appealed to a maternal sense of justice, insisting that women should be "organized and fighting shoulder to shoulder with our men."[118] The paper also provided a springboard for the participation of local women in the communist women's movement at national and transnational scales. Annie Whitfield, a CPC member and leading activist in the militant New Aberdeen WLL, wrote letters to the *Herald* attacking Besco executives and reactionary union officials by name.[119] Upon the demise of the *Herald*, Whitfield would become a frequent correspondent to *The*

Woman Worker (1926–29) and was selected by Buhay in 1930 to join the Women's Delegation to the Soviet Union, where she reportedly caused trouble by refusing to "immediately admit admiration for Russian socialism."[120] Upon the return of the delegation to Canada, Whitfield also refused to participate in the cross-country promotional tour organized to publicize the Soviet ideal.[121] Whitfield's willingness to defy CPC directives suggests her independence of thought, but not a lack of commitment to the communist cause. As Manley points out, Whitfield took a leading role in the early 1920s by organizing the WLL's monthly political education meetings. She also "strongly supported McLachlan's conception of class struggle unionism," and it was under her leadership that the New Aberdeen WLL was reconstituted as the women's auxiliary of the "red breakaway miner's union" in 1932.[122] The region may have "produced no equivalent to Rose Henderson, Annie Buller, or Becky Buhay,"[123] but this was not for lack of women devoted to the cause. More significantly still, the *Herald* constituted a key forum in which more prominent socialist feminists could enter into dialogue with the working-class women of Cape Breton.

Together, these local, national, and international contributions redirected the *Herald* toward a more inclusive gender politics even as they entered into tension with the paper's masculinist rhetoric and the broader androcentrism of the Canadian radical left. And like other letters, news items, articles, and poems, the paper's socialist-feminist discourse transcended the nexus of local and national political affiliations. Women writers such as Henderson were already central to the paper's international scope, but the activities of the WLLs, reported on in the *Herald* and often providing financial support to the paper, added an institutional dimension to the internationalism of the communist women's movement. The CPC's women's department had been formed on the advice of the International Women's Secretariat, an auxiliary body of the Comintern Executive. Custance herself attended the Fourth World Congress of the Comintern, and WLLs in Nova Scotia, though enjoying "some local autonomy," were "guided by the general goals of the larger Federation of WLLs" under the direction of Custance.[124] In this way, the formal channels of communist internationalism had tangible if oblique consequences for organization at the local scale. More importantly, the *Herald* was a medium for transnational exchange, putting the voices of women at local and national scales into dialogue with contemporary intellectual currents across North America, Europe, and Russia.

If the paper's appeals to "workers" tacitly hailed men as the principal subjects of class struggle, then the introduction of gender-conscious and socialist-feminist discourse within and beyond the women's column marked a significant renovation to the collective class identity promoted in its pages. Increasingly, working-class women were called upon *as women* to participate in a common proletarian culture, to imagine their own struggles in solidarity with working-class women globally. This was not only accomplished through analyses by writers such as Henderson, Custance, and Buhay, which situated the plight of working-class women within the context of international capitalism, but also through the identification of local women with proletarian internationalism. Accordingly, Boone's invitation to local women to join the WLLs in the struggle against Besco became an invitation to partake in global revolution against the "capitalist class": "We workers are going to own [the means of production] and the organized working women of the world are going to help bring this about. Come join us!"[125] Boone positions herself not as a wife supporting her "worker" husband, but as a working woman "of the world," a subject in a transnational movement for working-class liberation. If Buhay's "Daughters Awake!" signalled a clarion call to the *Herald*'s women readers for an awakening political consciousness, an injunction to "demand the earth as right for all," then women such as Boone, Carter, and Whitfield were proof that that call had been answered.[126]

Ultimately, women would have a decisive influence on the *Herald*'s political, rhetorical, and poetic appeals to working-class readers. Attending to that influence is bound to be more rewarding than focussing on a comparative lack of women's voices. It is of no small significance that the only original poems besides Wallace's to exhibit formal experimentation came from the pen of Buhay. Unlike Wallace's poetry, however, Buhay's has been entirely forgotten. One poem, in particular, is noteworthy for anticipating the intersection of proletarian poetry and literary modernism. "The Machine Awakens," published in the 19 July 1924 issue, presents a dystopic montage of physical degradation and confinement in fifty-three lines of free verse. Unlike "Daughters Awake!," the poem is not addressed strictly to working-class women, nor does it deploy the masculine generic. Buhay casts her embodied working-class subjects in terms that reject the tacit coding of gender evident in the masculinist poems of Wallace and Fraser. The resulting poem re-inserts working-class women into the immediate space of class struggle and moves beyond the conventions of formal traditionalism.

Like Wallace's best poems, Buhay's "The Machine Awakens" confronts the alienating conditions of capitalist modernity directly and in an unmistakably modern poetic idiom. Its title and denouement, suggestive as they are of political awakening and impending revolution, uphold Proletkult dicta to avoid "bourgeois" pessimism; but its several paratactic tableaux are distinctly imagistic:

> Pale blood-sapped faces of the men bent over their ironing boards,
> Yellow, unhealthy puffed cheeks of the operators,
> Elderly women work-worn.[127]

Here, and through the first half of the poem, Buhay broadly eschews sentiment and discursiveness in order to register the violence of labour inscribed on the bodies of workers. If the poem sacrifices subtlety, abandoning the objective correlative for profuse zeal in its concluding lines, it is only to meet the political imperative to revolutionary inspiration. On the whole, the poem reads as a forgotten precursor to the canonical "prototype of the Canadian documentary poem," Dorothy Livesay's "Day and Night."[128] Both poems deploy choreography and acoustics to figure the factory as a site of confinement and resistance,[129] and Buhay's poem, like Livesay's, depends upon the juxtaposition of "contradictory concepts": "arduous, exhausting, repetitive labour and the exhilarating instant of historical change."[130] Livesay's workers' lives "[turn] / the other way";[131] Buhay's "automatons" are literally transformed into human agents as "the air becomes electric with new life."[132] And yet, unlike Livesay, Buhay was not responding to "the specific historical conjuncture of the mid-1930s."[133] Buhay's poem prefigures the poetic preoccupation of later modernists on the left, but it was in the context of working-class struggle in Nova Scotia, the context in which it was published, that it obtained immediate relevance. In the 1920s, few Canadian readers would have been as attuned to the revolutionary poetics of "The Machine Awakens" as those who encountered it in the pages of the *Herald*.

DECLINE AND LEGACY

The dynamism and militancy that characterized the *Herald* through its first four years never abated while it survived, but publishing the paper became increasingly unviable in the face of deteriorating working conditions, intensifying labour action, and repeated attacks by local authorities and company police. When, in March 1925, District 26 began its fourth major strike in four years, the *Herald* had to cut its issues down to just four pages. By mid-March, more than 12,000 were on relief in the mining towns of Cape Breton.[134] A month later, Agnes McPhail spoke to Parliament of the desperate conditions she had found there during a recent visit. The *Herald*, McPhail conceded, "prints wild things," but "we would print just as wild things if we had suffered what they had suffered."[135] The leaders of the country, McPhail averred, "have no idea how deep the resentment is, how intense it is, and how quiet it is. These people are not broken, do not ever think that."[136] Until then, the resentment that surfaced in the pages of the *Herald* could hardly be described as "quiet," but McPhail's remarks would prove portentous. Two weeks after her address, the *Herald*'s offices and printing plant were burned to the ground. "They burn down the Labor Herald right this time," McLachlan wrote to CPC Secretary Tim Buck, "[this] is four times I have been burned out since 1922, and three times raided."[137] The paper would eventually be revived at four pages per issue and run from January to July 1926, but it never regained the support it had enjoyed prior to the 1925 strike.

A convergence of local, regional, and international factors contributed to the decline of the radical left in Nova Scotia and the demise of the *Herald* in 1926. Defeated in the 1925 strike and forced to accept the original wage cut proposed by Besco, the miners were no longer prepared to occupy the vanguard in a class struggle that seemed increasingly unwinnable. Consequently, the CPC ceased to be a significant organizing force in the region.[138] Moreover, as Manley explains, though the 1925 *Royal Commission on the Coal Mining Industry of Nova Scotia* had little tangible impact on the lives and working conditions of miners and steel workers, it nevertheless fostered a "mood of retrenchment" among the "rank and file."[139] Adding to this, in his report, Andre Rae Duncan singled out the *Herald* as having made peaceable and diplomatic class relations "impossible."[140] Left-wing labour was also facing defeats at the international level. In early 1926, the UMWA international executive amended its constitution to ban Communists from membership.[141] When UMW Communists joined forces with other radical dissidents to form the "Save-the-Union Movement," making a bid to oust John Lewis in the 1926 executive elections, they lost.[142] Facing a newly elected moderate leadership at the local level and an increasingly reactionary international executive, the *Herald* struggled, and was finally unable, to recuperate the subscriptions it had lost during its nine-month hiatus. On 2 July 1926, Besco's steel-producing subsidiary Dominion Iron and Steel Company declared bankruptcy and went into receivership, and the National Trust Company began proceedings "to 'wind up' the parent company."[143] The *Herald* published its final issue a week later.

In his autobiographical history of the CPC, Buck cites the *Herald* as one of four[144] influential progenitors of the party's official paper, *The Worker*, and elsewhere refers to the *Herald* as the Maritime version of Lenin's "collective organiser."[145] His comments reflect the extent to which the *Herald*'s influence extended beyond the ambit of its immediate readership, forming one locus in a national and transnational network of journalists, editors, and activists. Buck's characterization of the *Herald* as a "collective organiser," however, also suggests another way to frame the *Herald* within the broader context of regional protest in the 1920s. In his 1901 essay "Where to Begin," Lenin articulated the centrality of newspapers to socialist revolution, arguing that the role of the newspaper was not only as a "collective propagandist" and "collective agitator," but also as a "collective organiser."[146] For Lenin, the proletarian newspaper provided a nucleus of political engagement that began with the material conditions of its production – which "make it necessary to create a network of local agents"[147] – and extended outward beyond the "local" to affect "various strata of the population."[148] Here, one supposes, is Lenin's response to the contradictions of a bourgeois public sphere that claimed universal accessibility while constituting itself through multiple exclusions. If, as Jürgen Habermas suggests, Marx critiqued the "public sphere of civil society" and imagined "the social conditions for the possibility of its utterly unbourgeois realization," then the labour-paper-as-collective-organizer might be seen as one form in which this anti-bourgeois public sphere would be realized and mediated.[149] Both as the site of localized, material engagement and as a primary channel of exchange between geographically disparate formations of the political left, the proletarian paper was preconditional to the emergence of a common proletarian culture. It was the point at which the proximal, material social relations of local class struggle entered the broader discursive arena of the political left – a counterpublic that was the antithesis of the bourgeois public sphere.

In the critical context of regional cultural historiography – that is, in light of the critical flattening of interwar regional culture into a conservative, antimodernist monolith – the very fact of a plurality of conflictual cultural-political formations appears as something of a revelation. This is particularly true as it concerns the emergent conservative and antimodernist mythomoteur so influentially described by McKay in *Quest of the Folk*. The proletarian poetry contributed by Fraser, Wallace, and Buhay stands in contradiction to the folk-laden romance with which interwar regional culture has been deemed synonymous. It was ideologically dogmatic, but it was also anathema to the acritical conservatism that formed the ideological core of Nova Scotian antimodernism. It rejected the modernist separation of aesthetic and moral norms, but it addressed itself directly to the contradictions of twentieth-century capitalism and the alienating, degrading conditions of modern industrial life. Wedding a critique of industrial exploitation to demands for revolutionary transformation, this poetry achieved a modern poetic sensibility that responded to its historical moment. It did so not by embracing individualism and modernization as the telos of social life, as did *The Busy East*, but by occupying a stance of uncompromising critique.

The greater body of this poetry, of which Fraser was representative, developed its critique of capitalism within traditional forms and modes of address. Key poems, however, best represented by Buhay and Wallace, broke beyond traditionalism to develop distinctly modern structures and forms. The significance of this development, one that anticipates the well-documented juncture of literary modernism and proletarian poetry in the 1930s, transcends its specific local and regional contexts. It was, in fact, born out of exchanges and currents that cut across spatial scales, from the highly localized space of labour action to the transnational space of shared symbols, meanings, and political affiliations. As such, poetry played a key function within the mixed format of the newspaper, mediating between the proximate and the distant. The newspaper itself constituted the textual and bibliographic field in which local, national, and global meanings collided; it was the medium through which local readers entered the shared space of an ostensibly global proletarian culture. The *Herald* thus attests not only to the existence of cultural forms that challenged an emergent antimodernist hegemony in the region, but also to the multiple ways of accessing broader arenas of public debate and political contest. Though the geographical scope of its circulation was limited, the discursive arena in which the *Herald* circulated exceeded provincial, regional, and national boundaries. In turn, the contributors and successive editors of the *Herald* mounted a challenge to both liberal-populist regionalism and the extension and consolidation of the Canadian liberal order.

In its critique of nationalism, the *Herald* was generally measured. Notwithstanding the paper's claim to represent so-called "patriotic Bolshevists," nationalism was deemed to serve the interests of the state, and the Canadian state, as such, was an "instrument of the capitalist class."[150] Whatever Bolshevist "patriotism" implied, it did not involve civic nationalism, which McLachlan condemned as "flag idolatry."[151] Here, a distinction between national particularity and nationalism was drawn. Canadian workers, McLachlan argued, had a "mentality" distinct from their American counterparts, but unlike American workers, they were not nationalists, "political idolaters falling down and worshipping an outworn document, the principles of which we outgrew many years ago."[152] The *Herald* was thus set in opposition to (bourgeois) nationalism and the purportedly outmoded constitutionalism on which it depended, but it did not reject notions of national cultural particularity. At the same time, the paper was no more amenable to regionalist arguments that fetishized proximity and place as the principal reference points for identity formation.

The editors and contributors of the *Herald* bore no illusion that the bourgeois regionalism of Maritime Rights spoke for their interests or those of their working-class readers. When the Nova Scotian Conservative Party drew up its Maritime Rights platform in 1922, McLachlan summarily dismissed it as "the last word in lickspittle subservience to the international labor skinners" who were then "plundering" the working classes of the Maritime Provinces.[153] The "regionalism" of the movement was thus not regionalist at all, but one scale at which capitalism, as a world system, operated to consolidate conditions favourable to its reproduction. For McLachlan, the vaunted "non-partisanship" of the movement simply masked a shared commitment to economic liberalism, and the "Liberal-Conservative regime" deployed regionalism as a means to achieve a "more efficient and less expensive machine to keep the workers in wage slavery."[154] The region, as wielded by the bourgeois elites of Maritime Rights, was but a particular configuration of the global geography of capitalism.

McLachlan's position did not, however, entail a rejection of the region as a coherent territorial space or as an appropriate scale for political action. To the contrary, the paper's inclusion of the "Maritime" demonym in its title clearly implied aspirations for dissemination and coordination at the regional level. As Frank observes, the coal miners and steel workers of Cape Breton "hoped to offer a regional labour movement that transcended the coal industry itself," and "underwriting" *The Maritime Labor Herald* was central to this broader aspiration.[155] But though such labour militancy was "re-enacted in more modest ways" in regional centres including Saint John, Moncton, and Halifax, those regional aspirations went unfulfilled.[156] It is important to recognize, however, that though regionality formed an important scale for coordinated and collective political action, it was not an end in itself, not a sufficient criterion for collective identity. Class, rather than proximity and place, was regarded as the axis of identity-formation, the proper basis for a shared cultural-political identity.

This class-conscious resistance to national, regional, and other territorial exclusivities did not, however, translate into a broadly inclusive identity politics. Though the socialist feminism championed by figures such as Buhay, Custance, and Whitfield marked a significant break toward an expanded conception of working-class identity – an expansion that was remarkable in its discursive force, if much more limited in practice – the *Herald* displayed remarkably little recognition of any racial or sectional diversity among the local working class. One notable exception serves to illustrate the particular problem confronted by racial and ethnic minorities within a movement that was nominally inclusive but effectively unresponsive to questions of race. During the coal miners' strike of 1922, a group of Black workers in Glace Bay and New Aberdeen calling themselves "the Colored Element" released a message in the *Herald* addressing "colored people in and out of Canada."[157] The Colored Element, the statement read, would "not tolerate" Black migrant workers and was "prepared to deal with all such Negro scabs and strike breakers – UNDERSTAND?"[158]

On the surface, the statement sought to place class solidarity before Black solidarity. The letter's subtext, however, suggested an altogether different situation, pointing to the fear among local Black workers of anti-Black racial violence. It was, in fact, the potential for "one of the race" to "discredit or disgrace" those "who are localized" that impelled the Colored Element to release its statement in the *Herald*.[159] And evident within this ostensible threat is a concern for Black workers outside the region who might be "seduced" to go there – a tacit caution that inflects the meaning of the final, capitalized question, "UNDERSTAND?"[160] In effect, the letter was much less a reflection of cross-racial solidarity than it was an attempt to safeguard local and migrant Black workers against reprisals from local whites.

Regardless of whether the *Herald* aspired toward a more inclusive politics, then, the reality for racialized minorities within colliery towns was a constant threat of violence, liable to erupt should their interests be seen to conflict with those of the predominantly white working class. For all its antifascism, for all its denunciations of Ku Klux Klan incursions into Canada, the *Herald* was effectively indifferent to the racial and cultural stratification that fragmented the labour movement from within. Obviously, this was not a tendency unique to the radical left in Cape Breton, but partly reflected the failure of classical Marxism to address itself explicitly to issues of race – to recognize race as a distinct basis of oppression and not merely a derivation of its "real" economic basis. Unsurprisingly, the local Black community sought other modes of resistance, aligning itself with a tradition of Black nationalism that was shaped by Garveyism and cognate with the political program of Walker and *Neith*. A Glace Bay chapter of the Universal Negro Improvement Association was formed in 1918, and chapters were subsequently established in New Waterford and Sydney.[161] *The Nova Scotian Gleaner*,[162] a Black newspaper devoted to the UNIA cause, began publication in 1929, and as late as 1937, Marcus Garvey visited Cape Breton where he called on an audience at Whitney Pier "to emancipate [yourselves] from mental slavery because whilst others might free the body, none but ourselves can free the mind."[163] As Jamaican historian Robert Hill points out, that speech was immortalized in Bob Marley's "Redemption Song" forty years later.[164] Such remarkable lines of influence – what Hill calls "the product of dispersed networks of belonging that bind us as a people"[165] – speak to the transnational linkages that both helped shape divergent forms of regional activism and help sustain their traces into the present; yet, this Black nationalist tradition has been largely forgotten outside local sites of commemoration in Glace Bay. It has been obscured, in part, by the relative salience of labour radicalism between the wars. Thus, if the extraordinary revolt of radical labour in the 1920s was all but "extinguished in collective memory" by the re-imposition of bourgeois hegemony in the 1930s, then the invisibility of the region's Black nationalist formations reveals the multiple forgettings that have effectively expunged racialized political cultures from interwar historiography.[166] And increasingly, the populist regionalism of Maritime Rights was deemed to have constituted the *only* significant response to the severe socio-economic crisis of the 1920s.

Ultimately, the collapse of Besco and the decline of the radical left in Nova Scotia reveals the extreme precarity created by deindustrialization and economic decline. In 1920s Canada, a period of relative prosperity, this problem was basically limited to the Maritime Provinces. Accordingly, McKay and Morton suggest that the failure to develop a robust regional analysis marked a critical misstep for the radical left: "Neither the labourists nor the radicals seem to have addressed, in a serious and sustained way, the problem of building a counter-hegemonic movement in so divided and heterogenous a region."[167] As such, the left failed to capitalize on the nascent regionalism that the Maritime Rights Movement so successfully exploited and that *Acadiensis* had helped inaugurate at the turn of the century. From the Marxist perspective of radical labour, however, regionalism alone could not solve deindustrialization and underdevelopment. Centralism and Canadian federal policy may have exacerbated the region's economic weaknesses, but underdevelopment was not the result of political machinations and central-Canadian business alone; it was, rather, the contradictions of capitalist modernity manifest in space and place. It was, to borrow David Harvey's exposition of Marx, "the creation of a physical landscape conducive to the organization of production in all its aspects."[168] In effect, underdevelopment in the Maritime Provinces was the necessary correlative to capital accumulation, agglomeration, and centralization. These were problems inherent to the system of capitalism, not merely the consequences of its manipulation by oligarchic interests elsewhere, and they required nothing short of what the *Herald* advocated week in and week out: "the complete overthrow of the capitalist system."[169] In this, the local left recognized what the proponents of Maritime Rights seemed to overlook: further integration into the national economy would only serve to increase, rather than lessen, the region's dependency on the Canadian state.

With the collapse of Besco, the incredible moment of working-class rebellion, waged discursively across the pages of the *Herald*, quickly fell into sharp decline. In some respects, this dramatic collapse was exceptional; whereas workers in more affluent regions could depend, at least, upon the availability of work – however poorly recompensed – workers in the Maritimes were faced with the very real prospect that employers and capital, when faced with radical labour action, might well leave or else risk financial collapse. For workers outside the coal and steel industries, whose skills afforded them greater mobility, this meant out-migration to more prosperous centres – more than 120,000 would leave the region by the end of the decade. For those who remained, it meant "[accepting] working conditions and wages inferior to those offered elsewhere, on the understanding that if they did not, they would have no work at all."[170] Significant opposition to the emergent liberal order now seemed impractical, if not impossible. In this – the foreclosure of any substantive alternative to the liberal order – the decline of the region's radical left after 1925 signalled the beginnings of regional post-politics. The success of Maritime Rights, the deepening of regional dependency, and the consolidation of the Maritime Provinces as client states to a more robust and centralized federal state all seemed to augur the passing of a movement whose revolutionary vision had been all but eclipsed as the decade came to a close.

This post-political condition did not so much mark the complete failure of the left as it did its accommodation to the emergent liberal order, an accommodation that anticipated the compromise of post-war consensus. In tangible ways, the region's most vocal moment of political protest would help shape the new liberalism of the 1930s. This "left liberalism" was championed by Nova Scotian figures such as Premier Angus MacDonald and Nova Scotian federal Minister of Labour Norman McLeod Rogers, both of whom made marked contributions to the intellectual tradition and political institution of the "progressive liberal order."[171] Both of these new liberals, argues McKay, were "unmistakably influenced by and responsive to" the labour radicalism initiated in the previous decade.[172] In 1937, recalling the labour revolt of the 1920s, MacDonald introduced the *Nova Scotia Trade Union Act* – Canada's "first legislation requiring union recognition and compulsory bargaining."[173] Yet, though this legacy is readily apparent in the realm of legislative politics, the significant role that periodicals played in initiating and sustaining the discursive formation of working-class culture in the region has been effectively lost to Canadian literary and cultural history. The demise of the *Herald* thus marked the passing and forgetting of an oppositional, insurgent tradition that long predated and prefigured the "cosmopolitan, sophisticated sensibility" of "contemporary culture" in Atlantic Canada.[174] The vision of a new social order, born of sudden and severe crisis, could not finally survive the palliative retreat to regional nostalgia and golden-age mythmaking in the decades that followed. But in its brief tenure, in its insurgent opposition to the emergent liberal order, the *Herald* had striven to offer nothing short of a "ruthless criticism," awakening in its readers that "reform of consciousness" that Marx once promised could make the world anew and rouse it "from its dream about itself."[175]

CONCLUSION

Old Truths, New Fictions

From the muddy rims of the tidal estuaries
the wrecks of tugs stick out, a tourist's emblem,
graphs of decay and a kind of awakening.

Alfred Bailey, "Here in the East"

Alistair MacLeod's "The Closing Down of Summer" appeared in the Fall 1976 issue of *The Fiddlehead.* The story is perhaps the most profound articulation of mobility and transatlantic dislocation in twentieth-century Atlantic Canada. Yet it begins with a scene on a remote, isolated beach of Cape Breton in a moment of utter stasis:

> All summer it has been very hot … The brooks that flow to the sea have dried to trickles and the trout that inhabit them and the inland lakes are soft and sluggish and gasping for life. Sometimes they are seen floating dead in the over-warm water, their bodies covered with fat grey parasites.[1]

Static, hot, slow, but without a trace of bucolic pastoral. MacLeod's modern Cape Breton is only barely idyllic, and this underpins his portrait of Cape Breton under the conditions of economic globalization and neoliberalism. Thus, the initial description is apt, evocative as it is of stagnation, decay, and lifelessness. Death is a central theme in the story. The shaft and development miners who are its subjects, the narrator included, are haunted by the spectres of dead relatives, coworkers, and ancestors. Yet even the memories of these are quickly fading. And so, as they cross the Atlantic to work in mines in "Africa," "Chile," "Bolivia," etc., they take with them accidental talismans (a spruce twig pulled from a fender, for instance) "so that in the closeness of their work with death they might find nearness to their homes and an intensified realization of themselves."[2] The greater part of MacLeod's story is concerned with communicating the profound dislocation these miners experience as a result of systematically traversing the Atlantic to work in deep-shaft mines. The effects of their work manifest as a series of contradictions: it is not in the remoteness of Cape Breton that these workers feel isolated, but in claustrophobic mine shafts, "the tightness of confined space."[3] Their work requires them to cross the globe while rendering them increasingly immobile, with "arms that [they] cannot raise above [their] heads."[4] And they labour for a thoroughly modern resource-extraction industry, yet they sing old Gaelic songs, unable to recognize the "popular songs" from the "modern hit parade."[5] Consequently, returning home is like returning from a "journey to the land of the dead."[6] When they do return for the summers, they return to homes and families with which they have lost all connection, telephones and telegrams inadequate substitutes for in-person intimacy.

The effects of economic globalization take the heaviest toll on these migrant labourers, but other signs betray the infiltration of global cultural influences. As isolated as the beach on which the miners lie may appear – "so inaccessible" with "no public roads," "cliffs protect[ing] the beach, slowing the winds from both north and south"[7] – Cape Breton is not a preserve for the premodern. Summers begin with tourists flocking to Nova Scotia, arriving on the ferry at Yarmouth or by "highways ... heavy with touring buses and camper trailers and cars."[8] Summer ends with "the August gale" that augurs "the hurricanes that will sweep up from the Caribbean."[9] And the wives of these miners too have changed; with absentee husbands they seek a world of "vicarious experiences provided by the interminable soap operas that fill [their] television afternoons."[10] While a sense of loss characterizes the story, it never devolves into sentimental wistfulness. As Herb Wyile observes of MacLeod's work more broadly, "sense of loss is situated within a subtle socio-political critique that makes MacLeod's work more mordant, astute, and contemporary than he is usually given credit for."[11] The plight of MacLeod's miners is an absolutely contemporary one. Unable to re-establish meaningful familial connections, the miners are left trying to preserve a sense of identity against a deracinating and debilitating existence.

Yet it is not so much the contemporaneity of the story as what that contemporaneity ostensibly tells critics about the past that has won it so much acclaim. The reception of the story, and of MacLeod's fiction generally, reveals much about cultural historiography of the east coast. To be sure, MacLeod's craft, the story's style, is its greatest achievement. One of MacLeod's "most enduring stories," it has been deemed a "perfect, sculpted" work,[12] "masterful in the tightness of form."[13] Jane Brox regards the narrator of "The Closing Down of Summer" as the most memorable of MacLeod's "unforgettable" narrators,[14] and Bronwen Wallace celebrates the collection in which it appears for "language that is rich, lyrical, multifaceted."[15] But critics also note, almost invariably, the story's mournful qualities, its sense of loss. Laurent Lepaludier remarks that "'The Closing Down of Summer' conveys the sense of coming to an end,"[16] striking what Laurie Ricou calls a "tone of thoughtful nostalgia."[17] And Mark Levene sees the "anguish of [its] losses balanced with the resonance … of [the characters'] collective past."[18] But what exactly is being lost here, and what sort of past remembered? For many critics, what is lost is not the relative rootedness of a modern extractive economy replaced by transnational migrancy, but rather the coherence and stability of place. Writing "elegiacally" about his "region,"[19] MacLeod is "haunted by a sense of lost authenticity."[20] In MacLeod's fiction, according to these critics, modernity has finally destroyed the innocence of premodern rurality; as John Sutherland puts it, MacLeod's "fiction articulates the pathos of social progress."[21] And, for Sutherland, the (recent) past this progress supplanted was indeed authentic, almost medieval: "an essentially peasant existence," in fact.[22] MacLeod's work, then, at once captures and transcends what his modern sensibilities have effectively displaced.

Of course, other critics have offered more nuanced loco-materialist readings of MacLeod's fiction. Wyile's attention to MacLeod's "subtle socio-political critique" is exemplary of such work.[23] Caitlin Charman reads MacLeod's "nostalgia" for its "ambivalence," noting that it is not "lost authenticity" that haunts his fiction, as Sutherland suggests, but "the spectre of uranium extraction and its effects on male Cape Breton bodies."[24] Similarly, Peter Thompson sees a need to read MacLeod's fiction within the context of "the destabilizing and ongoing period of deindustrialization," for the ways in which it "questions romanticized ideas" about extractive industries and the region's past.[25] Nevertheless, while these critics offer a much-needed corrective to the tacit nostalgia that characterizes much *criticism of* MacLeod's fiction, there remains a sense that MacLeod was something of an anomaly, set apart from other "regionalist" writers not only by virtue of aesthetic merit, but also by the sophistication of his worldview. As David Carpenter remarks, "[if] he is a regionalist, he is not bound by the parochial snares of a limited vision."[26] The obvious implication is that "regionalists" before MacLeod *were* parochial. Indeed, even MacLeod's most perceptive readers appear to suggest that he was among the first to "[challenge] the central underlying assumptions of Folk ideology."[27] It is unsurprising, then, that Ian McKay should point to MacLeod as "the best single example of the new voices that are unsettling the old truths of the folk."[28] What the critical reception of MacLeod's work suggests, then, is that it is only with the "progressive cultural change" attending the rise of a *post*modern condition that the apparent verities of the stable, static, authentic region are called into question.[29] But when were those "old truths" settled? Even in the post-political moment precipitated by the collapse of the left, the incredible success of Maritime Rights, and the triumph of liberalism, discussed in chapters 4 and 5, a cultural politics of antimodernism did not reign unchallenged. Consistently, older regionalisms and concomitant expressions of romantic nostalgia were being questioned by writers and artists who, though less visible than their popular antimodernist counterparts, nevertheless responded to their modern moment by developing new cultural forms. In so doing, they reimagined the valence of place to articulate an evolving modernity from and beyond the nation's periphery.

To appreciate the countervailing discourse of modernity that continued into the 1930s through the 1960s, one need only look to the periodical in which MacLeod's "classic story"[30] was published: *The Fiddlehead*. Founded in 1945 by the Bliss Carman Society, *The Fiddlehead* began as a little magazine that sought to renovate tradition by fostering a modernism that was at once place-based and outward-looking. Centred in Fredericton, New Brunswick, this mid-century modernism not only consciously reacted against the ascendant antimodernist mythomoteur, but also sought to reconceptualize the relationship between the local and the global. As Tony Tremblay documents in *The Fiddlehead Moment* (2020), through the 1940s and 50s, "The Fiddlehead School," led by poet-ethnographer Alfred Bailey, advanced a "localist avant-garde" that would "hybridize urban modernism so that it could be both cosmopolitan and local."[31] In so doing, mid-century modernists offered a new politics of place, "reimagining the nation as a constellation of interdependent subjectivities and localisms."[32] In effect, these writers and critics – among them Bailey, Elizabeth Brewster, Fred Cogswell, and Desmond Pacey – challenged the spatial coherences and boundedness upon which earlier regionalisms depended, foregrounding the translocal linkages that constituted both cultural production and the production of place under the conditions of twentieth-century modernity. For Bailey, in particular, "acting locally had both proximate and distant effects" and "it was worth risking … the chauvinism of the local to avoid the erasure of the global."[33] Ultimately, it was this notion of "a modernist-infused localism" that would come to define editorial practice in *The Fiddlehead*.[34] Thus, when Bailey published "Here in the East" in *The Fiddlehead* in 1959, he was looking back to a nascent sense of localist activism that had taken root in the 1930s and emerged from an environment that was marked, paradoxically, by both "decay" and an impending sense of "awakening."[35] Even as the Fiddlehead Group sought to renovate tradition – to "develop it to the point of contemporaneity," as Bailey wrote in the magazine's inaugural manifesto – that historical sense was always tied to an evolving theory of places and cultural identities as "points" that were "forever in motion."[36] Accordingly, "a rebranding of the idea of place" was central to their cultural project.[37] Of course, this reinvigorated vocabulary of place did not align with the static, insular constructions of place upon which McKay's Folk depended. On the contrary, though it remained grounded in modernist sensibilities, it both pre-dated and anticipated the "resistance to closure" and "rigid categorical thinking" that would define postmodern geography in the decades to follow.[38]

The Fiddlehead and its associated writers and editors marked the most clearly defined tradition of literary modernism on the east coast after 1940, but mid-century modernism in the east was not confined to New Brunswick. As Bart Vautour's study of *The Song Fisherman's Song Sheets* (1928–30) perceptively argues, Halifax was host to similar "modernist experimentations" in the late 1920s.[39] In contrast to the relatively cohesive modernist formation that emerged in Fredericton, writers such as Kenneth Leslie, Martha-Ann Leslie, and Joe Wallace engaged modernist experiment from within the antimodern strictures of their coterie, dubbed the "Song Fishermen." These poets "work[ed] both with and against the dominantly antimodernist tenor of their periodical" in order to cultivate both "formal modernist qualities" and "a refiguring of the Maritime poetic subject in modernity."[40] Vautour's recuperation of these experiments thus reveals the instability of antimodernism itself, subject as it was to internal threats from aesthetic sensibilities antithetical to the Folk. This antithetical aesthetic provided an alternative to antimodernist spatial verities, responding to the "displacements" and "changing conditions of existence within a transnational modernity."[41] Vautour's work thus reveals the Song Fishermen – whom McKay identifies as the "only really organized movement" of antimodernist cultural producers[42] – to be internally fractured, their periodical as much a site of aesthetic and political contestation as a purveyor of settled truths.

Similar recovery work might look to Theodore Goodridge Roberts's *Acadie* (1930) – published in Fredericton nearly three decades after *Kit-Bag* appeared – as another example of a magazine divided. Intended, in part, to eulogize Bliss Carman, *Acadie*'s seven issues feature conventional forms interspersed with modern free verse. Significantly, it was in the depiction of place that these divergent tendencies toward traditionalism and modernism were most apparent. Writing in *The Dalhousie Review* in 1935, Grace Tomkinson saw in *Acadie* an animating tension between traditional pastoral and modern cosmopolitanism. For Tomkinson, "the new poetry" in *Acadie* was epitomized by Dorothy Livesay's "Prince Edward Island," which rejected the "conventionalized Arcady" of earlier writers in favour of a topographical poetry that was "unpretentious, unrhymed," "less romantic," and "more cosmopolitan."[43] Again, attention to these modernist incursions into the interwar antimodernist milieu upsets a temporal scope that sees even the early 1930s as a period of uniform romantic retreat. And these significant breaks toward modernism were not confined to literature.

A final example from Depression-era Saint John further complicates the picture of "regional" antimodernism developing post-1933, suggesting that the "decay" of which Bailey wrote became preconditional to the "awakening" of new cultural forms well before mid-century. When

Northrop Frye wrote Helen Kempe of his impression of Saint John in 1936, he described "a very impressive, dingy, dirty, dilapidated, poverty-stricken city" and "the greatest and sharpest contrast between rich and poor ways of living to be found anywhere in Canada." Frye could not then imagine that anyone there bore even "the slightest trace of social conscience."[44] What Frye failed to consider was that the same conditions were stimulating a politically conscious modernism among the city's visual artists. In fact, new forms had been taking shape there since Miller Brittain, Julia Crawford, Ted Campbell, and Jack Humphrey returned to Saint John from Europe and the United States between 1928 and 1932.[45] These artists brought with them "a modern artistic sensibility" influenced by the "avant-garde European modernists" and "representative of a new subjectivity within Canadian Art."[46] By the mid-1930s, Ted Campbell's studio on Prince William Street had become "a social milieu and place of stimulation, exchange, and dissemination of artistic, social, or political ideas."[47] Again, the periodical form was central to these artists' social vision; Saint John's artists were integral to the formation of the Maritime Art Association in 1935 and to the founding of *Maritime Art* in 1940. Edited by Walter Abell and produced by Violet Gillet, *Maritime Art* sought to decentralize artistic practice, advocating for a modern art that was not regionalist but "generational and ideological," and envisioning "a new social role for Canadian artists."[48] Social realism in Saint John thus arose from the same intersection of modernist culture and leftist politics that produced social modernisms elsewhere in Canada, yet this concurrence has generally gone unrecognized in Canadian art criticism.

The sum of these distinct modernist formations in Saint John, Fredericton, and Halifax dispels any notion that the east coast was unproductive of modernism after the 1920s. Until very recently, however, these developments received almost no critical treatment in cultural histories of modern Canada. Though nationally oriented criticism has generally explained this critical paucity by appealing to notions of lack or isolation – there are no studies of east coast modernism because there were no significant modernisms there to study – the actual reason is more complicated. In part, the east coast might be said to have formed a space against which narratives of modernist innovation elsewhere could be constructed and read: a dialectic that antimodernist cultural producers helped to construct from within. But that same critical gesture reveals a more fundamental aversion to the place politics of east-coast modernism itself. As Niergarth argues, Saint John's Depression-era artists have been considered peripheral to cultural modernity in Canada not because they were never recognized as modernists, but because they were "local and cosmopolitan" without appealing to a national imaginary.[49] They were not the only artists reacting against what Abell called "the fetish of nationalism,"[50] but they took as their subjects neither the symbolic matrix of Great Lakes–St Lawrence nor the frontier of the Pacific Northwest. Yet, though frequently celebrated as individual artists, they have been deemed "regional" and "isolated" in a "selective tradition of Canadian art history."[51] In other words, the "regionalism" of these artists has little to do with their aesthetic practice and much to do with a critical tradition working to maintain the coherence of one particular trajectory of Canadian artistic modernity.

The same critical neglect has met the periodicals in which modernism took shape on the east coast in the 1930s and 1940s, all of which have been deemed merely regional. The irony of the "regionalist" designation is epitomized by the fact that Canada's leading art magazine, *Canadian Art* (1943–), was created when the country's first art magazine, *Maritime Art* (1940–43), moved to Toronto and nationalized in 1943. Yet even this can be reframed in national histories to suggest rather the dismal state of Canadian art criticism before mid-century than the dynamism of arts cultures beyond Canada's metropoles. As Andrew Horrall bemoans, Canada's first art magazine began "only as a mimeographed, regionally focused journal," apparently strong evidence that "Canada still lacked the professionals and institutions" necessary to promote its modern artists.[52] Critical treatments of *The Fiddlehead* are similarly contradictory. Despite providing one of the only venues dedicated to the publication of literature in 1950s Canada, *The Fiddlehead* was consistently deemed aberrant in a climate of intense literary nationalism. Under Cogswell's editorial direction, the magazine's catholicity, its "tactic of seeding the local by showcasing the international," appeared to many as paradoxically too narrow and expansive.[53] As Andrew Moore observes, "*The Fiddlehead* was both un-Canadian and too provincial" and it was thus "under pressure to justify its presumptive position on the Canadian national literary landscape."[54] In a cultural climate that subordinated the local to the national, a *translocalist* modernism – as cosmopolitan as it was localist – had little purchase in

Canada's urban centres. These periodicals were neglected, then, not because the east coast was inhospitable to modernism, but because Canadian modernism was inhospitable to conceptions of place that figured rural and smaller urban centres as sites productive of, and not merely receptive to, modernity.

The recent work of several critics – most significantly Tremblay, but also those contributing article-length studies such as Vautour's and art criticism such as Niergarth's – has begun to correct the metropolitan bias of modernist studies in Canada. An important part of that recovery work has been to articulate and clarify the spatial politics of modernism on the east coast. And yet, the countervailing discourses of place and modernity, all of which found expression in periodicals, did not constitute a rupture in spatial understanding nor a complete break from the past. As I have argued throughout this study, the "old truths" – of a static, fixed region, of post-racial exceptionalism, of an authentic, premodern society – were *never* settled. Consciously political and socially activist literature emerged simultaneously with the construction of monolithic and exclusionary identities. Inasmuch as *Acadiensis* and *The Busy East of Canada* provided vehicles for the discursive production of region and regional identities, periodicals such as *Kit-Bag*, *Neith*, and *The Maritime Labor Herald* contested narrow definitions of space and identity by articulating alternative responses to modernity.

And those earlier periodicals, all of them, helped shape literary and political cultures in the decades that followed. Sometimes, that influence was direct. The Fiddlehead Group's Eliotonian conception of tradition looked back to Fredericton poets of the *fin-de-siècle*; a late-career Bailey poetically pondered what heights "the *Kit-Bag Magazine* in nineteen-two" might have reached had its editor not departed for Barbados in 1903.[55] The interwar modernist experiment that Joe Wallace brought to the Song Fishermen in 1928 and to *The Worker* before that had been developed in the pages of *The Maritime Labor Herald*. It was there, between 1922 and 1926, alongside other poet-polemicists such as Becky Buhay, that Wallace first conceived "alternative subjects in modernity."[56] For many critically acclaimed writers in the postwar period – including MacLeod, Ernest Buckler, and Alden Nowlan – *The Atlantic Advocate* (*The Busy East*'s successor) remained a viable publishing venue. And when a new Maritime historiography emerged in the 1970s, a revived *Acadiensis* served as the premier journal of regional history. But the consequences of earlier periodical cultures were often more diffuse than these straight lines of influence might suggest. The Black modernist poet Anna Minerva Henderson may well have "perused" copies of *Neith*, as George Elliott Clarke speculates,[57] but there can be little doubt that turn-of-the-century Afromodernism inflected the trajectory of Black protest and civil rights in the interwar period. Similarly, though *The Labor Herald* was short-lived, its role as the only significant forum for women on the far left in the early 1920s meant that its influence on socialist feminism far exceeded the ambit of its subscribed readership. And while the translocalist activism of mid-century modernism may have developed a new vocabulary of place by reacting against the liberal-populism of *The Busy East*, it was nevertheless cogent with the divergent strands of transatlantic cosmopolitanism that had defined earlier periodicals including *Kit-Bag*, *Neith*, and *The Maritime Labor Herald*. Attending to these earlier manifestations of modern periodical culture thus helps to alter the lines and geographies of influence by which we have come to define modern culture in Canada. In so doing, we can begin to recover and locate cultural agency in rural places, smaller cities, and towns, to acknowledge that modernity was not the sole jurisdiction of urban metropolitan centres.

But what is finally at stake in the recovery of early-twentieth-century periodicals is an historical sense of our own cultural moment, of the shifting values and relations we assign to the juncture of place, culture, and identity. In short, the alternative routes periodicals provide into the past reconfigure our understanding of the present. The uniqueness we are apt to ascribe to our contemporary moment of mobility and flows, for instance, is necessarily attenuated when we acknowledge the translocal linkages that shaped spatial understandings in the early twentieth century. Those were linkages that periodicals – inherently mobile, fluid, wrought by contradiction – were uniquely fit to register, but which dominant discourses of regionality and nationalism have since worked to obscure. A more measured assessment of contemporary writing and new media, then, may well be reached by reading current spatial sensibilities alongside the diverse discourses playing out in periodicals a century ago. At the very least, doing so can help us recognize and resist the persistent critical desire to read all non-metropolitan culture within a regionalist framework. Such recognition and resistance cannot only involve contesting the subordination of the local to regional, national, and transnational scales. It must also involve recuperating the inscriptions of place that settler-colonial geographies overwrite. These are inscriptions that cannot finally be accounted for by recourse to the archives of modern periodicals alone. But what periodicals do reveal is the incapacity of any place to finally contain and determine cultural identity. Ultimately, what the miners of MacLeod's "The Closing Down of Summer" look back to are not "old truths" – the assurances of an authentic and fixed regional space – but the fictions that sustain them through the experience of profound dislocation, an old poem or song remembered in moments of isolation. Those fictions may provide a sense of rootedness in place, but they are also an assertion of agency, an act of self-definition against narratives that would fix them as the living relics of an obsolete past. In the broader critical effort to understand and rethink the spaces and places we inhabit, turning to the mixed field of the periodical form can help us resist the impulse to fix the past as a foil to the present, to construct old truths from new fictions.

Notes

INTRODUCTION

1 Fauset, Interview.
2 Fauset to Elsie Clews Parsons, 11 August 1923.
3 Fauset, Interview.
4 Fauset, *Folklore*, viii.
5 Fauset, *Folklore*, vii.
6 Fauset, *Folklore*, x.
7 McKay, *Quest of the Folk*, 30.
8 McKay, *Quest of the Folk*, 12.
9 Scholes and Wulfman, *Modernism in the Magazines*, 43.
10 Creelman, *Setting in the East*, 11.
11 Davies and Swanick, "Print Culture."
12 Thompson, "Quest of the Folk," 239.
13 Tremblay, "Landscapes of Reception," 309.
14 Thornton, "Out-Migration," 5.
15 Wyile, *Anne of Tim Hortons*, 14.
16 Wyile, *Anne of Tim Hortons*, 20–1.
17 Davies, "Home Place," 199.
18 Conrad and Hiller, *Atlantic Canada*, 1.
19 Godard, "Cultural Field," 222.
20 Godard, "Cultural Field," 221, 222.
21 Godard, "Cultural Field," 238.
22 Massey, "Global Sense," 24.
23 Cresswell, *Place*, 87.
24 Lippard, *Lure of the Local*, 7.
25 Cresswell, *Place*, 83.

26 Tsing, *Friction*, 1.
27 Tsing, *Friction*, 3.
28 Hall, "Cultural Identity and Diaspora," 225.
29 Hall, "Cultural Identity and Diaspora," 226.
30 Davies, "Home Place," 194.
31 Davies, "Home Place," 195.
32 Davies, "Home Place," 199.
33 Bryant, *The Homing Place*, 6.
34 Bryant, *The Homing Place*, 4.
35 Bryant, *The Homing Place*, 28.
36 Bryant, *The Homing Place*, 28.
37 Troulliot, *Global Transformations*, 34.
38 Massey, *For Space*, 65.
39 Tremblay, Globalization and Cultural Memory," 36.
40 Troulliot, *Global Transformations*, 36.
41 Troulliot, *Global Transformations*, 35.
42 Troulliot, *Global Transformations*, 36.
43 Troulliot, *Global Transformations*, 35.
44 Rak, "Translocal Representation," 182.
45 Rak, "Translocal Representation," 182.
46 Anderson, "Staging Antimodernism," 97.
47 Weiss, "Popular Short Story," 88.
48 Ballantyne, Dvořák, and Irvine, *Translocated Modernisms*, 8, 6.
49 Connolly, "Print Culture," 7.
50 Beetham, "Publishing Genre," 98.
51 Beetham, "Publishing Genre," 98.
52 Latham and Scholes, "Periodical Studies," 517–18.
53 Ardis and Collier, "Transatlantic Print Culture," 1.
54 Ardis and Collier, "Transatlantic Print Culture," 2.
55 Moretti, *European Novel*, 165.
56 Moretti, *European Novel*, 165.
57 Haveman, *Making of America*, 12.
58 Piesse, *British Settler*, 21.
59 Piesse, *British Settler*, 21.
60 Piesse, *British Settler*, 26.
61 Jack, "Acadian Magazines," 200.
62 Massey, "Global Sense," 25.
63 Beetham, "Publishing Genre," 97.
64 Haveman, *Making of America*, 6.
65 Haveman, *Making of America*, 6.
66 More, "Hurricane Juan," 995.

67 Bundale, "Halifax's Brooklyn."
68 CMM, "Ecological Knowledge," 24.
69 Remes, "Mi'kmaq," 453.
70 Quoted in Remes, "Mi'kmaq," 454.
71 Parnaby, "Cultural Economy," 71.
72 Remes, "Mi'kmaq," 446.
73 Remes, "Mi'kmaq," 452.
74 Lonecloud, "Letter," 303.
75 Quoted in Walls, "Maritimes First Nations," 156.
76 Brown, "American Indian Modernities," 290.
77 Remes, "Mi'kmaq," 456.
78 Bryant, *Homing Place*, 24.
79 Remes, "Mi'kmaq," 459.
80 Bryant, *Homing Place*, 6.
81 The term "*fin-de-siècle*" here is used to refer not to specific aesthetic movements represented by Aestheticism or Decadence, but to the transitional period between the late nineteenth and early twentieth centuries, what Michael Saler terms "a socio-cultural moment within the larger story of Western 'modernity'" ("Introduction," 2). This period is especially significant both as the cradle of modern geopolitics and as an inherently global movement that "featured expansionist imperialism, the deployment of worldwide communications and transport networks, large migrations of populations … and the wider diffusion of mass production and mass culture to all parts of the world" (Saler, "Introduction," 5–6). Chapter 1 documents the extent to which these processes transformed society and culture on the east coast, inflecting the "sense of newness" that D.M.R. Bentley sees as a defining feature of Canada's *fin-de-siècle*, a period spanning the 1880s to the onset of the First World War in 1914 ("Canada," 217).

CHAPTER ONE

1 "Repeal," 1.
2 Howell, "W.S. Fielding," 34.
3 C. Roberts, "Acadia's Field," 3.
4 C. Roberts, "Acadia's Field," 3.
5 McCabe, "Contesting Home," 240.
6 Bentley, *Confederation Group*, 78.
7 Sutherland, "Mr. Smith," 51.
8 Fingard, "Paradoxes of Progress," 112. In fact, at the time Roberts was writing, the term "Maritime Provinces" was used to denote the easternmost provinces of Canada; according to the *OED*, the word "Maritimes" (denoting "the

Maritime Provinces") and the demonym "Maritimer" (denoting "A native or inhabitant of the Maritime Provinces of Canada") had not yet entered the lexicon. The OED cites the first instance of "Maritimes" as appearing in 1926 in *The Daily Colonist* (Victoria, BC) and the first instance of "Maritimer" as appearing a decade later in 1931 in *The Canadian Geographical Journal*. Actually, "Maritimes" appears at least as early as 1895 in the first issue of the Amherst, NS, monthly *Marshlands*. It was used outside the Maritime Provinces as early as 1908, when it appeared in a short story by Roger St. Stephen in the *Home Journal*. In 1917, *The Canadian Municipal Journal* adopted "Maritimes" as a heading under which it listed the cities of Halifax, Sydney, and Saint John. And the federal government had begun using the term "Maritimes" in press publicity material by at least 1918 when it referred to "The War Industries of the Maritimes." Similarly, "Maritimer" appears in print in 1907 in the eleventh issue of *The Maple Leaf* and the term begins to appear in Canadian magazines around 1910. Thus, in 1910 *The Canadian Courier* refers to Alex Johnston, deputy minister of Marine and Fisheries, as "a maritimer from Sydney"; and, in 1916, Augustus Bridle chastises "the Maritimer who, after he has seen Halifax or St. John, [*sic*?] takes a trip to Boston or New York and thinks he has traveled enough." The significance of the distinction between "Maritime Provinces," on the one hand, and "Maritimes" and "Maritimer," on the other, is considerable. The former clearly denotes a grouping of three distinct provinces. The term "Maritimes" maintains some of that sense as a plural noun, but clearly denotes an added sense of singularity, coherence, and cohesiveness. The emergence of the demonym "Maritimer" is especially marked, with the term functioning as a predicate in identity statements. *OED*, s.v. "Maritime," 5.B.1.b.; *Marshlands*, "Political and Personal," 2; St. Stephen, "Cask of Gasoline," 10; *Canadian Municipal Journal*, "Building in Canada," 112; "The War Industries of the Maritimes," 5; Maritimer, *The Maple Leaf*, 3; Johnston, "Men-of-Today," 9; Bridle, "What Is a Canadian," 3.

9 Fingard, "Paradoxes of Progress," 112.

10 Maritimer, "Maritimer Visits Oakland," 3.

11 Throughout this chapter, "regionalism" refers broadly to an "areally defined, non-nation-state [form] of political, economic or cultural organization or collective solidarity" and more specifically to the active construction, promotion, and mobilization of a regional identity through appeals to cultural particularity and distinctiveness (Entrikin, "Region and Regionalisms," 350). This definition is closely connected to Frank Davey's argument that "regionalism is cultural rather than geographic, and represents not geography itself but a strategically resistant mapping of geography" ("Ends of Regionalism," 4). Accordingly, "regionalist," as it is used herein, retains

that sense of active construction. Conversely, "regional" is intended to denote anything deemed to be or constructed to be of or related to the region; a regional magazine could thus be a magazine with a readership that roughly extends throughout the conventionally defined region and/or takes the region as its focus (even if not explicitly or consciously "regionalist" in its editorial polemic). These definitions are not meant to foreclose the polysemic qualities of these terms, but to provide some disambiguation in order to argue that they are not, in fact, signifiers of discrete processes, but interrelated concepts that refer to mutually constitutive processes of territorialization, identity-formation, and cultural selection.

12 This argument aligns with Herb Wyile's contention that "regionalism is not a discrete field of literary practice, but the nexus of a series of debates, contestations, critical prescriptions, and a territorializing of literary practice" ("Regionalism," 152).

13 Distad and Distad, "Canada," 75.

14 Jack, "Kind Words," 104.

15 Sugars and Moss, "E. Pauline Johnson," 392.

16 Nicholas, "Gabriel Acquin."

17 Graham, "Saturday Night," 348.

18 Jack, "Kit-Bag," 70.

19 Soja, *Postmodern Geographies*, 151.

20 Wyile, *Anne of Tim Hortons*, 2.

21 Wyile, *Anne of Tim Hortons*, 2.

22 Wyile, *Anne of Tim Hortons*, 2, 20.

23 Howell, "Industry, Urbanization, and Reform," 164.

24 Howell, "Industry, Urbanization, and Reform," 164–5.

25 Brookes, "Out-Migration," 29.

26 Acheson, "National Policy," 4.

27 Conrad and Hiller, *Atlantic Canada*, 142.

28 McCann, "New Social Order," 130.

29 Acheson, "National Policy," 2.

30 Conrad and Hiller, *Atlantic Canada*, 145.

31 Conrad and Hiller, *Atlantic Canada*, 145.

32 Howell, "Industry, Urbanization, and Reform," 157.

33 Howell, "Industry, Urbanization, and Reform," 158.

34 McCann, "New Social Order," 121.

35 Acheson, "National Policy," 25.

36 Howell, "Industry, Urbanization, and Reform," 190.

37 McKay, *Quest of the Folk*, 26–7.

38 Howell, "Industry, Urbanization, and Reform," 163.

39 Forbes, *Maritime Regionalism*, 12.
40 McKay, *Quest of the Folk*, 36.
41 Frank, "Geography of Centralization," 195.
42 Gerson, "Canadian Literature," 76.
43 Amin, "Regions Unbound," 40.
44 Paasi, "Place and Region," 806.
45 Massey, *For Space*, 64–5.
46 Massey, *For Space*, 64.
47 Massey, *For Space*, 64.
48 Larocque, "David Russell Jack," 526.
49 Wyile, "Regionalism," 142.
50 Davey, "Ends of Regionalism," 8.
51 Fiamengo, "Regionalism and Urbanism," 265.
52 Jack, "Acadian Magazines," 202.
53 Jack, "Acadian Magazines," 173, 179, 194.
54 Jack, "Salutary," 6.
55 Dawson, *Acadian Geology*, 1.
56 Dawson, *Acadian Geology*, 2.
57 Goldsmith, "Rising Village," 40.
58 C. Roberts, "Canada," 356.
59 Carman, "Low Tide," 16.
60 Sladen, *On the Cars*, 10.
61 McKay and Bates, *Province of History*, 77.
62 McKay and Bates, *Province of History*, 229.
63 Jack, "Salutary," 4–5.
64 Buckner, "Acadiensis II," 5.
65 Taylor, *Promoters, Patriots, and Partisans*, 213.
66 Bell, "Introduction," v.
67 Lochhead, "Introduction," 1.
68 Jack, "Salutary," 5.
69 Jack, "Salutary," 5.
70 Ganong, *Cartography of the Province*, 313.
71 Rees, *New Brunswick*, 17.
72 Ganong, *Cartography of the Province*, 314.
73 Wynne, "W.F. Ganong," 7.
74 Ganong, *Evolution of the Boundaries*, 142.
75 Taylor, *Promoters, Patriots, and Partisans*, 216, 4.
76 Wynne, "W.F. Ganong," 6.
77 Painter, "Cartographic Anxiety," 346.
78 Ganong, "Great New Brunswick Survey," 77.

79 Painter, "Cartographic Anxiety," 346.
80 Pickles, *Cartographic Reason*, 197, quoted in Painter, "Cartographic Anxiety," 346.
81 Ganong, *Cartography of the Province*, 314.
82 Ganong, *Origins of Settlements*, 142.
83 Wynne, "W.F. Ganong," 7.
84 Ganong, "Animal Romancers," 303.
85 Carman, "Supplication," 74.
86 Bentley, *Gay]Grey Moose*, 244.
87 Bentley, *Gay]Grey Moose*, 244.
88 Bentley, "Carman and Mind Cure," 85.
89 Cappon, *Bliss Carman*, 28.
90 Carman, "Supplication," 74.
91 Chamberlain, "Primitive Life," 82–3.
92 Chamberlain, "Primitive Life," 83.
93 Jack, "Salutary," 5.
94 Chamberlain, "Primitive Life," 75.
95 Clarke, "Glooskap," 87.
96 Davey, "Ends of Regionalism," 11.
97 I. Jack, "Aesthetic Attributes," 170.
98 I. Jack, "Aesthetic Attributes," 172.
99 De Mille, "Literary Possibilities," 129.
100 De Mille, "Literary Possibilities," 130.
101 Blair et al., "Introduction, " xxi.
102 Jack, "Indians," 189, emphasis added.
103 McAdam, "Indian Mound," 101.
104 Cody, an Anglican clergyman and novelist, would become better known for his short fiction and nearly two dozen popular novels published between 1910 and 1937. Among his best-selling novels was *The King's Arrow: A Tale of United Empire Loyalists* (1922).
105 See, for instance, John Frederic Herbin's "A Marshland River" in vol. 1, no. 2, or Marie Gill Currie's "The River Saint John" in vol. 2, no. 3.
106 Brewster, "Days," 113.
107 Carman, "Song," 1; "House at Lower Lachine," 2.
108 Jack, "Salutary," 5.
109 Jack, "Salutary," 6.
110 Smith, "Loyalist History," 9.
111 Harris, "Advantages of the Union," 182.
112 Harris, "Maritime Provinces," 240.
113 Frank, "Acadiensis, 1901–1999."
114 "Acadiensis," 63.

115 Larocque, "David Russell Jack," 526.
116 Buckner, "Acadiensis II," 8.
117 Exact numbers are difficult to determine. Most of the magazine's subscribers were in Nova Scotia. Ironically, this led Jack to highlight apparent social differences between the provinces; he proclaimed that Nova Scotians "are, as a class, more literary and artistic in their tastes and aspirations" ("Past," 5). Likewise, he lamented the fact that, by 1902, only 122 subscribers lived in the city of Saint John, where the magazine was published. Jack, however, suggested that the magazine had a substantial number of subscribers from elsewhere in Canada and the United States, and a small number of subscribers in Europe, demonstrating "a wide sphere of influence" ("Past," 5; "Acadian Magazines," 200–1).
118 Distad and Distad, "Canada," 75.
119 Bowles, "International," 1.
120 Reynolds, "Introduction," 3.
121 Reynolds, "Writers," 57.
122 "Publisher's Note," 29.
123 E. MacLeod, "Owen, Elizabeth, Anne."
124 Gerson, *Canadian Women*, 134.
125 Siadhail, "Hughes, Katherine Angelina."
126 See Irvine, "Little Magazines in English Canada," 602–4; Doyle, "Canadian Writers and American Little Magazines in the 1890s," 178; and Mount, *When Canadian Literature Moved to New York*, 24.
127 T. Roberts, "For the Thousand," 2.
128 T. Roberts, "For the Thousand," 2.
129 T. Roberts, "For the Thousand," 1.
130 Ware, "Cosmopolitan Nationalism," 296.
131 Bentley, *Confederation Group*, 62.
132 Ware, "Cosmopolitan Nationalism," 296.
133 Ware, "Cosmopolitan Nationalism," 296.
134 Ware, "Cosmopolitan Nationalism," 299.
135 Irvine, "Little Magazines," 605.
136 T. Roberts, "No Name," 5, 6.
137 T. Roberts, "No Name," 6, 7.
138 T. Roberts, "No Name," 9.
139 T. Roberts, "No Name," 9.
140 T. Roberts, "Story Writer," 23.
141 "The Kit-Bag," 4.
142 "January Magazines," 178.
143 Jack, "Kit-Bag," 71.
144 Jack, "Kit-Bag," 70.

145 Jack, "Kit-Bag," 70, 71.
146 Jack, "Kit-Bag," 70.
147 Jack, "Charles," 65.
148 Dole, "Some Fine Art," 47.
149 Dole, "Some Fine Art," 46.
150 T. Roberts, "My Comrade," 40.
151 T. Roberts, "My Comrade," 40.
152 Macdonald, "Inlander," *Acadiensis*, 6.
153 MacDonald, "Inlander," *Kit-Bag*, 10.
154 MacDonald, "Inlander," *Kit-Bag*, 10.
155 Mount, *Canadian Literature*, 7.
156 Frank, "Acadiensis, 1901–1999," 5.
157 Davey, "Ends of Regionalism," 3.
158 Wyile, *Anne of Tim Hortons*, 14.
159 "Sons and Daughters," 23.
160 Rhomberg, *No There There*, 27.
161 Rhomberg, *No There There*, 28.
162 D. Morris, "Maple Leaf," 31.
163 Robb, "Michael A McInnis," 16.
164 "Next Meeting," 7.
165 Robb, "Michael A McInnis," 16.
166 Robb, "Michael A McInnis," 17.
167 Paasi, "Place and Region," 804.

CHAPTER TWO

1 "Harriet Beecher," 4.
2 "City Cornet Band," 1.
3 "City Cornet Band," 1.
4 "Uncle Tom's Cabin," 2.
5 "Harriet Beecher," 4.
6 Stowe, *Uncle Tom's Cabin*, 282.
7 "Race Distinction," 4.
8 "Carleton Cornet Band," 1.
9 Siemerling, *Black Atlantic Reconsidered*, 182.
10 Siemerling, *Black Atlantic Reconsidered*, 147.
11 Shadd, "Notes of an Immigrant," 11.
12 A. Walker, "Prefatory Remarks," 1.
13 A. Walker, "Prefatory Remarks," 1.
14 Chariandy, "Black Canadian Literature," 542.

15 Cahill, "First Things," 376.
16 Winks, *Blacks in Canada*, 398.
17 Clarke, *Directions Home*, 32.
18 Clarke, *Directions Home*, 36.
19 Clarke, *Directions Home*, 35.
20 Clarke, *Directions Home*, 34.
21 Johnson and Johnson, *Propaganda and Aesthetics*, 1.
22 A. Walker, "Editorial Announcements," no. 1, 59.
23 A. Walker, "Editorial Announcements," no. 1, 60.
24 Du Bois, *Dusk of Dawn*, 135, 136.
25 Lemons, *Womanist Forefathers*, 56.
26 Lemons, *Womanist Forefathers*, 56.
27 A. Walker, "Editorial Announcements," no. 1, 60.
28 McGann, "Socialization of Texts," 70.
29 A. Walker, "Negrophobes," 6.
30 A. Walker, "Negrophobes," 6.
31 A. Walker, "Hayti and Its Enemies," 2.
32 A. Walker, "Tillmanism or Mob Rule," 19.
33 A. Walker, "Tillmanism or Mob Rule," 22.
34 Winks, *Blacks in Canada*, 400.
35 Winks, *Blacks in Canada*, 400.
36 A. Walker, "Tillmanism or Mob Rule," 17.
37 A. Walker, "Tillmanism or Mob Rule," 17.
38 A. Walker, "Tillmanism or Mob Rule," 20.
39 A. Walker, "Tillmanism or Mob Rule," 20.
40 A. Walker, "Tillmanism or Mob Rule," 17.
41 A. Walker, "Tillmanism or Mob Rule," 18.
42 Du Bois, *Souls of Black Folk*, 41.
43 A. Walker, "Negro Problem," part 1, 23.
44 A. Walker, "Negro Problem," part 1, 23.
45 A. Walker, "Negro Problem," part 1, 24.
46 Clarke, *Directions Home*, 35.
47 Du Bois, "Talented Tenth," 203.
48 A. Walker, "Tillmanism or Mob Rule," 19.
49 A. Walker, "Negro Problem," part 4, 180.
50 Clarke, *Directions Home*, 31.
51 Siemerling, *Black Atlantic Reconsidered*, 151.
52 Siemerling, *Black Atlantic Reconsidered*, 151.
53 Willmott, *Unreal Country*, 13.
54 Irvine, *Canadian Modernists*, 5.

55 Brandt, "New Genealogy," 4, 21.
56 Irvine, Lent, and Vautour, "Introduction," 17.
57 Irvine, Lent, and Vautour, "Introduction," 5.
58 Dobson, "Altermodernities," 235.
59 Iton, *Black Fantastic*, 14.
60 Troulliot, "Otherwise Modern," 222.
61 Gilroy, *Black Atlantic*, 37.
62 Troulliot, "Otherwise Modern," 228.
63 Hardt and Negri, *Commonwealth*, 102–3.
64 Siemerling, *Black Atlantic Reconsidered*, 30.
65 Siemerling, *Black Atlantic Reconsidered*, 30.
66 Dobson, "Altermodernities," 237.
67 Siemerling, *Black Atlantic Reconsidered*, 28.
68 Iton, *Black Fantastic*, 212.
69 Campbell, "Museum Shell," 26.
70 A. Walker, "Negro Problem," part 1, 25.
71 A. Walker, "Literary Notes," no. 1, 56.
72 G. Walker, "Realism in Fiction," 229.
73 G. Walker, "Realism in Fiction," 231.
74 Hill, "Introduction," xxix.
75 Hill, *Modern Realism*, 38.
76 Willmott, *Unreal Country*, 22, 23.
77 A. Walker, "Literary Notes," no. 2, 96.
78 A. Walker, "Emile Zola," 4.
79 G. Walker, "Realism in Fiction," 231.
80 A. Walker, "Emile Zola," 4.
81 A. Walker, "Emile Zola," 5.
82 A. Walker, "Emile Zola," 5.
83 Du Bois, "Criteria of Negro Art," 103.
84 A. Walker, "Emile Zola," 5.
85 Du Bois, "Criteria of Negro Art," 103.
86 Iton, *Black Fantastic*, 9.
87 Iton, *Black Fantastic*, 9.
88 Iton, *Black Fantastic*, 9.
89 Simmons and Crank, *Race and New Modernisms*, 16.
90 Simmons and Crank, *Race and New Modernisms*, 17.
91 Baker, *Harlem Renaissance*, 8.
92 Baker, *Harlem Renaissance*, 31.
93 Gilroy, *Black Atlantic*, 130, 115.
94 Hartman, *Scenes of Subjection*, 9.

95 A. Walker, "Tillmanism or Mob Rule," 18.
96 A. Walker, "Tillmanism or Mob Rule," 21.
97 Hartman, *Scenes of Subjection*, 3.
98 Hartman, *Scenes of Subjection*, 3.
99 A. Walker, "Tillmanism or Mob Rule," 21.
100 A. Walker, "Tillmanism or Mob Rule," 23.
101 Hartman, *Scenes of Subjection*, 9, 10.
102 A. Walker, "Tillmanism or Mob Rule," 17.
103 A. Walker, "Tillmanism or Mob Rule," 17.
104 A. Walker, "Tillmanism or Mob Rule," 21.
105 A. Walker, "Lynching in the South," 168.
106 A. Walker, "A Reasonable Protest," 170.
107 A. Walker, "Tillmanism or Mob Rule," 22.
108 A. Walker, "Tillmanism or Mob Rule," 21.
109 Moten, "Case of Blackness," 177.
110 Parker, *Book Trade in Canada*, 119.
111 Ronnick, "Henry Alexander Saturnin Hartley," 127.
112 Ronnick, "Henry Alexander Saturnin Hartley," 126.
113 Fingard, "Tale of Two Preachers," 26.
114 A. Walker, "Address by A.B. Walker," 1.
115 Hartley, *Ta Tou*, 138.
116 Fingard, "Tale of Two Preachers," 28.
117 "St. Philip's Church."
118 "N.B. and P.E.I. Conference," 5.
119 Fingard, "Tale of Two Preachers," 28.
120 A. Walker, "Negro Problem," part 3, 132.
121 Adejumobi, "Ethiopianism."
122 Adejumobi, "Ethiopianism."
123 A. Walker, "Negro Problem," part 3, 133.
124 A. Walker, "Negro Problem," part 3, 133.
125 Keita, "Believing in Ethiopians," 29.
126 Keita, "Believing in Ethiopians," 25.
127 Keita, "Believing in Ethiopians," 29.
128 Rankine, *Ulysses in Black*, 28.
129 Rankine, *Ulysses in Black*, 30.
130 Rankine, *Ulysses in Black*, 38.
131 A. Walker, "Late Coal Strike," 1.
132 Quoted in A. Walker, "Late Coal Strike," 1; translation by Ruden, *Aeneid*, 133.
133 Quoted in A. Walker, "Late Coal Strike," 2; translation by Zetzel, *On the Laws*, 159.

134 Rudd and Powell, "Introduction," xxvi.
135 A. Walker, "Late Coal Strike," 2.
136 A. Walker, "Philosophy of Society," 103.
137 A. Walker, "Philosophy of Society," 103.
138 A. Walker, "United States," 126.
139 A. Walker, "Tillmanism or Mob Rule," 20, 22.
140 West, "Prophetic Tradition," 93.
141 West, "Prophetic Tradition," 92.
142 West, "Prophetic Tradition," 93.
143 A. Walker, "Tillmanism or Mob Rule," 22.
144 Sorett, *Spirit in the Dark*, 6.
145 Sorett, *Spirit in the Dark*, 6.
146 Baker, *Harlem Renaissance*, 8.
147 In *Crossroads in the Black Aegean* (2007), Barbara Goff and Michael Simpson posit the "Black Aegean" as an extension of Gilroy's Black Atlantic. The Black Aegean is "a triangle, projected from within the Black Atlantic and symmetrical with it, but with its third point radiating eastwards so that it links Africa to ancient Greece and Asia Minor as well as to the imperial West" (38–9).
148 Du Bois, *Souls of Black Folk*, 3.
149 A. Walker, "Negro Problem," part 1, 23.
150 A. Walker, "Negro Problem," part 4, 181.
151 Chariandy, "Black Canadian Literature," 542.
152 A. Walker, "Hayti and Its Enemies," 3.
153 le Roux, "Creating a British World," 1.
154 A. Walker, "Boer and Black," 6.
155 Louw, *Legacy of Apartheid*, 19.
156 Raymond, "Negro in New Brunswick," 34.
157 McKeown, "Progress of Canada," 40.
158 Wilson, "Canadian Outlook," 36.
159 Clarke, *Directions Home*, 36.
160 Wilson, "Canadian Outlook," 36.
161 "Our New Settlers," 68; "Chinese to Pay," 1.
162 A. Walker, "Editorial Announcements," no. 1, 60.
163 Knowles, *Strangers at Our Gates*, 91.
164 "Neith," *Saint John Star*, 4.
165 "New Magazine," 209.
166 "Neith," *Guardian*, 2.
167 "New Magazine," 209.
168 "Neith," *Saint John Star*, 4.

169 Jack, "Acadian Magazines," 199.
170 Jack, "Acadian Magazines," 199, emphasis added.
171 Jack, "Acadian Magazines," 199, emphasis added.
172 "Neith," *New Freeman*, 7.
173 A. Walker, "Editorial Announcements," no. 2, 98.
174 A. Walker, "New Freeman," 63.
175 A. Walker, "New Freeman," 64.
176 Winks, *Blacks in Canada*, 401.
177 A. Walker, "Tillmanism or Mob Rule," 21.
178 Winks, *Blacks in Canada*, 401.
179 Distad, "Newspapers and Magazines," 293.
180 A. Walker, "Editorial Announcements," no. 5, 238.
181 "Notes of an Immigrant," 11.
182 Winks, *Blacks in Canada*, 401.
183 "Saint John," 8.
184 Green, "Present Demands," 215.
185 McKittrick and Woods, "No One Knows," 5.
186 McKittrick and Woods, "No One Knows," 4.
187 Jemmott, "Publisher's Announcement," 10.
188 McKittrick and Woods, "No One Knows," 6.
189 *Charter of the City*, 15; emphasis added.
190 "Act in Further Amendment," 203.

CHAPTER THREE

1 Prince, *Catastrophe*, 19, 20.
2 Scanlon, "Disaster's Little Known Pioneer," 214.
3 Prince, *Catastrophe*, 35.
4 Prince, *Catastrophe*, 32.
5 MacLennan, *Barometer Rising*, 302.
6 Culligan and MacPhee, "Racism and Relief," 7; D. Sutherland, *Rehabilitation Efforts*, xxi, 7, 58, 399.
7 Remes, "Committed as Near Neighbours," 29.
8 MacLennan, "Voltaire Said …," 137.
9 There is, admittedly, disagreement among critics as to whether MacLennan should be deemed a modernist or antimodernist writer. Reviewing T.D. MacLuluich's critical biography *Hugh MacLennan*, for instance, Paul Goetsch states matter-of-factly that MacLennan was a "highly conservative and antimodernist writer" (34–5). In "Hugh MacLennan's Ambivalent Portrait of the Highlander in *Each Man's Son*," André Dodeman offers a more measured

assessment, writing: "The modernity of MacLennan's fiction may not lie in its narrative techniques and formal characteristics, but it successfully tackles the major social, political and religious changes that were reshaping Canada in the second half of the twentieth century." For an extended discussion of modernism in MacLennan's unpublished novels, see Colin Hill, "Modernism, Antimodernism, and Hugh MacLennan's Novels of the 1930s."

10 Prince, *Catastrophe*, 19.
11 Anderson, "Staging Antimodernism," 97.
12 Forbes, *Maritime Rights*, 61.
13 McKay and Morton, "Maritimes," 75.
14 Tremblay, *Fiddlehead*, 35.
15 Savoie, *Looking for Bootstraps*, 92.
16 Sharma and Tygstrup, "Introduction," 2.
17 R. Williams, *Marxism and Literature*, 132.
18 Masters, "Maritime Board," 26.
19 Thompson, "Quest of the Folk," 246.
20 J. Cooper, "People and Affairs," 23:376.
21 J. Cooper, "People and Affairs," 23:376, 23:377.
22 Cunningham, "Maritimes Doctor," 42.
23 Underhill, *Image of Confederation*, 63.
24 Pentland, "Western Canadian," 60.
25 Bercuson, "Labour Radicalism," 163.
26 B. Cooper, "Regionalism," 97.
27 Willmott, *Unreal Country*, 153.
28 Willmott, *Unreal Country*, 179.
29 Willmott, *Unreal Country*, 153.
30 New, "Maritime Cadences," 3.
31 McKay, *Quest of the Folk*, 27.
32 McKay, *Quest of the Folk*, 30.
33 McKay, *Quest of the Folk*, 35.
34 McKay, *Quest of the Folk*, 31.
35 Wyile, *Anne of Tim Hortons*, 23.
36 Thompson, "Quest of the Folk," 240.
37 Thompson, *Foord Street*, 93.
38 Wyile, *Anne of Tim Hortons*, 22.
39 Creelman, *Setting in the East*, 11.
40 For direct critical responses to McKay's *Quest* beyond those discussed in this chapter, see the contributions of David Creelman, Stephen Dutcher, Greg Marquis, and Miriam Wright in *Acadiensis* 35, no. 1 (2005): 132–80.
41 McKay, *Quest of the Folk*, 36.

42 McKay, *Quest of the Folk*, 42.
43 McKay, *Quest of the Folk*, 33, 36.
44 Davies, *Studies in Maritime Literary History*, 196.
45 McKay, *Quest of the Folk*, 244.
46 Creelman, *Setting in the East*, 11.
47 Wyile, *Anne of Tim Hortons*, 25.
48 McKay, *Quest of the Folk*, 306.
49 McKay, *Quest of the Folk*, 216.
50 McKay, *Quest of the Folk*, 33, 36.
51 Lears, *No Place of Grace*, xvii.
52 McKay, "Helen Creighton," 3.
53 Tremblay, "Politics of the Centre," 37.
54 Lears, *No Place of Grace*, xv.
55 McKay, *Quest of the Folk*, 151.
56 MacMechan, "Private Journal."
57 MacMechan, "Private Journal."
58 Prince, *Catastrophe*, 32.
59 MacMechan, "Halifax Disaster," 59.
60 Metson, "Halifax Disaster," 11.
61 McKay, "Helen Creighton," 5.
62 Vautour, "Modernism, Antimodernism," 34.
63 Narbonne, "Antimodernist Antecedents," 407.
64 McKay, *Quest of the Folk*, 50.
65 McKay, *Quest of the Folk*, 56, 243.
66 MacMechan, *Headwaters*, 8.
67 Stewart, "Salutation," 3.
68 Stewart, "Salutation," 3.
69 Bush, "Varied Hues," 271.
70 Fairley, "Goethe the Poet," 158.
71 Djwa, "E.J. Pratt," 59.
72 Kennedy, "Exile," 520.
73 Klein, "Summer," 209.
74 Eliot, *The Waste Land*, 5.
75 Stewart to Frances Starr, 25 November 1933.
76 Gerson, "Literary Culture," 66.
77 Ritchie, review of *Heliodora*, 400.
78 Ritchie, review of *Heliodora*, 400.
79 Ritchie, review of *Roosevelt*, 140.
80 Ritchie, review of *Iron Door*, 283.
81 Ritchie, review of *Newfoundland*, 266.

82 Ritchie, review of *Dream Tapestries*, 130.
83 Ritchie, review of *Dream Tapestries*, 130.
84 Ritchie, review of *Dream Tapestries*, 130.
85 Trehearne, "Audrey Alexandra Brown," 187.
86 Gerson, "Mid-Century Modernity," 339.
87 Bowman, "Dragon Orchard," 156.
88 Bowman, "Just Before Dawn," 498.
89 Bowman, "Follow – Follow," 304.
90 Bowman, "Follow – Follow," 304.
91 Campbell, *Hidden Rooms*, 340.
92 Tomkinson, "Colonialism and Art," 147.
93 Tomkinson, "Watched Pot," 466.
94 Tomkinson, "Watched Pot," 467.
95 Stephen, "Dr. Samuel Johnson," 500.
96 Lears, *No Place of Grace*, xv.
97 "Communist Movement," 4.
98 Rouillard et al., "Working-Class History"; Frank, "Class and Region," 244.

CHAPTER FOUR

1 "The Busy East," 8.
2 "What's the Busy East?," 5.
3 "Good Advertising," 5.
4 Department of Commerce, *Factors in Foreign Trade*, 14.
5 "Good Advertising," 5.
6 Forbes, "Maritime Historiography," 8.
7 "Publications Received," 32.
8 Earl, "Mike Wardell's," 35.
9 Ferré-Rode, "Atlantic Canada," 178.
10 Ferré-Rode, "Atlantic Canada," 178.
11 Vipond, "Canadian Nationalism," 52.
12 Vipond, "Canadian Nationalism," 52.
13 Logan, "Maritime Provinces," 13.
14 Quoted in Forbes, *Maritime Rights*, 12.
15 Gray, *Promise of Canada*, 273.
16 McKay and Morton, "The Maritimes," 77.
17 For arguments positing the incompatibility of populism and liberalism, see Jan-Werner Mueller's *What Is Populism?* (2016), as well as Cas Mudde and Cristobal Rivera Kaltwassers's *Populism: A Very Short Introduction* (2017).
18 Laclau, *Populist Reason*, 117.

19 Forbes, *Maritime Rights*, vii.
20 Forbes, *Maritime Rights*, 37.
21 Laclau, *Populist Reason,* 74.
22 Marquis, "Commentary," 145.
23 Marquis, "Commentary," 145.
24 "Some Essentials," 4.
25 "Charity Begins," 3.
26 "Maritime Industrial," 21.
27 Sharp, "Do You Know," 13.
28 Hayward, "Sea Coast," 9.
29 "Dawn of a New," 3.
30 "Mental Sloppiness," 4.
31 "New Era," 3, 4.
32 Congdon, "Right of the Maritimes," 17.
33 Mason, *Home Feelings*, 9.
34 Avard, "Supreme Test," 12.
35 Avard, "Supreme Test," 12.
36 Avard, "New Spirit," 4.
37 Avard, "New Spirit," 4.
38 Quoted in Savoie, *Looking for Bootstraps*, 1.
39 Conrad and Hiller, *Atlantic Canada*, 167.
40 Forbes, *Maritime Regionalism*, 16; Frank, "Class and Region," 234.
41 Conrad and Hiller, *Atlantic Canada*, 170.
42 Forbes, "Maritime Rights."
43 Masters, "Maritime Board," 26.
44 Nerbas, "Revisiting the Politics," 111–12.
45 Nerbas, "Revisiting the Politics," 112.
46 Nerbas, "Revisiting the Politics," 127.
47 Nerbas, "Revisiting the Politics," 126.
48 Nerbas, "Revisiting the Politics," 127.
49 Paterson, "Maritime Disabilities," 7.
50 Nerbas, "Revisiting the Politics," 129.
51 McCurdy et al., "Annual Meeting," 4.
52 McCurdy et al., "Annual Meeting," 13, 19.
53 Paterson, "Maritime Disabilities," 6–7.
54 Paterson, "Maritime Disabilities," 5, 16.
55 Nerbas, "Revisiting the Politics," 126.
56 Frank, "Class and Region," 256.
57 As Frank, Forbes, Nerbas, and others point out, the region was disadvantaged by inordinate increases in freight rates relative to western Canada, it had been

only partially integrated into the national transportation network, it was losing political representation with each federal redistribution of seats, and none of the Maritime Provinces benefited from the new federal subsidies, subsidy increases, and school lands granted other Canadian provinces between 1905 and 1912. Forbes, *Aspects*, 13; Frank, "Class and Region," 257; Nerbas, "Revisiting the Politics," 112.

58 Frank, "Class and Region," 261.

59 As Jody Mason points out in her recent monograph *Home Feelings: Liberal Citizenship and the Canadian Reading Camp Movement*, citizenship was not a legal category in Canada before the *Canadian Citizenship Act* came into effect in 1947. The use of "citizenship" here is meant to refer to its conception and circulation within the "discourse of citizenship" that Mason argues emerged prior to mid-century "in relation to the various reform movements of the late nineteenth and early twentieth centuries, as well as in the context of the class struggles of the interwar period" (7).

60 "Spelling of Place Names," 7.

61 McKay and Bates, *Province of History*, 145.

62 Bird, *And We Go On*, 4.

63 Bird, *And We Go On*, 5.

64 Bird, *And We Go On*, 4.

65 Berlant, *Cruel Optimism*, 7.

66 Berlant, *Cruel Optimism*, 3.

67 Berlant, *Anatomy of National Fantasy*, 5.

68 Hodd, "Introduction," 2.

69 Vance, "Soldier as Novelist," 28.

70 McKay and Bates, *Province of History*, 131.

71 "Voltaire," 26.

72 Smyth, review of *And We Go On*, 15.

73 Vance, *Death So Noble*, 40.

74 McKay and Bates, *Province of History*, 135.

75 McKay and Bates, *Province of History*, 133.

76 McKay and Bates, *Province of History*, 162, 197.

77 McKay and Bates, *Province of History*, 136.

78 Hodd, "Introduction," 3.

79 Hodd, "Casualty of Genre," 103.

80 Hodd, "Casualty of Genre," 103.

81 Bird, "Priscilla's Private," 74, 75.

82 Bird, "Priscilla's Private," 87, 76.

83 Bird, "Priscilla's Private," 88.

84 Avard, "Banishing the Fear," 4.

85 Avard, "Banishing the Fear," 5, 6.
86 Avard, "Banishing the Fear," 6.
87 Avard, "Banishing the Fear," 6.
88 Bird, "Priscilla's Private," 81.
89 Avard, "Banishing the Fear," 6.
90 Bird, "Priscilla's Private," 88.
91 Bird, "Major's Prisoner," 10.
92 Bird, "Major's Prisoner," 12.
93 Bird, "Umpty-Ump," 12.
94 Bird, "Umpty-Ump," 13.
95 Hodd, "Casualty of Genre," 112.
96 Bird, *Private Timothy*, 7.
97 Bird, "His Deputy," 15.
98 Bird, "Boots," 14.
99 Bird, "His Brother," 14.
100 For a discussion of Bird's use of silent film conventions in his memoir, see David Williams, "Spectres of Time: Seeing Ghosts in Will Bird's Memoirs and Abel Gance's *J'accuse*" (2013).
101 Bird, "Boots," 14.
102 Bird, "Major's Prisoner," 10.
103 Bird, *And We Go On*, 4.
104 Bird, "Umpty-Ump," 13.
105 Bird, "Umpty-Ump," 14.
106 Bird, "His Brother," 17.
107 Bird, "Boots," 14.
108 Bird, "Boots," 16.
109 Bird, "His Brother," 14.
110 Bird, "His Brother," 15.
111 Bird, "His Brother," 16.
112 Bird, "Major's Prisoner," 17.
113 Bird, "Boots," 17.
114 Bird, "Boots," 17.
115 Bird, *Private Timothy*, 7.
116 Vance, "Soldier as Novelist," 28.
117 Hodd, "Casualty of Genre," 106.
118 C. Hill, "Generic Experiment," 61.
119 C. Hill, "Generic Experiment," 61.
120 C. Hill, "Generic Experiment," 61.
121 McKay, "Liberal Order Framework," 623.
122 Avard, "Old and New," 3.

123 Avard, "Old and New," 3–4.
124 McKay, "Liberal Order Framework," 130.
125 Simms, "Past Year," 9.
126 "Development in Construction," 18.
127 "Some Notable Changes," 7.
128 "Some Notable Changes," 7, emphasis added.
129 Frank, "Class and Region," 258.
130 Savoie, *Looking for Bootstraps*, 93.
131 Forbes, *Maritime Rights*, 191.
132 Nerbas, "Revisiting the Politics," 130.
133 Nerbas, "Revisiting the Politics," 130.
134 McKay, *Quest of the Folk*, 37.
135 With the notable exception of his story "47 Dollars Worth of Life," Bird's war fiction was mostly free of the cultural antimodernism that would dominate his later writing. Bird did publish several historical and contemporary romance stories alongside his war fiction in *The Busy East* prior to 1930, but, as McKay and Bates observe, it was in the early 1930s that Bird began to focus his efforts on producing "romantic Nova Scotiana," which became "fantastically popular in Canada during the 1940s and 1950s" (156).

CHAPTER FIVE

1 Reilly, "Toilers," 40.
2 Reilly, "Toilers," 38.
3 Reilly, "Toilers," 40.
4 "Barrett Brothers," 1.
5 Reilly, "Toilers," 38.
6 "Our Position," 2.
7 Frank, *J.B. McLachlan*, 556n66.
8 Kealey, "Canadian Socialism," 90.
9 Mellor, *Cape Breton Miners*, 135; Frank, *J.B. McLachlan*, 214.
10 Frank, *J.B. McLachlan*, 215.
11 Sclater, "Labor and Radical Press."
12 See John Manley's "Preaching the Red Stuff: J.B. McLachlan, Communism, and the Cape Breton Miners, 1922–1935" (1992); Ian McKay and Suzanne Morton's "The Maritimes: Expanding the Circle of Resistance" (1998); David Frank's *J.B. McLachlan: A Biography* (1999); John Mellor's *J.B. McLachlan and the Cape Breton Coal Miners 1900–1925* (1983); and Richard MacKinnon's "Protest Songs and Verse in Cape Breton Island" (2008).
13 Buchanan, "Yours for the Revolution," 134.

14 Irvine, *Editing Modernity*, 48.
15 Irvine, *Editing Modernity*, 49.
16 Nelson, *Revolutionary Memory*, 145.
17 Nelson, *Revolutionary Memory*, 145.
18 Fraser, "Case of Jim O'Coughlin," 4; Chaplin, "Industrial Heretics," 1.
19 Nelson, *Revolutionary Memory*, 55.
20 Frank, "Class and Region," 244.
21 Nelson, *Revolutionary Memory*, 145, 147.
22 Frank, "Class and Region," 244; MacGillivray, "Cape Breton," 50.
23 MacGillivray, "Cape Breton," 50.
24 Frank, "Class and Region," 245.
25 MacGillivray, "Cape Breton," 53.
26 Frank, *J.B. McLachlan*, 194, 239.
27 Quoted in Ludlow, *Canny Scot*, 130.
28 Frank, "Cape Breton Strikes."
29 Cotton, "Mission of Cape Breton," 4.
30 I adopt here the distinction, made by historians of the British, American, Australian, and Canadian labour movements, between the radical left and labourism, a reformist ideology "resembling but differing from agrarian populism, contemporary liberalism, and socialism" that rejected "industrial unionism" and "full-scale socialism" (Heron, "Labourism," 45, 71). For more on this distinction in the Canadian context, see Craig Heron's "Labourism and the Canadian Working Class," and, in the Nova Scotia context, Suzanne Morton's "Labourism and Economic Action: The Halifax Shipyards Strike of 1920."
31 Molinaro, *Exceptional Law*, 6.
32 Cotton, "Future Subjects," 4.
33 Cotton, "Our Position," 2.
34 The use of this analogy between wage labour and chattel slavery, generally evoked by the phrase "wage slavery," is pervasive in the *MLH*. It is by no means unique to the paper. In fact, American historian Lawrence Glickman observes of the late-nineteenth-century American labour movement that "[r]eferences [to wage slavery] abounded in the labor press, and it is hard to find a speech by a labor leader without the phrase" (19). Use of the "wage slavery metaphor," Glickman maintains, continued well into the twentieth century, and the analogy remained popular when Glickman was writing in the 1990s.
35 Cotton, "Our Position," 2.
36 "Industrial Democracy," 1; "Private Initiative," 1; Woodsworth, "New MP," 1.
37 "Russia Will Accept," 2.

38 "Yellow Legs," 6.
39 "Jobs for Soldiers," 6.
40 "UMW Take Great Stand," 6.
41 Manley, "Preaching the Red Stuff," 68.
42 Spector, "Great Stand," 1.
43 McKay and Morton, "Maritimes," 70.
44 Frank, *J.B. McLachlan*, 259; McKay and Morton, "Maritimes," 74.
45 Dogliani, "Socialist Internationalism," 38.
46 Cotton, "United Front," 7.
47 "Gazette and Labor," 1.
48 "Remedy for Strikes," 4.
49 "Strikers Threaten," 2.
50 Quoted in Manley, "Preaching the Red Stuff," 86.
51 McKay and Drachewych, "Introduction," 6.
52 Studer, *Transnational World*, 4, 5.
53 Lévesque, "Transnational Experience," 184.
54 Lévesque, "Transnational Experience," 184.
55 Manley, "Preaching the Red Stuff," 75.
56 "Married Under," 1.
57 Henderson, "Capital Internationalism," 1.
58 Campbell, *Rose Henderson*, 93.
59 Frank, "Fillmore."
60 Fillmore, "Peas, Potatoes," 2.
61 Fillmore, "Travelling in Russia," 3.
62 Fillmore, "Travelling in Russia," 3.
63 Fillmore, "Travelling in Russia," 3.
64 "Japanese Earthquake," 3.
65 "Japanese Earthquake," 3.
66 Doyle, *Progressive Heritage*, 82.
67 Doyle, *Progressive Heritage*, 82.
68 Doyle, *Progressive Heritage*, 83.
69 Fraser, "Case of Jim O'Coughlin," 4.
70 "Miners Demonstrate," 1.
71 Fraser, "Cape Breton Miner," 4.
72 MacKinnon, "Protest Songs," 44.
73 Doyle, *Progressive Heritage*, 66.
74 Doyle, *Progressive Heritage*, 64, 69.
75 Wallace, "Awake," 4.
76 Vautour, "Modernism, Antimodernism," 34.
77 Wallace, "Rise of the Red," 4.

78 Nelson, *Revolutionary Memory*, 157.
79 Nelson, *Revolutionary Memory*, 157.
80 Nelson, *Revolutionary Memory*, 157.
81 Nelson, *Revolutionary Memory*, 145.
82 Nelson, *Revolutionary Memory*, 145.
83 Wallace, "Voice of the Worker," 4.
84 "Blankets and Bedding," 3; "Tea," 3.
85 Mellor, *Cape Breton Miners*, 137.
86 Penfold, "Gender and Class," 25.
87 Bartholomew, "Steel Slaves," 8.
88 "Social Influence," 2.
89 Fraser, "Wearing of the Red," 8.
90 Wallace, "Awake," 4.
91 Buhay, "Daughters Awake," 3.
92 Buhay, "Daughters Awake," 3.
93 Buhay, "Women and Capitalism," 3.
94 Sangster, *Dreams of Equality*, 28.
95 Custance, "Some Facts," 7.
96 "Women's Labor," 1; "Women of Sydney," 1.
97 Custance, "International Women's Day," 6.
98 Custance, "International Women's Day," 6.
99 Custance, "International Women's Day," 6.
100 Sangster, "Communist Party," 25.
101 Sangster, *Dreams of Equality*, 28.
102 "Women's Club Meets at Dominion No. 4," 3.
103 Buhay, "Women and Capitalism," 3.
104 Buhay, "Women and Capitalism," 3.
105 Buhay, "Women and Capitalism," 3.
106 Buhay, "Women and Capitalism," 3.
107 Buhay, "Women's Place in History: 1," 3.
108 Eller, "Feminist Appropriation," 3.
109 Buhay, "Women's Place in History: 1," 3; Engels, "Origin of the Family," 744.
110 Engels, "Origin of the Family," 739.
111 Buhay, "Women's Place in History: 1," 3.
112 Buller, "Women and War," 3.
113 McPhail, "Women's National League," 3; Sangster, "Communist Party," 38.
114 Konikow, "Mother's League," 3.
115 Storch, *Red Chicago*, 26.
116 Carter, "Anti-Lenin Lies," 4.
117 Carter, "Anti-Lenin Lies," 4.
118 Boone, "Women Should Organize," 5.

119 Penfold, "Gender and Class," 38; Whitfield, "Miner's Wife," 3.
120 Sangster, *Dreams of Equality*, 70.
121 Sangster, *Dreams of Equality*, 70.
122 Manley, "Preaching the Red Stuff," 87.
123 McKay and Morton, "Maritimes," 59.
124 Sangster, *Dreams of Equality*, 29.
125 Boone, "Women Should Organize," 5.
126 Buhay, "Daughters Awake," 3.
127 Buhay, "Machine Awakens," 3.
128 Vellino, "Machine-Age," 46.
129 This connection merits further investigation, not so much for potential poetic influence as for situating their poetics within a common tradition of Canadian proletarian modernism that begins before the 1930s. Buhay, as a leading communist, was almost certainly known to Livesay. As Sangster records, the two were among several communist women to attend the founding convention of the Canadian League against War and Fascism in 1934, during which the women in attendance "met separately one evening and formed a National Women's Council" (Sangster, *Dreams of Equality*, 144). Of course, acquaintance does not suggest poetic influence. Livesay's poem is longer and adopts more regular metres and rhythms. The broad setting and subject of the poems – both poems register the violent inscription of labour upon the bodies of workers with emphasis on the tactile and sonic space of the factory – is not unique to these poets. Nevertheless, the similarities are striking. In Buhay's poem, "living automatons" move in "rhythm" "backwards and forwards" to the "tumult of the machines"; in Livesay's, workers take "one step forward / two steps back" to the "smashing rhythm" of "machines" and a "roaring voice." In both poems, this industrial choreography figures as a dance: Livesay's workers "dance in time to the machines" while in Buhay's poem, the "rhythm of their feet and hands" quickens as "the roar of machines breaks into song." Buhay's workers are literally suffocating within their factory jail, as they "puff and blow, trying to inhale the air"; meanwhile, Livesay's workers "blow [their] breath" and are "smothered" (Buhay, "Machine Awakens," 3; Livesay, "Day and Night," 155–60).
130 McCallum, "Race, Class," 192.
131 Livesay, "Day and Night," 160.
132 Buhay, "Machine Awakens," 3.
133 McCallum, "Race and Class," 192.
134 Forbes, *Maritime Rights*, 60.
135 McPhail et al., *House of Commons Debates*, 1731.
136 McPhail et al., *House of Commons Debates*, 1731.
137 Quoted in Frank, *J.B. McLachlan*, 378.

138 Manley, "Preaching the Red Stuff," 93.
139 Manley, "Preaching the Red Stuff," 93.
140 Frank, *J.B. McLachlan*, 428.
141 Manley, "Preaching the Red Stuff," 94.
142 Howard, "National Miners Union," 101–2.
143 Forbes, *Maritime Rights*, 61.
144 The others cited by Buck are *New Democracy* (Hamilton, 1919–23), the *BC Federationist* (Vancouver, 1911–25), and the short-lived *The Worker's Guard*, which was replaced by *The Worker* in 1922.
145 Buck, *Thirty Years*, 26; Manley, "Preaching the Red Stuff," 86.
146 Lenin, "Where to Begin," 22.
147 Lenin, "Where to Begin," 23.
148 Lenin, "Where to Begin," 22–3.
149 Habermas, *Structural Transformation*, 124.
150 "The Capitalist State," 4.
151 McLachlan, "Dead Hand," 5.
152 McLachlan, "Dead Hand," 5.
153 McLachlan, "Conservative Convention," 1.
154 McLachlan, "Conservative Convention," 8.
155 Frank, "Class and Region," 249.
156 Frank, "Class and Region," 249.
157 "Notice," 4.
158 "Notice," 4.
159 "Notice," 4.
160 "Notice," 4.
161 Beaton, "Religious Affiliation," 119.
162 Only a single issue of *The Nova Scotian Gleaner*, vol. 1, no. 3, survives.
163 Quoted in R. Hill, "Redemption Works," 205.
164 R. Hill, "Redemption Works," 205.
165 R. Hill, "Redemption Works," 207.
166 McKay and Morton, "Maritimes," 43.
167 McKay and Morton, "Maritimes," 77.
168 Harvey, *Spaces of Capital*, 81.
169 "UMW Take Great Stand," 6.
170 McKay and Morton, "Maritimes," 76.
171 McKay, "Note on Regionalism," 99.
172 McKay, "Karl Marx," 5.
173 Frank, "Class and Region," 287.
174 Wyile, *Anne of Tim Hortons*, 240.
175 Marx, "Ruthless Criticism," 15.

CONCLUSION

1 MacLeod, "Closing Down," 180.
2 MacLeod, "Closing Down," 185.
3 MacLeod, "Closing Down," 198.
4 MacLeod, "Closing Down," 183.
5 MacLeod, "Closing Down," 194.
6 MacLeod, "Closing Down," 194.
7 MacLeod, "Closing Down," 182.
8 MacLeod, "Closing Down," 144.
9 MacLeod, "Closing Down," 181.
10 MacLeod, "Closing Down," 193.
11 Wyile, *Anne of Tim Hortons*, 58.
12 Grady, "Complexity Graces," E10.
13 Levene, "Letters in Canada," 11.
14 Brox, "Mirroring the Passage," B1.
15 Wallace, "True Test," 1.
16 Lepaludier, "Everyday," 8.
17 Ricou, "Story and Teller," 117.
18 Levene, "Letters in Canada," 11.
19 Carpenter, "Writing Home," 154.
20 J. Sutherland, "Out with the Tide," 6.
21 J. Sutherland, "Out with the Tide," 6.
22 J. Sutherland, "Out with the Tide," 6.
23 Wyile, *Anne of Tim Hortons*, 58.
24 Charman, "Seems to Bust," 75.
25 Thompson, *Nights Below*, 38.
26 Carpenter, "Writing Home," 154.
27 Wyile, *Anne of Tim Hortons*, 56.
28 McKay, *Quest of the Folk*, 310.
29 McKay, *Quest of the Folk*, 276.
30 "Song of the Race," 1.
31 Tremblay, *Fiddlehead Moment*, xiv, xvii.
32 Tremblay, *Fiddlehead Moment*, 8.
33 Tremblay, *Fiddlehead Moment*, 76.
34 Tremblay, *Fiddlehead Moment*, 78.
35 Bailey, "Here in the East," 28.
36 Bailey, "Fiddlehead," 1.
37 Tremblay, *Fiddlehead Moment*, 96.
38 Soja, *Postmodern Geographies*, 73.

39 Vautour, "Modernism, Antimodernism," 19.
40 Vautour, "Modernism, Antimodernism," 19, 31.
41 Vautour, "Modernism, Antimodernism," 18.
42 McKay, *Quest of the Folk*, 227.
43 Tomkinson, "Watched Pot," 467.
44 Frye, Letter, 539.
45 Niergarth, *New Brunswick Artists*.
46 Leroux, "Concrete Artistic Vision," 2, 3.
47 Herring, *Creating a Centre*, 100.
48 Niergarth, *New Brunswick Artists*, 31.
49 Niergarth, *New Brunswick Artists*, 163.
50 Quoted in Niergarth, *New Brunswick Artists*, 84.
51 Niergarth, *New Brunswick Artists*, 164.
52 Horrall, "Century of Canadian Art," 156.
53 Tremblay, *Fiddlehead*, 194.
54 Moore, "Fiddlehead."
55 Bailey, "Ballad of John Bodkin," 18.
56 Vautour, "Modernism, Antimodernism," 34.
57 Clarke, "Anna Minerva Henderson," 33.

Bibliography

"A Remedy for Strikes." [Moncton] *Daily Times*, 25 August 1922: 4.

"Acadians (1752 to 1784)." *Censuses of Canada 1665 to 1871*, Statistics Canada, 26 August 2015. http://www150.statcan.gc.ca/n1/pub/98-187-x/4064810-eng.htm.

"Acadiensis." *Review of Historical Publications Relating to Canada* 12 (1909): 63.

Acheson, T.W. "The National Policy and the Industrialization of the Maritimes, 1880–1910." *Acadiensis* 1, no. 2 (1971): 3–28.

Adejumobi, Saheed. "Ethiopianism." *BlackPast.org*, 22 February 2020. https://www.blackpast.org/global-african-history/ethiopianism.

Amin, Ash. "Regions Unbound: Towards a New Politics of Place." *Geografiska annaler: series 8: Human Geography*, no. 86 (2004): 33–44.

Anderson, Benedict. "Staging Antimodernism in the Age of High Capitalist Nationalism." In *Antimodernism and Artistic Experience: Policing the Boundaries of Modernity*, edited by Lynda Jessup, 97–103. Toronto: University of Toronto Press, 2001.

Angell, Stephen W., and Anthony B. Pinn. "George Gilbert Walker." In *Social Protest Thought in the African Methodist Episcopal Church, 1862–1939*, edited by Stephen W. Angell and Anthony B. Pinn, 143. Knoxville, TN: University of Tennessee Press, 2000.

Angus, Frances. "The Lagoon." *Dalhousie Review* 17, no. 3 (1937): 310.

Appiah, Anthony. *In My Father's House: Africa in the Philosophy of Culture*. Oxford, UK: Oxford University Press, 1993.

"An Act in Further Amendment of the Charter of the City of Saint John. Passed 14th April 1849." In *The Revised Statutes of New Brunswick*, edited by William B. Kinnear, 129–38. Fredericton: J. Simpson, 1855.

Ardis, Ann L., and Patrick Collier. "Transatlantic Print Culture, 1880–1940: Emerging Media, Emerging Modernisms." In *Transatlantic Print Culture,*

1880–1940: Emerging Media, Emerging Modernisms, edited by Ann Ardis and Patrick Collier, 1–15. London: Palgrave Macmillan, 2008.

Avard, Clement C. "Banishing the Fear Bogey." *Busy East of Canada*, September 1930: 3–4.

– "Merit Is the Supreme Test." *Busy East of Canada*, March 1923: 12.

– "The New Spirit of the Age." *Busy East of Canada*, February 1920: 3–4.

– "The Old and the New." *Busy East of Canada*, January 1930: 3–4.

Bailey, Alfred. "Here in the East." In *Thanks for a Drowned Island*, 28. Toronto: McClelland and Stewart, 1973.

– "The Ballad of John Bodkin." In *The Sun the Wind the Summer Field*, 49–50. Fredericton: Goose Lane, 1996.

– "The Fiddlehead." *The Fiddlehead*, no. 1, 1945: 1.

Bailey, Joseph W. "Some Features of the Rivers of New Brunswick." *Acadiensis* 2, no. 2 (April 1902): 114–18.

Baker, Houston A. *Modernism and the Harlem Renaissance*. Chicago: University of Chicago Press, 1987.

– *Turning South Again: Re-Thinking Modernism / Re-Reading Booker T.* Durham, NC, and London: Duke University Press, 2001.

Ballantyne, Emily, Marta Dvořák, and Dean Irvine. "Introduction." In *Translocated Modernisms: Paris and Other Lost Generations*, edited by Emily Ballantyne, Marta Dvořák, and Dean Irvine, 1–19. Ottawa: University of Ottawa Press, 2016.

"Barrett Brothers Raided Newspaper." *Montreal Gazette*, 12 May 1923: 1.

Bartholomew, H.M. "Steel Slaves of Sydney." *Maritime Labor Herald*, 3 February 1923: 1, 8.

Beaton, Elizabeth. "Religious Affiliation and Ethnic Identity of West Indians in Whitney Pier." *Canadian Ethnic Studies* 20, no. 3 (1988): 112–31.

Beetham, Margaret. "Towards a Theory of the Periodical as a Publishing Genre." In *Investigating Victorian Journalism*, edited by Laurel Brake, Alex Jones, and Lionel Madden, 19–32. London: Macmillan, 1990.

Bell, D.G. "Introduction." In *The Judges of New Brunswick and Their Times*, 2nd ed., by Joseph W. Lawrence, v–xxi. Fredericton: Acadiensis Press, 1985 [1907].

Bell, Frank M. *A Romance of the Halifax Disaster*. Halifax: Royal Print & Litho, 1918.

Bentley, D.M.R. "Canada." In *The Fin-De-Siècle World*, edited by Michael Saler, 213–25. London and New York: Routledge, 2014.

– "Carman and Mind Cure: Theory and Technique." In *Bliss Carman: A Reappraisal*, edited by Gerald Lynch, 85–110. Ottawa: University of Ottawa Press, 1990.

– *The Confederation Group of Canadian Poets, 1880–1997.* Toronto: University of Toronto Press, 2004.
– *The Gay]Grey Moose: Essays on the Ecologies and Mythologies of Canadian Poetry, 1690–1990.* Ottawa: University of Ottawa Press, 1992.
Bercuson, David. "Labour Radicalism and the Western Industrial Frontier: 1897–1919." *Canadian Historical Review* 58, no. 2 (1977): 154–75.
Berlant, Lauren. *The Anatomy of National Fantasy: Hawthorne, Utopia, and Everyday Life.* Chicago: University of Chicago Press, 1991.
– *Cruel Optimism.* Durham, NC, and London: Duke University Press, 2011.
Bird, Will R. *And We Go On.* 1930. Reprinted with an introduction by David Williams. Montreal and Kingston, ON: McGill-Queen's University Press, 2014.
– "Boots." *Busy East of Canada*, January 1930: 12–17, 31.
– "His Brother." *Busy East of Canada*, October 1929: 14–20.
– "His Deputy." *Busy East of Canada*, April 1927: 12–18.
– "The Major's Prisoner." *Busy East of Canada*, August 1927: 10–17.
– "Priscilla's Private." In *A Soldiers Place: The Stories of Will R. Bird*, edited by Thomas Hodd, 74–89. Halifax: Nimbus, 2019.
– *Private Timothy Fergus Clancy.* Ottawa: Graphic Publishers, 1930.
– "Umpty-Ump." *Busy East of Canada*, July–August 1930: 12–18, 31.
Blair, Jennifer, et al. "Introduction." In *Recalling Early Canada: Reading the Political in Literary and Cultural Production*, edited by Jennifer Blair et al., xiii–l. Edmonton: University of Alberta Press, 2005.
"Blankets and Bedding for Cold Weather." *Maritime Labor Herald*, 6 October 1923: 3.
Boone, Bert. "Women Should Organize." *Maritime Labor Herald*, 3 May 1924: 5.
Bowles, J.S. "The International." *International*, July 1901: 1.
Bowman, Louise Morey. "Dragon Orchard." *Dalhousie Review* 7, no. 2 (1927): 156–8.
– "Follow – Follow." *Dalhousie Review* 14, no. 3 (1934): 304.
– "Just Before Dawn." *Dalhousie Review* 5, no. 4 (1926): 495–8.
Boyd, Barbara Weiden. *Ovid's Literary Loves: Influence and Innovation in the Amores.* Ann Arbor, MI: University of Michigan Press, 1997.
Brandt, Di. "A New Genealogy of Canadian Literary Modernism." In *Wider Boundaries of Daring: The Modernist Impulse in Canadian Women's Poetry*, edited by Di Brandt and Barbara Godard, 1–28. Waterloo, ON: Wilfrid Laurier University Press, 2009.
Brewster, Herbert L. "The Days that Are Not." *Acadiensis* 2, no. 2 (April 1902): 113.
Bridle, Augustus. "What Is a Canadian?" *Canadian Courier*, July 1916: 3–4.

Brookes, Alan. "Out-Migration from the Maritime Provinces, 1860–1900: Some Preliminary Considerations." *Acadiensis* 5, no. 2 (1976): 27–55.

Brown, Kirby. "American Indian Modernities and New Modernist Studies' 'Indian Problem.'" *Texas Studies in Literature and Language* 59, no. 3 (2017): 287–318.

Brox, Jane. "Mirroring the Passage of Cape Breton Ways." Review of *Island: The Complete Stories*, by Alistair MacLeod. *Boston Globe*, 18 Feb 2001: B.1.

Bryant, Rachel. *The Homing Place*. Waterloo, ON: Wilfrid Laurier University Press, 2017.

Buchanan, David. "'Yours for the Revolution': Communication and Identity in the *Western Clarion*." *English Studies in Canada* 41, nos. 2–3 (2015): 133–64.

Buck, Tim. *Thirty Years, 1922–1952: The Story of the Communist Movement in Canada*. Toronto: Progress Books, 1952.

Buckner, Philip A. "Acadiensis II." *Acadiensis* 1, no. 1 (1971): 3–9.

Buhay, Rebecca. "Daughters Awake!" *Maritime Labor Herald*, 16 August 1924: 3.

– "The Machine Awakens." *Maritime Labor Herald*, 19 July 1924: 3.

– "Women and Capitalism." *Maritime Labor Herald*, 12 July 1924: 3.

– "Women and the Trade Union Movement." *Maritime Labor Herald*, 27 February 1926: 3.

– "Women's Place in History: 1 – Women of the Earliest Times." *Maritime Labor Herald*, 16 August 1924: 3.

– "Women's Place in History: 7 – Women Under Capitalist Society." *Maritime Labor Herald*, 1 November 1924: 3.

"Building in Canada on the Increase." *Canadian Municipal Journal* 13, no. 4 (1917): 121.

Buller, Annie. "Women and War." *Maritime Labor Herald*, 7 June 1924: 3.

– "Working Class Movies." *Maritime Labor Herald*, 13 December 1924: 6.

Bundale, Brad. "Halifax's Brooklyn: Downtown Dartmouth One of Country's Hippest Neighbourhoods." *The National Post*, 6 November 2017. http://nationalpost.com/pmn/news-pmn/canada-news-pmn/halifaxs-brooklyn-downtown-dartmouth-one-of-countrys-hippest-neighbourhoods.

Bush, Douglas. "The Varied Hues of Pessimism." *Dalhousie Review* 9, no. 3 (1928): 271–81.

"The Busy East." [Moncton] *Daily Times*, 15 September 1910: 8.

Cahill, J.B. "First Things in Africadia: Or, The Trauma of Being a Black Lawyer in Late Victorian Saint John." *University of New Brunswick Law Journal* 47 (1998): 367–77.

– "Walker, Abraham Beverly." In *Dictionary of Canadian Biography*, vol. 13. Toronto and Laval, QC: University of Toronto / Université Laval, 1994. http://www.biographi.ca/en/bio/walker_abraham_beverley_13E.html.

Campbell, Charles. "The Museum Shell." *Neith* 1, no. 1 (February 1903): 26.

Campbell, Peter. *Rose Henderson: A Woman for the People*. Montreal and Kingston, ON: McGill-Queen's University Press, 2010.

Campbell, Wanda. *Hidden Rooms: Early Canadian Women Poets*. London, ON: Canadian Poetry Press, 2000.

"Capitalism in China." *Maritime Labor Herald*, 28 October 1921: 6.

"The Capitalist State." *Maritime Labor Herald*, 29 July 1922: 4.

Cappon, James. *Bliss Carman and the Literary Currents and Influences of His Time*. Toronto: Ryerson Press, 1930.

"Carleton Cornet Band." [Saint John] *New Freeman*, 21 February 1903: 4.

Carman, Bliss. "Low Tide on Grand Pre." In *Low Tide on Grand Pré: A Book of Lyrics: by Bliss Carman*, 15–18. Cambridge: Stone and Kimball, 1894. https://archive.org/details/lowtideongrandproocarmuoft.

– "Song of the Four Worlds." *Acadiensis* 6, no. 1 (April 1906): 1.

– "A Supplication." *Acadiensis* 2, no. 2 (April 1902): 74.

Carpenter, David. "Writing Home." Review of *The Lost Salt Gift of Blood: New & Selected Stories*, by Alistair MacLeod. *Canadian Literature*, no. 129 (1991): 152–4.

Carter, Blanche. "Anti-Lenin Lies." *Maritime Labor Herald*, 23 February 1924: 4.

Chamberlain, Montague. "Primitive Life of Wapanaki Women." *Acadiensis* 2, no. 2 (April 1902): 75–86.

Chaplin, Ralph. "The Industrial Heretics." *Maritime Labor Herald*, 31 May 1924: 1.

Chariandy, David. "Black Canadian Literature: Fieldwork and 'Post-Race.'" In *The Oxford Handbook of Canadian Literature*, edited by Cynthia Sugars, 540–63. Oxford, UK: Oxford University Press, 2015.

"Charity Begins at Home." *Busy East of Canada*, November 1923: 3.

Charman, Caitlin. "'It Seems to Bust Your Balls': Coal Nostalgia, Masculinity, and Energy History in Alistair MacLeod's Short Fiction." *Studies in Canadian Literature / Études en littérature canadienne* 43, no. 2 (2018): 60–78.

"Chinese to Pay a Tax of $500 in the Dominion." *Saint John Semi-Weekly Telegraph*, 7 March 1903: 1.

The Charter of the City of Saint John in the Province of New Brunswick. Saint John: William Durant, 1811. https://archive.org/details/cihm_48078.

"City Cornet Band." *Saint John Globe*, 21 February 1903: 2.

Clarke, George Elliott. "Anna Minerva Henderson: An Afro-New Brunswick Response to Canadian (Modernist) Poetry." *Canadian Literature* 189 (2006): 32–48.

– *Directions Home: Approaches to African-Canadian Literature*. Toronto: University of Toronto Press, 2012.

– *Odysseys Home: Mapping African-Canadian Literature*. Toronto: University of Toronto Press, 2002.

Clarke, Jeremiah S. "Glooskap." *Acadiensis* 2, no. 2 (April 1902): 87–9.

"Classical Translations." *Saint John Daily Sun*, 15 November 1889.

"The Communist Movement." *Maritime Labor Herald*, 23 December 1923: 4.

CMM Environmental Services and the Confederacy of Mainland Mi'kmaq. "Mi'kmaq Ecological Knowledge Study: Highway 107 Sackville to Porters Lake." 2010. http://novascotia.ca/nse/ea/highway-107-burnside-to-bedford/Appendix_I-K.pdf.

Cody, H.A. "Loyalists' Reception." *Acadiensis* 4, no. 2 (April 1904): 119.

Congdon, H.S. "The Right of the Maritimes to the Trans-Atlantic Trade of Canada." *Busy East of Canada*, November 1923: 12–21.

Connolly, James J. "Print Culture Histories beyond the Metropolis: An Introduction." In *Print Culture Histories beyond the Metropolis*, edited by Patrick Collier et al., 3–28. Toronto: University of Toronto Press, 2016.

Conrad, Margaret, and James K. Hiller. *Atlantic Canada: A Region in the Making*. Oxford, UK: Oxford University Press, 2001.

Constantinides, Zoë. "The Myth of Evangeline and the Origin of Canadian National Cinema." *Film History* 26, no. 1 (2014): 50–79.

Cooper, Barry. "Regionalism, Political Culture and Canadian Political Myths." In *Regionalism and Party Politics in Canada*, edited by Lisa Young and Keith Archer, 92–112. Oxford, UK: Oxford University Press, 2002.

Cooper, John A. "People and Affairs." *Canadian Magazine* 17, no. 4 (August 1901): 387–90.

– "People and Affairs." *Canadian Magazine* 23, no. 4 (August 1904): 376–8.

Cotton, William U. "Future Subjects of Discussion." *Maritime Labor Herald*, 3 December 1921: 4.

– "The Mission of Cape Breton Labor." *Maritime Labor Herald*, 29 October 1921: 4.

– "Our Position." *Maritime Labor Herald*, 17 June 1922: 2.

– "The United Front." *Maritime Labor Herald*, 29 July 1922: 7.

Courtney, E. *A Commentary on the Satires of Juvenal*. London: Athlone Press, 1980.

Craig, Terrence L. *Racial Attitudes in English-Canadian Fiction, 1905–1980*. Waterloo, ON: Wilfrid Laurier University Press, 1987.

Creelman, David. *Setting in the East: Maritime Realist Fiction*. Montreal and Kingston, ON: McGill-Queen's University Press, 2003.

Culligan, Mark, and Katrin MacPhee. "Racism and Relief Distribution in the Aftermath of the Halifax Explosion." *Journal of Law and Social Policy* 31 (2019): 1–33.

Cunningham, Herald. "Can the Maritimes Doctor Themselves?" *MacLean's Magazine*, 15 October 1926: 3–4, 42, 45.

Custance, Florence. "International Women's Day." *Maritime Labor Herald*, 15 March 1924: 6.

– "Some Facts About Women's Participation in Industry and the Trade Unions." *Maritime Labor Herald*, 27 October 1923: 7.

Cresswell, Tim. *Place: An Introduction*. Oxford, UK: Wiley-Blackwell, 2015.

Davey, Frank. "Towards the Ends of Regionalism." In *A Sense of Place: Re-evaluating Regionalism in Canadian and American Writing*, edited by Christian Riegel and Herb Wyile, 1–17. Edmonton: University of Alberta Press, 1998.

Davies, Gwendolyn. "The 'Home Place' in Modern Maritime Literature." In *Studies in Maritime Literary History, 1760–1930*, 192–9. Fredericton: Acadiensis Press, 1991.

– *Studies in Maritime Literary History*. Fredericton: Acadiensis, 1991.

Davies, Gwendolyn, and Eric Swanick. "Print Culture in the Maritimes (Nova Scotia, New Brunswick, & Prince Edward Island): An Overview." In *History of the Book in Canada*, May 1997. http://www.hbic.library.utoronto.ca/fconfmarit_en.htm.

"Dawn Fraser's New Book." *Maritime Labor Herald*, 19 April 1924: 2.

"The Dawn of a New Era." *Busy East of Canada*, May 1919: 3–4.

Dawson, J. William. *Acadian Geology: The Geological Structure, Organic Remains, and Mineral Resources of Nova Scotia, New Brunswick and Prince Edward Island*, 2nd ed. Saint John: Macmillan, 1878.

De Mille, A.B. "On Certain Literary Possibilities." *Acadiensis* 1, no. 3 (July 1901): 126–30.

Department of Commerce and Labor. *Factors in Foreign Trade: Language, Currency, Weights and Measures, Postal Rates and Parcel Post Facilities, Miscellaneous Series No. 7*. Washington, DC: Government Printing Office, 1912.

"Development in Construction Work Marks Revival of Progress in the Maritimes." *Busy East of Canada*, January 1930: 18–19.

Distad, N. Merrill. "Newspapers and Magazines." In *History of the Book in Canada*, vol. 2, *1840–1918*, edited by Fiona A. Black et al., 293–303. Toronto: University of Toronto Press, 2005.

Distad, N. Merrill, and Linda M. Distad. "Canada." In *Periodicals of Queen Victoria's Empire: An Exploration*, edited by J. Don Vann and Rosemary T. VanArsdel, 61–174. Toronto: University of Toronto Press, 1996.

Djwa, Sandra. "The 1920's: E.J. Pratt, Transitional Modern." In *The Pratt Symposium*, edited by Glenn Clever, 55–68. Ottawa: University of Ottawa Press, 1977.

Dobson, Kit. "Altermodernities: Thankfully, We Have Never Been Modern." In *Translocated Modernisms: Paris and Other Lost Generations*, edited by Marta Dvorak et al., 235–42. Ottawa: University of Ottawa Press, 2016.

Dodeman, André. "Hugh MacLennan's Ambivalent Portrait of the Highlander in *Each Man's Son*." *Études écossaises* 22 (2023). https://doi.org/10.4000/etudesecossaises.4131.

Dogliani, Patrizia. "The Fate of Socialist Internationalism." In *Internationalisms: A Twentieth-Century History*, edited by Glenda Sluga and Patricia Clavin, 38–60. Cambridge: Cambridge University Press, 2016.

Dole, W.P. "Some Fine Art." *Acadiensis* 3, no. 1 (January 1903): 41–50.

Doyle, James. "Canadian Writers and American Little Magazines in the 1890s." *Canadian Literature*, no. 110 (1986): 177–83.

– *Progressive Heritage: The Evolution of a Politically Radical Literary Heritage in Canada*. Waterloo, ON: Wilfrid Laurier University Press, 2004.

Du Bois, W.E.B. "Criteria of Negro Art." In *The Portable Harlem Renaissance Reader*, edited by David Levering Lewis, 100–5. New York: Viking, 1994.

– *Dusk of Dawn: An Essay Toward an Autobiography of a Race Concept*, edited by Henry Louis Gates Jr. Oxford, UK: Oxford University Press, 2007.

– *The Souls of Black Folk; With "The Talented Tenth" and "The Souls of White Folk."* 1903. New York: Penguin, 2018.

– "The Talented Tenth." 1903. In *The Souls of Black Folk; With "The Talented Tenth" and "The Souls of White Folk,"* 201–23. New York: Penguin Books, 2018.

Dumontet, Monique. *"Lest We Forget": Canadian Combatant Narratives of the Great War*. PhD diss. Winnipeg: University of Manitoba, 2010.

Earl, Lawrence. "Mike Wardell's Tempestuous Love Affair with the Maritime Provinces." *MacLean's*, 28 February 1959: 26–7, 33–5.

Eliot, T.S. *The Waste Land*. Edited by Michael North. New York: W.W. Norton, 2001.

Eller, Cynthia. "The Feminist Appropriation of Matriarchal Myth in the 19th and 20th Centuries." *History Compass* 3, no. 1 (2005): 1–10.

Engels, Friedrich. "The Origin of the Family, Private Property, and the State." In *The Marx-Engels Reader*, edited by Robert C. Tucker, 734–59. New York: W.W. Norton, 1978.

"The English Language for English Countries." *Cape Breton and Nova Scotia Magazine* 2, no. 1 (1902): 56–8.

Entrikin, J. Nicholas. "Region and Regionalism." In *The SAGE Handbook of Geographical Knowledge*, edited by John Agnew and David Livingstone, 344–56. Los Angeles: SAGE Publications, 2011.

Fairley, Barker. "Goethe the Poet." *Dalhousie Review* 12, no. 2 (1932): 143–58.

Fanon, Franz. *The Wretched of the Earth*. New York: Grove Press, 2004 [1961].

Fauset, Arthur H. *Folklore from Nova Scotia*, Memoirs of the American Folklore Society 24. Philadelphia: American Folklore Society, 1931.

– Interview by Carole Carpenter, 27 February 1970. CD-F1012, audio recording, Memorial University Folklore and Language Archive, St John's, NFLA.

– Letter to Elsie Clews Parsons. 11 August 1923. Subcollection II, Series IV, Research Notes, Nova Scotia Notebook #9b, Mss. Coll. 29, Elsie Clews Parsons Papers, American Philosophical Society Library, Philadelphia, PA.

Ferré-Rode, Sandrine. "Atlantic Canada." In *History of the Book in Canada*, vol. 3, *1918–1980*, edited by Carole Gerson and Jacques Michon, 178–81. Toronto: University of Toronto Press, 2007.

Fiamengo, Janice. "Regionalism and Urbanism." In *The Cambridge Companion to Canadian Literature*, edited by Eva-Marie Kröller, 261–82. Cambridge: Cambridge University Press, 2017.

Fillmore, Roscoe. "May Day in Petrograd." *Maritime Labor Herald*, 6 October 1923: 6, 8.

– "Peas, Potatoes, and the Proletariat in Kuzbas." *Maritime Labor Herald*, 29 September 1923: 2.

– "Travelling in Russia." *Maritime Labor Herald*, 6 October 1923: 3.

Fingard, Judith. "The 1880s: Paradoxes of Progress." In *The Atlantic Provinces in Confederation*, edited by Ernest R. Forbes and D.A. Muise, 82–118. Toronto: University of Toronto Press, 2001.

– "A Tale of Two Preachers: Henry Hartley, Francis Robinson and the Black Churches of the Maritimes." *Journal of the Royal Nova Scotia Historical Society* 5 (2002): 23–43.

Forbes, Ernest. *Aspects of Maritime Regionalism, 1867–1927*. Ottawa: Canadian Historical Association, 1983.

– "In Search of a Post-Confederation Maritime Historiography." *Acadiensis* 8, no. 1 (1978): 1–21.

– "Maritime Rights." In *The Canadian Encyclopedia*, 16 December 2013, Historica Canada. https://www.thecanadianencyclopedia.ca/en/article/maritime-rights.

– *The Maritime Rights Movement*. Montreal and Kingston, ON: McGill-Queen's University Press, 1979.

Frank, David. "The 1920s: Class and Region, Resistance and Accommodation." In *The Atlantic Provinces in Confederation*, edited by E.R. Forbes and D.A. Muise, 232–71. Toronto: University of Toronto Press, 1993.

– "Acadiensis, 1901–1999." *Acadiensis*, 1999. http://www.acadiensis.ca/acadiensis-frank-essay.

– "Cape Breton Strikes 1920s." In *The Canadian Encyclopedia*, 23 January 2014, Historica Canada. https://www.thecanadianencyclopedia.ca/en/article/cape-breton-strikes-1920s.
– "Fillmore, Roscoe Alfred." In *The Oxford Companion to Canadian History*. Oxford, UK: Oxford University Press, 2004. *Oxford Reference*. https://www.oxfordreference.com/display/10.1093/acref/9780195415599.001.0001/acref-9780195415599-e-560.
– "The Geography of Centralization." *Acadiensis* 20, no. 2 (1990): 190–206.
– "Introduction." In *Industrialization and Underdevelopment in the Maritimes 1880–1930*, edited by David Frank. Toronto: Garamond, 1989, vii–x.
– *J.B. McLachlan: A Biography*. Toronto: James Lorimer, 1999.
Fraser, Dawn. "Cape Breton Miner and Besco." *Maritime Labor Herald*, 26 April 1924: 4.
– "The Case of Jim O'Coughlin." *Maritime Labor Herald*, 16 February 1924: 4.
– "The Crime of Johnny Kyle." *Maritime Labor Herald*, 26 July 1924: 6.
– "The Wearing of the Red." *Maritime Labor Herald*, 1 May 1924: 8.
Frye, Northrop. Letter to Helen Kemp, 25 August 1936. In *The Correspondence of Northrop Frye and Helen Kemp, 1936–1939*, vol. 2, edited by Robert Denham, 537–40. Toronto: University of Toronto Press, 1996.
Ganong, William F. "The Great New Brunswick Survey." *Acadiensis* 4, no. 1 (January 1904): 76–9.
– *A Monograph of the Cartography of the Province of New Brunswick*. J. Durie, 1897. http://archive.org/details/cihm_12512/page/n11.
– *A Monograph of the Evolution of the Boundaries of the Province of New Brunswick*. Ottawa: J. Hope, 1901. http://babel.hathitrust.org/cgi/pt?id=mdp.39015011406769&view=1up&seq=11.
– *A Monograph of the Origins of Settlements in the Province of New Brunswick*. Royal Society of Canada, 1904.
– "New Brunswick Animals and the Animal Romancers." *Bulletin of the Natural History Society of New Brunswick* 5, no. 23 (1905): 299–304. https://books.google.ca/books?id=S04GIq8uq-EC&pg=PP7.
– "On the Uses and Value of Historical Museums." *Acadiensis* 3, no. 2 (July 1903): 131–5.
"The Gazette and Labor." *Maritime Labor Herald*, 17 June 1922: 1.
Gerson, Carole. "Canadian Literature at Home and Abroad: International Contexts of W.D. Lighthall's *Songs of the Great Dominion* (1889) and Robert Weaver's *Canadian Short Stories* (1960)." *Studies in Canadian Literature / Études en littérature canadienne* 41, no. 2 (2016): 61–80.
– *Canadian Women in Print, 1750–1918*. Waterloo, ON: Wilfrid Laurier University Press, 2011.

– "The Literary Culture of Atlantic Women Between the Wars." In *Myth and Milieu: Atlantic Literature and Culture 1918–1939*, edited by Gwendolyn Davies, 62–70. Fredericton: Acadiensis, 1993.

– "Mid-Century Modernity and Fiction by Women, 1920–1950." In *The Oxford Handbook of Canadian Literature*, edited by Cynthia Sugars, 337–51. Oxford, UK: Oxford University Press, 2016.

Gilroy, Paul. *The Black Atlantic: Modernity and Double Consciousness*. Cambridge, MA: Harvard University Press, 1993.

Glickman, Lawrence B. *A Living Wage: American Workers and the Making of Consumer Society*. Ithaca, NY: Cornell University Press, 1999.

Glicksberg, C.I. "Poetry and Social Revolution." *Dalhousie Review* 17, no. 4 (1938): 493–503.

Godard, Barbara. "Notes from the Cultural Field: Canadian Literature from Identity to Hybridity." *Essays on Canadian Writing*, no. 72 (2000): 209–47.

Goldie, Terry. "The Man of the Land / The Land of the Man: Patrick White and Scott Symons." *SPAN* 36 (1992). https://freotopia.org/readingroom/litserv/SPAN/36/Goldie.html.

Goldsmith, Oliver. "The Rising Village." In *The Rising Village, with Other Poems*, 13–41. Saint John: John McMillan, 1834. https://archive.org/details/risingvillagewit00gold/page/n1/mode/2up.

"Good Advertising for Maritime Provinces." *Saint John Standard*, 11 June 1910: 5.

Grady, Wyne. "Complexity Graces MacLeod's Stories: Short Works Soar with Details Worthy of a Novel." *Calgary Herald*, 13 May 2000: E10.

Graham, Jean. "Saturday Night." Review of *The Imperialist. Saturday Night*, 4 June 1904. Reprinted in *The Imperialist* by Sara Jeanette Duncan, edited by Misao Dean, 343–9. Peterborough, ON: Broadview, 2005.

Gray, Charlotte. *The Promise of Canada: 150 Years – People and Ideas that Have Shaped Our Country*. Toronto: Simon & Schuster Canada, 2018.

Green, Adam S. "The Present Demands for an Educated Negro Ministry." *Neith* 1, no. 5 (January 1904): 214–16.

Greenwood, Emily. "Re-Rooting the Classical Tradition: New Directions in Black Classicism." *Classical Receptions Journal* 1, no. 1 (2009): 87–103.

Goetsch, Paul. Review of *Hugh MacLennan*, by T.D. MacLulich. *International Fiction Review* 13, no. 1 (1986): 34–5.

Habermas, Jürgen. *The Structural Transformation of the Public Sphere*. Cambridge, MA: MIT Press, 1991.

Hall, Stuart. "Cultural Identity and Diaspora." In *Identity: Community, Culture, Difference*, edited by Jonathan Rutherford, 222–37. London: Lawrence and Wishart, 1990.

Hammill, Faye, and Mark Hussey. *Modernism's Print Cultures*. London: Bloomsbury, 2016.

Hanchard, Michael. "Afro-Modernity: Temporality, Politics, and the African Diaspora." *Public Culture* 11, no. 1 (1999): 246–68.

Hanses, Mathias. "Cicero Crosses the Color Line: Pro Archia Poeta and W.E.B. Du Bois's The Souls of Black Folk." *International Journal of the Classical Tradition* 26, no. 1 (2019): 10–26.

Harcourt, Peter. "Speculations on Canadian Cinema." *Queen's Quarterly* 111, no. 2 (2004): 237–48.

Hardt, Michael, and Antonio Negri. *Commonwealth*. Cambridge, MA: Harvard University Press, 2009.

"Harriet Beecher Stowe's Uncle Tom's Cabin." *The New Freeman*, 21 February 1903: 4.

Harris, Reginald. "The Advantages of the Union of the Maritime Provinces." *Acadiensis* 8, no. 4 (October 1908): 238–49.

– "The Union of the Maritime Provinces." *Acadiensis* 6, no. 3 (July 1906): 172–84.

– "The Union of the Maritime Provinces (Continued)." *Acadiensis* 6, no. 4 (October 1906): 247–59.

Hartley, H.A.S. *Classical Translations*. Saint John: J. & A. McMillan, 1889.

– *"Ta Tou Pragma Emou Biou", Or, Some Concerns of My Life*. Amherst, NS: 1890.

Hartman, Saidiya V. *Scenes of Subjection: Terror, Slavery, and Self-Making in Nineteenth-Century America*. Oxford, UK: Oxford University Press, 1997.

Harvey-Jellie, W. "T.S. Eliot Among the Prophets." *Dalhousie Review* 18, no. 1 (1938): 83–90.

Harvey, David. *Spaces of Capital: Towards a Critical Geography*. London and New York: Routledge, 2001.

Haveman, Heather. *Magazines and the Making of America: Modernization, Community, and Print Culture, 1741–1860*. Princeton, NJ: Princeton University Press, 2015.

Hayward, Victoria. "Sea Coast Homes of Our Maritime Provinces." *Busy East of Canada*, December 1921: 5–9.

Henderson, Rose. "Capital Internationalism." *Maritime Labor Herald*, 12 August 1922: 1.

– "The Civil War in Ireland." *Maritime Labor Herald*, 15 September 1922: 1.

– "England's Surplus Women." *Maritime Labor Herald*, 19 August 1922: 2.

Heron, Craig. "Labourism and the Canadian Working Class." *Labour / Le Travail*, no. 13 (1984): 45–76.

Herring, Karen. "Creating a Centre / Recreating the Margin: Ted Campbell and His Studio, Saint John, New Brunswick, in the 1930s and 40s." MA thesis. Ottawa: Carleton University, 1993.

Hill, Colin. "Generic Experiment and Confusion in Early Canadian Novels of the Great War." *Studies in Canadian Literature / Études en littérature canadienne* 34, no. 2 (2009): 58–76.

– "Introduction." In *Waste Heritage* by Irene Baird, edited by Colin Hill, ix–li. Ottawa: University of Ottawa Press, 2007.

– *Modern Realism in English-Canadian Fiction.* Toronto: University of Toronto Press, 2012.

– "Modernism, Antimodernism, and Hugh MacLennan's Novels of the 1930s." In *Making Canada New: Editing, Modernism, and New Media*, edited by Dean Irvine, Vanessa Lent, and Bart A. Vautour, 327–50. Toronto: University of Toronto Press, 2017.

Hill, Robert A. "Redemption Works: From 'African Redemption' to 'Redemption Song.'" *Review: Literature and Arts of the Americas* 43, no. 2 (2010): 200–7.

Hodd, Thomas. "A Casualty of Genre: The War Short Stories of Will R. Bird." *Canadian Literature*, no. 243 (2020): 102–17.

– "The Celtic Twilight in Canada: William Sharp's Early Occult Influence on Charles G.D. Roberts and Bliss Carman." *Canadian Poetry*, no. 54 (2004): 37–55.

– "Introduction." In *A Soldier's Place: The War Stories of Will R. Bird*, edited by Thomas Hodd, 2–5. Halifax: Nimbus, 2019.

Horrall, Andrew. "'A Century of Canadian Art': The Tate Gallery Exhibition of 1938." *British Journal of Canadian Studies* 27, no. 2 (2014): 150–62. https://doi.org/10.3828/bjcs.2014.10.

"House at Lower Lachine of La Salle, Voyageur and Explorer." Photograph and caption. *Acadiensis* 6, no. 1 (January 1906): 2.

Howard, Walter. "The National Miners Union: Communists and Miners in the Pennsylvania Anthracite, 1928–1931." *The Pennsylvania Magazine of History and Biography* 125, nos. 1–2 (2001): 91–124.

Howell, Colin D. "1900s: Industry, Urbanization, and Reform." In *The Atlantic Provinces in Confederation*, edited by Ernest R. Forbes and D.A. Muise, 155–91. Toronto: University of Toronto Press, 2001.

– "W.S. Fielding and the Repeal Elections of 1886 and 1887 in Nova Scotia." *Acadiensis* 8, no. 2 (1979): 28–46.

"In and Out of the Union." *The Maple Leaf* 1, no. 1 (1907): 3–4.

"Industrial Democracy Will Soon Triumph." *Maritime Labor Herald*, 17 June 1922: 1.

Irvine, Dean. *Editing Modernity: Women and Little-Magazine Cultures in Canada, 1916–1956*. Toronto: University of Toronto Press, 2008.

– "Introduction." In *The Canadian Modernists Meet*, edited by Dean Irvine, 1–16. Ottawa: University of Ottawa Press, 2005.

– "Little Magazines in English Canada." In *The Oxford Critical and Cultural History of Modernist Magazines*, vol. 2, *North America, 1894–1960*, edited by Peter Brooker and Andrew Thacker, 602–28. Oxford, UK: Oxford University Press, 2009.

Irvine, Dean, Vanessa Lent, and Bart Vautour. "Introduction." In *Making Canada New: Editing, Modernism, and New Media*, edited by Dean Irvine, Vanessa Lent, and Bart Vautour, 3–30. Toronto: University of Toronto Press, 2017.

Iton, Richard. *In Search of the Black Fantastic: Politics and Popular Culture in the Post–Civil Rights Era*. Oxford, UK: Oxford University Press, 2008.

Jack, David R. "Acadian Magazines." *Transactions of the Royal Society of Canada* 2nd s. 9, Sect. II (1903): 173–203.

– "Adieu." *Acadiensis* 8, no. 4 (October 1908): 235–7.

– "Charles Gamage Eastman." *Acadiensis* 3, no. 1 (July 1903): 62–6.

– "Gabe Acquin." *Acadiensis* 1, no. 4 (October 1901): 250–4.

– "Indians of Acadia." *Acadiensis* 1, no. 4 (October 1901): 187–201.

– "Kind Words." *Acadiensis* 1, no. 2 (April 1901): 104–9.

– "Kit-Bag." *Acadiensis* 1, no. 2 (April 1901): 70–1.

– "Past and Future." *Acadiensis* 2, no. 1 (January 1902): 3–6.

– "Salutary." *Acadiensis* 1, no. 1 (January 1901): 3–6.

Jack, Isaac Allen. "Aesthetic Attributes of Acadia." *Acadiensis* 1, no. 3 (July 1901): 169–77.

"January Magazines." *The Educational Review* xvi, no. 8 (1903): 178.

"Japanese Earthquake and B.C. Lumber Prices." *Maritime Labor Herald*, 6 October 1923: 3.

Jemmott, M.F. "Publisher's Announcement." *Atlantic Advocate* 1, no. 1 (April 1915): 10.

"Jobs for Soldiers." *Maritime Labor Herald*, 17 June 1922: 6.

Johnson, Abby Arthur, and Ronald Maberry Johnson. *Propaganda and Aesthetics: The Literary Politics of African-American Magazines in the Twentieth Century*. Amherst, MA: University of Massachusetts Press, 1991.

Johnson, Alonzo. *Good News for the Disinherited: Howard Thurman on Jesus of Nazareth and Human Liberation*. Lanham, MD: University Press of America, 1997.

Johnston, Alex. "Men of To-Day." *Canadian Courier*, June 1910: 9.

Kantrowitz, Stephen David. *Ben Tillman and the Reconstruction of White Supremacy*. Chapel Hill, NC: University of North Carolina Press, 2000.

Kealey, Linda. "Canadian Socialism and the Woman Question, 1900–1914." *Labour / Le Travail*, no. 13 (1984): 77–100.

Keita, Maghan. "Believing in Ethiopians." In *African Athena: New Agendas*, edited by Daniel Orrells, Tessa Roynon, and Gurminder K. Bhambra, 19–39. Oxford, UK: Oxford University Press, 2011.

Kennedy, Leo. "Exile." *Dalhousie Review* 11, no. 4 (1932): 520.

"King and Murdock Make Bolsheviks." *Maritime Labor Herald*, 4 February 1922: 1.

"The Kit-Bag." *The Daily Gleaner*, 27 November 1902: 4.

Klein, Abraham. "Summer." *Dalhousie Review* 12, no. 2 (1932): 209.

Knowles, Valerie. *Strangers at Our Gates: Canadian Immigration and Immigration Policy, 1540–1997*. Toronto: Dundurn Press, 1997.

Konikow, Antoinette. "Mass. Mother's League Show Way for Organization of Working Class Women for Fight." *Maritime Labor Herald*, 19 July 1924: 3.

"Labor's Gun." *Maritime Labor Herald*, 30 January 1926: 1.

Laclau, Ernesto. *On Populist Reason*. London and New York: Verso, 2018.

Larocque, Peter. "David Russell Jack." In *Dictionary of Canadian Biography*, vol. 14. Toronto and Laval, QC: University of Toronto / Université Laval, 1998. http://www.biographi.ca/en/bio/jack_david_russell_14E.html.

Latham, Sean, and Robert Scholes. "The Rise of Periodical Studies." *PMLA* 121, no. 2 (2006): 517–31.

le Roux, Cheryl S. "Creating a British World: British Colonial Teachers and the Anglicising of Afrikaner Children." *Yesterday and Today*, no. 15 (2016): 1–20. http://doi.org/10.17159/2223-0386/2016/n15a1.

Lears, T. Jackson. *No Place of Grace: Antimodernism and the Transformation of American Culture, 1880–1920*. Chicago: University of Chicago Press, 1994 [1981].

Lemons, GARY. *Womanist Forefathers: Frederick Douglass and W.E.B. Du Bois*. Albany: SUNY Press, 2009.

Lenin, Vladimir. "Where to Begin." In *Lenin Collected Works,* vol. 5: *May 1901–February 1902*, 13–24. London: Lawrence and Wishart, 1961.

Lepaludier, Laurent. "The Everyday in 'The Closing Down of Summer' by Alistair McLeod." *Journal of the Short Story in English*, no. 38 (2002): 1–12. http://journals.openedition.org/jsse/202.

Leroux, John. "A Concrete Artistic Vision." *Journal of the Society for the Study of Architecture in Canada* 45, no. 1 (2020): 2–9.

Levene, Mark. "Letters in Canada 1986: Fiction." *University of Toronto Quarterly* 57, no. 1 (1987): 1–22.

Lévesque, Andrée. "The Transnational Experience of Some Canadian Communists." In *Left Transnationalism: The Communist International and the National, Colonial, and Racial Questions*, edited by McKay and Drachewych, 183–203. Montreal and Kingston, ON: McGill-Queen's University Press, 2019.

Lippard, Lucy. *The Lure of the Local: Senses of Place in a Multicentered Society*. New York: New Press, 1998.

Livesay, Dorothy. "Day and Night." *In The Self-Completing Tree*, 155–60. Vancouver: Beach Holme, 1999.

Lochhead, Douglas G. "Introduction." In *An Index to Acadiensis 1901–1908*, edited by Dorothy Cooke, 2–3. Halifax: Dalhousie University, 1983.

Logan, H.J. "The Maritime Provinces Now and After the War." *Busy East of Canada*, May 1918: 12–15.

Lonecloud, Jeremiah. Jeremiah Lonecloud to the Secretary of the Department of Indian Affairs, 27 November 1917. In *The Old Man Told Us: Excerpts from Micmac History 1500–1950*, edited by Ruth H. Whitehead, 303–04. Halifax: Nimbus, 1991.

Longfellow, Henry W. *Evangeline: A Tale of Acadie*. Boston: Ticknor, Reed, and Fields, 1850. http://www.canadiana.ca/view/oocihm.42271/1?r=0&s=1.

Louw, P. Eric. *The Rise, Fall, and Legacy of Apartheid*. Westport, CT: Praeger, 2004.

Ludlow, Peter. *The Canny Scot: Archbishop James Morrison of Antigonish*. Montreal and Kingston, ON: McGill-Queen's University Press, 2016.

MacDonald, Elizabeth Roberts. "The Inlander." *Acadiensis* 3, no. 1 (January 1903): 6.

– "The Inlander." *Kit-Bag*, no. 1 (November 1902): 10.

MacGillivray, Donald. "Cape Breton in the 1920s: A Community Besieged." In *Essays in Cape Breton History*, edited by Bryan Tennyson, 49–67. Windsor, NS: Lancelot Press, 1973.

MacKinnon, Richard. "Protest Songs and Verse in Cape Breton Island." *Ethnologies* 30, no. 2 (2008): 33–71.

MacLennan, Hugh. *Barometer Rising*. 1941. Toronto: McClelland and Stewart, 2007.

– "Voltaire Said …" In *Thirty and Three*, 132–7. London: MacMillan, 1955.

MacLeod, Alistair. "The Closing Down of Summer." In *Island: The Complete Stories*, 180–99. New York: W.W. Norton, 2000.

MacLeod, Evelyn. "Owen, Elizabeth Anne." In *Dictionary of Canadian Biography*, vol. 13. Toronto and Laval, QC: University of Toronto / Université Laval, 2003. http://www.biographi.ca/en/bio/owen_elizabeth_lee_13E.html.

MacMechan, Archibald. "The Halifax Disaster." In *The Halifax Explosion December 6, 1917*, edited by Graham Metson, 12–71. Toronto: McGraw-Hill Ryerson, 1978.

– *Headwaters of Canadian Literature*. Toronto: McClelland & Stewart, 1924.

– "Private Journal of Archibald MacMechan, September 14, 1917 – April 1, 1920." 1920. Manuscript. Archibald MacMechan Fonds, MS-2-82, box 1, file 4, Archives and Special Collections, Killam Memorial Library, Dalhousie University.

Manley, John. "Preaching the Red Stuff: J.B. McLachlan, Communism, and the Cape Breton Miners, 1922–1935." *Labour / Le Travail* 30 (1992): 65–114.

"Maritime, 5.B.n.b.plural." *OED Online*, Oxford University Press, June 2019. http://www.oed.com/view/Entry/114163 (accessed 15 July 2019).

"Maritime Industrial Development." *Busy East of Canada*, December 1919: 21–3.

"Maritimer, n." *OED Online*, Oxford University Press, June 2019. http://www.oed.com/view/Entry/239558.

"Married Under Red Flag." *Maritime Labor Herald*, 31 May 1924: 1.

Marquis, Greg. "Commentary: *The Quest of the Folk*." *Acadiensis* 35, no. 1 (2005): 144–7.

Marx, Karl. "For a Ruthless Criticism of Everything Existing." In *The Marx-Engels Reader*, edited by Robert C. Tucker, 12–15. New York: W.W. Norton, 1978.

Massey, Doreen B. *For Space*. London: SAGE, 2015.

– "A Global Sense of Place." In *Space, Place and Gender*, 146–56. Minneapolis: University of Minnesota Press, 1994.

Mason, Jody. *Home Feelings: Liberal Citizenship and the Canadian Reading Camp Movement*. Montreal and Kingston, ON: McGill-Queen's University Press, 2019.

Masters, J.E. "Echoes of the Maritime Board of Trade Meeting." *Busy East of Canada*, November 1920: 20–6.

Maritimer. "Maritimer Visits Oakland." *The Maple Leaf* 1, no. 11 (1907): 3.

McAdam, N. "The Indian Mound." *Acadiensis* 4, no. 2 (April 1904): 101–2.

McCabe, Hauna. "Contesting Home: Tourism, Memory, and Identity in Sackville, New Brunswick." *Canadian Geographer* 42, no. 3 (1998): 231–45.

McCallum, Pamela. "'They cut him down': Race, Class, and Cultural Memory in Dorothy Livesay's 'Day and Night.'" In *Wider Boundaries of Daring: The Modernist Impulse in Canadian Women's Poetry*, edited by Di Brandt and Barbara Godard, 191–212. Waterloo, ON: Wilfrid Laurier University Press, 2009.

McCann, Larry. "The 1890s: Fragmentation and the New Social Order." In *The Atlantic Provinces in Confederation*, edited by Ernest R. Forbes and D.A. Muise, 119–54. Toronto: University of Toronto Press, 2001.

McCurdy, F.B., et al. "The 21st Annual Meeting of the Maritime Board of Trade." *Busy East of Canada*, September 1919: 4+.

McGann, Jerome. "'The Socialization of Texts.'" In *The Book History Reader*, edited by David Finkelstein, 66–73. London and New York: Routledge, 2010.

McKay, Ian. "The 1960s: The Stillborn Triumph of Progressive Reform." In *The Atlantic Provinces in Confederation*, edited by Ernest R. Forbes and D.A. Muise, 192–230. Toronto: University of Toronto Press, 2001.

– "Helen Creighton and the Politics of Antimodernism." In *Myth & Milieu: Atlantic Literature and Culture 1918–1939*, edited by Gwendolyn Davies and Carrie MacMillan, 1–16. Fredericton: Acadiensis, 1993.

– "The Liberal Order Framework: A Prospectus for a Reconnaissance of Canadian History." *Canadian Historical Review* 81, no. 4 (2000): 617–45.

– "A Note on 'Region' in Writing the History of Atlantic Canada." *Acadiensis* 29, no. 2 (2000): 89–101.

– "Of Karl Marx and the Bluenose: Colin Campbell McKay and the Legacy of Maritime Socialism." *Acadiensis* 27, no. 2 (1998): 3–25.

– *The Quest of the Folk: Antimodernism and Cultural Selection in Twentieth-Century Nova Scotia*. Montreal and Kingston, ON: McGill-Queen's University Press, 1994.

McKay, Ian, and Robin Bates. *In the Province of History: The Making of the Public Past in Twentieth-Century Nova Scotia*. Montreal and Kingston, ON: McGill-Queen's University Press, 2014.

McKay, Ian, and Oleksa Drachewych. "Introduction: Left Transnationalism? The Communist International, the National, Colonial, and Racial Questions, and the Strengths and Limitations of the 'Moscow Rules' Paradigm." In *Left Transnationalism: The Communist International and the National, Colonial, and Racial Questions*, edited by McKay and Drachewych, 3–45. Montreal and Kingston, ON: McGill-Queen's University Press, 2019.

McKay, Ian, and Suzanne Morton. "The Maritimes: Expanding the Circle of Resistance." In *The Workers' Revolt in Canada, 1917–1925*, edited by Craig Heron, 43–86. Toronto: University of Toronto Press, 1998.

McKeown, H.A. "The Progress of Canada." *Neith* 1, no. 1 (February 1903): 39–45.

McKittrick, Katherine, and Clyde A. Woods. "No One Knows the Mysteries at the Bottom of the Ocean." In *Black Geographies and the Politics of Place*, edited by Katherine McKittrick and Clyde A. Woods, 1–13. Toronto: Between the Lines, 2007.

McLachlan, James B. "The Conservative Convention." *Maritime Labor Herald*, 8 July 1922: 1, 8.

– "The Dead Hand of German George the Third." *Maritime Labor Herald*, 11 November 1922: 1, 5.

McPhail, Agnes. "Report on the Women's National League." *Maritime Labor Herald*, 17 May 1924: 3.

McPhail, Agnes, et al. *House of Commons Debates, 14th Parliament, 4th Session*. Vol. 2, Government of Canada, 1925. *Canadian Parliamentary Historical Resources*, Library of Parliament / Bibliothèque du Parlement. Accessed 9 December 2020. https://parl.canadiana.ca/view/oop.debates_ HOC1404_01.

McSorley, Tom. "Search and Rescue: Restoring Varick Frissell's 'The Viking.'" *Take One* 8, no. 46 (2004): 18–20.

Mellor, John. *J.B. McLachlan and the Cape Breton Coal Miners 1900–1925*. Sydney, NS: Breton Books, 2012.

"Mental Sloppiness." *Busy East of Canada*, March 1923: 4–5.

Metson, Graham. "The Halifax Disaster by Archibald MacMechan." In *The Halifax Explosion December 6, 1917*, edited by Graham Metson, 11. Toronto: McGraw-Hill Ryerson, 1978.

"Miners Demonstrate on the Return of Jim McLachlan." *Maritime Labor Herald*, 15 March 1924: 1.

Molinaro, Dennis. *An Exceptional Law: Section 98 and the Emergency State, 1919–1936*. Toronto: University of Toronto Press, 2017.

Moore, Andrew. "The Fiddlehead." In *New Brunswick Literary Encyclopedia*, edited by Tony Tremblay. Fredericton: New Brunswick Studies Centre, 2010. https://nble.lib.unb.ca/browse/f/fiddlehead.

More, Marylin. "Hurricane Juan – Gov't. (N.S.): Residents – Assistance Provide." In *Hansard*, Nova Scotia Legislature, 59th General Assembly, 1st Sess., Res. 341, 2003. https://nslegislature.ca/legislative-business/hansard-debates/assembly-59-session-1/59_1_house_03oct10.htm.

Moretti, Franco. *Atlas of the European Novel, 1800–1900*. London and New York: Verso, 1998.

Morris, Peter. *Embattled Shadows: A History of Canadian Cinema 1895–1939*. Montreal and Kingston, ON: McGill-Queen's University Press, 1992.

Morris, Dorothy. "The Maple Leaf – A Labour of Love." *Atlantic Advocate* 76, no. 10 (1986): 31–3.

Morton, Suzanne. "Labourism and Economic Action: The Halifax Shipyards Strike of 1920." *Labour / Le Travail*, no. 22 (1988): 67–98.

Moss, Laura, and Cynthia Sugars. "E. Pauline Johnson (Tekahionwake)." In *Canadian Literature in English: Texts and Contexts*, vol. 1, edited by Laura Moss and Cynthia Sugars, 390–94. Toronto: Pearson Longman, 2009.

Moten, Fred. "The Case of Blackness." *Criticism* 50, no. 2 (2008): 177–218.

Moulton, Louise. "Our Aeroplane." *Dalhousie Review* 14, no. 4 (1935): 428.

– "Process." *Dalhousie Review* 16, no. 4 (1937): 472.

Mount, Nick. *When Canadian Literature Moved to New York*. Toronto: University of Toronto Press, 2006.

Mudde, Cas, and Cristóbal Rovira Kaltwasser. *Populism: A Very Short Introduction*. Oxford, UK: Oxford University Press, 2017.

Müeller, Jan-Werner. *What Is Populism?* Philadelphia: University of Pennsylvania Press, 2016.

"N.B. and P.E.I. Conference." *Wesleyan*, 26 June 1890, 5.

Narbonne, André. "Antimodernist Antecedents in Early Canadian Modernism: Archibald MacMechan's 'A Ballade of Canadian Literature' and F.R. Scott's 'The Canadian Authors Meet.'" *American Review of Canadian Studies* 49, no. 3 (2019): 394–412. https://www.doi.org/10.1080/02722011.2019.1650084.

"Neith." *The Guardian*, 17 March 1903: 2.

"Neith." *The New Freeman*, 7 March 1903: 7.

"Neith." *Saint John Star*, 24 February 1903: 4.

Nelson, Cary. *Revolutionary Memory: Recovering the Poetry of the American Left*. London and New York: Routledge, 2013 [2002].

Nerbas, Don. "Revisiting the Politics of Maritime Rights: Bourgeois Saint John and Regional Protest in the 1920s." *Acadiensis* 37, no. 1 (2008): 110–30.

"The New Era – What Is Coming." *Busy East of Canada*, December 1919: 1–2.

"New Magazine." *The Educational Review* 16, no. 10 (March 1903): 209.

New, W.H. "Maritime Cadences." *Canadian Literature*, no. 68–9 (1976): 3–6.

"Next Meeting." *The Maple Leaf* 3, no. 8 (1909): 7.

Nicholas, Andrea Bear. "Gabriel Acquin." In *Dictionary of Canadian Biography*, vol. 13. Toronto and Laval, QC: University of Toronto / Université Laval, 1994. http://www.biographi.ca/en/bio/acquin_gabriel_13E.html.

Niergarth, Kirk. *"The dignity of every human being": New Brunswick Artists and Canadian Culture Between the Great Depression and the Cold War*. Toronto: University of Toronto Press, 2014.

"Notice: To Members of the Colored Race." *Maritime Labor Herald*, 26 August 1922: 4.

Paasi, Anssi. "Place and Region: Regional Worlds and Words." *Progress in Human Geography* 26, no. 6 (2002): 802–11.

Painter, J. "Cartographic Anxiety and the Search for Regionality." *Environment and Planning A: Economy and Space* 40, no. 2 (2008): 342–61.

Parker, George L. *The Beginnings of the Book Trade in Canada.* Toronto: University of Toronto Press, 1985.

Parnaby, Andrew. "The Cultural Economy of Survival: The Mi'kmaq of Cape Breton in the Mid-19th Century." *Labour / Le Travail*, no. 61 (2008): 69–98.

Paterson, A.P. "Maritime Disabilities within Confederation." *Busy East of Canada*, February 1929: 5–16.

Penfold, Stephen. "'Have You No Manhood in You?': Gender and Class in the Cape Breton Coal Towns, 1920–1926." *Acadiensis* 23, no. 2 (1994): 21–44.

Pentland, H. Clare. "The Western Canadian Labour Movement, 1897–1919." *Canadian Journal of Political and Social Theory* 3, no. 2 (1979): 53–78.

Pickles, John. *A History of Spaces: Cartographic Reason, Mapping and the Geo-coded World*. London and New York: Routledge, 2004.

Piesse, Jude. *British Settler Emigration in Print, 1832–1877*. Oxford, UK: Oxford University Press, 2016.

Pinder, Kymberly N. *Painting the Gospel: Black Public Art and Religion in Chicago*. Champaign: University of Illinois Press, 2016.

"Pity for Hugh Ross." *Maritime Labor Herald*, 11 March 1922: 1.

"Political and Personal Polities." *Marshlands* 1, no. 1 (1895): 1–2.

Pratt, E.J. "The Dear Illusion." *Dalhousie Review* 4, no. 4 (1925): 437.

Prince, Samuel H. *Catastrophe and Social Change: Based on a Sociological Study of the Halifax Disaster*. New York: Columbia University Press, 1920. http://archive.org/details/catastrophesocia00prinuoft/page/n5/mode/2up.

"Private Initiative." *Maritime Labor Herald*, 17 June 1922: 1.

"Publications Received." *Canadian Printer and Publisher* 26, no. 1–12 (1917): 32. https://archive.org/details/canprinterpublish1917toro.

"Publisher's Note." *Cape Breton and Nova Scotia Magazine* 2, no. 1 (1902): 30.

"Race Distinction." *The New Freeman*, 11 April 1903: 1.

Rak, Julie. "Translocal Representation: Chief Buffalo Child Long Lance, Nello 'Tex' Vernon-Wood, and CanLit." In *Critical Collaborations: Indigeneity, Diaspora, and Ecology in Canadian Literary Studies*, edited by Smaro Kamboureli and Christl Verduyn, 175–98. Waterloo, ON: Wilfrid Laurier University Press, 2014.

Rankine, Patrice D. *Ulysses in Black: Ralph Ellison, Classicism, and African American Literature*. Madison: University of Wisconsin Press, 2006.

Raymond, W.O. "The Negro in New Brunswick." *Neith* 1, no. 1 (February 1903): 27–34.

Reilly, Norman Rein. "Toilers Under the Sea II." *McLean's*, 15 January 1925: 20, 38–40.

Remes, Jacob. "'Committed as Near Neighbors': The Halifax Explosion and Border-Crossing People and Ideas." *American Review of Canadian Studies* vol. 45, no. 1 (2015): 26–43.

– "Mi'kmaq in the Halifax Explosion of 1917: Leadership, Transience, and the Struggle for Land Rights." *Ethnohistory* 61, no. 3 (2014): 445–66. https://doi.org/10.1215/00141801-2681732.

Rees, Ronald. *New Brunswick Was His Country: The Life of William Francis Ganong*. Halifax: Nimbus, 2016.

"Repeal." *The Colonial Standard*, 18 May 1886: 1.

Reynolds, William K. "By Way of Introduction." *New Brunswick Magazine* 1, no. 1 (1898): 1–5.

– "Writers and Workers." *New Brunswick Magazine* 1, no. 1 (1898): 57–61.

Rhomberg, Chris. *No There There: Race, Class, and Political Community in Oakland*. Berkeley, CA: University of California Press, 2004.

Ricou, Laurie. "Story and Teller." Review of *As Birds Bring Forth the Sun and Other Stories*, by Alistair MacLeod. *Canadian Literature*, no. 76 (1978): 116–18.

Ritchie, Eliza. Review of *Dream Tapestries*, by Louise Morey Bowman. *Dalhousie Review* 6, no. 1 (1926): 130–1.

– Review of *Heliodora and Other Poems*, by H.D. *Dalhousie Review* 4, no. 3 (1924): 400.

– Review of *The Iron Door*, by E.J. Pratt. *Dalhousie Review* 10, no. 2 (1930): 282–3.

– Review of *Isles of Paisley*, by Jennie N. Smith. *Dalhousie Review* 8, no. 4 (1929): 575–6.

– Review of *Newfoundland Verse*, by E.J. Pratt. *Dalhousie Review* 3, no. 2 (1923): 266–7.

– Review of *Roosevelt and Antinoe*, by E.J. Pratt. *Dalhousie Review* 10, no. 1 (1930): 140–1.

– Review of *The Tower*, by W.B. Yeats. *Dalhousie Review* 8, no. 4 (1929): 572.

Robb, Andrew. "Michael A McInnis, The Maple Leaf and Migration from Prince Edward Island." *Island Magazine*, no. 17 (1985): 15–19.

Roberts, Charles G.D. "The Outlook for Literature: Acadia's Field for Poetry, History and Romance." *Halifax Herald*, 1 January 1886, 3.

– "Canada." In *Canadian Literature in English: Texts and Contexts*, vol. 1, edited by Laura Moss and Cynthia Sugars, 354–6. Toronto: Pearson Longman, 2000.

Roberts, Theodore G. "At a Place that Has No Name." *Kit-Bag* 1, no. 1 (November 1902): 4–9.

– "For the Thousand." *Kit-Bag* 1, no. 1 (November 1902): 2.

– "My Comrade." *Acadiensis* 3, no. 1 (January 1903): 40.

– "The Story Writer." *Kit-Bag* 1, no. 1 (November 1902): 23.

Ronnick, Michele Valerie. "In Search of Henry Alexander Saturnin Hartley, Black Classicist, Clergyman, and Physician." In *Classicisms in the Black Atlantic*, edited by Ian Moyer, Adam Lecznar, and Heidi Morse, 119–32. Oxford, UK: Oxford University Press, 2020.

Rouillard, Jacques, et al. "Working-Class History." In *The Canadian Encyclopedia*, 4 March 2015. *Historica Canada*. http://www.thecanadianencyclopedia.ca/en/article/working-class-history.

Rudd, Niall, and Jonathan Powell. "Introduction." In *The Republic and the Laws*, by Cicero, edited by Niall Rudd and Jonathan Powell, ix–xxxi. Oxford, UK: Oxford University Press, 1998.

Ruden, Sarah, trans. *The Aeneid*, by Virgil. New Haven, CT: Yale University Press, 2008.

"Russia Will Accept Canadian Loan." *Maritime Labor Herald*, 17 June 1922: 2.

"Saint John, New Brunswick, Falls in Line for African Redemption." *Negro World*, May 1922: 8.

Saler, Michael. "Introduction." In *The Fin-De-Siècle World*, edited by Michael Saler, 1–8. London and New York: Routledge, 2014.

Sangster, Joan. "The Communist Party and the Woman Question, 1922–1929." *Labour / Le Travail*, no. 15 (1985): 25–56.

– *Dreams of Equality: Women on the Canadian Left, 1920–60*. Toronto: University of Toronto Press, 2015.

Savoie, Donald. *Looking for Bootstraps: Economic Development in the Maritimes*. Halifax: Nimbus, 2017.

Scanlon, Joseph. "Disaster's Little Known Pioneer: Canada's Samuel Henry Prince." *International Journal of Mass Emergencies and Disasters* 6, no. 3 (1988): 213–32.

Scholes, Robert, and Clifford Wulfman. *Modernism in the Magazines: An Introduction*. New Haven, CT: Yale University Press, 2010.

Sclater, Karla. "The Labor and Radical Press 1820–the Present." *Labor Press Project*, University of Washington, 2001. https://depts.washington.edu/labhist/laborpress/Kelling.htm.

Scott, William R. "Ethiopianism." In *Encyclopedia of Black Studies*, edited by Molefe Asante and Ama Mazama, 233–4. London: SAGE, 2005.

Seaman, Andrew. "Roberts, Theodore Goodridge." *The Oxford Companion to Canadian Literature*, 2nd ed., edited by Eugene Benson and William Toye, 1010–11. Oxford, UK: Oxford University Press, 1997.

See, Scott W. "The Orange Order and Social Violence in Mid-Nineteenth Century Saint John." *Acadiensis* 13, no. 1 (1983): 68–92.

Shadd, Adrienne. "'Where Are You Really From?' Notes of an 'Immigrant' from North Buxton, Ontario." In *Talking about Identity: Encounters in Race, Ethnicity, and Language*, edited by Carl James and Adrienne Shadd, 10–16. Toronto: Between the Lines, 2001.

Sharma, Devika, and Frederik Tygstrup. "Introduction." In *Structures of Feeling: Affectivity and the Study of Culture*, edited by Devika Sharma and Frederik Tygstrup, 1–19. Berlin: De Gruyter, 2015.

Sharp, R.V. "Do You Know Who We Are?" *Busy East of Canada*, December 1919: 9–13, 16.

Shaw, Melissa. "'Most Anxious to Serve Their King and Country': Black Canadians' Fight to Enlist in WWI and Emerging Race Consciousness in Ontario, 1914–1919." *Social History* 49, no. 100 (2016): 543–80.

Siadhail, Pádraig Ó. "Hughes, Katherine Angelina." In *Dictionary of Canadian Biography*, vol. 15. Toronto and Laval, QC: University of Toronto / Université Laval, 2003. http://www.biographi.ca/en/bio/hughes_katherine_angelina_15E.html.

Siemerling, Winfried. *The Black Atlantic Reconsidered: Black Canadian Writing, Cultural History, and the Presence of the Past*. Montreal and Kingston, ON: McGill-Queen's University Press, 2015.

Simmons, Merinda, and James Crank. *Race and New Modernisms*. London: Bloomsbury, 2019.

Simms, L.W. "Past Year Marked by Prosperity and Progress." *Busy East of Canada*, June 1929: 5–10, 31.

Sladen, Douglas. *On the Cars and Off*. London: Ward, Locke & Bowden, 1895.

Smiley, Cal. "Novels in English: 1900 to 1920." In *The Oxford Companion to Canadian Literature*, 2nd ed., edited by Eugene Benson and William Toye, 815–17. Oxford, UK: Oxford University Press, 1997.

Smith, Watson. "Loyalist History." *Acadiensis* 1, no. 1 (January 1901): 7–18.

Smyth, Hannah. Review of *And We Go On: A Memoir of the Great War* by Will R. Bird. *British Journal of Canadian Studies* 29, no. 1 (2016): 15–16.

"Social Influence." *Maritime Labor Herald*, 3 February 1923: 2.

Soja, Edward. *Postmodern Geographies: The Reassertion of Space in Critical Social Theory*. London and New York: Verso, 1989.

"Some Essentials for Success." *Busy East of Canada*, January 1920: 3.

"Some Notable Changes in the Maritime Provinces." *Busy East of Canada*, February 1930: 7–8.

"Song of the Race." Review of *No Great Mischief*, by Alistair MacLeod. *The Toronto Star*, 3 October 1999: 1.

"Sons and Daughters of Maritime Provinces to Give Entertainment and Ball." *San Francisco Call*, 13 March 1910: 23.

Sorett, Josef. *Spirit in the Dark: A Religious History of Racial Aesthetics*. Oxford, UK: Oxford University Press, 2016.
Spector, Maurice. "Great Stand Against Capitalism." *Worker*, 1 August 1922: 1.
"Spelling of Place Names in the Province." [Moncton] *Daily Times*, 17 March 1930: 7.
Spray, W.A. *The Blacks in New Brunswick*. Fredericton: Brunswick Press, 1972.
"St. Philip's Church." [Saint John] *Daily Sun*, 9 November 1988.
St. Stephen, Roger. "A Cask of Gasoline." *Home Journal* 5, no. 6 (1908): 10.
Stewart, Herbert L. Letter to Frances Starr. 25 November 1933. UA-35, box 6, file 3, Archives and Special Collections, Killam Memorial Library, Dalhousie University.
– "Salutation." *Dalhousie Review* 1, no. 1 (1921): 3–4.
Stephen, A.M. "Dr. Samuel Johnson Views Our Poets." *Dalhousie Review* 11, no. 4 (1932): 493–506.
Storch, Randi. *Red Chicago: American Communism at its Grass Roots, 1928–1935*. Champaign: University of Illinois Press, 2007.
Stowe, Harriet B. *Uncle Tom's Cabin; or Life Among the Lowly*. 1852. New York: R.F. Fenno, 1904.
"Strikers Threaten to Wreck Property by Use of Dynamite." *Globe and Mail*, 16 July 1923: 2.
Studer, Brigitte. *The Transnational World of the Cominternians*. Translated by Dafydd R. Roberts. London: Palgrave Macmillan, 2015.
"The Successful Man's Creed." *Busy East of Canada*, January 1930: cover.
Sutherland, David. *"We Harbour No Evil Design": Rehabilitation Efforts After the Halifax Explosion of 1917*. Halifax: Champlain Society, 2017.
Sutherland, John. "Mr. Smith and The 'Tradition.'" In *The Making of Modern Poetry in Canada*, 3rd ed., edited by Louis Dudek and Michael Gnarowski, 47–61. Montreal and Kingston, ON: McGill-Queen's University Press, 2017.
– "Out with the Tide." Review of *Island: The Collected Stories of Alistair MacLeod*, by Alistair MacLeod. *New York Times Book Review*, 18 February 2001: 6.
Taverner, Percy A. "In Memoriam – Montague Chamberlain." *Canadian Field-Naturalist* 39, no. 20 (1925): 20.
Taylor, Martin B. *Promoters, Patriots, and Partisans: Historiography in Nineteenth Century English Canada*. Toronto: University of Toronto Press, 1989.
"Tea Is High but Not Here!" *Maritime Labor Herald*, 6 October 1923: 3.
Thomas, Rebecca. "Remember Turtle Grove." *CBC News*: The National, 10 December 2017, 1:57. https://x.com/i/status/938622671876755461.
Thompson, Peter. "'If you're in quest of the Folk, you've come to the wrong place': Recent Trends in Atlantic Canadian Literary Criticism." *Acadiensis* 41, no. 1 (2012): 239–46.

– *Nights below Foord Street: Literature and Popular Culture in Postindustrial Nova Scotia*. Montreal and Kingston, ON: McGill-Queen's University Press, 2020.

Thornton, Patricia. "The Problem of Out-Migration from Atlantic Canada, 1871–1921: A New Look." *Acadiensis* 15, no. 1 (1985): 3–34.

"To Our Readers." *Nova Scotia Illustrated Magazine* 1, no. 1 (1895): 1.

"To the Fainthearted." *Maritime Labor Herald*, 10 June 1922: 1.

Tomkinson, Grace. "Colonialism and Art." *Dalhousie Review* 11, no. 2 (1931): 147–54.

– "The Watched Pot of Canadian Poetry." *Dalhousie Review* 14, no. 4 (1935): 459–70.

Trehearne, Brian. "Audrey Alexandra Brown, 1904–1998." In *Canadian Poetry, 1920 to 1960*, edited by Brian Trehearne, 187. Toronto: McClelland and Stewart, 2010.

Tremblay, Tony. *The Fiddlehead Moment: Pioneering an Alternative Canadian Modernism in New Brunswick*. Montreal and Kingston, ON: McGill-Queen's University Press, 2019.

– "Globalization and Cultural Memory: Perspectives from the Periphery on the Post-National Disassembly of Place." In *Canadian Literature and Cultural Memory*, edited by Cynthia Sugars and Eleanor Ty, 24–38. Oxford, UK: Oxford University Press, 2014.

– "Landscapes of Reception: Historicizing the Travails of the New Brunswick Literary Modernists." In *Making Canada New: Editing, Modernism, and New Media*, edited by Dean Irvine, Vanessa Lent, and Bart Vautour, 307–26. Toronto: University of Toronto Press, 2017.

– "'Lest on too close sight I miss the darling illusion': The Politics of the Centre in 'Reading Maritime.'" *Studies in Canadian Literature / Études en littérature canadienne* 33, no. 2 (2008): 23–39.

Trouillot, Michel-Rolph. *Global Transformations: Anthropology and the Modern World*. London: Palgrave Macmillan, 2007.

– "The Otherwise Modern: Caribbean Lessons from the Savage Lot." In *Critically Modern: Alternatives, Alterities, Anthropologies*, edited by Bruce M. Knauft, 220–40. Bloomington: Indiana University Press, 2002.

Tsing, Anna L. *Friction: An Ethnography of Global Connection*. Princeton, NJ: Princeton University Press, 2015.

"UMW Take Great Stand." *Maritime Labor Herald*, 1 July 1922: 1, 6.

"Uncle Tom's Cabin." *The St. John Daily Sun*, 24 February 1903: 8.

Underhill, Frank. *The Image of Confederation*. Toronto: Canadian Broadcasting Corporation, 1964.

Vance, Jonathan. *Death So Noble: Memory, Meaning, and the First World War*. Vancouver: University of British Columbia Press, 1999.

– "The Soldier as Novelist: Literature, History, and the Great War." *Canadian Literature*, no. 179 (2003): 22–37.
Vautour, Bart. "Modernism, Antimodernism, and the Song Fishermen." *Canadian Poetry: Studies, Documents, Reviews*, no. 70 (2012): 15–44.
Vellino, Brenda Carr. "Machine-Age Discourse, Mechanical Ballet, and Popular Song as Alternative Document in Dorothy Livesay's 'Day and Night.'" *Studies in Canadian Literature / Études en littérature canadienne* 32, no. 2 (2007): 43–58.
Vernon, Charles W. *Cape Breton, Canada at the Beginning of the Twentieth Century*. Toronto: Nation, 1903. https://www.canadiana.ca/view/oocihm.74577/1.
– "An Idyll of Acadie." *Cape Breton Magazine* 1, no. 1 (1901): 3–4.
Vipond, Mary. "Canadian Nationalism and the Plight of Canadian Magazines in the 1920s." *Canadian Historical Review* 58, no. 1 (1977): 43–65.
"Voltaire." *Busy East of Canada* 10, no. 3, October 1929: 24–6.
Walker, Abraham Beverly. "Address by A.B. Walker, LL.B." *St. John Daily Sun*, 17 August 1888: 1.
– "Editorial Announcements." *Neith* 1, no. 1 (February 1903): 59–60.
– "Editorial Announcements." *Neith* 1, no. 2 (March 1903): 98–100.
– "Editorial Announcements." *Neith* 1, no. 5 (January 1904): 238.
– "Emile Zola." *Neith* 1, no. 1 (February 1903): 4–5.
– "Hayti and Its Enemies." *Neith* 1, no. 1 (February 1903): 2–3.
– "Industrial Schools for British Negroes." *Neith* 1, no. 2 (March 1903): 8–11.
– "Keep Negrophobes Out of Africa." *Neith* 1, no. 1 (February 1903): 6.
– "The Late Coal Strike." *Neith* 1, no. 1 (February 1903): 1–2.
– "Let the Natives of South Africa Have Justice and Education." *Neith* 1, no. 1 (February 1903): 13–15.
– "Literary Notes." *Neith* 1, no. 1 (February 1903): 53–8.
– "Literary Notes." *Neith* 1, no. 2 (February 1903): 92–7.
– "Lost Israel Found." *Neith* 1, no. 1 (February 1903): 5.
– "Lynching in the South." *Neith* 1, no. 4 (August 1903): 167–9.
– "The Negro Problem, and How to Solve It, No. 1, Part 1." *Neith* 1, no. 1 (February 1903): 22–6.
– "The Negro Problem, and How to Solve It, No. 1, Part 3." *Neith* 1, no. 3 (July 1903): 131–3.
– "The Negro Problem, and How to Solve It, No. 1, Part 4." *Neith* 1, no. 4 (August 1903): 180–2.
– "Neith Is Canadian." *Neith* 1, no. 2 (March 1903): 63.
– "The New Freeman." *Neith* 1, no. 2 (March 1903): 63–4.
– "Our New Settlers." *Neith* 1, no. 2 (March 1903): 68.

– "The Philosophy of Society." *Neith* 1, no. 3 (July 1903): 103–5.
– "Prefatory Remarks." *Neith* 1, no. 1 (February 1903): 1.
– "A Reasonable Protest." *Neith* 1, no. 4 (August 1903): 170–1.
– "A Special Note to Our Friends." *Neith* 1, no. 5 (January 1904): 199.
– "Tillmanism, or Mob Rule in the South." *Neith* 1, no. 1 (February 1903): 16–22.
– "Treat Boer and Black Alike." *Neith* 1, no. 1 (February 1903): 6.
– "The United States." *Neith* 1, no. 3 (July 1903): 125–7.

Walker, Barrington. "Finding Jim Crow in Canada, 1789–1967." In *A History of Human Rights in Canada*, edited by Janet Miron, 81–98. Toronto: Canadian Scholars' Press, 2009.

Walker, George Gilbert. "Realism in Fiction." *Neith* 1, no. 4 (August 1903): 228–31.

Walker, James W. St. G. *"Race," Rights and the Law in the Supreme Court of Canada: Historical Case Studies*. Waterloo, ON: Wilfrid Laurier Press and Osgoode Law Society, 1997.
– *Racial Discrimination in Canada: The Black Experience*. Ottawa: Canadian Historical Association, 1985.

Wallace, Bronwen. "The True Test of Fiction." Review of *As Birds Bring Forth the Sun and Other Stories*, by Alistair MacLeod. [Kingston, ON] *Whig-Standard*, 23 May 1986: 1.

Wallace, Joe. "Awake!" *Maritime Labor Herald*, 23 June 1923: 4.
– "The Rise of the Red River." *Maritime Labor Herald*, 5 July 1924: 4.
– "Voice of the Workers." *Maritime Labor Herald*, 6 October 1923: 4.

Walls, Martha E. "Confederation and Maritimes First Nations." *Acadiensis* 46, no. 2 (2017): 155–76.

"The War Industries of the Maritimes." [Fredericton] *Daily Gleaner*, 2 November 1918: 5.

Ware, Tracy. "Cosmopolitan Nationalism: Canadian Literature of the Confederation Period, 1867–1914." In *The Oxford Handbook of Canadian Literature*, edited by Cynthia Sugars, 295–313. Oxford, UK: Oxford University Press, 2016.

"Wearing the Pants." *Maritime Labor Herald*, 8 April 1922: 6.

Weiss, Allan. "Rediscovering the Popular Short Story." In *Dominant Impressions: Essays on the Canadian Short Story*, edited by Gerald Lynch and Angela Arnold Robbeson, 87–97. Ottawa: Ottawa University Press, 1999.

West, Cornel. "The Prophetic Tradition in Afro-America." In *Let Justice Roll: Prophetic Challenges in Religion, Politics, and Society*, edited by Neal Riemer, 89–100. Lanham, MD: Rowman & Littlefield, 1996.

"What's the Busy East?" *Busy East of Canada*, June 1910: 5–6.

White, W.J. "The World in the Future." *Maritime Labor Herald*, 29 September 1923: 8.

Whitfield, Annie. "A Miner's Wife." *Maritime Labor Herald*, 1 March 1924: 3.

– "New Aberdeen's Women's Club Demands Action for Power Plant Victims." *Maritime Labor Herald*, 19 June 1926: 3.

Wightman, F.A. "To the Memory of Brave Loyalists." *Acadiensis* 8, no. 2 (April 1908): 94–6.

Williams, David. "Introduction." In *And We Go On*, by Will R. Bird, edited by David Williams, vii–xxi. Montreal and Kingston, ON: McGill-Queen's University Press, 2014.

– *Media, Memory, and the First World War*. Montreal and Kingston, ON: McGill-Queen's University Press, 2009.

– "Spectres of Time: Seeing Ghosts in Will Bird's Memoirs and Abel Gance's *J'accuse*." *Canadian Literature*, no. 219 (2013): 113–30.

Williams, Dorothy. "Print and Black Canadian Culture." In *History of the Book in Canada*, vol. 2, *1840–1918*, edited by Fiona A. Black et al., 40–3. Toronto: University of Toronto Press 2005.

Williams, Raymond. *Marxism and Literature*. Oxford, UK: Oxford University Press, 1978.

Willmott, Glenn. *Unreal Country: Modernity in the Canadian Novel in English*. Montreal and Kingston, ON: McGill-Queen's University Press 2002.

Wilson, Robert. "The Canadian Outlook." *Neith* 1, no. 1 (February 1903): 35–8.

Winks, Robin. *The Blacks in Canada: A History*, 2nd ed. Montreal and Kingston, ON: McGill-Queen's University Press, 2014.

– "Negroes in the Maritimes: An Introductory Survey." *Dalhousie Review* 48, no. 4 (1968): 453–71.

"Women of Sydney Form Labor League." *Maritime Labor Herald*, 29 March 1924: 1.

"Women's Club Meets at Dominion No. 4." *Maritime Labor Herald*, 23 May 1924: 3.

"Women's Labor Club Makes Rapid Progress." *Maritime Labor Herald*, 5 April 1924: 1.

Woodsworth, J.S. "Notes of a New MP." *Maritime Labor Herald*, 17 June 1922: 1.

Wyile, Herb. *Anne of Tim Hortons: Globalization and the Reshaping of Atlantic-Canadian Literature*. Waterloo, ON: Wilfrid Laurier University Press, 2011.

– "Regionalism, Postcolonialism, and (Canadian) Writing: A Comparative Approach for Postnational Times." *Essays on Canadian Writing*, no. 63 (1998): 139–61.

Wynne, Graeme. "W.F. Ganong, A.H. Clark and the Historical Geography of Maritime Canada." *Acadiensis* 10, no. 2 (1981): 5–28.

"Yellow Legs." *Maritime Labor Herald*, 17 June 1922: 6.

Zetzel, James, trans. *On the Commonwealth and On the Laws* by Cicero. Cambridge: Cambridge University Press, 1999.

Index